THE
RED ARMY
AND
THE WEHRMACHT

Russian Studies Series
Valery Kuvakin, General Editor

GENERAL INTEREST

History of Russian Philosophy, 2 volumes, edited by Valery Kuvakin
The Basic Bakunin: Writings 1869–1871,
    translated and edited by Robert M. Cutler
Anton Chekhov: Stories of Women,
    edited and translated by Paula Ross

FROM THE SECRET ARCHIVES
OF THE FORMER SOVIET UNION

Lenin's Will: Falsified and Forbidden, by Yuri Buranov
*The Red Army and the Wehrmacht: How the Soviets
    Militarized Germany, 1922–33,
    and Paved the Way for Fascism,*
    by Yuri Dyakov and Tatyana Bushuyeva
Out of the Red Shadows: Anti-Semitism in Stalin's Russia,
    by Gennady V. Kostyrchenko
The Struggle for Power in Russia in 1923,
    by Valentina P. Vilkova (Fall 1995)

THE
RED ARMY
AND THE WEHRMACHT

HOW THE SOVIETS MILITARIZED GERMANY, 1922-33, AND PAVED THE WAY FOR FASCISM

YURI DYAKOV & TATYANA BUSHUYEVA

From the Secret Archives of the Former Soviet Union

 Prometheus Books

59 John Glenn Drive
Amherst, New York 14228-2197

Published 1995 by Prometheus Books

99 98 97 96 95   5 4 3 2 1

Library of Congress Cataloging-in-Publication Data

D'iakov, IU. L. (IUrii Leont'evich)
    The Red Army and the Wehrmacht : how the Soviets militarized Germany, 1922-33, and paved the way for Fascism : from the secret archives of the former Soviet Union / Yuri L. Dyakov and Tatyana S. Bushuyeva.
        p.   cm.
    Includes bibliographical references.
    ISBN 0-87975-937-2
    1. Soviet Union—Military relations—Germany. 2. Germany—Military relations—Soviet Union. 3. Soviet Union—History—1917–1936.
4. Germany—History—1918–1933. I.Bushuyeva, T. S. (Tat'iana Semenovna)
II. Title.
DK67.5.G3D5   1994
355'.03243'09042—dc20   94-37158
                                                                   CIP

Printed in the United States of America on acid-free paper.

Contents

Abbreviations   6

Preface   7

Introduction   13

1. Germany and Russia—Pariahs of Versailles   31

2. The Peculiar Basis of Relations
   between the RKKA and the Reichswehr   49

3. The Concept of Military Cooperation
   Seemed Simple and of Mutual Benefit   127

4. The Program of Cooperation Was Rather Wide   209

5. The Year 1933: Never Had Relations Been Maintained
   in a Tenser General Political Atmosphere   285

Epilog: Dearly Bought Collaboration   319

Index of Names   337

Abbreviations

AVIAChIM, AVIAKhIM	Society of Friends of Air and Chemical Defense and Industry of the USSR
CC	Central Committee
CK VKP(b)	See TsK VKP(b)
CPSU	Communist Party of the Soviet Union
CSASA	Central State Archives of the Soviet Union; see also TsGASA
F.	*Fond,* meaning "collection"
Gosplan	State Planning Commission
GPVU	Head Military-Industrial Department
MC	Moscow Committee; see MK
MFA	Ministry of Foreign Affairs
MK	*Moskovskii Komitet*—Moscow Committee
Narkom	People's Commissar
NIK	Scientific and Engineering Committee
NKID	*Narkomindel,* People's Commissariat for Foreign Affairs
NKRKI	Commissariat (*Narkomat*) of the Workers' and Peasants' Inspection
OGPU	*Obiediniennoie Gosudarstvennoie Politichieskoie Upravlenii*—United State Political Administration; see also USPA
OSOVIAKhIM	Society for the Promotion of Defense, the Furthering of Aviation, and the Chemical Industry
PCFA	People's Commissariat of Foreign Affairs
RCP(b)	Russian Communist Party (of bolsheviks); see VKP(b)
RKI	*Raboche-Krest'ianskaia Inspektsiia*—Workers' and Peasants' Inspection; see also WPI
RKKA	Workers' and Peasants' Red Army
RKKF	Workers' and Peasants' Red Navy
RVS	Revolutionary Military Council
RWM	*Reichswehrministerium*—German Ministry of Defense
sh.	sheet
SOVTchK	Secret Department of VTchK
SR	Social Revolutionary Party
SSNE	Supreme Soviet of the National Economy; see also VSNCh or VSNKh
SSSR	Soviet Union
TsKVKP(b)	*Tsentral'nyi Komitet Vsesoiuznoi Kommunisticheskoi Partii (bol'shevikov)*—Central Committee of the All-Union Communist Party (of bolsheviks)
TsGASA	Central State Archives of the Soviet Union; see also CSASA
USPA	United State Political Administration
UVVS	*Upravleniie Voenno-Vozdushnyie Sily*—Department of the Air Force
VKP(b)	All-Union Communist Party (of bolsheviks); see RCP(b)
VO GVF	Military Department of the Civil Air Fleet
VSNCh or VSNKh	*Vysshii Soviet Narodnogo Khoziaistva*—Supreme Soviet of the National Economy; see also SSNE
VTchK	All-Russian Extraordinary Commission
VTchK GPU	All-Russian Extraordinary Commission for Combating Counterrevolution and Sabotage
VVS	*Voenno-Vozdushnyie Sily*—Air Force
WPI	Workers' and Peasants' Inspection
WPRA	Workers' and Peasants' Red Army; see also RKKA
ZGASA	Central State Archives of the Soviet Army

Preface

Find the beginning of things—
And you will understand much.

Today's view of many events and stages of our history is quite different from the previous one. We strive to evaluate them more definitely and accurately. Ever-increasing interest in history is not accidental—it is caused by strong demand for renewal. While pondering the possible sources of the total crisis that seized Soviet society, we try to find the reasons for the upheaval in the historic past. Some of them originated in October 1917; some others, in the period that followed; the rest, in the years that we call perestroika. However voices are heard: "Stop digging up the past." Of course, the truth about our past does not inspire us with historical optimism. Nevertheless, we should not leave a single stone unturned when searching for truth. It is only this way that will lead to enlightenment, help us to escape from the historic labyrinth into which we were drawn by our illusions.

Although their approach to their own history may be different, for all people it is the foundation, the beginning of all common sentiments. Without such support one cannot build something new and enter the future.

History contains all sorts of pages, including gloomy ones. They cannot be extracted and forgotten. The Soviet problem consists not only merely in the fact that Stalinism and its heritage should be held up to shame, but also mainly in freeing the people's consciousness and

7

hearts of the Stalinist influence. However, such liberation is a process, and not a simple and swift one.

For years Soviet historical scholarship has borne the weight of totalitarianism, enduring the severe constraint of strict ideologists and vigilant clerks of personnel departments. This system excluded any opportunity for heterodoxy and, moreover, for struggle. Pressure was exerted upon people in ideological, political, repressive, and other forms. Thus were laid the foundations of a lying historiography. Thus was disturbed a correct ratio between scholarship, ideology, and politics. Historiography was identified with ideology, communist party membership was set off against objectiveness. The Stalinist regime created its own history to falsify the past by the use of historic means. As a result, historic scholarship has lost one of its principal functions—to study the lessons of the past in the name of the present and of the future. Priests of politics deprived people of truthful information.

The time has come to realize that totalitarian power and a scholarship that is first and foremost humanitarian are not compatible with one another. It is necessary to overcome ideological and political dictates that deformed the functions of historic scholarship and brought it to a deadlock. In this case it is important to remember that historic scholarship cannot come out of the crisis state without gaining freedom of action. This is an axiom. And, we have no right to exercise freedom in only a single sphere—that of moral responsibility before ourselves, society, and progeny.

The bread of historic scholarship is facts. A hypothesis will never become a theory unless it is supported by facts. However, today we feel an obvious shortage of information and, consequently, knowledge. Society has been stricken by a syndrome of secrecy, the roots of which are in our past. The Bolshevik conspiracy, so natural before the revolution, brought after it the cult of secrecy and suspiciousness that has inflicted irreparable losses on the country and on the people.

Even at that time, in the first year after the revolution Lenin, Trotsky, Dzerzhinsky, Frunze, and other Bolsheviks, guided by the notorious dogmas of class struggle and dictatorship of the proletariat, established concentration camps and antiprofiteer detachments, introduced a hostage system, liquidated all other parties, exiled the fleeing Russian intelligentsia, set up censorship, etc. Stalin was only an original successor of the cause, and it was not he who invented the cult of the leader.

Stalin surrounded himself with secrecy—it was one of the basic springs of his power. Explointing it, he has managed to turn the history of the people into the history of monstrous crimes against them. Sometimes historical memory of the "Great Helmsman" hindered him, for it revealed the discrepancy, inconsistency, or absurdity of the words and actions of "leaders." Therefore all the measures were taken to prevent people from revealing the past, so that they never know it.

The strictly guarded documents contain much shame and sorrow, much information on mercenary honor, the triumph of meanness over honesty and true devotion. "And I tell you: wherever you see people who are ruled by secrecy, this secrecy contains evil. If the devil suggests an idea that this or that thing is terrible for your eyes look at it. If he says that something is awful for your ears, listen to it. . . . And if it seems to you that a certain truth is intolerable try to tolerate it." G. K. Chesterton wrote these words, which were spoken by his hero in a classic of English literature; they have something in common with our history.

According to Chesterton, "an admirer of the devil is a proud and sly person; he likes to rule and frighten innocent people by something incomprehensible. . . . That is why satanism is secrecy." Therefore, everything was hidden in the GULAG of archives and special depositories. Disagreeable publications were withdrawn from libraries. At the same time temples, icons, and other material and spiritual carriers of memory were annihilated. The past for the people seemed to be dead, to have ceased its existence. Instead of it was created a distorted history that formed public consciousness and fixed itself in it so that until even now many scientists are not in a position to renounce it.

The prevailing historical memory in a society is always formed by the power within it. It becomes more difficult for historical scholarship to struggle against this tendency, as it is enfolded in the arms of that power, which are now not so tight but still hold strongly.

Until recently, "inconvenient" themes were crushed by ideological ban, and even now the path to them is thorny. The official ideology oriented its followers to justifying their own failures by means of other persons. Even now one can observe the phenomenon of the substitution of one lie or half-truth for another. The truth is not found not because it is impossible to find it, but because the truth is not asserted.

But time has come to tell the people a bitter truth: that none other than real fascism raged in our country, and that the totalitarianism that seized the destinies of the peoples of the USSR and Germany was one of the reasons for unleashing World War II. In many respects, Hitler's fascism was abetted by Stalin's. Few historians know that the German Wehrmacht (Reichswehr) evaded the Versailles bans by gaining strength on our soil. In the USSR, under conditions of high secrecy, joint military ventures were undertaken, airfields were built, and tank and flying schools were operated. The flower of the fascist Wehrmacht was trained there. This has been attested to in documents. Those that are available shock even professionals, but the papers constitute only a part of the secrets hidden from the people.

Totalitarian consciousness has nothing to do with the realities of life and it never becomes lucid. One should be aware that there are no arguments that can get at dogmatic Stalinists, no sensible arguments that can shake their theoretical aspirations. This is normal for those who have undergone a change of consciousness. This change is most dangerous when combined with bureaucratic departmental structures. To tear oneself away from the strong claws of dogmatic thinking is not a simple matter even for those who deliberately strive after this goal. That is why we say, "Stalin is alive, and followers of totalitarianism are trying now to place, to impose historical myths to exterminate scientific knowledge."

But our people are not able to make proper use of the lessons given to them. The fact is that the many years of ignorance, sameness of opinions, and depressing monotony were set up as examples for scientific analysis. The scientific community is unable not only to suggest new ideas and the right method of approach but also to perceive them. Scientists who lost the creative spirit constitute a majority. Progressively minded scientists suffer losses.

Haste is not pardonable in a historian. If a sufficient database does not exist, there is no opportunity to develop proper methods of approach to this or that problem. Until now, the truth about the past war, and the reasons that caused its unleashing, has been the most strictly hidden secret. The victory won in the conflict has justified the strength and stability of the totalitarian system built by Bolsheviks, while revealing the secrets threatened to destroy this myth. The answer to the question why we gained the victory lies in quite another plane—in the unique nature of our people.

The most horrible crimes of the twentieth century were committed by German fascism and Stalinism. If the first one brought down the sword on other peoples, the latter inflicted it—first and foremost—on its own people. This is truth, the terrible truth, about our recent past. Knowing about it is shameful for us, but it is also at the same time of vital importance. The sufferings of the people is that abyss at which one cannot cast a glance without being horrified. But it should be done to understand finally where we are and how we are to get away from it.

One can understand the throes of the generations of deceived people who are still alive, many of whom are protesting against the "slandering" of our "glorious history." But it is not that truth, which is rarely spoken about, and not the truth-loving authors who are at fault, but the lie that was implanted into the people's consciousness, that our life was cloudless and happy. The fertile ground for the direct lie and half-truth (which is worse than a lie) was ideological monopolism characterized by intolerance and secrecy. Secrecy and falsehood are sisters, as the people who admitted to secrets are just as obliged to lie. A powerful social and psychological factor rests at the base of lie phenomenon, as many people sincerely believe that the full truth is harmful. The "lie-for-good" problem is everlasting. Some people consider a critical approach to the past to be destructive; other people take it as liberation from filth. Though the exhumation of truth is taking place morbidly, it is extremely necessary.

That is why an idea coming from the progressive, small-in-number scientists hardly forces its way through the pile of barriers erected by the keepers of party and state secrets. Until now, there was no law on archives; therefore any official might declare: "I shall not give it to you, I shall not let you in, I shall not allow you to do this or that." An archive taboo continues to prevail against publication of the most valuable documents that could help us to perceive the truth. The ban syndrome is especially strong in the field of international policy problems in which historians could base their interpretations only on the official documents in general use.

Today, a critical reevaluation of our history is out of the question without a decisive break in the secrecy screen. Making something secret does more than protect that something from foreign eyes. The keepers of archive secrets do not take care of pure military secrets, which have fully lost their sense and meaning after fifty years; they care for stability of political principles, for the destiny of the Stalinist false socialism, as behind it hides the principal problem: what was the actual price paid by our long-suffering people for our Great Victory? Till now historians have been warned against the divulgence of any secrets under the pretense that they might cause damage to the international prestige of the country. The power takes vengeance on those who make its secrets open.

Thus we are facing two obstacles, subjective and objective. If an inner censor can be overcome, though with certain difficulties, learning the truth becomes much more complicated when we are facing bureaucratic counteraction.

There exists a real threat of the annihilation of archive documents. Because of this, an end should be put to the bans established by unknown bodies in the archive business, to open access to the archives of the KGB, CC of CPSU, MFA, and other archives containing the history of the destinies of the millions of people deceived by the system.

Reconstruction of historic scholarship is a complex process. It requires moral efforts and courage to oppose routine. It was not an easy matter to recover our sight, but we perceive it as a purifying process. If historians always remember their responsibility to those killed and our people, they will do their best to find out the truth, following the dictates of their own hearts under any circumstances, without taking into account the consequences. The historian who is not in a position to do that has failed in choosing a profession.

Nobody is insured against everything. But, compared with our predecessors, we have the advantage of possessing the lessons of historical memory. Now, since we have been changed, we know where we can come to if we fail to learn the lessons of history, if we refuse the binds and relationship of generations. Today, having lost the past, we may lose the future.

Time puts everybody in his proper place. History, like life, either exists or does not. Our country has a long, complex, and tragic history. And this history is with us. It is like a road traversed by a hiker, a path that never disappears behind the traveler's back. Life puts so many questions before us that it is almost impossible to give proper answers to many of them. The real truth is still to be disclosed in the future.

Yu. L. Dyakov
Doctor of History

T. S. Bushuyeva
Doctoral Candidate of History

Introduction

Wherever you see people who are ruled by secrecy, this secrecy always contains evil.

The rebirth of the German armed forces in Soviet Russia is one of the most striking chapters of modern history. For eleven years (1922–33), hidden from the whole world, the German military was being prepared for reemergence. To a considerable extent, it was here in Russia that the foundations of the future offensive armed forces of Germany were laid. In 1939 they became a horror for the whole of Europe; in 1941 they attacked the USSR.

In February of 1919 Karl Radek,[1] "the most clever and cunning head of his time," was arrested for his participation in an uprising of "Sparta" (an organization of German left-wing Social Democrats) and placed in a prison cell used for detaining prisoners under investigation in the Berlin district of Moabit. The first months of imprisonment were hard, with strict isolation and interrogation. But in the summer, after the signing of the Versailles treaty, the conditions of his detention were improved quite unexpectedly. He was transferred to a good cell, which was soon called the "political salon of Radek," and was given unlimited opportunity to receive visitors. The Reichswehr paid especially great attention to him.[2] Here, at Moabit prison, threads of secret cooperation between the Red Army and the Reichswehr were drawn out.

In December 1919 Radek returned to Moscow, having brought with him, as invisible luggage, thoughts about a possible alliance directed against the West and the Versailles treaty. According to the Versailles treaty Germany lost all its colonies and 67.3 thousand square kilometers of its territory in Europe. Germany was deprived of the right to have its own air force, submarines, and large armored ships; and to manufacture aircraft and dirigibles, armored vehicles and tanks, and chemical weapons. It had to pay the Entente multimillion-dollar reparations. In V. I. Lenin's opinion the Versailles treaty conditions were dictated to a "defenseless Germany" by the "robbers with knives in their hands."[3]

After the Russian civil war, the Allied intervention and the failed "Polish campaign" revealed how unprepared the Red Army was for carrying on combat actions on a foreign territory. Russian also found itself in international isolation and searched for a way out of the difficult position brought about by the alliance with Germany.

Thus, both Russia and Germany were ready to start cooperating on the basis of equality, mutual interests, and mutual respect with allowances made for common enemies.

Although contradictions existed in the capitalist world's postwar treatment of Germany, Russia's development of relations with Germany fully complied with the foreign policy course developed by the Central Committee (CC) of the Bolshevik party headed by Lenin. It should be noted that the process of active cooperation with the Reichswehr gained strength after Lenin's illness caused his departure from real political activity (1922).

On the Soviet side, support for the alliance with the Reichswehr came from the highest party and state leaders, famous military leaders, officials of VTchK (GPU), and various people's commissariats:[4] V. I. Lenin, L. D. Trotsky, M. V. Frunze, F. E. Dzerzhinsky, I. V. Stalin, K. B. Radek, G. V. Chicherin, L. B. Krasin, N. N. Krestinsky, V. V. Kuibishev, E. M. Sklyansky, K. E. Voroshilov, M. N. Tukhachevsky, A. I. Egorov, I. P. Uborevitch, A. I. Kork, I. S. Unshlikht, I. E. Yakir, Ya. K. Berzin, Ya. M. Fishman, and others.

German backers of the alliance included representatives of the country and the Reischswehr leadership: H. von Seeckt, I. Virt, U. Brockdorff-Rantzau, W. Rathenau, P. von Hasse, K. von Hammerstein-Ekword, V. Grener, V. von Blomberg, and others. It was these family names that were most frequently mentioned during talks, in the texts of agreements of various sorts, in the documents pertaining to the relations between the Workers' and Peasants' Red Army (RKKA) and the Reichswehr.

At the beginning meetings, the military and political leaders of the two states envisaged the possibility of establishing contacts in case one or the other of the parties fell into conflict with Poland, which served as the base of the Versailles system in eastern Europe. Russia and Germany acquired new ideas for future cooperation: Russia could raise its defensibility by receiving foreign capital and technical aid, while Germany, in return, could make use of a top-secret Russian base for illegal manufacture of weaponry, primarily tanks and aircraft.

One of the most active German supporters of friendly relations with the Red Army was General von Seeckt. It was he who, in practice, began the realization of a program of friendship with the Red Army.

Von Seeckt, who did not want the strengthening of the military potential of Soviet Russia in general, nevertheless supported the idea of developing its industry. In von Seeckt's opinion, the Russians could deliver ammunition for the Reichswehr, if required, and, at the same time, could maintain neutrality in the face of international complications. He considered that such an alliance could provide an opportunity for bypassing the military and technical limitations imposed by the Versailles treaty. In addition, in case of war on the Western front, Russia was, at least theoretically, in a position to deliver the required amount of manganese, molybdenum, nickel, tungsten, and other raw materials. Special significance was attached to access to manganese ores: without it, the production of German steel could be paralyzed.

To ensure cooperation with the RKKA, a special group was established in the Reichswehr ministry which was headed by Major Fisher, by the beginning of 1921. (At the end of 1923–beginning of 1924, a representation of this group headed by Colonel O. von Niedermeier appeared in Moscow under the name "Moscow Center.") In March of the same year an exchange of opinions took place on whether it would be possible, and under what conditions, to transfer into Russia the German defense industry banned by the Versailles treaty. As noted in the report of the RSFSR representative in Berlin V. L. Kopp to Trotsky, simultaneous with that exchange of opinions secret talks were conducted: directly with the *Albatross* works about aircraft construction, with industrialists Blum and Foss about submarine construction, with Krupp about erection of factories for production of ammunition.

Soviet-German cooperation gradually strengthened. In the summer of 1921 von Niedermeier came to Moscow with a military mission from

Germany, as if for "reconnaissance." That same year Major General von Hasse, chief of one of the departments of the General Headquarters of the Reichswehr, visited Russia and was received by the chief of Headquarters of the RKKA P. P. Lebedev.

A follow-up meeting took place in Berlin in September of 1921. Radek and the chief of the People's Commissariat for Foreign Trade Krasin represented the Russian side in the talks, and von Hasse and Major Kurt von Schleicher spoke for the German side. The talks resulted in the establishment of an organization called GEFU (*Gesellschaft zur Förderung gewerblicher Unternehmungen*—"Company for development of industrial enterprises"), with offices in Moscow and in Berlin. It dealt with the problem of technical and economic assistance rendered to military-industrial works in Soviet Russian territory and existed till February 26, 1927. After unsound economic practices and bribery of and among the attending personnel caused its collapse, the functions of GEFU fell to the so-called WIKO (*Wirtschaftskontor*—"Economic Office"), whose representatives in the USSR were air force Colonel von der Lit-Tomsen and Doctor Zur-Lois.

In such a way Moscow and Berlin worked toward a careful, almost indeterminate, intimacy: through trade talks, rough drafts of military cooperation, unofficial missions traveling there and back.

In 1922, on Sunday of Easter week, like a bolt from the blue, the word "Rapallo" struck Europe. In the whole history of diplomacy no other such important international treaty had been concluded at such lightning speed. Some members of the German party who participated in talks in Rapallo offer recollections on this point:

> All of a sudden a slight knock was heard at the door of the apartment of Mr. von Maltzan: "A person with a funny name wants to speak to you." Maltzan, wearing his nightshirt and slippers, went carefully down the staircase to the telephone booth located in the hotel foyer. Chicherin, the Russian minister of foreign affairs, was on the wire. He said: "We should have an urgent meeting tomorrow. It is of extreme importance. . . ." And thus a notorious "conference in pyjamas" was held in Ratenau's room. The whole German delegation: the Reichschancellor, minister of foreign affairs, officials and diplomats—all gathered wearing their pyjamas and nightshirts and discussed a new situation all through the night sitting on beds and pillows. Is it reasonable to get to an agreement with Russia?[5]

After dinner on the same day the Russian and the German ministers of foreign affairs affixed their signatures to the already prepared draft agreement. Though it did not contain secret articles pertaining to military matters, the treaty's most important result was the Soviet-German military cooperation that had started even before the Rapallo agreement was signed.

"The greatest threat at present"—the prime minister of Great Britain D. Lloyd George wrote—"consists, to my mind, in the fact that Germany can bind its destiny with Bolsheviks and may place all its material and intellectual resources, all its huge organizational talent at the service of revolutionary fanatics, whose dream is conquest of the world by force of weapon for Bolsheviks. Such a threat is not chimera."[6]

Was there any other choice at Rapallo? The available documents testify that the Germans signed the agreement because they had no other choice. Soviet Russia had an alternative: it could conclude an agreement with the West. Still, Russia gave preference to a pact with Germany.

On August 11, 1922, Germany and Soviet Russia concluded a temporary agreement on cooperation between the Reichswehr and the Red Army. The Reichswehr was given the right to organize military bases on Soviet territory for carrying out tests of materiel, gaining experience in tactics, and training personnel in those branches of the services that the Versailles treaty had banned from Germany. The Germans gave the Soviets an annual material "reward" for utilization of those bases and the right to participate in military-industrial tests and maneuvers.

In the summer of 1923 the participants of the conference in Berlin—minister of foreign affairs Baron von Rosenberg; minister of finance A. Germes; an advisor to the metallurgical company "Hutehoffnungs-hutte," P. Roisch; chief of the armament branch of the ground forces headquarters Lieutenant-Colonel V. Mentzel; and others—determined that a sum in the amount of 75 million marks be allotted to financing military expenditures in Russia. But during an unofficial meeting between Chancellor W. Cuno and Ambassador Brockdorff-Rantzau and the people's commissar of the USSR A. Rozengolts and deputy minister of foreign affairs N. Krestinsky, held at a private apartment in Berlin on June 30, 1923, the chancellor confirmed allotment of only 35 million marks, thus saving 40 million marks in reserve for further talks. Here, Rozengolts offered the German party cooperation in aircraft construction.

A West German historian, an expert on military contracts secured

by the RKKA and the Reichswehr, Rolf Dieter Müller holds the opinion
that the

> German-Russian military relations that were intensively developing
> starting from spring of 1922 entered the phase of trials in the next
> year of 1923. Neither Moscow nor Berlin was ready to take a step
> forward toward entering into a formal military alliance. In the face
> of existing parity of forces, neither Lenin nor Trotsky nor von Seeckt
> or Cuno was apt to resort to military decisions. Both parties tem-
> porized and tried to impel the other to fulfill the preliminary con-
> ditions without binding itself with obligations. An area for tactical
> maneuvering was the manufacture of weaponry in which both parties
> were equally interested.[7]

In autumn of 1923 bilateral talks turned into concrete agreements,
particularly with the "Junkers" Company, on delivery of aircraft and
erection of aircraft factory buildings in USSR territory. In a letter written
by Vaurik, a person empowered to act for the German war ministry,
Russia was clearly referred to as the "strong point of the German aircraft
industry."

An agreement was also reached with the Reichswehr leadership
on the erection of a mustard gas factory. And in 1924, the Soviet industry
accepted an order from the "Metachim" Company for the manufacture
of 400,000 shells for three-inch field guns. In 1926 the Russians delivered
the shells to the Germans. This action caused some political damage
to the Soviets, when the German Social Democrats learned of the transaction and made it public.

In a letter dated February 1, 1926, and addressed to Stalin, Kaminsky
suggested that the three-year period of cooperation with the Reichswehr
had yielded only few results for various reasons. Taking the idea into
consideration, Krestinsky, who had knowledge of the highest ranking
Soviet political and military leadership, offered to call a meeting to
discuss the problems to be solved. Von Seeckt agreed to hold it in
Berlin. As a result of the talks conducted March 25–30, 1926, the Soviet
and German representatives concluded that the military departments
of both countries should start acting immmediately. Von Seeckt became
responsible for solving all the problems in Berlin, Deputy Chairman
of VTchK (GPU) Unshlikht, in Moscow. Communication would be

maintained in Berlin by military attaché P. N. Lunev, in Moscow by Reichswehr representative Lit-Tomsen.

Cooperation between the militaries took various forms: mutual acquaintance of both armed forces with their counterpart's conditions and methods of training by sending commanding personnel to participate in the maneuvers, field exercises, and academic courses of the other side; joint chemical experiments; organization of tank and flying schools; deputation of representatives of the Soviet departments (UVVS, NTK,[8] artillery department, main sanitary department, etc.) to Germany for studying certain problems and getting acquainted with the organization of a number of secret operations.

The cooperation between the RKKA and the Reichswehr in three centers under the code names "Lipetsk," "Kama," and "Tomka" (or "Tomko") deserves special notice. Many servicemen of the Reichswehr were trained there.

The background of the emergence of those centers follows. In 1924 the RKKA leadership suddenly closed a just recently established high-flight school in Lipetsk. At its site the Reichswehr set up a flying school that existed for almost ten years, camouflaged as the Fourth Air Squadron of a flying school of the Red Air Fleet (sometimes in documents as "the 4th air detachment headed by comrade Tompson"[9]). The center was controlled by "Inspection No. 1" of the German defense department "Veramta." Lit-Tomsen was authorized to oversee fulfillment of the terms of the agreement on the flying school.

At the beginning, the school had at its disposal 58 aircraft ("Fokker D-13s," in the main), delivered by the Germans. But the Soviets continually insisted upon delivery of much more modern, first-class aircraft. As a result, by 1931 the school had at its disposal 4 ND-17s and 2 "Fokker D-7" aircraft.

From 1927 to 1928 20 pilots and 24 pilot-observers were trained there. In 1931 fighter pilots were trained at two bases. The study term ran from April 17 till October 5, which seemed to be a quite sufficient period of training for achieving the prescribed goals. A total of 21 persons received training.

Pilot training at both sites relied on the experience accumulated in the previous years. If the training of pilots in the year 1929 was rated as "good," and that of 1930 as "satisfactory in general," graduates in the year 1931 received a mark of "very good."

In 1931 high-altitude flights were planned, but they could not be carried out on a full scale, as much time had been spent on other exercises and there was a shortage of machines and a limited amount of oxygen issued for a flight. To get around these problems, they carried out a greater number of exercise at altitudes (5,000–6,000 meters) that allowed them to breathe regular air. This measure turned out to be well-advised.

Some innovations were made in the school curriculum. For instance, it included the following studies: fighter bombing, which possessed an actual-hit advantage over machine-gun fire; and machine-gun firing practice at a towed target. In summer of the year 1931, for the first time, German and "Russian" air squadrons cooperated in sorties testing a method of attacking daylight bombers.

The school not only trained flying personnel, but also served as the site for experimental and research work. Soviet researchers stressed the need for increasing the quality of their work, as well as involving their specialists in it.

The Reichswehr, which bore the whole expense of the organization, equipment, and maintenance of the school, carefully concealed its activity and did not show its involvement in anything. To provide complete secrecy, the Reichswehr transferred those officers and mechanics to be sent to Lipetsk to the reserve for the duration of their stay in the USSR and gave them the status of "employees of private enterprises."

The pilots wore civilian clothes during their service in the Soviet Union. They were prohibited from telling anybody where they were and what they did there. Falsified reports were issued on deaths resulting from flight accidents. Coffins with corpses were packed in boxes and designated as aircraft parts in the shipper's declaration; the crates were then delivered to the Fatherland by sea from Leningrad to Stettin (today's Szczecin—a seaport in Poland).

It is not groundless to propose that a lot, if not a majority, of German pilots (Blumensaat, Heinz, Makratsky, Foss, Teezmann, Blume, Ressing, and others) who later became famous were trained in Lipetsk. In 1933, 120 to 130 pilots had undergone combat training at the school.

In accordance with the Versailles treaty, Germany was deprived of the right to have tanks; the Reichswehr had to manage without them. But the farsighted von Seeckt, chief of the ground forces department, repeatedly suggested that tank warfare would become a special arm of the service, side by side with the infantry, cavalry, and artillery.

Therefore, adopting von Seeckt's thesis, beginning in 1926 the Germans started to organize a tank school, "Kama," in Kazan.

There they reconstructed on former school premises a workshop and a training ground at a cost of about 2 million marks. The Germans now had an armored-vehicle training ground at their disposal. Training tanks from Germany first began arriving in March 1929.

The school had at its disposal six 23-ton tanks equipped with BMW engines and armed with 75-mm guns, as well as three 12-ton tanks armed with 37-mm guns. In addition, thanks to the RKKA, British-made "Carsten-Lloyd" light tanks were provided for the school. The Reichswehr received them in exchange for auxiliary equipment needed by the USSR defense industry that Germany had given to the Red Army.

Chief of the school was General Lutz who in 1933 held the post of chief of the moto-mechanized troops of the Reichswehr.

The school was controlled by "Inspection No. 6" (motor transport) through the earlier mentioned "Moscow Center" of the German war ministry department.

The tank school trained not more than 12 persons at a time. The German officers to be trained at this school had to leave the service of the Reichswehr for a certain period of time. They reached the USSR via Poland, with passports citing fictitious occupations. As some German historians believe, the horde of tankmen trained at "Kama" school, among whom there were 30 officers, enabled the later creation of German armored troops. Those "Kama" specialists were well trained in both theoretical and technical respects. At this school the future colonel-general of the Wehrmacht, the future commanding general of an armored army, and the future author of works dealing with the use of armored troops, H. Guderian was trained.

The most secret of the Reichswehr operations in the USSR was "Tomka," the so-called chemical warfare school headed by Ludwig von Sicherer.

Chemical experiments began in the area of Podosinky borough in 1926, then they were continued in "Tomka." The enterprise was located in the Samara region on the Volga, not far from the town of Volsk. If you look at a Soviet map of those years, you will see that this installation was in close proximity to the German territory bordering on the Volga Autonomous Republic. One may suppose that was mere coincidence. The school required its personnel to know the German language and such personnel was drawn from the German republic. By this one could evidently explain the choice of location of the "Kama" school.

The Germans invested about 1 million marks in the "Tomka" training center. All this was carried out in spite of the Versailles treaty, according to which the location and erection of similar military enterprises were to be agreed to and approved by the governments of the main allied and united countries. But the German command, ignoring the "Versailles," decided to develop scientific and research works at "Tomka" on the rationalization that the Soviet side would be given new means of chemical warfare (poison gases [PG], instruments, gas masks).

At "Tomka" methods of dispersing poison gases by artillery and the air force, as well as means and methods of degassing of contaminated areas, were practiced and tested. The scientific and research branch of the school used tanks of the latest design in its tests of poison gases with instruments delivered from Germany; it had at its disposal the corresponding workshops and laboratories.

The Soviets attached great significance to industrial production of poison gases. Chief of the military-chemical department Ya. Fishman, in his top-secret report to Voroshilov of February 8, 1927, stressed that "the task of creation of chemical defense of the country is enormous." He drew Voroshilov's attention to the necessity "to start considering seriously" requirements of chemical defense and insisted on increasing production of PGs and gas masks, and erecting new chemical enterprises. To gain that objective our country planned to erect and make use of the productive capacity of the future factory "Bersol" (town of Ivastchenkovo) in cooperation with the Germans. It was supposed that the "Bersol factory would be able to produce about 6 tons of PGs daily. In 'Bersol' factory," Unshlikht noted, "we shall obtain the first and till now a single base for production of a large amount of PGs."

An important factor in the cooperation between the RKKA and Reichswehr became the journeys of the Soviet commanders to Germany for mastering the art of war.

On a mutual basis visits of the Germans to the RKKA were allowed.

The first such mission of the Soviet commanders to Germany for participation in maneuvers took place in 1925. "Paradoxes were following one after another," as FRG historian S. Haffner put it. "The Russians allowed the Germans to visit their country in order that they could develop their weapon and be trained how to use it. Some years later the Germans nearly managed to conquer this country with the use of that weapon and in that situation they became instructors of those who managed to gain victory over them."[10]

In various periods Germany was visited by Tukhachevsky, Uborevitch, Yakir, Triandafilov, Yegorov, Kork, Fedko, Below, Baranov, Dybenko, Unshlikht, Uritsky, Mejeninov, Katkov, Zomberg, Danenberg, Stepanov, Ventsov, Kalmikov, Dubovoi, Primakov, Levandovsky, Levitchev, Latsis, Longva, Kotov,[11] Germanovitch, and many others.

Uborevitch, who worked in Germany for thirteen months, wrote:

> The Germans serve for us as a unique distraction through which we can study the successes achieved in military field abroad, for the German Army in a number of fields has rather interesting achievements. We have learnt much, and we have to do much in our Army in order to get over to more perfect methods of combat training. Now we should focus our attention to making use of engineer achievements of the Germans, mainly in that field which can help us in studying methods of manufacture and use in combat of the latest means of fighting: tanks, perfection of aircraft materiel, anti-tank mines, means of communication, etc. . . . German specialists, including those engaged in the military field, are much more competent than ours.

In a report about large-scale maneuvers of the German Reichswehr conducted from September 14 till September 19, 1930, in Turingia and Bavaria, Germanovitch and Kotov, employees of the intelligence department, informed on the organization of the German troops and praised their high standards. The report noted that during their stay in Germany the Soviet representatives had a meeting with the Commander-in-Chief of the Reichswehr, General Heye.

When staying in Germany, commanding personnel of the RKKA worked in military academies, military schools, archives, and libraries; took part in maneuvers, war games, field exercises (operational and tactical, aviation, logistics supply); and were trained together with specialists on tactics. The Red Army officers got acquainted with the light machine-gun "Dreise" (they praised the German heavy machine-gun equipped to adjust for firing at air targets within 30 seconds), the German field artillery, guns, howitzers, action of anti-tank mines, etc.; studied the Germans' operational, tactical, organizational, and technical views on modern army methods of preparation and organization of education of general staff services—in other words they acquired the so-called "military culture." They were also very much interested in getting acquainted with materiel of the latest design.

Here are only some of the novelties demonstrated by the Germans: anti-aircraft (AA) gun of 7.5 cm caliber, muzzle velocity—88 m per second, effective firing ceiling—9.5 km, range of fire—16 km, i.e., a gun twice as good as the Soviet-made AA gun; the latest optical instrument for anti-aircraft firing designed by Professor Pschor and manufactured by "Siemens" and "Zeiss" companies, intended for firing at a flying enemy air squadron and hitting it at the first round; small-caliber gun used against both tanks and aircraft; AA machine-gun capable of piercing armor of more than 200 mm in thickness, i.e., armor of any light and medium tank, with a firing ceiling of 4200 m (firing ceiling of our heavy machine-gun was 1 km). After inspecting those machine-guns, Uborevitch and Triandafilov concluded that "our machine-guns are not fit to be used against tanks."

Apart from the opportunity to perfect the knowledge of the art of war in Germany, the German side—many companies in particular—gave the RKKA weaponry, ammunition, uniforms, and know-how in regard to various military productions. Thus, in the course of talks with the "Krupp" company in April 1929, an agreement was reached "in the field of special military production." The company undertook to place "experience accumulated in laboratories and training grounds in the field of exterior ballistics at the disposal of the Russian part," to "convey all the experience accumulated in the field of production of material used for making military outfit, methods of its treatment and the whole procedure of handling it," as well as the experience "relative to explosives and powders."

In the summer of 1931 General Kestring wrote to von Seeckt that the consequences of military support provided by Germany to the USSR manifest themselves everywhere in the Red Army. "Our views and methods run all through their military provisions." And no later than 1935, after the Soviet maneuvers, brilliantly carried out by the Red Army, Kestring remarked: "We can be satisfied with this praise. Still, those commanders and chiefs were trained by us."

Marshal Tukhachevsky also had a high opinion of the combat

abilities of the RKKA, but he expressed his opinion of that in a somewhat different, ideological way: "The Workers' and Peasants' Red Army is the only one in the world, force and strength of which are based on the masses of the working people. We are better organized than capitalists. We shall manage to solve the task we are facing more firmly, boldly, and accurately. Guarantee of this consists in our victorious building of socialism, the organizational art of our party, of its great leader comrade Stalin and his comrade-in-arms Voroshilov."

The training of German officers was also actively carried out in the USSR. In 1931 in Moscow additional training was provided to future military commanders of the Second World War: Model, Horn, Kruse, Faige, Brauchitsch, Keitel, Mannstein, Kretchmer, and others.

One may say—and quite reasonably—that a two-way process took place: the Red Army learned something from their better trained teachers. But on the one hand, secret bargains behind the back of the world public had the seal of immorality, while on the other hand the destiny of the Soviet commanders of the higher and medium levels who worked on probation in Germany will turn out tragically. Almost all of them will be annihilated, while the military knowledge and experience they have gotten in Germany will sink into oblivion. (Here is a clue for explaining the repressions of many officials of the RKKA.) Whereas the knowledge and experience acquired by the German specialists were not in vain; the military skills were fully applied when opposing the Red Army.

But as far back as in January 1931 von Seeckt, taking the floor at the Society of the World Economy meeting at the old Münster town hall, said: "Our relations with the Soviet Russia are closely connected with our aspirations for the future."

But history arranged things in another way. . . .

The fascists' taking power in Germany had fatal consequences for all mankind. It became a turning point in the origins of the Second World War and interrupted the joint activity of the Red Army and the Reichswehr.

On April 3, 1933, Krestinsky, in conversation with the ambassador of Germany von Dirksen and military attaché Hartman said:

Close cooperation between the Reichswehr and the Red Army has already been lasting for more than eleven years. I stood at the source of this cooperation and continue to further it all the time. I am well acquainted with all the stages of development of this cooperation, with all the features of improvement and deterioration of our relations, and I may say that these relations were never before realized under such a complex general political situation, as that of today.

On May 10, 1933, a group of five German higher officers headed by chief of the armament department of the Reichswehr General Bokkelberger came to Moscow on Tukhachevsky's invitation. The delegation returned a visit Tukhachevsky had made in 1932, where he got acquainted with some works of the German defense industry. When on tour in the USSR, the Reichswehr officers visited such enterprises of the Soviet defense industrty as TsAGI, the first aircraft building factory; artillery repair works in Golutvin, chemical works in Bobriky; Krasno-Putilovsky works, a range in Luga; a small-arms factory in Zaporojie, the Kalinin gun factory in Moscow; as well as other establishments.

An elated atmosphere reigned at the reception given by the ambassador of Germany on 13 May. Voroshilov spoke about the aspiration to maintain relations between the "friendly" armies in the future as well. During the talk with the Germans Tukhachevsky emphasized: "Do not forget that it is our policy that separates us and not our feelings, the feelings of friendship of the Red Army to the Reichswehr. And always think about the following: you and we, Germany and the USSR, can dictate our terms to the whole world if we are together."

However, despite such assurances, the Soviet-German friendship was gradually coming to naught. According to the evidence of von Dirksen, the USSR initiated the break: "The Soviet military leaders demanded that the Reichswehr should stop the realization of all their arrangements in Russia."

There is no doubt that the coming to power of such an odious figure as Hitler distinctly affected the foreign-policy course of both countries. Nevertheless the Soviet-German contacts still continued on various levels, though their character became different. During that period no important long-term agreements on cooperation were concluded, only agreements of little significance, bearing on the purchase of some samples of war machinery and armaments. The policy of smiles and assurances of friendship of any kind has a purely diplomatic character. In reality the parties show more and more distrust and suspicion of each other, keeping watch on each of its ally's steps to elucidate the character and prospects of subsequent military-political relations. And in that particular case, the actions of the Workers' and Peasants' Red Army and the Reichswehr only reflected (in specific form) those complicated, not simple, processes that were being furthered by the political leadership of the two states when forming their foreign policy.

The Soviet commanders who visited Germany in the thirties noted that the Reichswehr had secret connections simultaneously with other countries as well. The Germans actively cooperated with the plants of Sweden, Holland, and Spain. Some officers had access to the Edgewood Arsenal in America to study the organization of the chemical industry, and General Heye, for instance, acquainted himself with the military establishments in the United States during his mission in the autumn of 1927. In England representatives of the military forces were present at the air and tank maneuvers, and the war technique was worked through in Czechoslovakia.

For its part the Soviet Union also tried to establish many-sided contacts with the West—but this is already another page of history.

In the heat of the many years of mutually advantageous cooperation between the USSR and Germany, hardly a person could foresee that the Soviet Union cherished a snake in its bosom, the "gratitude" of which would later emerge on a tragic summer dawn in 1941. The German offensive military forces—the Wehrmacht—were brought in much under the cover of the deepest secrecy and with the full accord and support of the Soviet government. The fascist sword raised over the world was forged, however regrettable it is, on Soviet soil as well. But to create a powerful air force and the most powerful tank armaments of the time "from nothing" during six years—from 1933 to 1939— would not be possible for even a genius in the field of building-up military forces.

However, that sword was double-edged and was forged by both totalitarian states: the "Stalinist" USSR and fascist Germany. During the Second World War in the long run it would fall upon both the peoples of the USSR and the peoples of Germany.

When survivors of the Second World War related those events from it after the fact, from force of habit they still tried to conceal something and to belittle somehow the importance of what had happened. And so far much remains unclear. For the present, much in their narrations has to be interpreted and much in the documents of that time has to be read between the lines.

The documents presented in this collection are published here for the first time. All of them had been classified as secret, concealing from the world public the secret cooperation of Germany and the Soviet Union. Most of the materials being published are reproduced translations of the originals—quite often in manuscript form—with autographs, resolutions, and notes of their authors. The documents have been selected according to the problem-subject principle and are arranged in chronological order by chapters. Although the book does not have a strictly narrative character, it is being published with all the peculiarities of style and the phraseology of documents of that time maintained. In a number of them some extractions of the text have been made: they mostly involve information of little significance, not bearing directly on the subject. The italics are editorial additions. In the original documents the text is underlined.

The specific feature of the published documents is that most of them concern the activity of the intelligence services of the USSR and Germany. In this connection some names and family names have remained undeciphered, and one just has to speculate on the character of their work.

The texts of the documents are supplied with necessary scientific comments and remarks. Of necessity, the orthography and punctuation have been brought into conformance with up-to-date standards.

Naturally, the documents being brought forward do not pretend to completely elucidate the problem. It seems fruitful for Soviet and foreign historians to combine their efforts in the future to recreate a comprehensive picture of the military cooperation of the Red Army and the Reichswehr.

NOTES

1. K. B. Radek was a left-wing communist in the years 1919–24; a member of CC of RCP(b); a member of the Executive Committee of the Communist International; and a coworker on *Pravda* and *Izvestia* newspapers.

2. Reichswehr (Germ. *Reichswehr,* from *Reich*—state, empire + *Wehr*—defense)

is the German armed forces from 1919 to 1935, which the Versailles peace treaty of 1919 limited to 100,000 hired men. The Reichswehr leadership carried out concealed preparation for a massive armed forces. In March 1935 Germany abrogated the military articles of the Versailles treaty and introduced universal military service. The Wehrmacht was formed on the basis of the Reichswehr.

3. V. I. Lenin, *Collected Works,* 41: 353.

4. More detailed information on persons involved in the events is given, as a rule, when the individuals are first mentioned in the documents.

5. S. Haffner, *Devilish Pact* (Munich, 1965), p. 65.

6. D. Lloyd George, *Truth about Peace Treaties* (Munich, 1957), 1: 350.

7. R. D. Müller, *Das Tor zur Weltmacht* (Boppard am Rhein, 1984).

8. UVVS—Department of the Air Force; NIK—Scientific and Engineering Committee.

9. Actually, his name was Lit-Tomsen.

10. Haffner, *Devilish Pact,* p. 69.

11. Special attention should be paid to Kotov's personality (sometimes he bore the names of Lavrentyev, Naumov). His real name was Eitingon—an official of the intelligence department, an NKVD general, and an organizer of the assassination of Trotsky in 1940.

1

Germany and Russia—
Pariahs of Versailles

Russia and Germany are fighting for their places in world history,
for the predominance of their spirit, for the creation of their values,
for their movement. . . .

N. Berdiaev, Russian philosopher

Linked by native soil, linked by destiny Germany lies between the
West and the East. She must not merge into either. The foundation
of our foreign policy is the aspiration for our being again strong,
united, powerful.

H. von Seeckt, head of the Reichswehr

INTELLIGENCE REPORT.
SOURCE: MINISTRY OF DEFENSE, 2ND BUREAU[1]
RELIABILITY—DOUBTFUL[2]

1920
Warsaw

German-Soviet relations

According to the available information the following agreement was
concluded between Germany and the Soviet government in March 1920:

I. Germany undertakes:

1. To equip the Russian army and industry so that same could resist the English in Asia and in Poland.

2. In every possible way to support Russia in her peace negotiations with the Western States.

II. The Soviet government undertakes:

1. To place mines, railways, canals, and big enterprises for exploitation by the Germans.

The original text was signed by Lenin, Trotsky, and Chicherin,[3] on the one hand, and by Noske, Ertsberg, Bauer[4]—on the other hand.

A copy of that document was bought by an English agent for 18,000 livres, sent to Warsaw, and forwarded express to the British Ministry of Foreign Affairs. According to the same source the number of the German instructors in Russia comes to 20,000; they come by a regular sea lane from Szczecin.

Attention! The Ministry of Defense of Poland states that they received this information from an English person, and passes same "under question" and requests to inform, if possible, to what extent it is reliable.

The State Archives. Main. f. 1703. Inv. 1. F. 441. Sh. 80.
[The original is in German.]

*   *   *

TOP SECRET—TO COMRADE LEJAVA[5]

20 August 1920
Post-telegram No. 791

The Politburo[6] has decided to conclude immediately the transaction for arms proposed by comrade Unshlikht.[7] You have immediately, not losing an hour, to come to an agreement with comrade Obolensky,[8] so that under his responsibility the necessary sum (twenty-seven million marks) be remitted through Gukovsky[9] or Kopp. The matter is extremely important and urgent. Its practical execution is entrusted by the Politburo to you and to comrade Unshlikht; the remittance of the money, to comrade Obolensky.

Chairman of the Revolutionary Military Council—Trotsky
CSASA. F. 33987. Inv. 3. F. 52. Sh. 430.

*   *   *

TROTSKY—TO LENIN, CHICHERIN, KRESTINSKY,[10] BUKHARIN[11]

1920
Post-telegram No. 757

It is necessary to make preventive measures in respect of the stupid demand of the Germans[12] of satisfaction for Count Mirbakh.[13] If that demand is advanced officially and we are forced to enter into explanations, then rather unpleasant recollections will come to light (Alexandrovitch,[14] Spiridonova,[15] and others). I think that, since the matter has already come to light in the press, it is necessary that our press responds too and that comrade Chicherin in an interview or in some other way gives the understanding to the German government and to the Scheidemann[16] Social-Democrats supporting it that having advanced that demand they fall into the most stupid situation. The newspapers could ridicule that demand in prose and in verses, and the echo would reach Berlin by radio. It is much more advantageous than to explain officially at the talks on the substance of the matter.

Trotsky
CSASA. F. 33987. Inv. 3. F. 52. Sh. 383.

*   *   *

LETTER OF TROTSKY—TO KOPP

December 1920
Moscow
No. 1031

Dear Comrade!

Quite irrespective of whether the German bourgeoisie will fight with White Poland because of the parts of Silesìa, I believe—and this is general opinion here—that our policy must be strictly peace-oriented. Undoutedly, the state of our army and our transport is such that we could liquidate with a surplus the consequences of our failures of August at the Western front. But it is out of the question. The Party intends to pursue the policy of peace in the most firm and resolute way. All our forces are being concentrated now on economy problems.

I doubt very much that General Seeckt[17] is really conspiring with the British. If there is anything of this kind then it is most likely provocation on the part of the clique of Churchill. These scoundrels want to draw us into a new war at any cost. But we do not want a war—either in the West, or in the East.

CSASA. F. 33987. Inv. 3. F. 52. Sh. 759. Copy.

*   *   *

FROM THE DRAFT PLAN SETTING UP
A SECRET SERVICE IN GERMANY[18]

1920
Top secret

Germany requires a comprehensive investigation not only from diplomatic and political, but also from military and economic, points of view. . . . The Central Residents should pay the most serious attention. . . .

3) In the military sphere it is necessary to find out the real forces of Germany, those provided for by the Treaty of Versailles as well as those organized or being organized bypassing same, in the guise of various kinds of societies and organizations of internal guards, shooting, gymnastic, etc. Number of officers and noncommissioned officers recorded only nominally in the reserve. Further it is necessary to find out how units and various organizations of a military character are equipped, the extent of training and discipline of the latter, stocks of armaments and equipment of any kind being available in Germany, locations of warehouses, and also the extent of productivity of the factories. It is also important to ascertain the mood of units, possibilities of their use for inner purposes and for external fight, secret mobilization plans in case of war, real state of military training of the youth (in connection with the Treaty of Versailles), the mood of the officers and the influential

military spheres, this or that influences on them of political circles (the monarchist ones) and its importance as a political factor. . . .

It is necessary to find out the exact number of prisoners of war from Russia, their composition, location of camps, state, mood, propaganda of the reactionary Russian circles and the extent of support of the latter by the present German government, governmental agents, influential anarchist circles and representatives of the Entente. . . .

6) Transit via Germany of these or those cargoes for Poland, Czechoslovakia, or Ukraine; transport of the Russian and Ukrainian units being formed in those directions.

7) Possibility of manufacturing war orders in Germany for the needs of her neighboring states. . . .

> CSASA. F. 33987. Inv. 3. F. 25. Sh. 93–95.
> Copy.

*   *   *

IAGODÁ:[19] "WOULD THINK TO SETTLE THIS QUESTION ONCE AND FOR ALL IN THE FOLLOWING WAY. . . ."[20]

1920

. . . 1. Send all generals, colonels, and lieutenant-colonels to Moscow, put them in a camp there, and filter them.

2. Arrange rear camps in which there is no big conglomeration of military units for counterrevolutionary elements.[21]

3. After filtration on the spot, act according to the telegram of Vesnik.[22]

4. Stamp all documents of the former officers [to indicate] their former service with the Whites.

5. Oblige all military commissars of provinces and regions to complete the Special Department questionnaires on the arrival of officers and inform about their movement.[23]

> G. Iagodá[24]
> CSASA. F. 33987. Inv. 3. F. 25. Sh. 70.
> Original.

*   *   *

FROM CIRCULATING LETTER OF VTchK NO. 10[25]

1921
Moscow

After the liquidation carried out by Vecheka,[26] the old membership of the Central Committee of the SR party[27] was arrested in its considerable part, and namely the following members of the PSR CC were arrested: Gots, Abram Rafailovitch; Rakov (Osetsky), Dmitry Fedorovitch; Timofeev (Litvinov), Evgueny Mikhailovitch; Vedeniapin, Mikhail Alexandrovitch; Tseitlin, Mikhail Salomonovitch;[28] Donskoi, Dmitry Dmitrievitch; Ratner (Elkind), Evguenia Moisseevna; Morozov, Serguei Vladimirovitch; Berg, Efrem Solomonovitch.

A part of the members of the CC of the SR party had time to escape, including the leader of the party and a permanent member of its CC, Victor Tchernov.

The All-Russian conference of the SR party held in autumn 1920 elected a new CC. Undoubtedly that V. Tchernov is a member of that new CC as well. At present Tchernov is abroad. Previously he lived in Revel . . . , and then moved to Prague, where under the wing of the ruling part of the Czech national "socialists" a whole nest of the SR was set up, publishing the newspaper *Volia Rossii,* edited by Zensonov, Lebedev, Minkh. Kerensky, who has come to the surface anew, joins that group.

. . . To carry on the work aiming at the total destruction and liquidation of the SR party as such.

Chief of SOVTchK[29] Samsonov
Business Manager of VTchK G. Iagodá
CSASA. F. 33987. Inv. 3. F. 62. Sh. 147.

*   *   *

FROM CIRCULATING LETTER OF VTchK NO. 11[30]

1921
Moscow

For the three years of the existence of the Soviet Republic among the enemies against which it has had to fight, not the last place was occupied by Social Democrats (Mensheviks). The party of the proletariat was forced to be engaged in the fight before the October Revolution as well. What is the point and the cause of our fight against Menshevism? When the world capital in the person of Lloyd George and Co. comes out against us as well as the Russian White Guard generals, they strive openly for the return of the power of capital over the working people. . . . All the tactics of the Russian and foreign imperialists lead to the most part of the proletariat being consolidated against them in their aspiration to smash the hostile forces of capital, and as long as the revolutionary unity of the proletariat and its combat readiness are secured, the Soviet Republic is not so afraid of the danger on the part of world capital. The danger would be mortal if the proletariat lost the revolutionary unity and combat readiness. The activity of the socially treacherous parties on the whole, and the Mensheviks in particular, is reduced exactly to that. . . .

Thus we ascertain that the party of Mensheviks in Russia has not renounced the plan to overthrow the Soviet power. . . .

1) So far as the Mensheviks, under pressure of the historic events and the successful struggle of the Soviet power, have openly recognized it, have mobilized their members to the Red Army, and so on—the affiliation itself to the party of Mensheviks does not give ground to persecute them, to imprison them only for that without definite accusations. . . .

2) But since the petit-bourgeois nature of the Menshevist party incites them to a dual policy of vacillations and hesitations, the Soviet power must be on the watch and on the alert for their each step, suppressing any counterrevolutionary attempts. Resort to repressive measures must be engendered and motivated not by the affiliation to the Social-Democratic Party, but by concrete definite deeds. . . .

At the present moment all our attention must be concentrated on the information without which the work of the TchK apparatus will be amateurish—not achieving its objective—and blunders will eventually occur. At present the center of the burden of our work is placed on the informative apparatus because only on condition that TchK is sufficiently informed, [and] has the exact information to throw light upon both the organization and its individual members, will it be able to avoid mistakes [and] to take necessary measures in time to liquidate both a really harmful and dangerous group and an individual subject to isolation. . . .

> Chief of SOVTchK Samsonov
> Business Manager G. Iagodá
> CSASA. F. 33987. Inv. 3. F. 62. Sh. 1–5.

*   *   *

COLLAPSE OF THE COMMUNIST POWER

1921
Warsaw

Trotsky and Lenin are quarreling. Trotsky insists on renewing hostilities against Poland. Lenin speaks of the necessity of a [brief] "respite." Soon Trotsky would call Lenin a "counterrevolutionary," and the father of communism "Ilyich" would come to belong to the "White Guard." This is one sign of the collapse of the communist power. Rats desert the sinking ship. In February a plan was worked out for "evacuation" of commissars and communists abroad to Western Europe via [the town of] Kovno, for communists know that the day of the peoples' wrath is approaching. Having robbed the people of everything they could, many of the communists with their families are now residing in Berlin, Budapest, and other cities on account of the alleged treatment. This is another sign of the collapse of the communist power.

The communists have cancelled requisitions. They are imposing a land tax. They have given up the idea of communes in the villages, but none of the peasants will believe their sincerity, for one lie makes many. The communists who shot down peasants, who took away their cattle and bread, who ravaged villages—this time are playing friends to the people. And this is the third sign of the collapse of the communist power.

Fuel is lacking. Railways are deteriorated. Factories are closed, cities perish. Poverty in villages. And here is the fourth sign of the collapse of the communist power.

There is now hatred for communists in the Red Army. Workers hate them. All the people hate the communists. And this is the fifth sign of the collapse of the communist power.

The communists lie through their teeth that "everything is going on well," factories are operating, railways are in order, everybody in cities has much food and enjoys happiness, peasants in villages are thriving and blessing Lenin and Trotsky—in a word, Sovdepia is the earthly Paradise. The lie is a manifestation of weakness. This is the sixth sign of the collapse of the communist power. Their power is shaken. The communists do not have other foundations to rest upon except "Ch(e) K(a)" and "Special Boards." The hour of the revolution, of the peoples' liberation, is approaching. Down with the commune! Long live the Constituent Assembly!

> ZGASA.[31] F. 33987. Inv. 3. F. 62. Sh. 720.
> Rokov, V. [32]

*   *   *

AFRAID TO BE CALLED TO ACCOUNT

1921, Warsaw

Now that they have an answer for their deeds and try to save their skin—they sing out of tune more and more. Trotsky tries to shift Lenin, while Bukharin is bearing a grudge against Trotsky. And the main blood-sucker Dzerzhinsky wouldn't mind choking them to death altogether to reign himself thereon. For the time being they are certainly trying to conceal this struggle from the people, but murder will always out. The rumors about the squabbles and the plots the Soviet ringleaders are weaving against one another are even slipping into the Soviet press. Comrade Rykov[33] has been removed from his post of Sovnarkhoz Chairman. Comrade Lomov,[34] the one who went to Riga for organizing trade business (but failed to do it though), has been driven away as well, and many others have got the beating. As for Rykov, he kept insisting on acknowledging in a loud voice that the commune policy had been for nothing and should be liquidated.

—All they did for the past three-and-a-half years has come to nothing. Everything is to be started from the beginning—from the former way of life, without commune—he used to say. That is why he was driven away! . . .

ZGASA. F. 33987. Inv. 3. F. 62. Sh. 720.

*   *   *

VYGAND'S[35] CORRESPONDENCE TO NEW YORK

March 26, 1921, 16.50
Nauen

. . . Chicherin openly informs that the Russian-German agreement has not been signed as yet. The Ministry for Foreign Affairs has confirmed the information and notified me of the fact that only the Minutes of the Russian-German trade agreement were signed in Moscow in February, but the agreement itself has not been signed as yet. Chicherin's radio informs of the following: "Moscow. To Vygand, Berlin. The trade agreement with Germany gives England great advantages in trade dealings with Russia. Having concluded the agreement before Germany and America the English Government has gained great advantages. The trade agreement with England means for Russia radical change in its economic life which will later affect its methods. It will undermine the French economy and make it possible for Great Britain to occupy a more comfortable position for a long period of time. In due course we shall see for ourselves the great importance of this agreement."

Chicherin-Vygand.

CGASA. F. 33987. Inv. 3. F. 62. Sh. 370.

*   *   *

PRINTED ORDER NO. 171
OF VCIK PLENIPOTENTIARY COMMISSION

June 11, 1921
Tambov

From June 1 forth the decisive struggle against thuggery has brought relief to the regions.

The Soviet power is gradually recovering, the peasants are getting down to peaceful labor. Antonov's[36] band is destroyed by decisive operations of our troops; the members of the band are now scattered and captured one after another, each separately.

To root out the social-revolutionaries' bands, the VCIK Plenipotentiary Commission, further to the previous orders, decrees the following:

1) Those refusing to give their name shall be shot down on the spot without trial.

2) Upolitcommission or Raypolitcommission (the Authorized Political Commission and the Regional Political Commission) shall arrest hostages and shoot them down, should they not surrender weapons hidden in villages.

3) Should the hidden weapon be found, the head of the family shall be shot down without trial.

4) The family, sheltering a bandit in its house, shall be arrested and deported from the province, its property confiscated, and the head of such a family shall be shot down without trial.

5) The families sheltering family members of such bandits in their house will be regarded as bandit families and the head of such a family shall be shot down without trial.

6) Should the family of a bandit make an escape, the property of such a family shall be distributed among the peasants devoted to the Soviet Power; the houses of such families shall be burnt down.

7) This order shall be implemented severely and mercilessly.[37]

Chairman of VCIK Plenipotentiary Commision
Antonov-Evseenko

General Officer Commander
Tukhachevsky

Chairman of Gubispolkom (Province Executive Committee)
Lavrov

Secretary
Vasiliev

To be read out at villagers' meetings.
Published in the newspaper *Nasha Pravda* (Our truth).
The group of the Kozlovsk Executive Committee of RKP(b)-Russian
Communist Party (of Bolsheviks). 1921.

CGASA. F. 33987. Inv. 3. F. 62. Sh. 800.

* * *

EXTRACT FROM MINUTES OF THE SESSION
OF THE RUSSIAN NATIONAL COMMITTEE[38]

February 29, 1924
No. 140

Chairman: A. V. Kartashev[39]
Comrades of the Chairman: V. L. Burtsev, Yu. N. Danilov
Counts N. D. Dolgorukov, E. P. Kovalevsky, P. M. Fedorov
Committee members: A. I. Guchkov, V. K. Katenev, Ya. I. Savich,
K. I. Sychev, S. A. Smirnov, D. S. Pasmanik, Count I. A. Kurakin
Invited: I. P. Aleksinsky, Count; citizens N. Trubetskoy and P. N.
    Shatilov

1. Report from A. I. Guchkov on the news from Russia.
    . . . It is maintained, that the split is serious and irreparable, there
is no other way out but a violent upheaval. Only martial upheaval is
possible—of whatever form it may be—a coup d'etat or a larger scale
action. The power itself is so weak that its overthrow is inevitable. It
will be replaced by the red dictatorship. Tukhachevsky who is now in
Smolensk is a typical figure. According to one well-informed German,
Tukhachevsky has much appeal among the masses. Some time ago he
became suspected and was called to Moscow. He was supposed to be
charged with an honored but not influential post.

He refused to obey. Rabble-rousing anti-communist and anti-Semite moods now exist in Smolensk. Open propaganda is spread in the battalion (the group of Rykhov, Krasin, Sokolnikov responds best to the vital interests of Russia). (Trotsky could join them. Rykov is a man of will.)

There has been a change in the Germans' estimation of the situation in Russia. Before, they used to believe in evolution. Now they think that the military upheaval is more probable, though not inevitable. They point to Tukhachevsky. They do not only dare to predict who is to come to succeed the doomed power. They also acknowledge a full economical crash of the Soviet power. As the center grows weaker, the population becomes braver and braver. . . .

The center of the power is still strong, it is early to speak of its fall. Even Trotsky does not seem to present danger to the power. In the Army all the suspected have been exterminated.

> Chairman of the Committee A. Kartashev
> Chairman Comrade P. Fedorov
> CGASA. F. 33987. Inv. 3. F. 1295. Sh. 1–2.
> Copy.

*   *   *

"WE START AT THE POINT WHERE WE STOPPED SIX CENTURIES AGO"—A. HITLER

. . . Neither our orientation to the West nor our orientation to the East should be the future aim of our foreign policy in the sense of acquiring a piece of land for our German people. . . . The victory of the idea will become possible sooner, as the propaganda among the masses of the people becomes more comprehensive, and as the organization that carries on the practical struggle becomes more exclusive, stricter, and stronger. . . .

We start at the point where we stopped six centuries ago. We cease the holy campaign of the Germans to the South and West of Europe and fix our eyes on the land in the East. At last we are completing the colonial and trade policy of the pre-war period and are going over to the land policy of the future. But when in Europe today we speak of new domains, foremost we can think of Russia and its subordinated limitrophies. . . .[40]

A. Hitler, *Mein Kampf* (München, 1925–27),
pp. 653, 742, 757, 783
[Translated from German]

NOTES

1. The Ministry of Defense, the 2nd Bureau—the intelligence body of the Polish Ministry of Defense.

2. The document, as is seen from its contents, is of a secret-service character. To all appearances, it concerns the secret agreement between Russia and Germany. The only thing known is that Kopp, the envoy of Trotsky, arrived in Berlin in November 1919, not only to settle the questions of repatriation of the Russian prisoners of war, but also to extend the relations established by Radek. On 19 April 1920, the German Reich and the RSFSR signed the agreement on the repatriation of prisoners of war and interned persons on both sides. That agreement legally consolidated the existence of the missions of observation. In Moscow the mission was headed by Gustav Hilger, and in Berlin, by Victor Kopp.

3. L. D. Trotsky was Chairman of the Revolutionary Military Council (RVS) of the republic; G. V. Chicherin, in 1918–30, was Commissar of Foreign Affairs of the RSFSR, USSR.

4. G. Noske, M. Ertsberg, and O. Bauer were representatives of the German government.

5. A. M. Lejava was Deputy Chairman of People's Commissar of Foreign Trade.

6. Of the Russian Communist Party (Bolsheviks).

7. I. S. Unshlikht, in 1919–20, was a member of the RVS of the Western front; at the same time in 1920 he was a member of the Interim Polish Revolutionary Committee. In 1921, he was Deputy Chairman of the All-Russian Extraordinary Commission for Combating Counterrevolution and Sabotage (VTchK) (GPU). He submitted a proposal to make a transaction with Germany for the supply of arms. On 20 August 1920, Trotsky informed him by direct line in cipher: "In reply to ref. No. 3838/V 930/ III. Transaction is approved, that is, Lejava is instructed to remit money promptly. Hurry up to complete the transaction. Trotsky" ([CSASA]. F. 33987. Inv. 3. F. 52. Sh. 427). Side by side with that telegram there is also this unsigned document: "Gold will be delivered to you in German marks, partly in English pounds sterling" (ibid., sh. 438).

On the same day one more telegram was sent to Unshlikht: "Top secret. By direct-line (in cipher). Call Unshlikht. Further to my cable No. 790, informing: Sending of gold by ways mentioned to you extremely difficult. Do you have yourselves opportunity to deliver gold in bars directly to supplier? Do you also have opportunity to send another lot to Kopp with reliable persons? Trotsky" (ibid., sh. 439).

8. L. L. Obolensky was a representative of the RSFSR in Poland.

9. I. E. Gukovsky was a Menshevik, representative of the RSFSR in Germany.

10. N. N. Krestinsky was a member of the Politburo of the Central Committee of RCP (Bolsheviks), People's Commissar of Finance, and later on, Deputy People's Commissar of Foreign Affairs.

11. N. I. Bukharin was a member of the Politburo of the Central Committee of the RCP (Bolsheviks).

12. Trotsky called "stupid" the German demand for bringing a German battalion into Moscow for the protection of the diplomatic mission after the assassination of the German Ambassador Count V. Mirbakh in 1913. The Soviet government declined to honor the demand.

13. As is known, Mirbakh was assassinated by Bliumkin and Andreev, belonging supposedly to the party of the Socialist Revolutionaries. Lately, the Western press has advanced a point of view that the VTchK, not the Socialist Revolutionaries, was involved in the assassination of Mirbakh. We are not influenced by such documents. However, the reporters managed to find material of a later date (1927) showing that Bliumkin was on the staff of the IVth Intelligence Department of the RKKA Staff. These lines are from the document signed by the chief of the intelligence department Berzin:

> . . . Comrade Bliumkin . . . upon arrival in Urga started a row against our instructors and comrade Kangelari [chief of the staff of the Mongolian People's Army], stopping at nothing, right up to discrediting some Party functionaries in front of the Mongols and even to terrorizing. . . . At the meeting of the Party activists of the cell he put forward the idea of setting up in Urga the "Bliumkin" People's University. . . . Bliumkin's behavior has a very corruptive influence on all instructors and in the future it can affect the combat efficiency of the Mongolian Army. . . . I believe that in the nearest future he must be recalled from the Mongolian Army. Candidates are being selected.

> Berzin
> CSASA. F. 55987. Inv. 3. F. 126. Sh. 48.
> Original

14. V. Alexandrovitch was a Left Socialist Revolutionary, Deputy Chairman of VTchK.

15. M. A. Spiridonova was one of the organizers and leaders of the Left Socialist Revolutionaries. Murdered by NKVD in autumn 1941.

16. F. Scheidemann was one of the leaders of the German Social Democrats. He tried to hamper further development of the November Revolution (1918–19) in Germany.

17. H. von Seeckt, from 1920, was chairman of the Land Forces Department of the Reichswehr.

18. The document was worked out by the Registration Department of the field staff of the RVS of the republic. According to its chief Ausem, from December 1918

up to January 1920, about 6,000,000 rubles were spent on intelligence work. The number of agents totals 285 person (CSASA. F. 33987. Inv. 3. F. 25. Sh. 98).

19. G. G. Iagodá, in 1920, was business manager of the Special Department of VTchK.

20. The question is about the White Guard officers.

21. On 3 June 1920, the authorized envoys from the officers imprisoned in the second Tula forced labor concentration camp—Semisotov, Senitsky, Maliuguin, Beka-revitch, Voznesensky, and Nikultsev—applied to Moscow with a letter to the Chairman of the Special Meeting under Commander-in-Chief Brusilov:

> The Russian officers have always served the Motherland not for fear, but conscientiously, and are ready to serve her to the bitter end. . . . We believe that at that historic moment of our people's life this is not the place and not the time for a protracted exchange of proclamations and resolutions from behind the barbed wire of camps. If the Motherland and the Soviet government need us then we request the Special Meeting under the Commander-in-Chief to solicit granting us as soon as possible an opportunity to make use of our experience and knowledge.
>
> CSASA. F. 33987. Inv. 3. F. 25. Sh. 78

Such concentration camps for the White Guards were in Moscow, Petrograd, Orel, Riazan, and others.

22. Ia. I. Vesnik was a member of RVS. The text of the cable is unknown.

23. Such orders were reproduced voluntarily or not by the Germans during their time in their country.

24. The stressmark is put in the document exactly like that.

25. The document is marked with "copy No. 4 is handed to Trotsky."

26. VTchK.

27. The only party with which the Bolsheviks shared power in 1917 was the Socialist-Revolutionary party (SR). They were popular among peasants as they stood up for the "socialization" of land. The famous Decree on Land was a part of their program. In 1918 a split between the Bolsheviks and the SR came about on the question of the Brest Peace Treaty. The positions became extremely sharp after the Bolsheviks introduced the food dictatorship in the country, since the SR believed that such policy in the first place strikes the country as a whole, not the kulak.

28. Like this in the document.

29. The Secret Department of VTchK.

30. The document is marked with "copy No. 187 is handed to Bukharin."

31. ZGASA—The Central State Archives of the Soviet Army.

32. V. Rokov was a member of the SRs (Social Revolutionaries).

33. A. I. Rykov, in 1918–21, was people's commissar of internal affairs (*Narkom*).

34. G. I. Lomov (Appokov), in 1918–31, was deputy chief of *Gosplan* SSSR, CC member, VCIK SSSR.

35. Vygand—obviously a *New York Times* correspondent.

36. A. S. Antonov was a Social Revolutionary, leader of the peasant rebellion in the province of Tambov that broke out because of growing discontent with *prodrazverstka* and mobilization policy. The struggle against *antonovshchina* was guided by the VCIK Plenipotentiary Commission with Antonov-Evseenko and Tukhachevsky— General Officer Commander as leaders. Army Commanders Uborevich, Fed'ko also participated in the severe suppression of the rebellion. In the future all of them will closely cooperate with the Reichswehr.

37. Rykov's handwritten note to Trotsky of July 18, 1921, now kept in the archives, contains the following information concerning the order:

> Lev Davydovitch: In accordance with the Politburo resolution, attached is the order issued by Antonov-Evseenko and Tukhachevsky. The following proposal was made to the VCIK Presidium and supported by the majority of its members: 1) The order shall be cancelled. 2) Antonov-Evseenko and Tukhachevsky shall be recalled.
>
> To my account is a report to the VCIK Presidium on these proposals and on coordination with CK RKP(b). To my mind, VCIK Presidium must respond to this order after it is published in the local press.
>
> A. I. Rykov
> CSASA. F. 33987. Inv. 3. F. 62. Sh. 799–800.
> Original manuscript.

38. This document was found on the premises of the Raivola railway station in Finland after the Red Army had occupied it in the course of the Soviet-Finnish war. The minutes were sent to Voroshilov by Beria on January 3, 1940.

39. A. V. Kartashev was a religious thinker, a historian, a Constitutional Democrat. From January 1919 he headed the Russian National Committee in Finland. It consisted of former industrialists, ministers of the Provisional Government, members of the State Duma, scientists, and people involved in social activities.

40. Limitrophies (from Latin-Greek, *limitrophus,* frontier)—neighboring or adjacent states. In a narrow sense it implies Lithuania, Latvia, Estonia. In a broader sense it also implies Poland and Finland.

2

The Peculiar Basis of Relations
between the RKKA and the Reichswehr

All "friendship" and cooperation of the Reichswehr proceeded from
the desire to give us less and worse, but to exploit us as fully possible.
K. Voroshilov, Narkom (Peoples' Commissar
for Military and Naval Affairs)

Both states must rely upon one another and work together.
V. Adam, chief of the General Headquarters of Reichswehr

INTERCEPTED GERMAN SÉCRET-SERVICE REPORT[1] TO FRUNZE,[2]
CHAIRMAN OF RVS SSSR [REVOLUTIONARY
MILITARY COUNCIL OF THE USSR]

Copies to: Unshlikht, Chicherin

February 5, 1925
Strictly confidential

Implementing the ideas that formed the basis of the Dowers Plan,[3] the
Entente, and France in particular, rightly took into consideration the
fact that the adoption of this plan by Germany will naturally direct the
active economic policy of Germany to the west of Europe, and this will
cause a change of the political course with Soviet Russia outlined by
the Rapallo agreement, which was a continuation of the historical "Drang

49

nach osten" movement toward the Russian market. After the adoption of the Dowers Plan with Germany, Baron Maltzan and Count Brockdorff-Rantzau[4]—the most active adherents of the "eastern" political course of Germany—nevertheless tried to prevent the turn of policy from western tendencies. But [this is] due to the fact that now more than before considerations lying at the basis of the German policy are the industrial and financial interests of Germany, and due to the fact that since the adoption of the Rapallo treaty the years of practice have not yielded expected results, the reason for which was not only the impossibility of Germany's carrying on a wide-range policy in the USSR because of its financial and political situation, but also the inertia of the Russian government in facilitating Germany's interest in the east of Europe. . . .

After the adoption of the Dowers Plan, most of the German industrialists who had voted for it began to protect their interests—on their own accord without the government's assistance—by either conducting negotiations with French and English industrialists and their financial circles or being supported by Luther's cabinet,[5] which sympathizes with the western direction of the policy, and partly by Stresemann,[6] an adherent of this course as well.

Finally, part of the Rhine industry representatives supported by the government drew its attention to the west of Europe. Krupp's resistance is broken down, mainly owing to Widenfeld,[7] and the possibility to obtain credits in the UNSA.[8] Now Krupp also supports west industrial movement, the main leader of which is Tissen.[9] Such a direction of German policy brought out the necessity for the resignation of Maltzan who is in favor of the Rapallo policy way. At the same time the USSR policy has been giving Germany more and more grounds to deviate from the eastern direction. The USSR government tries to secure its position among the most powerful Entente countries.

Moscow is undoubtedly ready to sacrifice Germany's interests. Bolsheviks are disappointed in the revolutionary movement in Germany. Now Communist International seems to pin much hope on France. The Soviet military circles are trying to acquaint themselves not with the suppressed German military doctrine, but with a free, developing, military science based on French practice. For example, it is very important a fact that Junkers concession—the main implement of the Rapallo agreement—which has been working successfully in the USSR so far, has now entered its new stage.

Biased by the forthcoming French-Soviet negotiations, Bolsheviks seem to have lost interest in Junkers and are ready to sacrifice him, should it become possible to enlist credits for aeronautic purposes from the French industry. We have information that Moscow is prepared for discussions of aeronautic issues with France and is ready to make concessions to the French airplane industry.[10] . . . Trotsky's resignation[11] has had adverse effects on German-Soviet relations. Rantzau's work in Moscow meets with more and more difficulties.

Erbet's[12] arrival in Moscow has relegated him to the background. The government has called him to Berlin for report and also to acquaint him with the new directions of the German policy and with the ideas it is guided by. It can hardly be possible for Maltzan to attract American investments, a condition for which is recognition of the USSR by the USA—the principal idea of Maltzan's work in fulfillment of the behests of the "movement to the east of Europe" idea.

We have information reliable enough to say for sure that France is now developing its eastern policy and that Moscow is to become its center; we are also informed that by tying Germany's policy to the Dowers Plan, thus binding the interests of the German policy to the western movement, France is now preparing for active policy in the USSR. The French ambassador to the UNSA not only advocates the recognition of Moscow by Washington, but also seeks employment in Russia for Frenchmen. The old French plan is implemented, though much restricted, by English-American movement. De-Monzy[13] is right to say that much time has been wasted. Despite all this, we are actually not in a position to change the present situation.

Our interests now lie in the western part of Europe. Our industry works only on condition of the agreement with France and England. The present government is only drifting, guided by our industry. And, nevertheless, the stronger are our specialists, the more powerful is our west political movement. All the political parties except the extreme right-wings and the extreme left-wings are instigating and leading our policy in the western direction.

Germany's joining the Nations League will become one more obstacle in our past "movement to the east" policy, but there is no other way out. From the logical point of view, we cannot lean on Russia and look for salvation in that country. We cast in our lot with the west of Europe now.

It must be admitted, however, that the Rapallo agreement has made many things easier for us and has given us a certain weight in international policy, but on an even larger scale it was used by Bolsheviks who are in every respect now ready to regard its use in all ways exhausted. ... From the psychological and political point of view, the activities of France in the USSR are more advantageous and convenient than was our work; therefore it may be expected that it will yield better results for France than did our Rapallo policy. Economically and industrially Russia and Germany are separated from each other, and although, to a certain extent, the USSR can exist independently, we with our political situation and Dowers Plan and Versailles treaty cannot do that. Our industrial isolation is impermissible for us, therefore we must seek help in the West on the grounds that the conditions of the East cannot offer it to us.

Of course, it is problematic that the Junkers plans in Russia will be frustrated, but in this situation the decisive point is the behavior of the Soviet government, for it is Junkers who can work principally on the Russian market, since under the existing circumstances its work in the west of Europe does not seem possible. But Moscow, however, is interested in the treaty with France. In this treaty it will drink to the dregs all its disappointment in Germany, since however peculiar our situation, Moscow had expected much more from us (and probably not without reasons), but our internal policy and the hesitant character of our international policy prevented us from taking advantage of the time and the favorable situation that existed. Now it is too late, and there is no use doing it.

Probably we shall soon face the necessity not only to develop, but also to defend, the advantages we have in the Rapallo agreement. It may be expected, however, that in due time, when the present situation of our industry has been overcome, and we have entered the stage of industrial stabilization, our growing industry, thanks to the Dowers Plan, may once again turn to the East, but it may also be expected that by the time it will have happened, we shall not be able to compete with the international industry and investments already soundly settled, since the idea of laying hold of the key branches by industry for the future in Russia was not fulfilled for many reasons. It may also be that the Entente itself will send us to the Russian market to the extent necessary for British industry, but we shall certainly not be drawn together politically by this. Such a new situation makes easier our struggle against Communist International and its bodies, and against Bolshevik agents.

> Verified: Chief of the Second Department[14]
> [Signature][15]
> ZGASA. F. 33987. Inv. 3. F. 98. Sh. 153–57.
> Certified copy.

*   *   *

BERLIN. STRICTLY CONFIDENTIAL. LUNEV[16]

August 13, 1925[17]

I have inspected Hertz optics plant on August 12, 1925. Director Ipan[18] particularly insisted on the inspection of the glass plant, all the time trying to convince me that it was very inexpedient to have built our own plant of optical glass in Russia and that it was more advantageous to purchase glass abroad (from Hertz, for instance). He tried to persuade me that even now that the plant is already built, it would still be more advantageous to abandon it and to purchase a stock of glass abroad. . . . Glass processing, manufacturing of mechanical parts of optical devices and calculators at the plant are mechanized and even automatized.

At one time they had sold us filming equipment, and comrade Ershov, who accepted the equipment, promised to forward the pictures that were taken in the region of Pervomaisk for further experiments at the second stage of the work.

All the devices are complicated and bear high accuracy. . . . Plant divisions are engaged in the production of military devices (panoramas, stereotubes, range-finders) and are located in Pressburgh, Wien. We have failed to learn whether there are any other production branches. Due to lack of time I did not inspect . . . the photographic materials (tapes and plates). Though allowed to visit the plant at any time, I doubt if frequent visits would be expedient, for to derive a piece of some important information during an ordinary inspection visit is possible only for a good expert.

> ZGASA. F. 33987. Inv. 3. F. 98. Sh. 70–71.
> Copy.

*   *   *

"SOURCE OF INFORMATION IS PERFECTLY CREDIBLE"[19]

August 17, 1926

There were two periods in the political thought of all the right wings of the politically maneuvering Germany. The first period originated from first expectations in Berlin at the time when the German guarantee proposal first appeared on the international political scene and when the ideas it reflected seemed to become true due to the promises of British diplomacy and all English policy both in the Baltics and in the USSR.

German politicians believed that the fact that Great Britain was seeking a base in Poland and that British imperialism was strengthening such a base in the Baltic states is the reason for its plans to struggle decisively against Moscow. In search of an ally England will also attract Germany to its Russian policy, in which place Germany will be compensated by changing the present status quo on the Reich eastern borders. Besides, England will not be an obstacle in the amalgamation of Austria with Germany. During the period when both official German policy and, in particular, its leader Stresemann were extremely optimistic, the German right-wing circles thought of the march campaign to Moscow and were ready to see in such an action the only way to break the chains of the Versailles treaty.

Part of the German industry that needed credits and conducted the appropriate negotiations in London and Washington supported such ideas and spoke in favor of the direction of the German political and economic course solely to the west of Europe, and in favor of reorganization of the position in the East, particularly, in the USSR, which was disadvantageous, at the same time tying the Reich's hands to foreign policy. No doubt that should the English policy indeed have continued in the direction it had been pursued in Berlin, i.e., should the French government have failed to paralyze the movement that was beginning in England and to place it within frames not wide enough to fulfill German expectations, the followers of the western orientation would have come out winners, and England's enemies and the few Russophile circles of that time would have had to surrender their positions.

The English policy, being bound with obligations to France, and the art of Soviet diplomacy contributed to a dramatic change in the situation, and despite the fact that social-democratic circles continue to adhere to the western orientation of Germany only, the democrats seek compromise for both eastern and western orientations. First political results of the German diplomatic negotiations and the exchange of diplomatic acts with ally countries have proven the fact that under no circumstances could Germany count on the fact that Great Britain wishes and is in a position to change the present situation of Germany, because this runs counter to the Versailles treaty. The latter is not subject for compensation on England's part, no less than the English policy itself in regard to the USSR is the policy of preparation for the future collision, the time of which depends on the general political situation of Great Britain. These same results have also proven the fact that even if, following England, Germany cannot count on obtaining more than the present situation in the French-English relations permits, London is far from planning to spoil its relations with Paris to the extent necessary to fulfill all German wishes. Finally, as a countermaneuver of the USSR, Russian-French negotiations were successful and nearly created a new situation in which England to a certain extent became dependent upon France in the Russian question.

This, British policy had to maneuver and this, in its turn, automatically resulted in the change of the cause of the German political circles. Thus it seems necessary for Stresemann, who has to stick to the middle line in between the two directions when discussing the guarantee pact,[20] to take up a position other than before when discussing the guarantee pact as well.[21] For adherents of the western orientation a German-Polish conflict regarding the question of optants[22] was untimely aroused, and the old idea of joint struggle in the future USSR against Poland has acquired new grounds.

The right-wing nationalistic groups changed their course in favor of Moscow as easy as they did it before against it. . . . Owing to the fact that the political board of the right-wing organizations was centralized . . . the right-wing circles have changed their orientation quickly and drastically. After the official announcement of the political program of the right-wing forces by Count Holtz and the order to adhere to it, the national organizations, still hostile to communism and its apostle in Moscow, acknowledged the necessity for German state interests to support the policy of having relations with the USSR and not to be under the thumb of England, for the whole guarantee project is aimed by the Entente at further restricting the German foreign policy and possibilities for the development of the German political system. . . .

By requesting foreign representatives from the West, the German government has learned that the exceptional orientation to the West does not lead to the expected results, that in this or that respect Germany must certainly maintain its relations with the USSR, and that it is these relations that are Germany's main trump card in its foreign policy. . . .

ZGASA. F. 33987. Inv. 3. F. 98. Sh. 73–76.
Copy.

*   *   *

VOROSHILOV TO MOLOTOV:[23] "THE CONTENTS OF
COMR. CHICHERIN'S LETTER DO NOT GIVE AN IMPRESSION
THAT CITIZEN RANTZAU WAS
DECISIVELY REPULSED BY OUR *NARKOMINDEL*"[24]

March 7, 1926
Moscow
Strictly confidential

Comrade Chicherin writes, in particular, the following in his letter in your name, with copies to the members of Politburo and Board NKID,[25] of March 5, current year, titled "Scandal with Germany": "The ambassador[26] said very excitedly that, as a matter of fact, this phrase was a mere report to the Entente on the secret armaments of Germany,[27] i.e., on one of the most sore subjects between the defeated country and the Versailles winners. This amounts to obsequiousness before the latter."

As Comrade Chicherin reports, this quotation consists of words said in "great excitation" by the German ambassador. And further are the words of our *Narkomindel* (and I wonder in what state he was when he wrote them): "This phrase indeed coincides with the reports of various French militarists on Germany. In his mouth it sounds unexpected and is fraught with unforeseen consequences."

I do not know whether my phrase about German armaments is identical to the reports of "various French militarists," but the tone of Comr. Chicherin's letter with regard to myself is lordly, as a matter of fact. In his letter Comr. Chicherin did not say a word about how he parried the pounce of "His Majesty"[28] in the speech of the *Narkomvoenmor*.[29] The contents of Comr. Chicherin's letter do not give an impression that Count Rantzau was decisively repulsed by our *Narkomindel*.

With regard to the subject of the question, I cannot see anything "flagrant" in my speech, the more so that it was made in the presence of three Politburo members: Comrades Stalin, Bukharin, and Kalinin, and they did not make any "reproof." . . .

It does no harm to know the reaction of the *Narkomindel* to the communique (TASS) of *Izvestia*[30] of February 25, the current year, No. 46, that a representative of the Naval Department in his speech in the Reichstag Chief Commission against communists and social democrats, supporting the increase of Morved estimates[31] by 47 mln. marks, "referred to the necessity of reinforcing naval defenses of the eastern coast, and mentioned the maneuvers of the Soviet Fleet in the Baltic Sea."

> With communist regards.
> Voroshilov
> ZGASA. F. 33987. Inv. 3. F. 151. Sh. 92–93.

*   *   *

UNSHLIKHT TO STALIN: "BOTH WE AND THEY WERE INTERESTED IN STRICT SECRECY"

> December 31, 1926
> Strictly confidential

The latest denunciations by the English and German press of the joint cooperation between the USSR and Germany is one of the moments that point to the change in Germany's foreign policy.[32] So far, the principal idea of cooperation of both parties was based on the usefulness of the attraction of foreign investments for strengthening the defense capacity of the country; for them it meant the necessity of having a completely hidden base for illegal armaments.

Both we and they were interested in strict secrecy. On our part, many a time did we remind them of that (I did it personally during my visit to Berlin, and in the letters of August 28, November 13–26, etc.).

In our estimations of the cooperation in the above aspect during the past period, we come to the conclusion that it has fallen short of our mutual expectations. We have obtained only part of the equipment of well-known enterprises, fit to be used only after its serious reconstruction; they have spent all their means, disgraced themselves, but among other political speculations, they used these enterprises as well.

After Germany's weakening its political dependence on the Entente countries and obtaining the right to vote in the League of Nations, there remains less and less room for illegal armaments and more and more fancied possibility to obtain the expected results legally. But it would not be right to maintain that Germany has fully denied illegal possibilities of strengthening its military potential. With the growth of its specific weight, the German diplomats will try to achieve their aims by means of legal negotiations, at the same time keeping some illegal possibilities in reserve, in case of failure.

Thus the main task we put forward at the beginning of our co-operation, i.e., improvement of the material bulk of RKKA (in the organization of the military industry), has not yielded the expected results and in future is leaving the Reichswehr, for, first, it has not enough means for this and, second, the government, while restricting the Reichswehr's independence, tries to make it dependent upon the interests of its foreign policy.

It is also necessary to repudiate mediation of RWM[33] in our relations with German firms, because besides bureaucracy and additional control it results in nothing. . . . I regard it necessary that our future joint work with the Germans be guided by the following main statements: to use their tactical and operative experience of the world war and further development of such experience (participation of our specialists in German military games, maneuvers, etc.) and also to use Germany's most important technical innovations in communication, artillery, aviation, tank engineering, both technically and tactically.

It should also be specified, however, that outwardly our line should not be seen to have changed so that they remain sure that we are still interested in their material support. But should in future the Germans follow their recent line (intensification of the course of western orientation, denunciations of the joint work), we may have to repudiate our joint work in this field.

By this day we have six joint ventures,[34] a brief description of which is given below.

1. Aviation school in Lipetsk. The school has been in existence since May 1925. As of December 1926, on our part, 16 military pilots have been trained on fighter aircrafts, 25 full-time mechanics and 20 part-time mechanics have studied a detailed course in maintenance and exploitation of the Napir-Lyon motor. A group of 40 qualified workers has been formed in repair shops at school to do different kinds of work with wood and metal under the supervision of the German engineers. New tactical techniques are also taught at school. The study of tactical innovations is of value to us, because the knowledge of the tactical methods of various types of aviation are acquired by German school instructors in America, England, and France during their visits there.

According to our competent comrades, the work of the school provides the following possibilities: (1) the capital equipment of the cultural aviation town; (2) the organization of joint work with building units; (3) training personnel as qualified specialists, mechanics, and workers; (4) teaching us new tactical methods of various types of aviation; (5) participation in testing the military equipment of the planes, photo, radio, and other auxiliary services, which allows our representatives to be always in the know of new technical innovations; (6) preparation of our pilot personnel for flights on plane-fighters; and finally (7) providing a refresher course for our pilots during their temporary stay at school. So, we can come to the conclusion that our work on aviation in the said direction is undoubtedly useful and our cooperation is to be continued in future.

2. Aviachemical tests. On August 21 of the current year an agreement was made on aerochemical tests. In accordance with the agreement, the work started late in September. The whole first part of the program has been fulfilled. Forty flights accompanied by liquid-spraying tests from on board the plane at different altitudes have been fulfilled. In their tests they used a liquid whose physical properties were similar to those of yperite [mustard gas]. The experiments proved the fact that application of toxic agents can be used on a large scale by our aviation. According to our experts, the experiments yield a conclusion that the

application of yperite against moving targets and for the purposes of contamination of localities and settlements is quite possible technically and presents great value. The second testing stage is scheduled for spring 1927 when it is planned to perform spraying at different altitudes of yperite that is supposed to be prepared here in February by using the German method. Simultaneously, tests will be made on the fitness of the gas-protective masks and chemical-defense uniforms and of other means of chemical defense. The post-yperite effects will be tested on laboratory animals.

Now the Germans develop sight devices. The completeion of the program is scheduled for autumn 1927. Speaking of the results, it should be noted that tests have been very useful for us. Apart from acquiring a new method of spraying, unknown to us before, we have also obtained all thoroughly investigated material and working techniques, because each of our specialists was taught by a specialist and in the course of the study adopted their experience.

Our material expenditures are small in comparison with the Germans. The completion of the first testing stage cost us about 2,000 rubles, not counting the payment to our specialists. Obviously it cost them several hundred thousand rubles, because they bore the equipment and transport expenditures, and their specialists cost them much more than ours.

This brief report makes us draw up the conclusion of the necessity of completing the experiments in question, for we shall obtain a thoroughly investigated and completed method for conducting a modern battle involving air fleet and for studying protection methods well in advance.

3. About Dreise machine guns. Continued talks on the production of Dreise machine guns have resulted in nothing due to unacceptable terms on the Germans' part. Taking into account the novelty of the design and good quality properties of the machine guns, in December 1925, Metachim[35] made an order for ten cavalry machine guns to be produced to accommodate the size of the Russian cartridge and to cost, tentatively, 6,000–7,000 marks per unit, and for ten pistol machine guns for 800–1,000 per unit.

The tests of the light and heavy machine guns adjusted to our cartridges' sizes, which were performed in Germany in the presence of our military attaché, gave good results. The military attaché reports that the first light machine gun will be forwarded for its further delivery to Moscow on January 1, ten ordered pieces will obviously be ready by April 1, and one heavy machine gun will be dispatched by February 1927.

I regard it necessary to insist on fulfilling the order within the deadline, without any give and take.

4. About the tank school. On December 2 an agreement was made on organization of a combined tank school. The work of the school can be estimated only after the school is newly equipped (at the expense of the German side) and the studying process begins.

5. About the "Bersoli." According to the Politburo Resolution of November 25, 1926, Minutes No. 71, I issued instructions to Comrade Krestinsky as to the necessity of instigating the Germans to break off with us, requesting him to inform me on the results of talks with Heye[36] and his advice on the most acceptable way of doing it, taking into consideration all the points of the present political situation. According to the report of our military attaché in Berlin, in the course of the talks with N.[37] the Germans again expressed their wish to share the work on Bersoli with us. Heye seems to be wishing to apply to his government for money for this purpose. Our opinion (in the Krestinsky and Lunev's version) is stated in written form and forwarded to Heye. The answer is expected one of these days. On our part, the issue is prepared and will be put for final decision of the Defense Commission as soon as Krestinsky's considerations are obtained. As far as the work at the plant is concerned, it should be noted that in accordance with Prof. Schpitalsky's report, all basic questions on design and project of T. and N. devices[38] have been solved.

6. About Junkers. The talk with the "Junkers Co." firm on liquidation of the concession treaty and the agreements on bomb carriers are not completed as yet. Glavkoncesskom agreed to pay the full sum of their claim of 3,500,000 rubles as compensation. The local representative of the firm reduced his claims to 2,500,000. Then the representative left for Berlin to report to the management board. On December 17, on his return from Berlin, the talks were resumed, but have not given any result as yet. In the light of the above said I am inclined to draw the following conclusions:

1. Our attempts to attract German investments in our military industry through RWM have failed. So in future we shall have to refuse the organization of joint (with RWM) military-industrial ventures.

2. Our further joint work with RWM, while outwardly continuing

to maintain a friendly spirit, must proceed in using the tactic and operational experience of the Germans and, most important, technical innovations (in artillery, tank engineering, communications, etc.). But we must bear in mind that we should not allow them to penetrate into the organism of our army.

3. To continue our joint work in tank school and aviation school and in aviachemical tests.

With communist regards.
Unshlikht
ZGASA. F. 33987. Inv. 3. L. 151. L. 18–23.
Original.

*   *   *

UNSHLIKHT TO LITVINOV

Copies to Stalin and Voroshilov

December 31, 1926
Strictly confidential

Writing this in reply to your letter of December 16 and stating my own considerations, I have as a sole object impartially approaching and examining the pressing questions connected with the latest exposures in the German press.

On the basis of materials dealing with Germany's foreign policy at my disposal at present, I am inclined to draw the following main conclusions:

1. Pursuing the policy of economic and political rapprochement with France . . . , and simultaneously playing on French-English contradictions, Stresemann has already achieved on this path a marked success. The available intelligence information shows that the German MFA[39] tends to pursue the following political line: while improving relations with France without, however, simultaneously worsening relations with England, Stresemann strives for resolving the German bourgeoisie's problems in the West (further relaxation of military control, liberation of the occupied regions and Saar, revision of Dawes Plan, etc.), with these western problems predetermining his policy in the East—in relation to Poland, Czecho-

slovakia, the USSR, and Lithuania. There are indications of England's willingness to lend him support in resolving problems on Germany's eastern borders as well as on the question of military control.

Stresemann thinks that he will achieve still greater successes in his gambling on English-French contradictions if he subjects to this task his policy in regard to the USSR. He assesses the importance of friendly relations with our country from the viewpoint of making use of the USSR as a chesspiece in pursuing his policy of maneuvering, as well as in Germany's economic interests, with every passing day taking less and less into account the USSR's genuine interests and aspirations.

2. In the internal policy there is a marked increase of economic and political influence of those bourgeoisie circles that are not connected with the Reichswehr's present leading circles and are striving for altering its orientation in the sense of giving up cooperation with the USSR. Simultaneously one observes an increase of influence of sea circles tending for rapprochement with England. With these forces' support Stresemann is carrying on a struggle for strengthening his influence on the Reichswehr, for subjecting the Reichswehr's policy to the German government's foreign policy and altering its "Russian" orientation.

Seeckt's resignation is Stresemann's major success in this direction, succeeded by the strengthening of those circles in national organizations (in particular in eastern Prussia, on both sides of the corridor in eastern Silesia), which have subjected their tactics to the MFA! Stresemann promised to these associations that he would carry on a more active policy in the east of Germany, stressing while doing it that he would proceed in this question from the point of England's potential rendering necessary support. Germany's success at the last session of the League of Nations in regard to Konigsberg's fortifications is to a significant extent explained by England's support. This strengthens the course of foreign policy Stresemann has embarked upon—the course showing that with England's support it is possible to gain results in regard to Poland earlier than when following a "Russian" orientation.

3. Stresemann is reluctant to oppose the present Reichswehr leadership more openly because he fears to strain his relations with it. Until recently Stresemann has not exercised any noticeable authority in the Reichswehr. Therefore, he had to make use of the struggle of other parties and persons (in particular Democrats and Social Democrats) against the Reichswehr, as well as to resort to a number of roundabout

maneuvers in order to appear in the end in the role of a staunch champion, guarding the Reichswehr against encroachments of radical elements seeking to republicanize it.

4. The campaign of "exposures" concerning the Reichswehr's connections with the USSR is in essence a roundabout maneuver of this kind. The results of negotiations at the last session of the League of Nations Council showed that these "exposures" had not exercised any influence on the course of negotiations and had as their main object an attack on the Reichswehr's eastern orientation. German Social Democrats, fully suporting the MFA's policy, simply could not dare venture "exposures" on their own without Stresemann's direct or tacit agreement.

There are ample grounds to surmise that the latter was fully in the know and made clever use of England's and France's as well as Social Democrats' demands, himself personally remaining in a very advantageous position.

The possibility of recurrence of such "exposures" in future cannot be excluded, if Stresemann again considers it necessary to prove to England his willingness to struggle against the Reichswehr's "pro-Soviet" attitudes of mind. In connection with the latest "exposure" very characteristic is our Berlin attaché's communication, running as follows: "Today the newspaper *Vorwärts* again carries a loathsome article: a speech in the Reichstag in which the orator, a Social Democrat, openly challenges Communists: ask Chicherin as to what is 'GEFU' or 'WIKO.' " The latter designation appears in the press for the first time. There is no wonder at all, because from all sides I am receiving numerous communications, depicting our friends' amazing unconcern in all these questions. Thus, for instance, the steamships *Artushof* and *Hotenhof* were unloaded in Szczecin in the daytime in the roadstead in an inopportune place, before the inquisitive eyes of people boating on the river. The German colony of Leningrad knows "GEFU" in all details.

Doctor Tiele expatiated at a banquet in Essen, in foreigners' presence, on his activities in the USSR, to which country he had arrived with a secret assignment from RWM,[40] and so forth. Materials, testifying against us as well as against them, are there in great abundance at the disposal of circles hostile to us. More than that, according to our intelligence reports, it was Stresemann himself who had opened the campaign in the press by passing appropriate materials to Social Democrats through his secretary.

5. Of late, Germany's interest in the USSR as a military base is

gradually diminishing. In particular, Germany's striving for making use of all kind of indulgences on the side of the enemy coalition for creating its own military industry is rather characteristic in this relation. As to aviation, it has been achieved mainly thanks to the concessions France has made in the questions of German aircraft construction [development of civil aviation]. In relation to the Navy (including submarines) one observes cooperation of Germany's Navy Department with England. It is rather significant that the greater part of Germany's naval circles is in regard to the USSR at one with the policy of England and disapproves of the Reichswehr's eastern orientation. The external base for Germany's heavy artillery is Sweden. Besides, Germans have got bases in Finland, Spain, Holland, and Argentina. Cooperation with Chile is also increasing of late [navy, aviation, hydro-aviation, gas production].

The strengthening of Germany's position in Turkey is also noticeable. The enumerated facts are amply sufficient for revealing the fact of Germany's interest in the USSR markedly tending to decrease both in the question of military-political cooperation as well as in that of cooperation of our military department with RWM. . . .

> With communist greetings.
> Unshlikht
> CSASA. F. 33987. Inv. 3. F. 151. Sh. 3–5.
> Original.

*   *   *

BERZIN TO VOROSHILOV:
"IT IS EXPEDIENT AND NECESSARY . . . TO KEEP GERMANY
FROM FINALLY PASSING OVER TO THE ENEMY CAMP"[41]

> January 29, 1927
> Moscow
> Strictly confidential

. . . 5. For the purpose of putting off the war of our country with the capitalist world and improving our military-political position, it is expedient and necessary:

a. to secure conclusion of the raw-stuff supply agreement with

Finland, guaranteeing Finland's neutrality in case of the USSR's war with a third party;

    b. to hamper settlement of Polish-German issues (Danzig corridor, Upper Silesia, etc.);

    c. to prevent conclusion of Polish-Baltic alliance;

    d. to keep Germany from finally passing over to the enemy camp;

    e. to promote aggravation of French-English relations;

    f. to continue struggle for establishing our influence upon Turkey and Persia;

    g. to proceed with all-sided promotion of strengthening our political positions in China, with making the most of that country's national-liberation and revolutionary forces.

    6. To further aggravation of Japan-USA relations, prevent conclusion of England-Japan agreement on the questions of Chinese policy.

> Fourth Department Chief
> Berzin
> Third Department Deputy Chief
> [Signature illegible]
> CSASA. F. 33987. Inv. 3. F. 128. Sh. 26.
> Original.

*   *   *

LUNYOV TO YUROVSKY,[42] FROM BERLIN

> February 21, 1927
> Strictly confidential

1. . . . . Friends[43] are carefully trying to keep it secret from us that Gessler[44] has already spoken before the Reichstag commission. To my question, asked in general form (what was the purpose of Gessler's speech and whether it might harm our future relations), Fr.[45] mentioned only the session of the Reichstag's commission on foreign affairs due on Wednesday, February 23. The same was also the result of Brodovsky's[46] talk with Schubert.[47] Both, Schubert and Fr., maintained that the substance of speeches on the Russian question would be preliminarily coordinated between Dirksen[48] and Fischer.[49] The latter stated that for this coor-

dination he would make a report to Generals Wetzel[50] and Heye. Not a single word was said about Gessler's having already made the statement at the budget commission's session. I believe they really intend (as Fr. affirms) to disclose at the secret commission's session (commission on foreign affairs is secret) all that is already known and maybe also some other things that are all the same very hard to be kept secret (Lipetsk after Klim's unmasking),[51] thereby depriving Social Democrats of the opportunity for further badgering them.

In this way they will demonstrate their loyalty to the League of Nations. At least Gessler has not so far told anything but what is already known, nor has he mentioned anything of the matters that has not yet percolated into the press. In reply to my question Fr. affirmed that coordination would be effected in such a manner that nothing new would be disclosed, for they were fully aware of the fact that everything told in Social Democrats' presence would become immediately known to Frenchmen, etc., and, besides, this coordination was to secure the possibility for our further cooperation (with Social Democrats' knowledge and blessing). I took this statement into account and promised to bring it to your notice. A definitive conclusion can be drawn only after Wednesday.

2. Fr. has handed me the translation of the intercepted wireless message, which I am enclosing. I told him that it was either a misinformation, designed to make us quarrel with each other, or it might be the question of other pilots, sent from the USSR to get the aircraft back, for, as I read already in Riga, in Latvian newspapers, the plane was to be returned to us. I personally think the first explanation more plausible.

3. The director of one of the enterprises having business relations with Fishman,[52] told me that, to his knowledge, a governmental ban on transfer to us of any kind of military production secrets was soon expected. I asked this of Fr., having tied up my question with Krupp firm's Director Esterlen's statement of RWM's having allegedly forbidden him to continue negotiations with us. Fr. called it all fabrications, and I fully agree with him in the first case; but as to the Krupp firm, here the matter is not yet clear. With such conversations I am getting on Fr.'s nerves, to make him more lenient.

4. I informed Fr. of your and Comrade Litvinov's consent in principle as to coordination of statements at the disarmament conference.

However, I am afraid, now it is already late to coordinate anything, for the conference is literally just round the corner, and of its transfer from Geneva there is not as yet anything definite.

5. Further, Fr. asked to speed up supplying him information about Bruchmüller.[53]

6. Frank said they had gotten fairly reliable information about Poles holding negotiations in Paris as to increasing the 400 million credits for placing orders for aircrafts and motorized heavy artillery. Besides, Poles had placed orders in Renault plants for 2,000 light and 500 average (25-hp engine) tanks.

The latter communication appears to me quite incredible, for the figures are too big. Please, let me know the verified data you dispose of.

7. I had a talk with Stolzenberg's[54] representative, who maintained that Stolzenberg had got a smoothly operating installation in Spain[55] and was willing to reestablish business relations with us without any kind of intermediaries. I said I was not sure there would be such a desire on our part because of a fairly disappointing former experience; perhaps it would be useful if St.[56] presented convincing proofs of not only his willingness but also being able to fulfil his obligations. His representative said that he would try to arrange for our specialists' being invited to work in Stolzenberg's plants in Spain. I answered that this offer was new to me, but I would report of it to Moscow. I am waiting for further instructions in this relation. . . .

Lunyov
CSASA. F. 33987. Inv. 3. F. 151. Sh. 87–89.

*   *   *

BERZIN REPORT: "ON COOPERATION OF WPRA AND THE REICHSWEHR"

December 24, 1928
Moscow
Strictly confidential

Negotiations on cooperation between the WPRA and Reichswehr began, as far as I know, in 1922 [exact data in the Fourth Department are lacking]. At that time they were carried on by the USSR Revolutionary War Council Member Comrade Rozenholz and assumed, in the autumn of 1923, after a long exchange of opinions, a concrete form of the following agreements:

a. with the Junkers Firm on delivery of aircrafts and erection of an aircraft works on the USSR territory;

b. with the Reichswehr High Command on joint erection of mustard gas works (joint stock companies "WIKO," "Metachim," "Bersoli"). Further, in 1924, Reichswehr's order for manufacture of 400,000 shells for three-inch field guns was received by our industry through the "Metachim" Firm.

The above-mentioned agreements (with the Junkers Firm and the agreement on the erection of mustard gas works) have not yielded us any positive results. The Junkers Firm did neither carry out its obligations concerning delivery of metallic aircrafts, nor erect an aircraft works. Therefore, the agreement with it was cancelled in 1926–27. The agreement on joint erection of mustard gas works also had to be cancelled, because the Stolzenberg Firm, to which the technical carrying out of the obligations under the agreement (delivery of equipment and organization of production) was later reassigned by the Reichswehr, in fact cheated both, the Reichswehr and us, having in good time received from the Reichswehr about twenty million marks. The equipment delivered by Stolzenberg did not conform to the specifications indicated in the agreement, and the methods of production of mustard gas were found by our, and subsequently also by German, specialists to be obsolete and inadequate.

As a result of this we have not suffered any material damage, but have lost almost three years for, sure of the works to be erected under the agreement, we have not taken steps toward organization of independent production of mustard gas.

The Reichswehr's order for three-inch field-gun shells was executed by us, and the shells were passed over to the Germans in 1926. However, the payments connected with this order were completed (true, through our industry's fault) only at the end of the current year. This delivery of shells has done a huge political damage to us, as is generally known, for the fact of our having manufactured field-gun shells for Germany is, through the Germans' own fault, known to German Social Democrats, who have (as far as we know) started a noisy campaign against us in the press, with Stresemann's blessing.

Thus, the first period of our cooperation with the Reichswehr did not yield us any positive results (I am not speaking of the purely political aspect of the question).

Starting with 1925, when the failure with the Junkers Firm and mustard gas works became amply obvious, the cooperation has been gradually put on different rails.

If by signing the agreements of 1923 the Germans—as seen from the secret letter of January 7, 1927, of the Reichswehr High Command to the name of its representative in Moscow Lit—strived for becoming our suppliers in the sphere of aviation as well as securing influence on the appropriate branches of our industry, they are since 1925 "first and foremost interested in speedily acquiring still greater influence over the Russian army, air fleet, and navy." So it is obviously a question of exerting influence upon the organization and tactical training of our army.

In this connection, as far back as 1925, the Germans agreed to admit (on mutual terms) five of our officers to their tactical field exercises and maneuvers, and in 1926 already raised a question of holding a joint conference on strategic questions with a view to work up common strategic views.

In 1926 our officers (Comrades Svechnikov and Krasilnikov) were for the first time admitted to the German Military Academy as its final year students (academic courses).

In the same 1926 the Germans concluded with us an agreement on organization of a tank school in Kazan and joint gas experiments in Podosinki (now "Tomka").

At present our mutual relations with the Reichswehr have got a specific expression in the following:

a. mutual acquaintance with the present state and methods of instruction and training of both armies by sending officers to maneuvers, on field trips, to attend academic courses;

b. joint gas experiments ("Tomka" enterprise);

c. joint organization of a tank school in Kazan ("Kama");

d. a flying school in Lipetsk ("Lipetsk");

e. a number of representatives of certain departments (AFD, STC,[57] Artillery Dept, Central Medical Dept, etc.) sent on official trips to Germany for studying certain questions and acquainting themselves with the organization of work.

1. Passing over to an evaluation of separate kinds of cooperation, it is necessary to state that the most appreciable results are yielded by our officers' maneuvers' observation and field trips as well as by their attending academic courses in Germany. By studying the organization of individual branches of the service, the arrangement of staff work, methods of instruction and training as well as development of military thought, our officers not only acquire a good amount of useful knowledge and broaden their outlook, but also get some stimulus to examining certain problems and trying to solve them independently as applied to our conditions. In short, our officers, enriching their knowledge, acquire so-called "military culture." Other west European armies being presently inaccessible to us, it is both expedient and necessary to retain this possibility of perfecting the professional grounding of a number of our officers.

2. The existing enterprises have not been of real great advantage to us so far. The oldest enterprise—the flying school in Lipetsk—was used very inadequately by us until 1928. This school, organized by Germans in 1923-24,[58] has got as its object not only training of the flight personnel (fliers and observers), but also experimental-research work. During the first two years it was poorly equipped, had old aircraft, and was not of any special interest to us. Starting in 1927 the school became more active, and our interest in it grew accordingly. All expenses on its organization, equipping, and maintenance are borne by Germans.

3. Chemical experiments in Podosinki and later on in "Tomka" have yielded positive results, and their continuation in the coming year is considered advisable by the Chemical Dept. The object of these experiments—testing of new devices and methods of application of PG[59] (artillery, aviation, special gas projectors, etc.) as well as new methods and means of decontamination of the contaminated area. Expenses on experiments are borne on an equal footing.

4. The tank school in Kazan has not yet started functioning; instructions in it will begin, according to the Germans' statement, only in the spring of 1929, after arrival from Germany of tanks required for it. Meanwhile, during the last two years Germans have completed construction work and equipped school premises, workshops, and training area. From this enterprise we shall be able to derive benefit only on commencement of instructions, for we are entitled to have in it an equal number of trainees with Germans. Expenses on equipping

and maintenance of the school, excluding maintenance of our future trainees, are borne by the Germans.

For organization and maintenance of the aforesaid enterprises Germans have been expending large sums of money; the exact amount is not known to us (besides straight expenditures on our territory on construction works and maintenance of personnel, one must also take into account the expenses on the equipment, all of which is being brought from Germany); but the expenses on "Tomka" (chemical experiments) are already reaching one million marks, the expenses on organization and maintenance of the tank school exceed 500,000 marks, and those on Lipetsk school—including equipment—exceed one million marks. Taking into account the Reichswehr's former expenses in the form of a grant to the Junkers Firm on the lines of cooperation with us and its loss of about 20,000,000 marks in the Stolzenberg business (mustard gas works), one cannot but state that the Reichswehr's financial expenditures on the "enterprises" in the USSR are very large and up to now far from being repaid by the concrete results these enterprises are yielding.

Beyond any doubt, all German enterprises, besides their direct object, also pursue the gathering of economic, political, and military information (espionage). This is already borne out by the circumstance that the post of supervisor over all these enterprises is held by such a double-dyed intelligence agent of the German General Staff as Niedermeier. From this viewpoint the enterprises are causing us certain damage.

However, this espionage is, by all indications, being effected by means of personal observation, conversations, and gathering verbal information and is not directed at procuring and collecting secret documents. Such an espionage is less dangerous than the clandestine one, for it confines itself only to fixing what one sees and does not yield documentary data. The Germans have got on the territory of our country more than enough people capable of making perfect intelligence agents; therefore, removal of German enterprises from our territory with a view to eliminate German espionage would be highly ineffective.

Until the beginning of 1928 (Colonel Mittelberger's arrival) the Germans' attitude toward cooperation was a wait-and-see one and fairly transparently reflected all the vacillations between the East and West that were present in German foreign policy. "Military cooperation" with the Soviet Union was only a trump in negotiations with France and

England for German diplomacy. However, with the commencement of a new rapprochement between England and France (beginning of 1928) and the ruin of German hopes for a solution favorable for Germany of the reparation question and "Rhine problem" (clearing the Rhine zone of French and Belgian troops), the attitude of the Reichswehr's ruling circles toward the question of cooperation with the WPRA is gradually changing. Such highly responsible persons as General Staff Deputy Chief Mittelberger and, later on, General Staff Chief General Blomberg are sent to the USSR to acquaint themselves with the WPRA and study possibilities of cooperation. The atmosphere of interrelations is getting noticeably friendlier than before. Of course, it is still early to speak of a serious, stable course for eastern orientation, but the Germans' failures in their attempts to reach agreement on the questions of reparations and clearing the Rhine zone of occupation troops will apparently strengthen the "eastern orientation," and it is this circumstance that explains the Reichswehr High Command's new proposals concerning "regularization and expansion" of cooperation of both armies, made through Niedermeier and Comrade Korka.

Specifically, these proposals come to the following:

1. Substitution of qualified officers of the active Reichswehr service for the enterprises' present personnel, consisting of reserve officers.

2. Opening of the tank school in Kazan in the spring of 1929; delivery there of new heavy and average German tanks of the latest design.

3. Signing of an agreement on carrying out gas experiments and expansion of these experiments. Delivery from Germany of gas shells and four field howitzers for experimental firing.

4. Supply of radio stations for coordination of the work of the Kazan tank and Lipetsk flying schools; air communication between schools and testing of the operation of radio stations aboard aircrafts to a greater distance than that allowed by the Lipetsk aerodrome.

5. Gradual rapprochement of the naval staffs of the two countries by means of our Navy representative's trips to Germany or the German Navy representative's trip to Moscow; establishment of personal contacts between responsible chiefs of two fleets, discussion of some common problems, etc.

6. Establishment of contacts in the intelligence activity of the two armies against Poland, exchange of intelligence materials on Poland,

and a meeting of the leaders of the two intelligence services for joint consideration of materials on the mobilization and deployment potentials of the Polish Army.

7. Joint work of designer forces in the sphere of artillery and machine-gun design, taking advantage of appropriate achievements of the industries of both countries on condition of equal utilization of the results of this designing work (proposal, passed to us through Professor Schmiz).

8. Continuation of mutual official trips to maneuvers, field trips; admission of our officers to the Reichswehr's Military Academy as final year students; coming of several German officers for probation service in our military units.

Besides, the Junkers Firm has unofficially raised before our military attaché in Berlin the question of resumption of its work in the USSR and, in particular, of erection of an aircraft works on a concession basis. The Junkers Firm is ready to concretize its proposals, providing there is our consent in principle to conduct appropriate negotiations.

Summing up the aforesaid, I consider it expedient to do the following:

1. To continue cooperation with the Reichswehr in the forms practiced at present.

2. To make maximum use of the opportunity for training and advanced training of our officers by means of sending them to the German Military Academy as students in its final year, for participation in field trips, maneuvers, etc. Likewise, to make arrangements for our specialists' acquiring knowledge and practical experience by studying various modes and methods of work in appropriate branches of the German military industry.

3. To insist on the Germans' most speedy opening of the tank school and make the most of its functioning for training our armored troops officers.

4. To make in future most wide use of the results of the Germans' experimental works in Lipetsk school by introducing into it a number of our students, allowed by the agreement.

5. To proceed with chemical experiments, having introduced into the agreement a clause as to our reserving the right to discontinue them when we find it necessary.

6. To accept the proposal concerning establishing contacts between commanders of both fleets, having restricted the contacts to their personal mutual acquaintance and discussion of questions of general nature.

7. To accept the proposal about exchange of intelligence materials relating to Poland and joint discussion of questions of mobilization and deployment of the Polish Army, with attempts at establishing organizational contacts between intelligence services to be declined.

8. To decide the question of joint designing work sujbect to further concretization of the proposal on the part of Reichswehr.

I am reporting the aforesaid for your judgment.

> WPRA General Staff's Fourth Dept Chief
> Berzin
> CSASA. F. 33987. Inv. 3. F. 98. Sh. 71–78.
> Original.

*　　*　　*

FROM THE TALK OF REPRESENTATIVES OF THE "KRUPP" FIRM AND SOVIET MACHINE-BUILDING INDUSTRY[60]

> April 17, 1929
> Moscow
> Strictly confidential

After a detailed exchange of opinions the representatives of the "Krupp" Firm formulated their proposals as follows:

1. The "Krupp" Firm proposes to pass over to the Russian side without exclusion the experience on all special designs (field-gun systems, shells, detonating fuses, fuses) gained by it before 1918, as well as all the experience it has got without exclusion on all designs devised after 1918. The latter designs have been worked out in close cooperation with the German government, and the present talks are being held with the German government's knowledge and sanction. The firm's representatives have made a reservation that as to the latest equipment and that devised by them after 1918, for each of these designs it will be necessary for them to obtain the government's authorization, maintaining nevertheless that on the whole the talks have been approved of.

2. For the purpose of rendering this technical assistance, planned as a large-scale operation, the "Krupp" Firm will strengthen its Design Office in Essen, where special Russian assignments, if such are there, will

be carried into effect. To this office can be sent Russian designers for coordination of work on particular assignments and, besides, at the Russian side's request, German designers can come to Moscow for a longer or shorter period of time in order to effect management at all the involved plants, work in Russian design offices, or supervise manufacture of test specimens. Besides, the "Krupp" Firm will place at the Russian side's disposal the experience on external ballistics, etc., gained in laboratories and on the testing grounds, as well as regularly pass over to it all the technical achievements that will be attained by it from the moment of the signing of the agreement up to the expiration of its validity period.

3. The "Krupp" Firm will pass over the designs that will be in future worked out by it on the German government's commission.

4. . . . An understanding has been reached that the experience obtained under Russian conditions while working with the system worked out by the firm's Design Office, or systems in which German designers in the Soviet Union have taken part in devising, should be reciprocally passed over to the "Krupp" Firm. . . .

6. At the same time the representatives of the "Krupp" Firm propose to pass over to us all the experience the firm has got in the sphere of production of fabric for military outfits, methods of its treatment, and the whole regime of handling it. Further, the firm's representatives propose to pass over the available experience in regard to explosives and gunpowder, emphasizing that here, too, whatever was devised before 1918 will be placed by them at our disposal with the German government's consent.

7. Passing over assistance on the last questions, the firm will also pass on the available experience in application of gunpowder and explosives. . . .

9. . . . As regards compensation for technical assistance in qualitative metallurgy and on special questions, . . . the "Krupp" Firm's representatives stated that they would like to get as much as two million dollars from the Russian side for all the technical assistance rendered by them.

10. Taking into consideration the political importance of the present agreement, the representatives of the "Krupp" Firm think it necessary to obtain for its signing authorization of appropriate government bodies in Germany, which circumstance should be brought to the Russian side's notice.

CSASA. F. 33987. Inv. 3. F. 295. Sh. 228.

* * *

"NEGOTIATIONS WERE CARRIED ON IN MOSCOW"[61]

May 3, 1929
Strictly confidential

Negotiations were carried on in Moscow from April 10 to April 20, 1929. On our behalf the participants were Comrades Ksandrov, Tolokontsev, Uryvayev, Budnievich, Korzun, and Ivanov.[62] For discussion of special questions were invited Comrade Oborin of Glavmashstroy,[63] Comrade Neumeier of Gomza,[64] Comrade Grigorovich of Scientific-Technical Council, Butyrin of Glavelectro,[65] Comrade Pastukhov of the Gun-Arsenal Trust, Comrades Molodtsov and Smirnov of AD[66] and the WPRA Supply Department Chief. A strictly limited circle of persons, appointed by Comrade Tolokontsev, took part in conferences on military questions.

The negotiations on behalf of the Krupp Firm were conducted by Professor Gerens—Member of Directorate of the Fried-Krupp Joint-Stock Company, head of delegation; Doctor Engineer Griesmann—Director of Magdeburg Works of the Fried-Krupp Joint-Stock Company; and Bamberger—Director of the Eastern Section of the Fried-Krupp Joint-Stock Company.

Representatives of the two sides held a number of conferences (protocols and shorthand records were regularly kept) on two main questions: *on technical assistance in the sphere of production of nonmilitary goods* (manufacture and procession of high-quality steel, pig iron; special methods of control over the process of production), and on technical assistance *in the special sphere—that of military production.*

The results of negotiations can be represented in the following propositions:

I. The period of validity of the agreement from the date of its signing and approval shall be fixed at ten years;

II. The object of the agreement shall be the *technical assistance* of the Krupp Firm to Soviet industry in the sphere of nonmilitary and military production. The Krupp Firm shall pass over to the Soviet side all the experience and knowledge gained by it in all the production spheres, which are its specialty or which it has had occasion to study.

For rendering this assistance, and in its framework, the Krupp Firm shall give the Soviet side an opportunity to study—at its plants, works, laboratories, and testing grounds—both the entire organization of the firm's work on the whole as well as its certain special aspects of our choice. The firm's Design Office in Essen shall be enlarged in accordance with the necessity of meeting Soviet requirements. In case the Soviet side wishes it, a design office shall be organized in the USSR. Besides directions regarding organization of new USSR production methods, borrowed from the Krupp Firm, the firm shall also be bound to give directions on the questions of technically sound and rational organization of production in general. At the Soviet side's request, the Krupp Firm shall be obliged to send to our country a necessary number of instructors possessing appropriate qualification and meeting our special requirements. The Soviet side shall be entitled to send a necessary number of its engineers and workers to all the enterprises of the Krupp Firm, including the Design Office in Essen.

III. The representatives of the Krupp Firm have, nevertheless, made the following essential reservations *in the sphere of special military production.*

1. Whatever the Krupp Firm had got in its possession in the sphere of production, experience, and knowledge before 1918 can be unreservedly "passed over" to us for studying and putting into production in our country.

2. Achievements attained in the period from 1918 to the date of signing of the agreement can be "passed over" to us only with the Reichswehr's consent, even though there is a preliminary guarantee of such consent being given.

3. New designs and inventions shall be "passed over" to us in the period of validity of the present agreement each time with the German government's authorization.

4. All the achievements attained by the Krupp Firm in cooperation with the Bofors Firm in Sweden shall be "passed over" to us with the Bofors Firm's consent. The Krupp Firm has offered mediator services in establishing cooperation between Soviet plants and the Bofors Firm, in case of our wishing it.

IV. Maintenance of the Russian section in the Design Office in Essen, upkeep of Soviet specialists due to be sent to work in the Krupp Firm's enterprises as well as that of Krupp Firm's designing engineers due to be sent to the USSR ought to be separately paid by the Soviet side, taking into account actual expenditures involved.

V. During the negotiations a more accurate definition of the "Volume and Character of Technical Assistance" has been worked out by the Soviet side, and an essential amendment inserted in it as to Soviet engineers sent to work in the Design Office in Essen having to be taken on the office's staff, instead of a just "Russian section" being formed, attached to this office.

VI. Essential differences have come to light during the discussion on the question of time and amounts of payments to be effected in due time on both parts of the agreement on technical assistance. The Krupp Firm's representatives, having abandoned their initial charge— 2 million American dollars with 1,500,000 American dollars paid in the first two years—have made the following statement. The Soviet machine-building industry shall pay to the Krupp Firm 1,850,000 American dollars in the following way: on the day of signing of the agreement— 500 ths [thousand] American dollars; six months later—125 ths dollars; nine months later still—100 ths dollars. . . .

CSASA. F. 33987. Inv. 3. F. 295. Sh. 227.

* * *

STOMONYAKOV[67] ON HIS TALK WITH DIRKSEN

July 5, 1929
Strictly confidential

During his talk with Mikoyan[68] and me, Dirksen said that he expected speedy termination of reparation negotiations and commencement, following that, of credits talks with us. However, the Paris negotiations had dragged on exceedingly. Besides, they had not allowed the concerned governments to settle the whole matter quickly by approving decisions of the Paris reparation conference, and there arose the necessity of new negotiations that would take place at the forthcoming political conference. The second circumstance that hampered the speedy commencement of credits talks was the occurrence of May events in Berlin and Moscow[69] and anti-German demonstrations in Leningrad. Not that the mentioned events had made the germpra[70] revise its attitude toward the necessity of a credit-extending act, but they had created an unfavorable atmosphere around Soviet-German relations and, as a result of this, decreased the German public's—and especially German industrial circles'—interest in further steps directed at expansion of German export to the USSR. In Germany they began to say openly that Comintern was staking on Germany and looking for an opportunity to organize German workers' open action against the government.

In Germany they also said that we were neither adequately reckoning with Germany's interests, nor taking due notice of its protests; the Leningrad incident, in particular, had been unsatisfactorily addressed: we had not even expressed regret in this regard.

The third circumstance was the increase of late of the German export, which during the last twelve months exceeded the corresponding figures of the previous year by 1.5 milliard marks. . . . The German interest in effecting a new credit-extending act diminished. . . . In Berlin it was now believed that it would be more expedient to start talks on credits on termination of the international conference that was expected to solve the reparation and political problems standing in the order of the day. . . .

I replied to Dirksen that I was grateful to him for these communications, which I intended to pass to Comrade Mikoyan and the PCFA[71] Board. Dirksen interrupted me by saying that he was passing these communications to me in private, on his own initiative, without instruction from Berlin. . . . Neither in Berlin nor in Moscow did the German side consider it necessary even to inform us why the German delegates were so slow in coming. After all, we were not desperate seekers after German credits. Starting with the December talks we had repeatedly declared in a plain and unambiguous form to the German side in reply to its inquiries that German credits were not absolutely indispensable for us, because our economy could well do also without them. . . . Many people in our country believed that the germpra's silence on the credits question after the German ambassador's statement concerning appointment of German delegates and their expected arrival in three weeks was accounted for exclusively by political reasons. In our country it was believed that influential circles in Germany were insisting on the germpra's reserving as free as possible a hand for the forthcoming political negotiations with the Entente. These circles apparently thought that one should not hurry with either credits and a credit-extending act, for Germany might conclude with the Enténte an agreement proving favorable both for itself and also in regard to the USSR, and it might be that after the international conference Germany would have before itself new vistas opened in relation to its export to the USSR as well. Germany's silence, therefore, produced a highly unfavorable impression here and was regarded as a result of the increase of anti-Soviet tendencies in Germany. Dirksen said that it was definitely not so and the main cause for it was and continued to be, as he had already told me earlier, a fear that extending credits to us might greatly affect Germany's position in final settlement of the reparation question.

Then I raised the question of "indiscretion" and said that in our opinion there was no doubt at all as to the "leakage of information" having occurred on the German side. Dirksen, however, believed as a matter of fact that indiscretion had occurred on the Soviet side.

In conclusion I told Dirksen that the most sad circumstance was the fact that the German side was shortsightedly inclined to exaggerating the importance of all sorts of temporary troubles and because of them, questioning the very foundation of our relations, though officials in Berlin would be expected to realize that, with such a great difference in our political and economic systems, a certain amount of conflicts, incidents, and frictions was absolutely unavoidable. One ought to meet these inevitable concomitants of the Soviet-German friendship with philosophical calmness and take all measures for their possibly prompt lessening and localization, without exaggerating their importance and letting them affect our countries' relations, resting on the parallelism of certain external-political and economic interests of long duration. One simply ought not to allow temporary impediments we come across in our journey to make us lose our way and perspective.

B. Stomonyakov
CSASA. F. 33987. Inv. 3. F. 295. Sh. 231–36.
Copy.

*   *   *

FROM VOROSHILOV'S TALK WITH REICHSWEHR OFFICIALS
GENERAL HAMMERSTEIN[72] AND COLONEL KÜLLENTAL

September 5, 1929
Strictly confidential

VOROSHILOV. . . . I would like to know what is your general impression of what you have seen.

GENERAL HAMMERSTEIN. My impression is that there is still plenty to be done in the work you have undertaken. But it was started with a good amount of ideology, according to rather impressive plans, laid well in advance, and your construction is, I am certain, proceeding along the line of ascent. But your question, I understand, refers first of all to enterprises in Lipetsk, Kazan, and Tomsk.[73] My general impression of them is satisfactory. In Kazan I was accompanied by Monsieur Kulik,[74] in Tomsk—by Monsieur Fishman. . . .

VOROSHILOV. . . . Last year I had a talk with General Blomberg on all specific questions involved, and the talk appears to have been mutually beneficial. I'll say it openly that in our relations there have been some hitches and frictions, but in the main the results we have obtained are positive. . . . I regard Herr General Hammerstein as a representative of a friendly state and a man well disposed toward the Red Army, of which circumstance I have been more than once informed by our comrades who studied in Germany. Therefore, the question of our discussion now can be only that of whether we can manage to find additional ways of improving and concretizing our relations to the benefit of both Germany and the USSR, but assuredly not that of mutual trust or distrust. . . .

HAMMERSTEIN. We should like to increase the number of students from ten to twenty, in order to make a better use of the expended capital. In the coming spring we intend to carry out experiments with the newer tanks.[75] We contemplate giving to ten students technical training at the German works supplying us with tanks, and tactical training—in the classrooms. . . .[76]

In the vicinity of the tank school in Kazan there is an artillery unit. It would be useful to have a tank platoon there also, for our object, besides mastering the technical side, consists also in tactical application of tanks, and therefore it would be good if Russian units also took part in our work. By that time in Kazan there will be also three light tanks, besides three heavy ones. . . .[77]

VOROSHILOV. Our relations are based on rather peculiar principles, and the objects we pursue in our joint work differ. The Reichswehr wishes to have a base for testing newly designed tanks, training professional tankmen, and studying the tactical and technical possibilities of tanks. As regards our interests, they also include, besides the aforesaid, getting technical assistance. Specifically, I should like Herr General Hammerstein and Herr Colonel Küllental to tell me openly how far our cooperation can go in the sense of our getting assistance from the Reichswehr. . . .[78]

HAMMERSTEIN. . . . On the whole I should say that the Russians' wishes in principle coincide with the Germans' intentions, but first it is necessary to complete the period of technical testing. . . .[79] One more addition: I share all the more Monsieur Voroshilov's view that in Germany, because of the Versailles treaty, it is impossible to organize mass production of tanks. . . .

VOROSHILOV. To us it is highly important to link the work on laboratory experiments, conducted by the Germans in Kazan, with our tank-building activity. If Germans consider creation of a design office in our country now inopportune, perhaps our engineers might be temporarily included in the staff of your design offices working on tanks. . . . I know that Germany, on account of the Versailles treaty, cannot produce tanks. The USSR is not bound by any treaties and can build tanks not only for itself but also for other countries. Besides, under certain conditions it is possible to build in our country several special enterprises. . . . We should like to establish—with the aid of Herren Generals Hammerstein, Blomberg, Heye, and other Reichswehr's high officials with whom we have good relations—relations also with the German industry, so that we should be able to get technical assistance for our army in the near future.

HAMMERSTEIN. As regards our work, I have—to my greatest regret—to place some restrictions. We shall be very pleased if Russian and German engineers conduct joint studies in Kazan. But as to Germany, one ought to take into account the fact that German firms are working in defiance of the Versailles treaty, so that, for instance, Krupp fears that it may cause trouble. . . .

VOROSHILOV.[80] . . . The Reichswehr has not rendered us assistance we are entitled to on the basis of reciprocity.

HAMMERSTEIN. For strengthening our relations I am proposing as intermediaries: on all industrial questions—General Ludwig; on all tactical-strategic questions—Colonel Halm . . . and on questions relating to our joint enterprises—Herr Niedermeier.[81] . . .[82] In your country the communist system is a state system, whereas in our country communism is hostile to the state system. . . . Friendly relations of our two countries are based on the following three factors: friendship of armies, as far as possible friendly foreign policy, and mutual respect for the internal policy of each country. . . .

VOROSHILOV. . . .[83] A few words on political questions. We must proceed from the fact that in regard to social-political systems, our states are antipodes. . . . Therefore, it stands to reason that our relations can be only business ones. Nevertheless, both sides, as I understand it, should avoid in their joint work such steps that may cause damage to our states. There is no point at all in our implicating the Third International or parties in our purely business relations. . . . The magazine *Militär Wochenblatt,*[84] no. 8, carried an article by the retired General Von Mirk on the USSR's military might in the Far East. The article is impregnated with hatred and hostility toward us and affords a "rich," perverted, and, most important, false material to the Enténte, against which we should, one would expect, hold a united front. . . . One may not like Bolsheviks, however, one ought to respect our people, carrying on a most cruel struggle for existence. . . .

HAMMERSTEIN. . . . Unfortunately we cannot make *Militär Wochenblatt* abstain from printing certain articles, because the magazine is a private enterprise. . . .[85] We do not have our press in our hands to the extent you are having yours.

VOROSHILOV. What are Herr General Hammerstein's wishes in regard to Tomka?

HAMMERSTEIN. Tomka has got much in common with Kazan. Here our joint research institute is located, and we should like it to remain so. We believe, Russians are going to expand the institute and then the experimental gas battalion will come to Chikhany. However, we should like both the institute and battalion to remain as they are at present, not merged into a military unit. . . . I agree with Monsieur Fishman on all major questions, but on that of separating Tomka from

Chikhany our views differ. Practically it could be reduced to the following: if there is a hangar for aircrafts in Chikhany, the same kind of hangar— true, a smaller one—should also be there in Tomka.

VOROSHILOV. . . .[86] We consider the German chemical industry to be still unsurpassed in the world. Therefore we are surprised at the modesty and scarcity of technical means and equipment at the specially organized testing ground. It suggests an idea of it here being the point of either misunderstanding or of unwillingness to acquaint us with new and old chemical means of warfare that the Reichswehr disposes of.

HAMMERSTEIN. . . . All we have got at our disposal has been brought to Tomka, and my impression is that in Tomka, under General Trepper's excellent command, everything possible is being duly done, but Monsieur Fishman, whom I like very much, is carried away by enthusiasm and insists on moving forward too quickly. We are not keeping anything a secret; all we have got is there in Tomka. . . . My proposal is in the same old spirit—to continue work at this small institute in Tomka. . . .

VOROSHILOV. . . . The question of the pace of arming and testing, especially of testing of chemical means of warfare, is of paramount importance. Nobody knows when the war may break out. . . . Now let me pass to the question of Lipetsk. The Lipetsk school is existing for a long time already; it is the oldest of our enterprises. The school has yielded good results to the Reichswehr, whereas we unfortunately have not derived any benefit from its existence. . . .[87]

HAMMERSTEIN. . . . I have got a request for the tactical exercises in Voronezh still taking place and their being retained in the program. As regards Lipetsk, in the future we are going to expand the research work and increase equipment. . . .[88]

CSASA. F. 33987. Inv. 3. F. 375. Sh. 1–13.

*   *   *

DRAFT RESOLUTION OF VKP(b) CENTRAL COMMITTEE:[89]
"ON EXISTING RELATIONS WITH THE REICHSWEHR"

1929
Top secret

Heard:

1. On existing relations with the Reichswehr.

Adopted:

(a) Demand from the Germans the enhanced conspiracy in cooperation of both armies, as well as guarantees of preventing leakage of any information concerning this cooperation into press.

(b) Demand from the Germans compensation in the form of a rent payment for the buildings and lands in Lipetsk, Kazan, and Tomsk used by them.

(c) Further existence of the above enterprises should be conditioned by the need of equipping them with the most up-to-date technique (the newest tanks, planes, toxic substances, etc.), establishing research divisions with attendant workshops and laboratories, and attracting our researchers and technicians to work there.

(d) Use the possibility of advancement of the commander staff most fully by sending commanding officers to a German military academy, for participation in maneuvers, field trips, games, and fire drills, etc.; permit the Germans visiting RKKA on the basis of mutuality.

2. About new proposals of the Germans

2. Replies of the Soviet side

(a) On cooperation of German and USSR engineers in the field of artillery and machine guns; on the use of the newest achievements in this field of Reichswehr and German industry, on the one hand, and Soviet industry, on the other hand.

(a) With a view to use German experience in designing new military technique, favor cooperation of engineers from both countries in the field of artillery and machine guns and in military chemistry, too. Admit as possible the visit of prominent German experts for participation in design and production works in the USSR.

(b) On establishing contacts between RKKF and the German Navy (first, a visit to the RKKF head to Berlin, and the German Navy to Moscow).

(b) To take a reserved attitude to the establishment of contacts between both navies, admitting single and beneficial contacts for RKKF (achievements in the design of submarines, etc.). Penetration of Germans into RKKF should be avoided.

(c) On contacts in intelligence activities of RKKA and RV of Reichswehr against Poland with a view to exchange intelligence information about Poland and joint analysis of information on mobilization and deployment of the Polish Army. . . .

(c) Exchange of intelligence information on Poland and joint discussion of mobilization and deployment of the Polish Army are considered to be appropriate. A proposal on carrying out joint organizational work of both intelligence services is to be rejected.

(d) On the proposal of Germans to set up radio sets to establish communication between a tank school and the Lipetsk air fleet school.

(d) Reject.

3. Proposals of the Junkers Company.

Start negotiations on building a plant in the USSR.

3. Enter into preliminary talks with the Junkers Company in order to make clear concrete proposals of the company. Then return to discussing this question once more.

TzGASA. F. 33987. Op. 3. D. 329. L. 146–47. D. 295. L. 69–70.

* * *

FROM LITVINOV'S DIARY: RECEPTION AT THE DIRKSENS'

February 20, 1930
Secret

1. Dirksen started with saying that on the suggestion of Britain, they are discussing in Geneva a problem of bringing some articles in the Statute of the League of Nations into conformity with the Kellogg's

Pact[90] and that the German government decided to submit its comments to this end in writing to an appropriate commission. Quite confidentially Dirksen gave me a copy of this note. The diversionary nature of this step was quite obvious; it ought to prove the readiness on the part of the German government to further maintain contacts with us as concerns international problems.

2. Then Dirksen, in his own words, related to me the content of the long telegram, which he got from Kurtzius[91] as an answer to my comments sent to Berlin. . . .

. . . According to Kurtzius, Germany demonstrated its loyalty to us in the previous year in connection with the Soviet-Chinese conflict and the proposals it got to establish an anti-Soviet front. . . . From himself Dirksen added that we ourselves, by some our steps, have caused the worsening of the Soviet-German relationships:

. . . (a) Official celebrations in Leningrad and other cities in honor of Max Helz,[92]

(b) Official reception of a delegation of red soldiers[93] by the Far-Eastern Army and Blyukher . . . ,

(c) Reception of delegates of red Bolsheviks at the Bolshoi Theatre on the occasion of the OSOVIAKhIM Congress, at which Voroshilov and other government members were present . . . ,

(d) Keeping in mind special relations between the Red Army and Reichswehr and some special agreements concluded with the knowledge of the German government that thus plunges it into a great political risk, the German government was especially "Fruppieren"[94] at the public demonstration of closeness between Comrade Voroshilov and red soldiers. . . .

4. Dirksen asked whether I consider a trip to Berlin of some member of the Politburo to be useful. Obviously, mere talks between members of both foreign affairs offices, between them and me and Kurtzius and Schubert with Krestinsky, are not enough and further discussions between higher rank officers are needed [this suggestion is a reaction to the opinion expressed in some secret German document about the complete lack of authority of Chicherin, Litvinov, and NKID as a whole, and about Politburo and OGPU as actual decisionmakers in foreign policy]. . . . I said to Dirksen once more that now the point is not only in mutual assurances of loyalty between governments' members, but also in taking some definite stand by the German government in public in the face

of the anti-Soviet campaign, unrolling in Germany, and anti-Soviet statements made by German authorities.

> Litvinov
> TzGASA. F. 33987. Op. 3. D. 349. L. 61–64.
> Original.

*   *   *

KRESTINSKY ON HIS CONVERSATION WITH KURTZIUS[95]

Wednesday, March 5, 1930

KURTZIUS. I was always an advocate of the closer ties with the USSR. I think that we have many common economic and political problems. . . .[96] And now, when in the public opinion of the bourgeois world, including Germany, negative attitudes to the USSR prevail, I want not only to maintain, but also extend and deepen friendly relations with the USSR. . . .

KRESTINSKY. . . . We have information that a campaign against Derop[97] was inspired by the Prussian Ministry of Foreign Affairs. This information[98] is proved by the fact that the police visited first the Derunaft's Office and then the Derop's Division in Baden and demanded a list of employees as well as a list of all persons who use pumps with the Derop petrol. This means a planned attack on the petrol export, which scares off both buyers and contragents, selling our petrol directly to customers. An absurd statement of *Vorwärts* that I subsidize *Rote Fahne* by purchasing 5,000 copies can cause only laughing in a sensible man.[99] . . . I do not dwell on each of the above facts, I do not give a full list of our claims, but from what I said Mr. Minister should certainly understand that irritation against the German side is rising in our public opinion, that quite naturally we start thinking, speaking, and writing about re-orientation against us of the German public opinion and German government. . . .

KURTZIUS. And, naturally, a question appears: how can we put together friendly relations between us, with these attacks and often unfriendly statements against us in the press [that are] fully dependent on your government? And then, the activities of Komintern and your party. Certainly, neither you nor your government provide direct money assistance to German communists, but only inspire them to anti-government actions. But this is done by Komintern, and this is done by the communist party of your Union. And it is so difficult for us to make a division between the Soviet government and Komintern in view of that enormous influence the leaders of your party, and especially Stalin, have both in Komintern and in the Soviet state.

It would be very essential if your party of Komintern have openly declared, in any form, their indifference in respect to the German communist party. This would quickly improve the situation and eliminate enmity in relation to you, which exists in some our public circles. . . .

My answer [Krestinsky]: You exaggerate the dependence of our press on the government. . . . I think that the possibility of influencing the press in our country is hardly more than that of the German government. . . .[100] In no measure can we take on responsibility for the actions of Komintern. We have one-and-a-half millions of members. All of them work, get their salaries, pay greater or lesser party dues.[101] This gives our party some dozens of millions of robles a year. Much of this sum is used, certainly, for the needs of VKP(b) proper, but some percentage (five or ten, I don't know exactly) goes to K.I. This makes up several millions a year.

[According to Kurtzius], if he returns every time to a question of Komintern and VKP, it is with the sole aim to "disarm" our opponents in Germany. . . . He understands that we cannot take up any obligations in the name of Komintern and in relation to Komintern. But he does want all. He does not need any statements. He wants only that Com. Stalin, who, for all that, has nearly a dictator's power in VKP, lets German communists know somehow that he does not show great interest in their statements, this will be quite enough. Kurtzius wants to give one more example. Never did he speak with me about relations between the Reichswehr and the Red Army. But he knows about them and treasures them. But, naturally, his attitude would have changed if offices in our Red Army, contacting with the Reichswehr, became involved in communist propaganda in the Reichswehr.

My answer: Mr. Kurtzius falls in the wrong thinking that there is a dictatorship of Stalin in the USSR. Certainly, Stalin is the most influential person in our party, the whole party listens to his opinion. But this does not imply that he could force some erroneous political line upon the party. His strength and origin of his influence lie in his contacts with wide circles of the party members and working nonparty masses of people in general. . . .[102]

Krestinsky

TzGASA. F. 33987. Op. 3. D. 349. L. 65–81.

Original.

* * *

HORATZIUS HUMBOLD[103] TO ARTHUR HENDERSON:[104]
INFORMATION SUBMITTED BY THE BRITISH MILITARY ATTACHÉ
IN BERLIN[105]

1930

. . . The original cost estimate of Reichswehr for 1929–30, submitted by General Grenner for consideration of the Reichstag in spring this year, made up 482,409,090 Reichsmarks. After criticisms and as a result of reductions the total expenditures for army maintenance were brought to 471,394,820 Reichsmarks. . . .

Armaments of Reichswehr can be considered outdated in comparison to armaments in use in the armies of other European countries. . . . It is also known, that despite articles of the [Versailles] treaty, Germany exports to Sweden remote-sensing tubes with a clock mechanism, to Holland periscopes for submarines, to Brazil capsules.

A promotion of Lieutenant-General von Blomberg is the most interesting case of quick promotion in ranks. Being a director of "Trapen AMT," he was nominated at the age of 50 a commander of the first division in Eastern Russia, an important commanding rank. The third and fourth infantry divisions are presently under command of cousins Joachim and Edward von Stülpnagel; at the same time Otto von Stülpnagel, a brother of Edwin, takes the post of a transport inspector. Two most important departments of the Ministry of Reichswehr—"Trapen AMT" and "Personal AMT"—are headed by brothers Kurt and Hender von Hammerstein-Ekword. . . .

Last year everything seemed as if advocates of rapprochement with the eastern neighbor took the upper hand in the military policy of

Germany. And that this policy concentrates around more close cooperation with Russia. Soviet officers were present more than once at the maneuvers in different areas of Germany, while General von Blomberg with a group of staff officers went off to Russia on some secret mission. However, at the same time, beginning from the First-May disturbances in Berlin and the important speech of Voroshilov at the Moscow parade delivered in the presence of the German ambassador,[106] a certain cooling of the Russian-German relations is observed. But notwithstanding this Major-General von Hammerstein-Ekword (assis. of Blomberg), escorted by Colonel Küllental and Captain Hofmeister, officers of the information division, visited September maneuvers of the Red Army. These officers have made a long journey over Russia. They visited Ukraine, the Volga and Ural regions, and also Caucasus and Crimea.

Although at present political relations between Germany and Soviet Russia cannot be called cordial, there still is an impression that the German military authorities have an intention to maintain close ties with their future powerful ally in case of a likely conflict with Poland.

The Reichswehr, as before, takes a reserved attitude to us. Of course, the main idea, he cherishes, is breaking-off of relations between us and France. . . .

I personally do not consider that the Reichswehr, as it is now, is a menace only to European peace. But truly speaking I had only limited possibilities to observe these forces at work. . . . Reichswehr possesses a perfect personnel, well-trained body of officers, but at present due to limitations under which it is developing, it cannot rank abreast with either the British or French armies. I have an impression that its leaders are preoccupied more with its future, than present and, thus, we should look upon it as a cell, which will be enlarged several times in the future, and not as a homogeneous fighting unit ready for direct use. In this context the Reichswehr requires and deserves the most serious attitude and study.

> Have the honor and so on.
> Colonel Marshal Kornuel,
> Military attaché
> TzGASA. F. 33987. Op. 3. D. 70. L. 153–62.

*   *   *

A MESSAGE OF KUIBYSHEV[107] TO TsK VKP(b) POLITBURO

April 22, 1930
Top secret

By the adopted armament system Revvoensovet has predetermined production of more advanced artillery armaments, especially anti-tank and anti-aircraft guns, as well as more up-to-date howitzer systems. Taking into consideration the great difficulties involved in setting up design bureaus for all systems of armaments within the assigned and desirable— for the Workers'-Peasant Army—period, the Military Department and industry considered it appropriate to acquire technical aid from the best European companies in order to reduce terms and make easier the problem of reequipment and gaining experience in design and production of the newest systems of European armaments.

In this connection measures were taken to find out which of the most well-known companies could be of use to this end. During 1929 there were preliminary talks on this subject both with the Krupp Company and the "Rheinmetall" Company, too. After careful study of this subject and when concluding a contract with the Krupp for technical assistance in respect to the specialty steels, the problem of inviting technical aid from the Krupp Company as concerns the artillery systems of armament was withdrawn in view of unsuitable conditions put forward by the company, which was timely reported to the Politburo. After this both Voenved and industry decided on the "Rheinmetall" Company, being at present the sole company in Europe with which we can start negotiations on getting technical aid. In the course of preliminary talks there were identified three likely and necessary systems manufactured by this company.

The first direction—concluding a contract on technical aid for developing production of the four systems of artillery armament already designed and built, and two systems designed, but not built.

These systems are:

(1) a 3-in anti-aircraft gun, surpassing in its ballistic characteristics the similar system in service now—zenith height is up to 10 km and horizontal range of shot 16 km at 20 shots per minute;

(2) a 15-cm howitzer; shell weight is 38 kg, a range of action is 5,000 m, and a system weight is 1,130 kg;

(3) a 37-mm anti-tank gun (a system meant for combating tanks

and which is not at present in service of RKKA), a system weight is 310 kg;

(4) a 2-cm automatic gun (machine gun) which is meant both for combating tanks and for firing at zenith targets;

(5) two systems—a 6-in howitzer and a 37-mm automatic anti-aircraft gun.

Technical aid for the above systems includes provision by the company of working drawings, technological processes applied at the company, and assistance in organizing production at our plants. For this purpose the company delegates ten specialists assigned with the task of devising a production plan for plants, organization of the production proper, and rendering advisory aid concerning production during the whole contract term. Realization of this contract supposes development and production of these systems in 1931, i.e., by the end of the 1931 calendar year, to the following extent: a 3-in anti-aircraft gun of 58 systems, a 15-cm machine gun of 168 systems, a 37-mm anti-tank gun of 390 systems, and a 2-cm automatic gun (machine gun) up to 270 systems.

The total value of this contract on technical assistance makes up 1,125,000 $US to be paid within a year and a half. . . .

Apart from payments stipulated by this contract, we also take up an obligation to provide dwellings for invited specialists who are working under this contract and provision of all everyday amenities for them.

The second line of technical assistance is setting up design bureaus for developing, according to our assignments, technical systems of artillery armaments, which are an integral part of a general plan (developed by RV Council) of re-equipment, which concerns mostly large- and medium-caliber systems. It is envisaged here to invite twenty skilled expert-designers as well as to provide the required company's archive materials, which are instrumental for developing corresponding designs, by our assignments, within shorter time periods, in comparison to ours. The design of these systems also envisages developments on shells, tubes, firing mechanism, and the whole shot in general. . . . This contract is signed with the company for five years and our side is to pay annually 200,000 $US by the following dates: 1 Sept. 1930—50,000 $US, 1 Dec. 1930—50,000 $US, 1 March 1931—50,000 $US: and 1 Apr. 1931—50,000 $US; and so on. After full-scale tests, which give satisfactory results for the first test prototypes in a new artillery system, provided by the project developed at the bureau by the company's specialists, extra bonuses are to be paid annually: for small-caliber (up to 12 cm) artillery systems—20,000 $US; for medium-caliber ones (from 12 to 24 cm)—30,000 $US; and for large-caliber (over 30 cm)—40,000 $US. On top of this we also take up expenditures connected with accommodation of these specialists. . . .

The third line of the contract envisages purchasing a number of artillery systems, some of them semi-finished, some, completely ready. In order to make shorter the period of organizing production of these artillery systems, mentioned in the first contract, i.e., four artillery systems, it is stipulated that the company should supply technological instruments, special measuring and cutting tools, devices, and dies.

By this third contract we ought to pay the company 1,082,000 $US. . . .

Thus, summing up the problem of technical assistance of the "Rheinmetall" Company, by these three contracts we have to pay the company all in all 2,493,000 $US.

Besides, it should be said that for realization of this contract we would have to spend about 2 mln rubles in the hard-currency equivalent for purchasing of the required equipment, re-planning of one weaponry plant chosen for this purpose (eighth plant in Mytischi). A sum of 1.5–2 mln rubles has to be spent this year for equipment and internal arrangements at the plant—starting production of cast steel shapes, quick storage of semi-finished articles, standard instrumentation (both cutting and measurement), enrollment and training of labor force, and all measures associated with this contract.

It should be noted that, taking into consideration the great secrecy of this contract and the urgency of its implementation, the work over this contract was carried out not in a regular order, i.e., enlisting here the authorities of the concession committee, but by a small group of specialists who were entrusted with this work, i.e., Armaments Head Com. Uborevich on the part of Voenved and GVPU[108] Head Com. Uryvayev and also a limited number of legal and engineering experts.

At present a contract with the "Rheinmetall" Company is initialed[109] by our side and by the company's side. I am asking you to make a decision concerning final signing of this contract and corresponding expenditures of hard currency above the adopted hard-currency plan.

V. Kuibyshev
TzGASA. F. 33987. Op. 3. D. 112. L. 74–77.
Copy.

*   *   *

FROM A CONVERSATION BETWEEN
GERSTENBERG AND MEZHENINOV

October 31, 1930
Top secret

GERSTENBERG. I've got a letter where Moltke writes that Putna approached him with a request to provide the Lipetsk aircraft proving grounds to test your bombs. And that Moltke is interested in this and is happy to participate in joint trial work and asks to give him bomb samples.

MEZHENINOV. I know nothing about a talk with Mr. Putna. Most likely this is a continuation of a conversation about regular training bombings with concrete bombs of our air squadron. These samples we have already passed.

GERSTENBERG. But here, in the letter, they speak about testing fighting bombs.

MEZHENINOV. I don't see the point. Will you allow me to read a paragraph in Mr. Moltke's letter?

GERSTENBERG. [Reads himself]: "Mr. Putna applied with a question on provision of aircraft proving grounds for testing bombs, and so on."

MEZHENINOV. This is, probably, a question of testing electronic bombs.[110] You have passed us several pieces. . . .

GERSTENBERG. No. Here your new fighting bombs are meant, which you are going to test.

MEZHENINOV. I don't now have at my disposal any data and cannot get any. . . .

GERSTENBERG. In a conversation with Alksnis[111] we spoke about a plan of joint works. A question concerning bombs will evidently be included there, and we could learn about the time of testings.

TzGASA. F. 33987. Op. 3. D. 349. L. 88.

*   *   *

ABOUT AIRSHIP BUILDING AND ABOUT
AERIAL TRIPS ON AIRSHIPS OF THE "ZEPPELIN"[112] TYPE
OVER RUSSIA AND SIBERIA[113]

1930[114]

Top secret

Doctor Ekkener: With a view to provide your future workers at the shipyard with the study and training possibilities, the necessity of which we have already mentioned, we are ready to accept at our design bureau one-two engineers sent by you approximately two months prior to the start of building on condition that after they know the work properly they must participate in design works. Of course, the chosen engineers should possess appropriate engineering qualifications and adequate practical experience, for instance, in ship building and bridge building. . . . After the airship becomes your property you should start training your crew. To this end we can suggest to you the following. We can provide one or two crews for the airship at the expense of the Russian government while they are trained at one of the German airports. . . .

As soon as your crew, after numerous flights, adequately masters the control and maintenance of the airship the latter can be transferred to a Russian airport. For flying to the USSR we will provide one or two more German crews on the same conditions as above. Then training of other Russian personnel can be started. With this in view we'll try to make up one highly skilled German crew that, however, must be enrolled in your staff; thus, you would have to sign contracts with each crew member. We will readily render you assistance in signing these contracts. We think that training of the Russian crew could take up about two months if you manage to select appropriate persons. For this period we could provide one crew at your disposal. We think it right that the command of the airship during training should be trusted to a person nominated from our side, but this problem deserves further exchange of opinions.

We are ready to provide you advisory help in building up a shipyard for an airship both in selecting a proper site and in constructing and equipping the hangar with regard to your wishes and possibilities. The same is true for the construction of airports for airships, masts, gas plants, etc. It should be kept in mind that the building of units producing combustible gas may require further negotiations and new contracts with corresponding companies concerning licenses.

For the building of airships planned by you, we are ready to provide you, on condition of signing a license agreement, all our patents and experience both at present and in the future. . . .

In addition we would like to note that board-and-lodging expenses for workers who are needed for participation in trial and research flights in the USSR should be taken up by you. Then we must stress that personnel sent by you should, of course, be obedient to German legislation, working conditions, etc., and should, in particular, be obliged to submit to acting rules, internal rules at a plant, and our directions.

We are asking you to study the above program and are eagerly waiting for your positive reply. We propose starting negotiations on details of their program and its realization.

> M. P. Luftshiffbau Zeppelin
> Dr. Ekkener
> TzGASA. F. 33987. Op. 3. D. 112. L. 148–51.
> Attested copy.

* * *

DRAFT RESOLUTION OF POLITBURO OF VKP(b)CC ON AIRSHIP BUILDING

> December 12, 1930
> Top secret

Proceeding from the Resolution of Politburo of Sept. 9, 1930, "On development of civil aviation and ways of its connection with the military one," which provides for starting construction of a shipyard for airship building so that by the end of a five-year period we can build no less than 10 airships:

1. Admit it is necessary to organize building of 4 types of airships in the USSR: nonrigid, semi-rigid, rigid, and all-metal types, keeping in mind that by the end of a five-year period the USSR airship fleet should include, apart from trial ones, the following:

Types	Q-ty	Volume
nonrigid	30	10,000 cu.m
semi-rigid	3	Up to 20,000 cu.m
rigid	5	No less than 150 t
all-metal	2	

2. Proceeding from this program, entrust VO GVF to get down to building trial and serial airships, relying upon Soviet experience and taking the most advanced ideas from world experience.

3. Entrust the USSR Gosplan to envisage construction of two bases in a five-year plan: one in the Volga area for building trial samples, production, and capital repair of airships; the other, in Central Siberia for operation and repair of airships. . . .

4. Entrust VSNH and NK RKI SSSR[115] within a two-month period to analyze carefully all developments on helium that have been made up till now and to make up a plan of wide-scale survey and production works. . . .

Entrust Gosplan to study a question on expediency of inviting foreign technical aid for improving helium production in the USSR.

5. Approve a program of capital construction in the field of airship building in 1931 in the following volume:

(a) Construction of 11 airships of various volumes, of which 5 are nonrigid (Soviet design), 2 semirigid (Soviet and Italian design), 2 rigid 150 thous. cu.m in volume (German design, order one in Germany and start building the other in the USSR), and 2 trial all-metal (Soviet design, using data of SASSh);

(b) Construction of a shipyard with appropriate structures, including 1 hangar 200 thous. cu.m in volume, workshops—VTUZ and a school of technicians and pilots.

6. Entrust:

Gosplan SSSR to envisage in a/p for 1931 financing of this construction project in the amount of 20 mln rbls.[116] and provision of building materials:

NK Trud SSSR to provide engineering, technical personnel, and workers;

VSNH SSSR to provide building organization and render assistance in design works:

NK Snab SSSR to provide corresponding supplies;

NK Vneshtorg SSSR to provide corresponding foreign contingent after verifying this with Com. Rozengoltz and Com. Goltzman.[117]

7. Entrust VO GVF[118] to start negotiations in Germany, Italy; SASSh about getting technical assistance in building corresponding types of airships and overland structures.

K. Mehonoshin
V. Zarzar
TzGASA. F. 33987. Op. 3. D. 112. L. 152–55.

* * *

VERY URGENT. SECRET. TO *NARKOMVOENMOR* VOROSHILOV: PROTOCOL OF THE MEETING OF THE COMMISSION PERMITTING FOREIGN FLIGHTS THROUGH THE USSR

October 1, 1931

Heard: a German pilot Elli Bainhorn applied for permission to fly through USSR territory on the way from Germany to Persia by route of the "Deruluft" line to Moscow and then by the route of the VO GVF lines through Kharkov, Rostov, Armavir, Vladikavkaz, Baku, and Pekhlevi. Elli Bainhorn would like to have a photocamera on board a plane to take shots of landing places, if she gets permission for this.

The OO OGPU,[119] Sixth Department of the Headquarters of RKKA, and VO GVF have no objections against the flight of Elli Bainhorn through the USSR territory, but all object against the part of the route along the Black Sea coast and against the photocamera on board the plane.

Decided. Allow the flight from Germany to Moscow by the route of the "Deruluft" line and farther on along the route of the VO GVF lines through Kharkov, Rostov, Armavir, Pyatigorsk, Vladikavkaz, Grozny, Baku, and Pekhlevi.

Refuse permission to have a photocamera on board the plane.

F. Goltzman
TzGASA. F. 33987. Op. 3. D. 112. L. 206.

*   *   *

VON DIRKSEN TO VON BYULOV:[120] PERSONAL AND SECRET[121]

October 17, 1931

Dear Byulov,

Allow me now to write you about one matter, which, in view of its secrecy, cannot be considered in regular working order. A week ago General Adam arrived here with two persons from the Ministry of Reichswehr and, thus, after some complications, this visit did happen. Fortunately, this visit has so far justified the hopes associated with it. A conversation between Adam and Voroshilov, People's Commissar on Military Affairs, took place. It lasted over three hours and Mr. Adam was highly satisfied with its results. . . . Voroshilov gave dinner. . . . He invited to dinner me with my wife, persons from the Ministry of Reichswehr accompanying Kestring,[122] as well as Mr. von Tvardovsky and Mr. Gelger[123] with their wives. Dinner was held not at a hotel, but in the Kremlin. Taking into consideration local conditions, this is quite an extraordinary event. We also met there Enukidze,[124] local "Meissner,"[125] Krestinsky, Tukhachevsky; a successor of Uborevich at the post of head of the Armament Department, Deputy Chairman of the Military Council, head of the General Headquarters Egorov (a former tzarist army officer), head of the Moscow Military Region Kork (a former tzarist army officer and former military attaché in Berlin) with their wives. . . .

After dinner I met Voroshilov to explain to him how seriously we keep an eye on the Soviet-Polish negotiations. Since Voroshilov is a member of the Politburo and one of the closest friends of Stalin, his words gave me a possibility to get acquainted with the intentions of the political center. . . .

Voroshilov, in a quite categorical manner, underlines the invariable feeling of friendship to Germany entertained here. By his words, both talks with France and talks with Poland are purely political and tactical events, which reason suggests. Lack of the inner value of the nonaggression treaty with Poland is most clearly realized here. Voroshilov believes, and he stressed this in his conversation with Adam, that the border with Poland is not final.

I spoke much with Tukhachevsky, who plays a decisive role in the matter of cooperation with "Rheinmetall" and that organization, which was headed until recently by Niedermeier.[126] He is far from being such a direct and likable person, openly speaking in favor of the German orientation, as Uborevich was. He is rather reserved, clever, restrained. I hope that he will show loyalty, too, after he understands the necessity and advantages of this cooperation. . . .

Von Dirksen
TzGASA. F. 33987. Op. 3. D. 70. L. 267–69.
Translated from the German.

*   *   *

INFORMATION ABOUT MEETING OF TUKHACHEVSKY WITH ADAM, KESTRING, HOFMEISTER, AND MANNSTEIN

November 10, 1931
Moscow
Secret

General Adam said that he is happy to meet personally such an eminent leader of the RKKA as Com. Tukhachevsky, and he expressed his wish to discuss with him numerous problems concerning enterprises.

Com. Tukhachevsky pointed out that despite some achievements and successes the pace of the work of joint enterprises is very low, and their technical base is so limited that the effect of joint activity is very unsatisfactory and is not justified either in financial or political terms. It is necessary to hasten the pace and get the highest benefit.

In particular, about Lipetsk—in the next year it's likely to test planes of the newest designs, with high-output engines working on heavy fuel. Besides it is necessary to test the Junkers plane with a hermetically sealed cabin in winter conditions and in flights at high altitudes, carrying out bombing from these altitudes and firing from heavy machine guns at cones.

Adam stressed that yesterday the People's Commissar[127] told him the same and that on returning to Berlin he will pay most close attention to the work of the enterprises.

Further on Com. Tukhachevsky pointed to the necessity of improving equipment both in Tomsk and Kazan. Not knowing the situation at enterprises properly, Adam asked Tukhachevsky to accept Hofmeister and speak with him on all problems of interest to us, for which he got a consent.

Com. Tukhachevsky asked about Adam's opinion concerning unification of artillery, as a result they got six samples. In the answers of Adam there was some uncertainty, while explanations of Tukhachevsky showed a deep knowledge of modern artillery technique and this correspondingly cannot but impress Adam. In his turn, Adam was interested in the experience of mechanical traction of artillery gained in the period of the Soviet-Polish campaign of 1920. Com. Tukhachevsky replied that in this period mechanization was at its initial stage and it was used only in the first days of attack.

> Head of the Foreign Relations Department
> Sukhorukov
> TzGASA. F. 33987. Op. 3. D. 375. L. 162–63.
> Original.

*   *   *

VOROSHILOV TO STALIN[128]

November 11, 1931

Dear Koba,

I am sending you a record of a conversation with Adam. Everything Adam said was put down in shorthand. I will tell you about my personal impressions at meeting.

> Best wishes.
> Voroshilov
> TzGASA. F. 33987. Op. 3. D. 375. L. 21.
> Copy.

*   *   *

VON DIRKSEN ABOUT A MEETING WITH TUKHACHEVSKY[129]

November 13, 1931

. . . I was particularly interested in the problem of cooperation in the field of specialty industry.[130] . . . I doubt much whether the construction plan, about which an agreement was concluded, can be realized, which is awaited by the Soviet government. The plants suffer from a great deficit of skilled workers and the demands of plants' administration for adequately skilled manpower are left unsatisfied in view of the lack of adequate labor resources. As a result, production of all three types, envisaged in the agreement, has not evolved, and only a 10-centimeter type is produced.

. . . Then Tukhachevsky put forward some more complaints that can be reduced to the following—that our supply of materials to the Soviet Government is unsatisfactory and that it gets more comprehensive information on many problems from Britain or Italy.

In this context he mentioned in particular new tanks of German design, which we, obviously, keep in secret, while the British side handed us working drawings. Then he also mentioned the oil engine of the Junkers Company, which is stirring great interest. As for a tank, Mr. Adam promised to find out about it and in case of favorable results he will meet his wish.

As for an oil engine, Mr. von Mannstein said that so far his office did not have means enough to buy such an engine.

To the Embassy Counselor
Mr. von Tvardovsky for notice.
TzGASA. F. 33987. Op. 3. D. 70. L. 259–62.

*   *   *

VOROSHILOV: "I WOULD LIKE TO ASSURE YOU
ONCE MORE THAT EVERYTHING MOST VALUABLE
AND MOST IMPORTANT IS PASSED TO YOU"[131]

November 19, 1931
Top secret

ADAM. Reichswehr is sure that in the future the same friendly relations that have existed so far will continue. We are of the opinion that both states should rely on each other and work hand-in-hand. I, personally, look with great respect upon Russian idealism, upon Russian strength and work. . . . Public opinion of our soldiers is slightly uneasy about your negotiations with France, but we are sure that this goes not from the heart, but from mere financial considerations. Certainly, we would be much more anxious if you, under pressure of France, start negotiations with Poland. . . . For the army it would be very unpleasant if, in the course of these negotiations with Poland, there has been proved the validity of our existing borders, which we cannot admit for Poland. . . . Both you and we need peace. . . .

VOROSHILOV. . . . I must assure you most firmly that in negotiations with France there is not, and cannot be, anything directed against Germany. Our country is interested in good-neighborly relations with all states. A possibility that we will negotiate a nonaggression pact with Poland cannot be dismissed. . . . But we are not going to speak about borders and least of all about Germany in general. We can speak with Poland only about mutual nonaggression obligations.

ADAM. I have already said, and you have stressed this, that you and we need peace. But although we are peace-loving we can be forced to wage a war. As far as the world exists, when someone wants to start a war, no pact can stop him. . . . I am of the opinion that there is a mutual suspiciousness between the Soviet Union and France. General Hammerstein . . . is ready to contribute to the promotion of these relations. . . . In your relations with Lithuania the problem of Memel[132] is so far a bleeding wound. But our and Lithuanian armies are tied by friendly relations that have been strengthened this year still more. Among our military men there are people who dream of a military convention with Lithuania.

VOROSHILOV. I quite agree that, despite the striving of our and your states for peace, there may arise a situation when we have to defend ourselves from an attack. I cannot argue the fact that a pact is not a full guarantee against war. But today, when the word "war" is still in the memory of peoples, a nonaggression pact acquires the peculiarity that public opinion can be mobilized around it, which, if a pact is available, can be doubly against an aggressor. In this very sense a pact can acquire certain importance. . . .

ADAM. We are interested in those things in your country that we do not possess, especially tanks. Heavy artillery and your great experience in applying large aviation forces.

VOROSHILOV. There is a vagueness in the relations between the USSR and Germany. . . . For instance, the Kazan school. It seems to me that something is not good with it. If I did not know the German army, then I would say directly that here is sabotage. You know the meaning of this term. . . . For three years there has been some fuss in Kazan, and nothing resulted from it. The same tanks as there were at the beginning. I said—send us designers—and you and we would have tanks.

ADAM. We approach a tank problem with great caution due to the lack of adequate means and also due to the fact that tanks are very costly and become quickly outdated. I will study this problem most carefully once more—maybe the fault is with us. . . .

VOROSHILOV. . . . Since these enterprises are joint ventures, their goals and objectives are to provide benefit to both sides. . . . We have already an industrial basis, but so far we feel the shortage of designers. But you have specialists, and we thus assumed that your side would provide prototypes, drawings, projects, concepts, designs, in other words, that we would get laboratories both for you and for us. But nothing like this happened. . . .There is much fussing about the school, both among Poles and Americans. . . . I don't understand why not all possibilities are used—maybe something is kept from us or you do not consider it necessary to do everything. Not only I think in such a way. It is not I who manage everything. I am a member of the government and am obliged to report to it. I am told—there is a risk, and where is the result? Show us tanks, and I have nothing to show; three years of joint efforts and no results. . . . I have no suspicions—this is not a conclusion—but I have doubts whether everything is done with an open heart.

ADAM. I am sure that we don't conceal anything. I will delve into this matter personally.

VOROSHILOV. . . . Allow me to ask you a question, maybe slightly not to the point. What do you think, as the head of the General Headquarters of the Reichswehr? In a future war will tanks be of primary importance or will they be some auxiliary means?

ADAM. I am strongly of the opinion that in a future war tanks will be given a subsidiary role, and that would have to pay special attention to anti-tank facilities; if anti-tank facilities are good enough, then the role of tanks will be not so great.

VOROSHILOV. If tanks are of no importance, then why do we need anti-tank facilities?

ADAM. Tanks are a very costly weapon, and only a wealthy state can afford them. . . .

VOROSHILOV. . . . I don't quite agree with you. If there is a need for anti-tank weaponry, then it is against good tanks. I am sure that you, despite a rather difficult situation in Germany, would use tanks, and good tanks. . . . Tanks you will have, therefore you are interested in developing a tank business. Tanks of Rheinmetall, Krupp, and the one you have brought lag far behind the up-to-date tank-building technique.

ADAM. Then this is a mistake; we should be well informed in tank-building developments and build modern tanks. . . . It's not correct to think that tanks had decided the outcome of the war, but one should have tanks to defend against tanks, to follow their development and to build them.

VOROSHILOV. Then how do you look upon Britain's orientation to a wide-scale development of mechanization of armed forces?

ADAM. The British are also limited by their finances and will abstain from wide-scale tank development. . . . The outcome of great battles will be decided not by tanks, but by people.

VOROSHILOV. . . . In Tomsk the situation is somewhat better than in Kazan. . . . We provide all necessary conditions and ask also in return a concrete financial compensation. . . . I think that the Reichswehr, similar to the Red Army, will not be the first to use gases. But remember that other armies are seriously involved in this matter. . . . My opinion to this end is that the school does not give the awaited and necessary effect.

ADAM. . . . I am very thankful that German pilots can study in your country. . . . Our intelligence activity against Poland is very unsatisfactory. Thank you for the materials we got from you, and I am asking for cooperation in acquiring them in the future. We know that your intelligence provides much better information than ours.[133]

VOROSHILOV. . . . It's very pleasing to hear such praises of our intelligence men, but I am afraid they do not quite deserve them.

ADAM. There is a proverb: "Only a bad man gives more than he has in his pocket." . . .

VOROSHILOV. . . . I would like to assure you once more that everything most valuable and most important is passed to you.

ADAM. And the last—I would like to speak in brief about a disarmament conference and our joint work in Geneva. It's the opinion of military men that one must fight for disarmament at every level. Our demands are equal security for all, unity of methods, unity of prohibitions. This should be fought for. If this is not attainable, then one should leave the conference. . . . I myself do not believe in this conference, hardly anything will come of it.

VOROSHILOV. . . . We will keep to a position of complete disarmament. If this is not attained, then we'll fight for partial disarmament in the form that was declared by Com. Litvinov. I, too, have weak belief in this comedy and think that everything is arranged to stir public opinion. But we treat this comedy quite seriously, since it provides a possibility to curb a mad run to a war, observed now everywhere.

ADAM. It would have been a serious step—to leave the conference.

VOROSHILOV. Please, do not take it so, that we go off from the conference. If we do this, we'll play into the hands of the League of Nations or the leading group of the League of Nations. The odium[134] of defeat will fall on us. We will not leave completely, but will be fighting for disarmament.

ADAM. I understand it just so—to stay till the end, but not sign. This is my personal point of view. . . .

VOROSHILOV. I think that further on our friendly relations will be developing and gaining in strength. . . .[135]

TzGASA. F. 33987. Op. 3. D. 375. L. 22–40.

*   *   *

VON DIRKSEN ABOUT HIS MEETING WITH VOROSHILOV[136]

December 12, 1931
Moscow
Top secret

. . . Voroshilov confirmed once more that even signing a treaty with Poland will not in any case entail some worsening or changing of the friendly relations of the Soviet Union and Germany. Voroshilov said that, of course, under no circumstance can one speak about any guarantees of the Polish western border; the Soviet government is a principled opponent of the Versailles treaty; it will never undertake anything that would somehow contribute to strengthening the Danzig corridor[137] or the Memel border. As for Poland's eastern border, the Soviet Union has concluded a peace treaty with Poland and, thus, to a certain extent recognized the border. During the conversation I had an opportunity to ask Mr. Voroshilov what he thinks about the present state of German-Soviet relations. For this I got an answer that at present the relations are satisfactory, both in political and economic terms.

TzGASA. F. 33987. Op. 3. D. 70. L. 253–58.

*   *   *

VON NIEDERMEIER TO TUKHACHEVSKY

December 17, 1931
Moscow

Dear Mr. Tukhachevsky,

I don't want to take up your precious time once more and, thus, I am asking you to allow me to say good-bye to you in this way. I much regret that I have no possibility to continue our joint work and look forward in the future to having an opportunity to display proofs of my friendly attitude to the Red Army and the Soviet State. I wish you every success in your work and am asking you not to forget the most devoted to you

Niedermeier
TzGASA. F. 33987. Op. 3. D. 72. L. 63.
Original.

*   *   *

ADAM[138] TO VOROSHILOV

December 23, 1931
Top secret

Dear Mr. People's Commissar,

I think that you have already returned to Moscow and I hurry to express to you once more, Mr. People's Commissar, my sincere thanks for the most amiable reception and hospitality that I have met at all institutions and authorities of the Soviet Union.

I was much impressed by the construction that is being waged in the Soviet Union.

I am especially thankful to you for the opportunity to acquaint myself with the troops and departments of the Red Army. I also managed to see the high level of preparedness and greatly improved armaments and equipment.

. . . . At the military Academy, the VTzIK school, and Kamenev's school[139] in Kharkov I saw great achievements of teachers and students, although I think that by German standards the methods of teaching could be still more free and less schematic. A visit to the sixty-second cavalry regiment gave me an idea of the good cavalry training of the commander's body. At a tank regiment I saw with great interest the introduction of three interesting machines that are undoubtedly quite suitable for war and whose engineering faults have been described to me by the regiment commander. Certainly, I don't know whether they intend using these modern machines parallel with the heavy, outdated machines available to the regiment during the war, too. But I would think this inappropriate. Then an acquaintance with a motorized intelligence detachment in Kiev was of great interest to me. I think that the detachment composition is most appropriate. However, it can be used only as an intelligence detachment of big formations (army corps, army), but not divisions. Quite outstanding are the achievements of the Kharkov air brigade, already known to you from the report of Captain Ashenbrenner.

In general, I have got an impression that the Red Army is systematically and consciously working over development of its preparedness and armament and as of today it makes up an enormous force. . . .

Most respectful and devoted to you

> Adam
> TzGASA. F. 33987. Op. 3. D. 375. L. 96–99.
> Original in German signed by Adam.

*   *   *

"THE REICHSWEHR IS 'FRIENDLY' WITH US (THOUGH IN ITS HEART HATING US)"[140]

> March 12, 1932
> Top secret

. . . Giving appropriate consideration to the political significance of the Reichswehr and its leaders for Germany, we, at the cost of material sacrifices, have done a lot to establish good relations with the Reichswehr. However, here we never forgot that the Reichswehr is "friendly" with us (though in its heart hating us) only because of the established conditions, because of the necessity to have a "safety valve" in the East, to have some trump card for threatening Europe. The friendship and cooperation of the Reichswehr went along the lines of giving less and worse, but using us more fully. . . .[141]

> Voroshilov
> TzGASA. F. 33987. Op. 3. D. 342. L. 179–80.
> Original.

*   *   *

NIEDERMEIER IS READY TO ORGANIZE
A MEETING WITH HERING:[142] A REPORT OF ALEXANDROVSKY,
COUNSELOR OF THE USSR PLENIPOTENTIARY REPRESENTATION
IN GERMANY

July 28, 1932
Top secret

ALEXANDROVSKY. . . . Stricly secret, Niedermeier said that beginning in autumn a military academy, prohibited by the Versailles treaty, will start functioning in Berlin. . . . Schleicher pursues a course to complete destruction of utterly outdated and unfavorable forms, ordered by Versailles to Reichswehr. Actually this means abolishing some of these forms. . . . Niedermeier thinks that the question of military aviation will take up quite another character. . . . Cautiously enough, Niedermeier hinted that such radical reorganization of the army is directed against the West (France) and will go on notwithstanding international prohibitions. . . . After his leave Niedermeier, if I am interested, is ready, after taking the necessary precautions, to organize a meeting with Hering and promote in every way the permanent contacts between the Plenipotentiary Representation and Nazi. . . .

TzGASA. F. 33987. Op. 3. D. 342. L. 191–96.
Original.

*   *   *

"WILL BE REPORTED TO BERLIN": NEGOTIATIONS OF
VOROSHILOV, TUKHACHEVSKY, ALKSNIS, AND DEREVTZOV
WITH ADAM AND HOFMEISTER

November 1932

Our wishes	Replies of Germans	Final replies of Germans
1	2	3

(a) About Lipetsk
I. Get acquainted in 1932 with the following trials and experiments:

Our wishes	Replies of Germans	Final replies of Germans
1. Experimental flights into the stratosphere.	Will be reported to Berlin.	
2. Possibilities to use oil engines in military aviation with experiments in Lipetsk.	Trials, on financial considerations, should be done in Germany. Our representatives can learn about the course of trials after they are delegated to Germany.	
3. Trial flights in mist.	Will be reported to Germany.	
4. Experiments on automatic stabilization of planes in air.	—"—	
5. Automatization of bombing.	—"—	
6. Making pictures at high altitudes in clouds.	—"—	
7. Experience of bombing from high altitudes.	—"—	
8. Analysis of objects, the list of which Com. Alksnis handed over to Hofmeister on 22.11.1932 for further transfer to Mittelberger (engines, planes, armament, aeronavigation, safety appliances, radio devices, photo, clothing).	—"—	

1	2	3
9. Transfer of image from a ship to the earth.	Will be reported to Germany.	
10. Control of planes from the ground and in air.	—"—	
11. Study the problem of inter-action of aviation and quick-moving units in maneuvers in war conditions (mechanized units, cavalry units).	—"—	
12. Study the problem of con-trolling ranging fire and correct-ing artillery firing in the condi-tions of a great concentration of their own and enemy aviation.	Will be reported to Berlin.	
13. Allow participation of our commanders in tactical trainings of aviation in Germany.	—"—	
14. Give the "Green book" on the use of aviation and in-structions on the aviation and troops interaction.	—"—	
15. Demonstrate in Lipetsk new high-altitude measurement in-struments, sighting devices, guns and machine guns on board a plane, improved means of com-munication.	—"—	
16. Trial firing from large-caliber machine guns from air upon air- and ground-based targets.	—"—	
17. Illumination service at night flights.	—"—	

1	2	3

18. Lipetsk turns solely into a school for training and education of pilots and, due to curtailing experimental works by Germans, its significance becomes nil.

This year the Lipetsk school must become more an experimental institution than an educational one. Educational purposes should recede to the background. However, this way of development is impeded by a poor financial situation in Germany.

19. In Lipetsk there were refusals to show some radio equipment and others alluding to a company's patent.

This is not admissible. If this happens in the future, please, report to us for taking immediate action.

(b) About Kazan

1. In Kazan there is no new equipment. For 3 years there are no results.[143]

Adam will consider this problem in Berlin.

2. The number of students will be the same as in 1931.

This depends on the number of teachers.

3. Germans as before will be responsible for general guidance and preparation of a study plan. Our students study by our regulations. These courses should be oriented to improving skills. For our students more important are the problems of tactics, not the technical equipment. Within a section they should be trained both in tactics and technique.

Have no objections against a parallel course.

1	2	3

4. The number of German teachers:
in tactics (one will be on firing)   3
in technique (dynamics—in particular for student-engineers)   2
in radioservice   1
in driving   1

This number is difficult to provide, but this will be reconsidered.

Each of them are given our assistant.

5. At the school both sides should have new models of tanks.

In 1932 it is impossible to send new machines. Questions put forward by the Germans:
(1) A request to send new machines to Kazan (Kristy and Vikkers). They themselves cannot send new machines.
(2) To increase the number of machines of the same speed (for training 60 persons).
(3) Reduce the number of German teachers required by the Soviet side (we have not replied).

(c) About Tomsk
Extend the experiments, have more equipment and facilities for active and passive work.

Maybe now we succeed in turning the chemical industry to us, before it wasn't in need of us. German wishes: Due to limited financial possibilities the experiments can be done no more than 2 months a year; thus, to go every year seems unnecessary. It's likely that VOHIM[144] takes up the following:

1	2	3
	(1) provision of "friends" of OV, (2) expenses on labor force, (3) expenses on burying animals.	
(d) General		
1. Let know about the following:		
(a) experiments on thermal treatment, carburizing, nitriding, and electrical welding of armor.	Will be inquired in Berlin.	
(b) stamping and molding of armor.	—"—	
(c) trials with facilities to control anti-tank mines.	—"—	
(d) production of nitrosilk.	—"—	
(e) production of powders.	—"—	
2. Sending of Soviet technicians for participation in experiments.	—"—	
3. Rejected forgings for heavy-caliber artillery guns, manufactured by Krupp as a technical aid.	RV is willing to help with advice.	
4. About distending of 37-mm barrel of Rheinmetall.	All misunderstandings can and must be settled down. Delays with payments are not welcome, since this will reduce the possibilities of the company.	
5. About technical aid in the production of liquid de-aerator.	Will be inquired in Berlin.	
6. About technical aid in the production of artificial silk for producing gun powder.	—"— (already inquired)	

1	2	3

Since these enterprises are joint ventures, their targets and objectives are to get benefit to both sides; naturally, we should assign out expenses in such a way that enterprises show the highest efficiency. We can improve much in Kazan, if your money is spent on technique and the technique itself is more real.

Wishes of Germans:
1. The Soviet side takes up salary payment to workers at enterprises while the German side pays a certain sum in German marks.
2. Payments for items and appliances from the implements of enterprises, sold to the Soviet side, can be done in exchange for fuel and materials.

TzGASA. F. 33987. Op. 3. D. 375. L. 16–20.

*   *   *

HAMMERSTEIN: "IN MY OPINION RUSSIA IS UNASSAILABLE . . ."[145]

On December 11, 1932, Hammerstein had the following conversation with Kaniya, the Hungarian envoy in Berlin.

KANIYA. . . . For all that Russia has achieved much by its nonaggression pacts and its diplomatic status has strengthened a lot.

HAMMERSTEIN. Of course, one should distinguish the diplomatic power and the actual power. But I still think that Russia is unassailable. And it will be the cause of much distress to its neighbors. The Russian army and the Russian workers will fanatically fight for their motherland. I know about the increasing number of military plants in Perm, but even if they are only ready for commencement, then even in this case Russia, by virtue of its advantageous geographical situation, is invincible. What can it mean to Russia, if one can capture even Moscow for some time!

TzGASA. F. 33987. Op. 3. D. 497. L. 2–5.

NOTES

1. The document was obtained by members of the staff of the fourth secret service board of the RKKA Headquarters and forwarded to Frunze by Zvonarev, chief deputy of the secret service board.

2. Appointed by CK VKP(b) in January 1925 after Trotsky's resignation from this post.

3. "Dower plan"—the Dawes Plan (named after Ch. Dawes—the wealthiest banker in the USA) was adopted by leading western states in August 1924 with the diplomatic and financial support of the USA. In accordance with the plan, German reparation obligations were to be fulfilled at the expense of international credit. This was the beginning of the process of reconciliation of the losers and winners in 1918.

4. Maltzan was Germany's foreign minister of that time; U. Brockdorff-Rantzau was German ambassador to the USSR in 1922–29.

5. Luther was a German Reich councilor.

6. G. Stresemann was German foreign minister, 1923–29.

7. Widenfeld (apparently Widfeldt) was Kruppe plant's director.

8. UNSA—spelling of the USA at that time.

9. F. Tissen was a German coal industry magnate.

10. Chapter 3 will give a detailed account of the cooperation with the Junkers firm.

11. Resignation of the RVS chairman.

12. J. Erbet was appointed ambassador to Moscow in 1924 after relations between France and Russia resumed. In 1931 Erbet was transferred to become ambassador to Spain.

13. De-Monzy was a French senator who stood for recognition of Soviet Russia.

14. Fourth Secret Service Board of RKKA Headquarters.

15. Signature on the document is illegible.

16. P. V. Lunev was a military attaché in Berlin.

17. Document was forwarded to Frunze.

18. The true name is Shpan—"Zeiss" commerical director, Russian White Guard officer (ZGASA, F. 33987. Inv. 3. F. 1128, K. 62).

19. The document was obtained by the Soviet secret service. The accompanying note read: "To: Frunze M. V., RVS SSSR Chairman. Strictly confidential. This is to forward copies of the secret service information obtained by the Japanese Embassy in Berlin. The source is perfectly credible. Secret service agency chief deputy. 22.8.25." Copies forwarded to Unshlikht, Voroshilov, Chicherin.

20. On February 90, 1925, Stresemann forwarded an official project of the guarantee pact to the French government. Germany undertook to keep to the status quo at its western borders, but at the same time it outlined its unwillingness to give whatever obligations to eastern borders.

21. Such coordination is in the text of the document.

22. An optant is a person who has the right to choose citizenship.

23. V. M. Molotov was the then secretary of the CK VKP(b).

24. *Narkomindel*—People's Commissariat for Foreign Affairs, abbreviated NKID.

25. The copy of the document was intended for Politburo members and members of the NKID Collegium.

26. Brockdorff-Rantzau.

27. Voroshilov's speech on February 23, 1926, in which he touched upon the questions of German armaments.

28. Brockdorff-Rantzau.

29. People's Commissariat of the Navy.

30. This is how the document runs.

31. Naval Department.

32. Publication in the *Manchester Guardian* and *Münchnerpost* newspapers of the names of Reichswehr officers sent on a mission to the USSR.

33. RWM—Reichswehrministerium, Germany's Ministry of Defense.

34. Chapter 3 will discuss five joint ventures with the Germans. The sixth one is Dreise machine-gun production. We have only fragmentary information on this subject.

35. A joint stock company.

36. Heye was a Reichswehr general.

37. A. I. Kork was troops commander of a number of military districts.

38. Chemical devices.

39. MFA—Ministry of Foreign Affairs.

40. See note 33.

41. The document, entitled "Assessment of the USSR's International and Military Position at the Beginning of 1927," was drawn up by the Fourth Intelligence Department of the Workers' and Peasants' Red Army Headquarters and reported by Berzin to Voroshilov. The document being rather voluminous, only an extract of it is given here.

42. S. S. Yurovsky was deputy minister of foreign affairs.

43. So were the Germans cooperating with the Soviet side often called in documents.

44. Gessler was minister of defense.

45. Apparently, Frank, who was a member of the Control Council, regulating the interrelations between the Junkers firm and the Soviet side.

46. Brodovsky was secretary of the Soviet mission in Berlin.

47. Von Schubert was Reichswehr lieutenant-colonel, von Seeckt's proxy.

48. G. von Dirksen was Germany's ambassador to the USSR in the twenties.

49. Fischer was von Dirksen's adviser.

50. Wetzel was the General Staff chief.

51. Flying school in Lipetsk. See chapter 3.

52. Ya. M. Fishman was the Military-Chemical Department chief.

53. Information on Bruchmüller not found.

54. Stolzenberg was the chemical firm's director.

55. Obviously, chemical arms.

56. Stolzenberg.

57. AFD—Air Force Department; STC—Scientific-Technical Council.

58. The protocol of the agreement between the WPRA Air Force Department

and representatives of the Special Group regarding organization of a flying school and arrangement of a depot for aviation materials in Lipetsk was signed by WPRA AFD Chief P. I. Baranov and on behalf of the Germans by Lit-Tomsen on April 15, 1925.

59. Poison gases.

60. Information has been prepared by the Fourth Intelligence Department of the WPRA General Staff.

61. Information prepared by the Fourth Intelligence Department of the WPRA General Staff.

62. Chiefs and representatives of industrial and military People's Commissariats.

63. Glavmashstroy—Central Machine-Building Management.

64. Gomza—Central Management of State Amalgamated Machine-Building works.

65. Glavelectro—Central Electric Power Management.

66. AD—Artillery Department.

67. B. Stomonyakov was a PCFA board member.

68. The text of this talk, which took place earlier, is not available. A. I. Mikoyan was at that time People's Commissar of External and Internal Trade.

69. Anti-Soviet and anti-German actions in Berlin and Moscow, respectively.

70. Germpra—German government.

71. PCFA—People's Commissariat of Foreign Affairs.

72. K. von Hammerstein-Ekword was the Reichswehr's Land Forces Department Chief, successor to von Seeckt in this post.

73. Reference to "Tomka."

74. G. I. Kulik was at that time WPRA Artillery Department Chief.

75. In the tank school in Kazan ("Kama").

76. Further, Hammerstein-Ekword suggested sending to Germany Soviet military school students who knew German.

77. Hammerstein-Ekword expresses a desire to invite Russian engineers' services for working at the all-around perfection of tanks.

78. Voroshilov states a desire to get drawings of German tanks and for Soviet engineers to be able to work in the Design Office in Germany.

79. Hammerstein-Ekword recommends General Ludwig as an intermediary between the Reichswehr and German industry.

80. Voroshilov points out that there is an agreement on cooperation with the Krupp Firm.

81. It is necessary to dwell especially on Colonel O. von Niedermeier—German military intelligence service agent. In the twenties he was known in Moscow under the name of Neuman. In the years of the Second World War he was in command of Wehrmacht units consisting of "Russian turncoats." By the end of the war, von Niedermeier, having joined the ranks of fascist regime opponents, found himself in a concentration camp, from which he was released by the Americans. Subsequently, on appearance in the Soviet zone, he was arrested on suspicion of espionage and kept in Butyrsky prison until 1949, after which his traces are lost.

82. Hammerstein-Ekword advises to maintain contact through the Soviet military attaché Putna.

83. Voroshilov approves of candidacies of Ludwig, Halm, Niedermeier, Putna.

84. *Militär Wochenblatt*—a military weekly.

85. Hammerstein-Ekword asks Voroshilov to send a counterarticle refuting the *Militär Wochenblatt* author's allegations and promises to have it published.

86. Voroshilov maintains that the German side is not giving to "Tomka" what is due to it under the agreement. Existence of the institute becomes problematic.

87. Voroshilov appeals to Hammerstein-Ekword with a request to allow Soviet specialists to come to Germany for training. Hammerstein-Ekword gave his assent to it.

88. In conclusion Hammerstein-Ekword insists on permitting duty-free carriage of German cigarettes to the USSR and light wines for German specialists.

89. One of the located copies of this document bore a handwritten note by Berzin: "Resolution of the Commission of M.[ilitary] I.[ndustry]."

90. The Briand-Kellogg Pact was signed in Paris on August 27, 1928. It is also known as the Paris Treaty on the prohibition of war as a tool of national policy and a means of settling international disputes. Its authors, French Minister of Foreign Affairs A. Briand and the USA Secretary of State F. Kellogg, were striving to create an organization parallel to the League of Nations but headed by the USA. This pact was signed by fifteen states, including Germany and Japan. Then it was joined by forty-eight more states. The USSR was the first to ratify it (August 29, 1928), inviting neighbor countries to sign a protocol of putting it into force without waiting for general ratification. Such a protocol was signed in Moscow on February 9, 1929.

91. Kurtzius was minister of foreign affairs of Germany.

92. Max Helz was leader of the German workers-communists, participant of the Revolution in Germany.

93. "A delegation of red soldiers"—a workers' self-defense organization in Germany in 1924–39, illegal since 1929. From February 1925 it was headed by Ernst Telman. In 1925 the Fourth Intelligence Department of the RKKA Headquarters submitted a detailed report on this union to Frunze.

94. From the German *fruppieren*—astonish, strike.

95. This conversation took place at Daleme, at a house of Kurtzius.

96. Further on they spoke about mutual claims of the Soviet and German sides to each other.

97. Derop—representation of petroleum companies in Germany.

98. Krestinsky mentions unfriendly, provocative actions on the part of German authorities, department heads in relation to Soviet officers.

99. *Vorwärts* and *Rote Fahne* were German newspapers of various orientation.

100. Krestinsky dwells on the independence of the Soviet press from the Soviet government directives.

101. To Komintern.

102. Krestinsky's reasonings justifying Stalin go on further.

103. H. Humbold was British ambassador in Berlin.

104. A. Henderson was minister of foreign affairs of Great Britain.

105. This document was obtained through agents and handed over to Voroshilov by Messing, the OGPU Deputy Chairman.

106. On the eve of May 1, 1929, the police chief of Berlin, Tzergibel, prohibited a First-of-May demonstration in Berlin. At the First-of-May parade in Red Square in Moscow, Voroshilov, speaking about the international movement of working-class solidarity and the class struggle in capitalist countries, touched upon this question, which gave rise to a noisy anti-Soviet campaign in Germany. Voroshilov's speech was regarded as interference into the internal affairs of Germany.

107. V. V. Kuibyshev was from 1926, VSHN Chairman; from 1930, chairman of Gosplan.

108. GVPU—Head military-industrial department.

109. Initialing is signing of an international agreement with the initials of the persons who participated in the work over it, in order to confirm a preliminary agreement prior to official signing.

110. Most likely, electronic; the original text is damaged.

111. Ya. I. Alksnis was, in 1926-31, deputy head of VVS; in 1931-37, a head of VVS RKKA

112. A name of a German company. The building of zeppelins at that time was a world monopoly of "Der Zeppelin" in Friedrichshafen. This company had more than thirty years' experience in the construction and operation of rigid airships.

113. From a conversation between Dr. Ekkener, head of "Zeppelin & Co.," which took place in Moscow after the descent of an airship "Count Zeppelin" (named in honor of Count F. Zeppelin, a national hero of Germany and designer of the airship used by the Germans as a powerful air-attacking weapon), with Baranov, head of VVS SSSR.

114. Is dated by the content.

115. Commissariat (*Narkomat*) of the Workers-Peasant Inspection.

116. In actual prices.

117. A. Goltzman was the head of GVF who suggested the organization of a base not in the Volga area, but in Pereslavl-Zalesski.

118. Military department of the Civil Air Fleet.

119. Special department of OGPU.

120. "Von Byulov" [von Bülow] was probably a close friend of von Dirksen. Other information is absent.

121. This document was obtained by the Soviet intelligence service.

122. Kestring was a colonel of the Reichswehr and a military attaché of Germany in the USSR.

123. Von Tvardovsky and Gelger were counselors of the German Embassy.

124. A. S. Enukidze was, in 1932-35, secretary of the Presidium of TzIK SSSR.

125. "Meissner" is a kind of a minister of the court and a confidential person of Hindenburg [Translator].

126. German intelligence service.

127. Voroshilov.

128. In 1937, at the meeting of the Military Council, Stalin accused military chiefs of the Red Army of spying in the interests of Germany. The impression was given that he himself knew nothing of contacts between RKKA and the Reichswehr. This

small note proves that Stalin did know about contacts of RKKA and the Reichswehr. Moreover, it's quite obvious that nothing was decided without Stalin knowing it.

129. This document is obtained through the Soviet intelligence service.

130. Military is meant here.

131. From a text of the conversation between Voroshilov and Adam.

132. From 1871 to 1918 the Memel region belonged to the German Empire, then it was under the control of the Entente, and in 1923 was returned to Lithuania. Thus, the Memel problem appeared.

133. Adam passes a request of Fisher, head of the intelligence service of the Reichswehr, to get information from the Soviet intelligence service.

134. From the German word *Odium*—disgrace, dishonor, shame.

135. Present at the reception were Colonel Kestring, the military attaché of Germany (translator for General Adam), and Petrenko, the RKKA officer (translator for Narkomvoenmor Voroshilov).

136. The document was obtained through intelligence agents and reported to Voroshilov by the head of the OGPU Special Department Leplevsky on December 21, 1931.

137. The Danzig corridor is a name given to a strip of land obtained by Poland in accordance with the Versailles treaty, which opened up for Poland a way out to the Baltic Sea.

138. A brief description of Major-General Wilhelm Adam, prepared by Sukhorukov, the head of the Foreign Relation Department, was enclosed with the document. It says:

> Major-General Adam was born on 15.09.1877. He graduated from the Military Academy. During the war the last post he held was the head of the operations section of the Eighth Bavarian reserve division (first officer of G[eneral] H[eadquarters]) in the rank of major. In 1921 he was an officer of the headquarters of the seventh division of the Reichswehr (in the rank of major). In 1925—head of the headquarters of the seventh division. In 1926 he was transferred to the headquarters of troops of the first military district (an officer of the GH). In 1929 he was appointed chief of the headquarters of the first military district troops. From February 1930 he was chief of the Reichswehr headquarters (Truppenamt). In 1925 he was in the rank of lieutenant-colonel, in 1926 he became colonel, in 1929—major-general. Was awarded the Iron Cross Order of the first degree.
>
> Major-General Adam is considered one of the most capable young generals of the Reichswehr. He doesn't play a politically independent role; he is associated with the group of "eastern" orientation of Hammerstein-Shleiher. (TzGASA. F. 22987. Op. 3. D. 375.)

The following postscript to this text of the characteristics was made by Shtern, the head of the sector of military and military-naval attaché:

By my personalri pressions Adam is a very lively, pink-cheeked, quick person, who, by his looks and behavor, is younger than his 54. He is a brave soldier, likes to drink, crack jokes, quick to laugh and promise, a little bit rough like a simple militaryman. In general, he is much more a soldier than a colonel. Putna called him a "German Kovtyuh" [E. I. Kovtyuh—a komkor]. This is not exactly so; Adam is livelier than Kovtyuh. Adam is Bavarian, and, according to our observations of Bavarian officers, out of all Germans they are especially cold to us. Apart from the German nationalistic feelings, they also have their own, Bavarian ones. Bavarian officers (in Bavaria there are practically no Prussians in the troops; before the war there was even a separate military academy and a headquarters in Munich), most often nobility, monarchists, have the closest ties with the Steel Helmet and fascists. Stern. (TzGASA. F. 22987. Op. 3. D. 109–109 ob. Original.)

139. Military-educational institution preparing military personnel of different categories and specialities.

140. From a letter of Voroshilov to Hinchuk, the Soviet plenipotentiary in Berlin.

141. Further on in this document, Voroshilov spoke about a consent to joint, together with Germany, intelligence against Poland. The same is mentioned in Hinchuk's letter to Moscow dated March 1, 1932 (TzGASA. F. 33987. Op. 3. D. 342. L. 180).

In 1932 Tukhachevsky personally (the authors' analysis of his manuscripts proves this) worked out a detailed plan of operation for crushing Poland, where he envisaged "attacks of heavy aviation on the Warsaw Region." In his draft project on disorganization in case of a concentration of Polish troops in the western Ukraine and western Byelorussia it was said: "Based upon a new program of tank building, we have a full possibility, by the end of 1932, to turn rifle divisions, located in the near-front zone of BMR [Byelorussian Military Region] and MUR [Ukrainian Military Region], into mechanized brigades and corps."

At the same time Tukhachevsky stressed: "In this note I did not touch either upon Romania or Latvia. By the way, such an operation can be easily organized against Bessarabia. . . . (TzGASA. F. 33987. Op. 3. D. 400. L. 14–19. Handwritten original of Tukhachevsky.)

142. H. Hering was chairman of the Reichstag from July 31, 1932.

143. Data on it are not available.

144. VOHIM—a military-chemical department.

145. The document was obtained by the Soviet intelligence service, and Berzin reported about it to Voroshilov on January 14, 1933, as strictly top-secret information.

3

The Concept of Military Cooperation Seemed Simple and of Mutual Benefit

In Germany we witness an amazing industrial progress and achievements which open up great possibilities for creating the newest battle means.

I. Uborevich, head of the RKKA armament

We should be fighting against our political isolation, and in this struggle our agreements and treaties with Russia should further on serve as a springboard that has already brought us so many political benefits. . . .

G. von Dirksen, German ambassador in the USSR

"JUNKERS" FLIES TO THE USSR

We are always ready to a wide and open cooperation with the "Junkers" Company. . . .

P. Baranov, *Narkom* of VVS RKKA

Still prior to signing the Rapallo Treaty on March 15, 1922, the Soviet government has signed a contract with the "Junkers" Company on the construction of a military plant on the territory of the USSR. This contract was secret. Niedermeier, a military secret-service man, signed it as Neuman; the town of Dessau, where a plane-building plant was located, turned into Leipzig, while the types of planes were not openly mentioned. During talks it was arranged that the company took up the whole risk of this venture. The German side allotted 600 mln. marks to the "Junkers" Company. The Soviet side granted it the right to build and equip plane-building plants in Fili (then in the vicinity of Moscow) and in Kharkov with a view to manufacture planes and engines for them. . . .

*   *   *

REPORT FROM LUNEV[1]

August 18, 1925
Berlin
Top secret

The letters of the fifth and twelfth are received. As to items 2 and 3 of my report of 7 August on which you request the details, I can report the following: Junkers A.20 airplane has already taken off today; this Junkers airplane is intended for ties of Litt with Lipetsk.[2] It will be followed by two other ones of the same type. I requested your instruction on this airplane as far back as 28 July, then I reminded you of it in every report, with no answer having been received until the present time, and now it doesn't matter: it took off under the German number; if owing to this there are troubles in Kovno or in Smolensk it will be through no fault of mine and it was impossible for me to detain it here for more time.

As for Telefunken,[3] you will receive the most detailed information from Landsberg, the authorized representative on Russian affairs. He has obtained a visa and goes to Moscow on the twentieth. I gave him a letter addressed to Yashka,[4] being very neutral in content, without giving the address, and indicated the telephone of the first house of the RVS [Revoliutsionnyi Voennyi Soviet-Revolutionary Military Soviet, RMS], and there, I say, he will learn. It may be better for Comrade Yashka not to have dealings with him personally and to bring him into contact with the proper person. For the second time I ask you to allow me to spend 75 dollars on a steel box for confidential papers. I see from your information about comrades being sent on a mission to maneuvers that I am described among them. Certainly, I shall still be present there in order to participate in subsequently summing up the maneuvers by the Germans.

In the twenties of the month I go to Vienna. I succeeded in getting into contact with Zeiss,[5] the latter seems to make advances with us. In addition, I have a chance of seeing the works of Prof. Ezau about which I wrote you the last time (by radiotelegraph at a wavelength of 1 meter); after returning I shall report at greater length. I ask to inform Comrade Ginsburg[6] that I have received and fulfilled his letters 2348, 2408, and 2423. The last letter for Schwarz[7] I shall give tomorrow and at that time shall talk about tests of Dreise.[8]

N. L. L[unev]
TsGASA. F. 33987. Op. 3. D. 98. L. 64.
Copy.

*   *   *

FROM FISHER[9] TO LIT-TOMSEN:
"WE ARE MOST INTERESTED IN . . . GAINING MORE INFLUENCE
OVER THE RUSSIAN ARMY, AIR FORCE, AND NAVY"

January 7, 1926
Berlin
Top secret

. . . Unshlikht's position with respect to our joint work is neatly characterized by you.[10] He considers all supply questions as a focus of attention whereas we are most interested in before long gaining more influence over the Russian Army, Air Force, and Navy.

Because of this, Professor Geller recognizes with gratitude that in the very first case you were in search for ways through Unshlikht to Voroshilov and specifically to Tukhachevsky. . . .

The state of the Junkers matter to date is as follows.

Before the meeting of the extended control council on January 4, 1926, in our small circle (Geller, Schwarz, Volkmann, Wilde, Frank), various possibilities of subsequently considering the Junkers matter were discussed. It was stated that from political considerations we must keep to the idea of the enterprise in Fili, with technical considerations, however, no longer playing the role that they did in 1922.

Since we do not want to make an additional contribution to the enterprise in Fili, when discussing various possibilities those among them that mean a financial load on us fall away. . . .

TsGASA. F. 33987. Op. 3. D. 151. L. 60.
Attested copy.

*   *   *

FROM ONUFRIEV TO COMRADE STALIN[11]:
"I CONSIDER IT TO BE A COMMUNIST'S DUTY FOR ME TO
FOREWARN, IN YOUR PERSON, THE WHOLE OF THE PARTY
ABOUT REPEATING THE MISTAKES."

March 11, 1926
Top secret

In addition to my reports of Nov. 11, Oct. 6, Oct. 16, and Dec. 3, 1924, and in addition to what I said at the meeting of the Politburo of TsK VKP(b) on March 6, 1926,[12] by the present report I consider it to be a communist's duty for me to forewarn, in your person, the whole of the Party about repeating the mistakes that have been committed by the UVVS over the last three years and which (according to facts) have taken the form of the rule. As the primary idea in the above-mentioned reports I set off the intolerable extravagance of the gold fund on foreign purveyance of airplanes and the fettering of the Republic to a concession agreement with Junkers Company as well as the intolerable inattention on the part of directing bodies like the UVVS to our own aircraft industry as a primary basis of the Air Force, on the development of which the development and power of the latter depend.

I considered and consider now the extravagance of the gold fund that is thrown out abroad and to the concessioner, as a principle in general, to be intolerable and criminal by the results obtained from these purveyances. As characteristic examples of these, the following facts of 1923–1924 can serve.

1. Giving the order to Junkers Company for D-11 type fighters,[13] the model of which was recognized as unfit for adopting during preliminary tests by a commission of the Scientific and Experimental Aerodrome.[14] In spite of this, the order was nevertheless given for 125 units that came to the USSR in such a state that they had to be repaired on the spot.

2. Giving the order to the concessioner for 100 metal airplanes the acceptance of which was accomplished without preliminary testing at the Scientific and Experimental Aerodrome and only after almost the whole of the order had been completed 2 airplanes were transferred for testing and they were recognized as not conforming to the agreement and, by virtue of this, in no way meeting the requirements being imposed on them as on military airplanes. Despite such an opinion of the competent organ like Scientific and Experimental Aerodrome the airplanes were adopted to detachment service. As a result, the operation of these airplanes confirmed all imperfections detected through testing, which is stated in the Bulletin No. 6 of January 6, 1926, of the N.K.UVVS [Narodnyi Komissariat Upravleniia Voienno-Vozdushnykh Sil—People's Kommissariat of the Air Force, PC AF].

The order for Fokker airplanes was at the cost of 3,600,000 rubles and the order for Junkers airplanes given to the concessioner cost 2,500,000 rubles, which in aggregate cost 6,100,000 rubles and gave the Air Force the low-quality airplanes that can be categorized as ordinary training airplanes but not under any circumstances as combat airplanes, since Junkers and Fokker airplanes are not equipped with devices for arranging and dropping bombs and have no sets for firing through propeller disks, and all this work after an actual acceptance is fulfilled at the ex-Duks factory.[15]

But in all, over the 1923–1924 period, a sum of 11,700,000 rubles was expended for foreign orders and for the concessioner. The laid-down system of foreign orders for the 1923–1924 period exists at the present time as well, but it has taken a somewhat different form, and as for essence, it is directed to weakening our own industry. Purchased over the past year are 160 motors of BMW company in Germany, 200 motors of Lorent-Dietrich in France, 200 Siddley-Puma motors at government depots in Great Britain, and at the moment a procurement in the USA is conducted of 500 Liberty motors remaining after the World War. . . .

The BMW motors are low-powered and of no value to combat Air Force.[16] . . . In the spring of 1925 a twin-motor airplane was built by Junkers Company in Dessau, which came flying to Moscow where it was demonstrated by representatives of the company to the UVVS with a proposal to convert it into a bomber. . . .

All purchases abroad in 1924–1925 are expressed in a sum of 11,000,000 rubles plus 3,600,000 rubles of the agreement for 12 bombers, which together with expenses of the 1923–1924 period adds up to 26,300,000 rubles. . . .

The crisis experienced now by the aircraft industry must not be considered as casual; it is inevitable and results from expending a colossal means on a foreign market, which is equivalent to 52,600,000 rubles in the domestic market, under the assumption of the recalculation coefficient being equal to two.

The lack of ordinary economy and proper care for the own aircraft industry of the UVVS resulted in an inevitable and at the same time intolerable deficit in pinewood necessary for airplane production at the moment, not to mention the mobilization stocks of pinewood and other materials with which factories are in no way provided. The amount of money expended over three years on the foreign market has a disastrous impact on providing factories with currently needed materials as well as on development of the aircraft industry in the future. Duks factory being the sole and large-scale aircraft production enterprise calls for 75 percent replacement of equipment only due to wearing. . . .

Buildings of the factory are so ramshackle and homely that all expenses for their repair are a waste of time and means. . . . Certainly, expending millions abroad and thus promoting development of the enemy's Air Forces, activities of our own new design organs must not be laid up.[17] . . . Reporting to you on the present critical and besides inevitable state of affairs in the aircraft industry, together with the air fleet, I insistently say another time to call more serious attention to this, since it is now impossible for many things to be saved but many things can be remedied, for objective conditions in the country and the industry give a prerequisite in favor of the development of the air fleet foundation.

The orientation to foreign countries taken since 1923 and pursued up to now (purchases of fighters in France) must be stopped and corrected by the Party in your person.

> Acting director of the AVIAKhIM[18] GAZ [*Gosudarstvennyi Aviatsionnyi Zavod*—State Aviation Factory, SAF] No. 1
> Onufriev
> TsGASA. F. 33987. Op. 3. D. 151. L. 77–79.
> Duplicated from a copy. The document is typed in one copy: for Voroshilov.

*   *   *

TO COMRADE DZERZHINSKY, CHAIRMAN OF THE VSNCh[19]
OF THE USSR: "THERE WERE CONNECTIONS BASED ON
BRIBERY BETWEEN . . . THE JUNKERS COMPANY
AND RESPONSIBLE PERSONS IN THE UVVS."

April 29, 1926
Top secret

Conclusion

The question posed by Comrade Onufriev in his reports addressed to Comrade Stalin, from our standpoint, needs not only comprehensive inspection but exploration as well. The point is that, as ascertained by materials of the GPU [same as OGPU—(United) State Political Administration], there were connections based on bribery between foreign companies, in particular the Junkers company, and responsible persons in the UVVS. Because of this, it is quite possible that these persons playing a large part in the UVVS influenced not only the purchase of airplane and motor types, maybe not corresponding distinctly with their purpose, at companies in which they were interested, but also the acceptance itself by accepting faulty materiel, more precisely, low-quality products of foreign companies.

Among the persons arrested recently in connection with the case of derangement of work at aircraft factories is the engineer Lino, a ringleader and inspirer of every bribery adventure in the UVVS and Avaitrust. According to Olsky's[20] statement, this "knight" has confessed to his taking bribes from foreign companies. Certainly, the bribes are not given for nothing, and it should be believed that these companies, in particiular Junkers, together with the "hero" Lino, robbed our treasury over a long period of time supplying us with the trash. Unfortunately, we have succeeded only in ascertaining that motors and airplanes were delivered in such a state that they must not be put into operation without repairs. But we have not succeeded in ascertaining whether or not all the airplanes and motors that came from abroad for the UVVS were faulty, as well as in ascertaining to what extent in general these airplanes and motors purchased since 1921 up to now meet the requirements of operation in the Air Force fleet, how many among them went out of service and how many were rejected very early, that is, on coming from abroad, and what was done with them. Without the data indicated above, it is generally difficult to judge serviceability (of airplanes) not only called for in Onufriev's reports, as such, but also according to their purpose itself. An effort was made to obtain these data through the NAMI[21] and TsAGI research institutes. But as a response to our request we have received answers written for form only, that these institutes have not the data in their disposition and that in general they were not involved in these matters. Even a quite harmless question of whether such-and-such types of airplanes and motors are serviceable in the Air Force fleet was not answered neither by the NAMI nor by the TsAGI.

It has become clear that the research institutes have no desire to draw a conclusion on the serviceability of one or other type of materiel in the Air Force fleet.

But whoever must make an analysis and draw conclusions? What are research institutes formed for and what do they exist for if a required response cannot be obtained from them at a proper moment? This circumstance only confirms with greater evidence that everything is not all right with importing motors and airplanes, to say nothing of prices that for some units are many times higher than those of products of our factories that are still in the experimental phase of development. In addition to research institutes, we also requested a scientific committee of the UVVS regarding the quality of imported airplanes and motors and whether they all are serviceable in accordance with their purpose; but now nine days have already passed and we do not have any answer and, it should be believed, shall not have.

Comparing all these circumstances, namely:

(1) Onufriev's reports where he points out a variety of crying facts with references to documents;

(2) Lino's testimonies;

(3) dread or unwillingness of research institutes to answer in essence the openly posed questions; and

(4) silence of the N.K.UVVS;

one can draw a conclusion that this matter should be investigated in order to know all about foreign orders at Junkers company and this can be done only by the GPU which, in our opinion, must be charged with clearing up the following:

1. What motivated annual purchase of airplanes and motors abroad since 1921 at rates indicated above over the elapsed time?

2. What quantity of airplanes and motors purchased in this time period is in operation according to their purpose?

3. What quantity of imported airplanes and motors failed to operate annually and what was done with them?

4. General data about quality of every type of imported airplanes and motors and about their serviceability in the VVF [Voienno-Vozdushnyi Flot—Air Force Fleet, AFF] as compared to VVF of other countries: Poland, Italy, Germany, France, and Great Britain.

5. Total value of purchases and prices of every type of imported both airplanes and motors and for every consignment.

6. How much money was spent altogether in this time of foreign purchases of motors and airplanes, and how many units of airplanes and motors totally were received for this money?

7. How much money was allotted to our aircraft industry, and how many products were manufactured for this money?

Only after the questions enumerated above have been elucidated shall we have a possibility of judging this matter quite objectively

Deputy chairman of the management board of the Glavmetall
Mezhlauk

Member of the management board of the Glavmetall
Budniak
TsGASA. F. 33987. Op. 3. D. 151. L. 74–76.
Original.

*   *   *

FROM VAURIK TO GILDER:[22]
"I DO NOT WANT TO PRESENT MYSELF IN MOSCOW
IN CONNECTION WITH THE JUNKERS MATTER."

June 8, 1926
Top secret

. . . The situation is very complicated here. Only in my departing I told you it is necessary to advise the ambassador[23] to wait a little with writing letters addressed to the professor[24] until one clears up who is the owner of Junkers enterprises. But up to now it remains to be seen. In fact, the management of the plant is now in hands of a financial committee.

The contact with the professor himself who has a certain minority in his disposition, as chairman of the control council, is disturbed, to put it mildly. A comprehensive inspection under the leadership of Simons[25] has come close to such a decision that is declined by the other side (the imperial ministry of defense). In accordance with the decree of the council of ministers, this has now to become obligatory or, as is now demanded by the imperial ministry of defense, legal proceedings must be instituted in regular order. This means, therefore, that in the short run or maybe only after another year one will be able to ascertain who is the owner of Junkers enterprises.

To be sure, for the time being I was able to partly thrust Russian affairs on attention of the professor whose head is stuffed with care for local German affairs. Mr. Schlez[26] who also already talked with separate persons can explain many things to you. I agree with his appraisal. It is most proper to follow a temporizing policy with respect to the course of events.

The decision, factors of which in this phase cannot already be affected, demands to temporize. And hence, the problem will again become urgent ("What is going on in Russia?") when the matter concerns the conservation of this base of the German aircraft industry.

And if then the Junkers Company is taken into account, the first thing that should be done is to fulfill technical prerequisites of suitableness for Russian airplanes. As is reported to me from Dessau, this will occur just in autumn. If it is so, all Russian doubts can be overcome as well as doubts associated with the present circumstance.

Until this technical problem is solved it would make no sense to talk about Junkers in Moscow. . . . Professor Junkers wanted that I should go there now, too, but until technical promises are fulfilled I do not want to present myself in Moscow in connection with the Junkers matter.

TsGASA. F. 33987. Op. 3. D. 151. L. 58.
Attested copy.

*   *   *

STATEMENT OF MR. SCHLIEBEN[27]

June 15, 1926
Moscow

I am grateful to Mr. Baranov for his giving me an opportunity to talk with him. Having learned that serious clashes between you and representatives of Junkers Company took place, I must tell you that in order to recreate the atmosphere of mutual confidence favoring fruitful activities, Junkers Company has entirely discharged Mr. Sacks, he will no longer work at Junkers Company, and Mr. Schöl is transferred to other enterprises of Junkers Company so that he will not participate in interrelations with the Russian air fleet. Mr. Heisemann, a representative of Junkers Company in Moscow who is present here, is appointed to his post. It is self-evident that in doing so Junkers does not admit any guilt, but for the atmosphere to be more clear all the above-mentioned persons were put out from here. Junkers Company has received a letter from the concession committee containing the proposal of terminating the concession. The company designedly delayed the reply to the letter. We hope to find some way to settle the question through personal talks. The results may be of different kinds. Resumption of functioning at the factory in Fili is possible under the management of the Soviet government but with financial and technical aid of Junkers Company. The company management board considers as inexpedient the conclusion of the new agreement. Why to conclude agreements when there is no certitude of their being performed completely? Such an output should be found that the company would work here in the atmosphere of mutual confidence. Now Junkers Company is working on new airplane models.

Both the political and economical interests of Germany and the USSR are coinciding on this question: for your army to be supplied with airplanes of the latest models. Favorable conditions for collaboration with the Junkers Company should be created. Favorable output should also be found on the agreement for bombers and motors.

It is now inexpedient to talk about old deliveries, but as for the current delivery, all in our power should be done for completing it all right. Junkers Company will do its utmost to remove all existing shortcomings. We are waiting for a telegram tomorrow or the day after with the news about elimination of the trouble hindering the achievement of the airplane's ceiling. My earnest request to you is to solve a question on arming airplanes in the shortest possible time so that this problem will not affect delivery dates.

As for dates, Junkers Company will hardly be able to perform the agreement punctually. But technical defects will be eliminated whatever happens. Utmost is being done for this. It seems to me, that full agreement can be made by personal talks with Mr. Heisemann rather than by exchanging letters. To do this would require mutual confidence and goodwill. Junkers can do much in the matter of reinforcing your army's combat power. A close connection should be set between German and Russian aviation. We are relying on your assistance, Mr. Baranov, in this direction. The aim of today's sitting is to outline general questions and common opinions. The details will be discussed later on. I ask you to not press Mr. Heisemann with technical questions. He is a new hand at it and the matter is not yet entirely mastered by him. As for me, I am going to Germany. I must also report to the German government about our talk and only thereafter are some concrete decisions possible. As for subornation of some Russian officials by representatives of Junkers Company, this, to my knowledge, took place after concluding the agreement for airplanes, and Junkers Company will hardly be able to make a concession on the agreement price. The company made an entire calculation and it is of no use for it to operate at a loss. But my statement regarding possibilities of reducing the agreement price does not mean that talks on this matter are impossible.

These questions should be discussed with Mr. Heisemann. I must once again thank Mr. Baranov for good words that he told me and state that our wishes regarding collaboration are in agreement. Mr. Mülich-Hofmann declares on behalf of the German government: the German government, on economical and political considerations, declares its readiness to remove all obstacles preventing the Junkers Company from the fruitful activity in the USSR. The interests of the German Republic and the USSR in aviation affairs are in agreement. Owing to our experience and our technical knowledge, we can render aid in the matter of arming your Red Army.

Mr. von Schlieben once again thanks Mr. Baranov.

Translated and written by Krianga.[28]
TsGASA. F. 33987. Op. 3. D. 151. L. 64–66.

＊　　＊　　＊

ON NEW PROPOSALS OF THE JUNKERS COMPANY:[29]
PROTOCOL OF A MEETING OF THE GLAVMETALL,
UVVS, AND AVIATRUST

June 25, 1926
Strictly confidential.

Was present: Comrades D. F. Budniak (Glavmetall), V. K. Averin (Aviatrust), Baranov (UVVS).
Was heard: On new proposals of Junkers Company.
Was resolved: With the presence of new circumstances and new proposals of Junkers Company, it is considered as expedient to use
the proposal of Schlieben's company:

First, on technical aid in the airplane-production field, with the technical aid must primarily be reduced to the company developing and
transferring to the Aviatrust for realization with the use of modern
structural technology metal airplanes fitted and meeting all conditions
of military service.

Second, on organization of production using foreign technology.
On the basis of these two primary requirements an agreement with the
company regarding its technical aid must be drawn up, regardless of

the old concession agreement, within the framework of a special technical commission.

As for the old agreement and mutual monetary payments, the Glavmetall, UVVS, and Aviatrust propose:

(1) to terminate the concession agreement, and

(2) to solve the mutual monetary payments within the framework of a mixed technical and financial commission with the participation of the government and Junkers Company.

Schlieben's stated proposals concerning his financial participation in this new undertaking can be evaluated after liquidating the concession. The form of this participation now does not have to be determined and supposedly can take the form of the credit that the German government and the Junkers Company will give to this enterprise for developing jigs, constructions, importing foreign materials, some equipment, etc., with all this must be included in the agreement on the technical aid of the company.

D. Budniak
TsGASA. F. 33987. Op. 3. D. 151. L. 62.
Original.

*   *   *

FROM BARANOV, CHIEF OF VVS RKKA, TO VOROSHILOV

Report

Presented here are (1) the material characterizing the situation with the concession of Junkers Company; (2) the situation with the last orders at this company.

According to the agreement of July 1, 1925, of the Air Force Command concluded in Moscow with Junkers-Dessau, an airplane production joint stock company, we were to receive as scheduled deliveries:

(a) three JuG-1 prototype airplanes with L-5 motors, accessories, tools, and spare parts; (b) two L-5 motors; (c) one flotation gear kit with two equipped floats, right and left, for the G-1 airplane.

Prices of delivery subjects were determined as follows:

(a) 228,000 gold rubles per each of the airplanes with motors, accessories, tools, and spares (the price is conjectural and relates to the case when the command orders 45 units under the next agreement. The order being absent, this value should be increased by 86,000 rubles).

(b) 15,000 rubles per each L-5 motor with accessories and spares, which the UVVS pays to the Junkers Company.

(c) 35,000 rubles per one flotation gear kit with floats.

Total cost of delivery under the agreement is 744,000 rubles. According to the agreement of November 24, 1925, with the same Junkers Company also concluded in Moscow, we were to receive deliveries of (1) 12 G-1 airplanes with accessories including L-5 motors with tools and spares; (2) 18 L-5 spare motors; (3) 12 flotation gear kits; (4) one additional kit.

The established price per airplane with motors, tools, and spares is 105,913 US dollars (the price is conjectural and stipulated by our purchasing additionally 5–8 airplanes; we would be obliged to additionally pay 24,672 US dollars). The price per kit of flotation gear is 15,935 US dollars. To date it has become clear that the persons who drew up the agreement accepted bribes from representatives of the company in Moscow. Ill-intended actions of the Air Force Command and their agreements with representatives of the Junkers Company in Moscow resulted in concluding the disadvantageious agreeement at increased price with terms of payment being advantageous for the company.

Considering the prices for motors according to information of the Foreign Department of the Air Force Command and taking into account the peculiarities of markets, one can conclude that the average price per motor with a power of 300–450 HP[30] should be 9,500 rubles under condition of purchasing in batches.

When delivered together with motor spares, this price should be increased up to 10,000 rubles. This calculation is a reference and rather approximate. Based on this calculation, one can say that for 65 motors Junkers Company obtained 325,000 rubles in excess.

Considering foreign prices for heavy airplanes, one can ascertain that the minimum reference cost of a large metal airplane without motors can be about 100,000 rubles. If taking the airplane cost according to minimum prices for airplanes and motors, total cost of the airplane will be about 130,000 rubles. Under the agreement for 12 G-1 airplanes the value is fixed at 205,471 rubles 22 kopecks.

Thus, if the reference price is taken as an accounting price, one talks about overpayment of 205,471 – 130,000 = 75,471 rubles per each batch of airplanes with motors; 75,471 × 12 = 905,672 rubles for 12 airplanes; 600 × 20 = 100,000 rubles for 20 spare motors; and 1,005,652 rubles totally for the airplanes and motors ordered in batch. . . .

An approximate cost of the G-1 airplane derived from the calculation of manufacturing the airplane can be determined in the following way:

(1) Under the assumption of completely manufacturing the airplane in Dessau: structural weight is as great as 2,600 kg, material cost is 14,404 rubles, payment of wages is 8,450 rubles (35 kopecks hourly), overhead charges (300 percent) are 25,350 rubles. Trade expenses (130 percent) are as great as 10,985 rubles. Altogether it is 59,189 rubles, and totally with accounting for a 20 percent profit (11,838 rubles) it is as great as 71,027 rubles.

The cost per kilogram of structural weight is equal to 27 rubles 32 kopecks.

(2) When constructing the airplane at the factory in Fili, the cost of manufacturing will be significantly higher, since actual wages at the factory for production workers were as great as 60 kopecks hourly. Overhead charges can range from 450 to 400 percent. Then, when constructing in Fili, the price for a weight unit is equal to 41 rubles.

(3) Thus, when constructing the airplane partially in Dessau and partially at the factory in Fili, as the agreement stipulates, and under assumption that only final assembly is carried out in Fili, the airplane cost will be as follows. We take the quantity of man-hours worked for manufacturing the airplane equal to 24,143 (rather to excess). Let the assembly in Fili take about 15 percent of man-hours, for ease of calculating we assume it to be 4,143 man-hours (3,621 exactly). The cost of materials let be equal to that at Dessau plant.

Cost of materials	14,404 rubles
Wages in Dessau and Sweden (20,000 man-hours, 20 kopecks hourly)	4,000 rubles
Wages in Fili (4,143 man-hours, 60 kopecks hourly)	2,486 rubles
Overhead charges in Dessau (300 percent)	21,000 rubles
Overhead charges in Fili (450 percent)	11,187 rubles
Trade expenses in Dessau (130 percent)	9,100 rubles
	65,177 rubles
Freight charges and miscellaneous costs (10 percent)	6,518 rubles
Profit (20 percent)	13,035 rubles
Total	94,730 rubles

Thus, a value of 545,652 rubles[31] can be considered as the most probable overpayment according to the agreement.

The situation with tests and acceptance of subjects under the agreement is as follows: (1) Two motors No. 5 tested in the NAMI are adequate in design but motor shafts were found to be weak: the shaft of the first motor broke in 89 hours and the shaft of the second motor broke in 35 hours. The company showed the motor with a reinforced shaft. . . .

(4) The tested airplane revealed an imperfection associated with stabilizer vibration. In addition, the airplane is overweighed by 120 kg and does not achieve the negotiated ceiling (2,800 instead of 5,000 mt[32]).

Concerning the motors, the company is charged with claims on elimination of shortcomings, otherwise the acceptance of motors will be impossible.

. . . According to the batch order, the first airplane is to be delivered by the company on May 15, but this did not take place. Before July 1 six airplanes were to be delivered, but representatives of the company have stated that the time of delivery will not be kept. Our Trade Delegation in Berlin has announced to the representative of the company about 50 percent discount on the sum of the agreement, but the company did not give an answer to this. In response to our representation, Schöl is dismissed and replaced by a new person. Mr. von Schlieben, the representative of the company, stated during talks that price revision should be discussed with Heisemann, the new representative in Moscow.

Baranov, chief of the Air Force of the RKKA
TsGASA. F. 33987. Op. 3. D. 151. L. 36–37.
Original.

*   *   *

BARANOV'S STATEMENT TO THE REPRESENTATIVE OF THE JUNKERS COMPANY: "I AM READY TO ADMIT THAT THE TIME OF DELIVERING MOTORS AND AIRPLANES WILL NOT BE KEPT"

June 1926

We are always ready for widely and frankly collaborating with the Junkers Company. But both the execution of separate orders and the ful-

fillment of the concession agreement have brought a lot of disappoint-
ments to us: over four years the factory yielded 100 airplanes that are
of rather lower quality as compared to foreign products. We were certain
that the company had serious resolutions to work in our country, and
we strained every nerve for joint work, considering that this collaboration
based on political and economical cooperation would be advantageous
both for the company and for us. Nevertheless, the last period of work
and particularly the behavior of representatives of the company brought
such a deep disappointment that we had to take decisive steps. Technical
problems regarding both motors and airplanes that within the last order
to date are not solved by the company are well known to you.

I am ready to admit that the time of delivering motors and airplanes
will not be kept. As this takes place, it is desirable to know what the
company will do for eliminating shortcomings and in what time span
this will be done. But I must state with full frankness that subsequent
collaboration with the company would be open and useful only after
revising the amount of the last agreement. You know our presentation
of facts about the lack of conscientiousness of some representatives of
the company and the bribing of our officials, which entailed the conclusion
of an agreement commercially disadvantageous for us. This is the primary
question of the day. A wide collaboration and its form can be found,
since your statements argue that common language can be found more
easily after personal rearrangement.

TsGASA. F. 33987. Op. 3. D. 151. L. 67.
Copy.

*   *   *

REPORT ON INSPECTION OF THE
AIRPLANE-PRODUCTION FACTORY IN FILI

January 20, 1927

On January 20, 1927, the commission of the Air Force Command under
the chairmanship of Comrade Fradkin, with the participation of Comrades
Mark and Oradovsky, and with the presence of Mr. Vitkovsky and Mr.
Rosenbaum inspected the factory premises and ascertained the following.

The first half of the building (main) is sufficiently heated, glazed, and work on assembling airplanes is carried out in it. This half of the building is protected enough from snow penetration. Machine tools located here are in satisfactory condition. In the second half of the building, more than a third of the roof glazing is broken. Snow penetrates freely into the building through empty window frames, and at this inspection the snow is seen in heaps across the floor, despite the fact that snow is removed regularly. In view of machine tools and other machine elements being covered only by separate roofing-felt sheets, they are not protected enough from being snow-covered and in spring will in no way be protected from rusting in the course of thawing. Examination of external parts of machine tools showed that they are lubricated satisfactorily with grease. . . . The commission notes the presence of snow on one of the milling machines and on transmission parts (pulleys) placed on the floor. Snow cover was found on mounted transmissions. This half of the building is not heated at all. The remainder of the factory premises . . . is kept in the proper state.

> nn[33] A. Fradkin, Vitkovsky, V. Oradovsky, Rosenbaum, Mark
> TsGASA. F. 33987. Op. 3. D. 249. L. 60.
> Attested copy.

*   *   *

REPORT OF VOROSHILOV TO STALIN AT POLITBURO TsK VKP(b):
"THE FACTORY IN FILI IS KEPT VERY BADLY:
SNOW IS IN THE SHOPS . . ."

> January 26, 1927
> Top secret

In connection with the Junkers Company systematically not meeting obligations of the concession agreement and unsatisfactorily fulfilling current deliveries of bombers under separate agreements with the UVVS RKKA, a decision was taken to liquidate the concession and to cancel the delivery agreement. On August 13, 1926, the GKK [*Glavnyi Kontsessionnyi Komitet*—High Concession Committee, or HCC] proposed to

Junkers to conduct this liquidation on the basis of mutual consent and simultaneously advanced the following proposals:

(a) mutually giving up losses,

(b) immediately transferring the former Russian-Baltic factory in Fili to the VVS Command, . . .

(d) in parallel, handling negotiations of the UVVS with the Junkers Company on reducing prices for bombers of the current order.

Simultaneously with this, our delegation was formed for the supposed parity commission under the chairmanship of Ginsburg.[34] To the GKK's letter of August 13 Junkers replied on November 1 that he agrees, first, to give up his claim for damages and, second, to form a parity commission for determing the amount of compensation under a new agreement but providing that bomber prices not be reduced.

On September 1, 1926, the VVS Command, due to the company not keeping delivery time and elementary technical terms of the agreement, on the basis of the corresponding article of the agreement, declared cancellation of the same agreement for 12 bombers and demanded the company to return the advance and to pay a penalty. The agreement with the company for 3 bombers was cancelled as far back as on June 16, 1926. After this, the UVVS proposed to Junkers Company to make a new proposal for delivering the same bombers under different, reduced technical specifications and with accordingly decreased prices.

On September 10, 1926, negotiations took place between the GKK and the company, where the representatives of the latter took back its consent for giving up losses provided agreements for bombers not be renewed and the bombers not be accepted. The GKK declined this proposal of the company.

Subsequently, Junkers put forward a proposal: to simultaneously discuss the matters on compensation for bombers and for material values invested by the company in the concession. This proposal was accepted by the GKK at its sitting on September 22 and already on September . . .[35] negotiations continued on the basis of this proposal.

In its letter of October 2, 1926, the company asks the government for compensation (for the factory and the bombers) in the amount of 4,000,000 rubles, but the GKK offered in response a sum of 1,400,000 rubles. Since that time a wrangle has started that is still going on. The latest offer of the GKK is a sum of 2,400,000 rubles, but Junkers Company insists on 3,500,000 rubles.

Thus, the wrangle did not culminate in final results over five months, and it is quite unknown when one will be able to carry out the negotiations to its conclusion with the present course of events.

Meanwhile, the factory in Fili, which already has stood for nearly two years and is a large industrial unit by its equipment, is kept badly: snow lies in shops as a snowdrift, machine tools are rusting. Airplanes are losing their value every month since they are removed from one place to another, disassembled and assembled, and, as a consequence, they cease to be new airplanes and take an appearance of stored assets. All these circumstances, together with the profound importance and necessity of quickest restoration of our own production of metal airplanes at the former Russian-Baltic factory in Fili, strongly require the most decisive measures to be taken for liquidating the concession and reaching an understanding concerning cancelled agreements for bombers. By virtue of the foregoing, I believe that the following decisions must be taken:

1. To demand from the German Junkers Company by February 15, 1927, either to finally accept or to finally decline the last GKK's proposal as being final on our side.

2. In the case of the Junkers Company declining our proposal, the GKK must occupy the factory and offer to the company to transfer the consideration of questionable monetary claims into the arbitration court.

3. To charge the GKK no later than on February 1 of the present year with issuing the ultimatum to the company corresponding to items 1 and 2 of this proposal.

The arbitration court, by the GKK's interpretation, must act in accordance with laws of the USSR.

> Voroshilov, people's commissar of military and naval affairs, chairman of the Revolutionary Military Soviet.
> TsGASA. F. 33987. Op. 3. D. 249. Sh. 57–59.
> Copy.

*　　*　　*

TROTSKY: "WE HAVE TO CONSENT TO THE PAYMENT
OF THREE-AND-A-HALF-MILLION RUBLES . . ."[36]

February 3, 1927
Top secret

1. The reply from Junkers is received. It agrees on all essentials with that rough copy the content of which I set forth in my letter of January 31.[37]

2. We are, thus, faced with the necessity of deciding today without fail: either to pay 3.5 million (for the concession and for the bombers) instead of 2.5 million proposed by our side or to enter the arbitration court. The new lawyer's conclusion does not add anything to considerations of my last letter. The arbitration court means for us a possibility of surprises only in the direction of deteriorating rather than improving conditions of the liquidation.

3. Lawyers discussed the question of whether or not we can take the factory in our hands based on considerations of state necessity and came to a conclusion that neither the concession agreement nor the Soviet-German treaty give any opportunity for us. In other words, our unilaterally taking possession of the factory would mean a diplomatic conflict and additional payments associated with the arbitration court.

4. Thus, if we apply to the court, which will drag on several months at the minimum, the fate of the factory will hang poised in mid-air for this time. Or we take the factory in our hands unilaterally at the risk of additionally paying an imposing sum for this. The last question remains: if not going by the law, is it possible to gain anything by peaceable way? Since the opposite party poses the question alternatively: either 3.5 million or the arbitration court, no place remains for trading, in my opinion, the more so as we have made the last attempt of squeezing out some fairness between the rough copy of Junkers' letter and its final draft, but we have obtained nothing. The attempt of evading the arbitration court and continuing the trade shall only reveal our weakness.

Taken together this leads me to a conclusion that we have to consent to the payment of 3.5 million rubles so as not to risk the payment of the large sum and delay the matter of the factory.

L. Trotsky
TsGASA. F. 33987. Op. 3. D. 249. L. 77–78.
Copy. The document is attested by S. Yoffe, secretary of the people's commissariat of military and naval affairs.

*   *   *

FROM ALKSNIS TO VOROSHILOV

Report

June 23, 1929

On the transference of two Junkers society's airplanes through the USSR's territory for the Persian airline piloted by Haal and Hönischen.

Junkers airline society in Berlin has made a request for allowing its two B-33 airplanes piloted by Haal and Hönischen to be transferred through Moscow and Baku to Teheran for Persian airlines by routes: from Berlin to Moscow—of the Deruluft society and from Moscow to Teheran—of the Ukrvozdukhput.

There are no objections to this transfer flight on the side of the UVVS, the RKKA staff, and the OGPU. I ask for your instruction on possibility to allow this transfer flight.[38]

Ya. I. Alksnis, acting chief of the RKKA Air Force
TsGASA. F. 33987. Op. 3. D. 295. L. 225.
Original.

*   *   *

"LIPETSK"

The commander-in-chief of the Reichswehr expresses the Reichswehr's particular thanks to the Red Army and the Red Air Fleet for hospitality of many years in Lipetsk. . . .

> From the letter of Kestring, military attaché of Germany in the USSR, to Voroshilov. July 22, 1933. Moscow.

From information of the Fourth Intelligence Division of the RKKA staff:

" 'LIPETSK' is a school of the air fleet established in 1925. There are 58 airplanes in the school, which were delivered by Germans. In 1927–1928 20 pilots and 24 observer pilots were trained. The school sets itself as an object the scientific and experimental work in addition to flight training of flying personnel (pilots and observer pilots). Germans bear all expenses on organization and maintenance."

The protocol of the agreement betwen the Air Force Command of the RKKA (hereinafter referred to as the R.L.)[39] and representatives of the Special Group (hereinafter referred to as the S.G.M.)[40] on establishing the aviation school and aircraft materials depots in Lipetsk.

1. General part

(a) The R.L. gives its consent to establish the aviation school at the Lipetsk aerodrome[41] with the S.G.M.'s assistance. The aviation school must be immediately adjacent to the R.L.'s installations located there.

(b) The R.L. transfers to the S.G.M., which resides in Lipetsk, its former plant for using as premises for storing airplanes and aviation accessories and as lodging for supposed aviation school personnel and store administration. The aerodrome and the plant are given to the S.G.M. for use with the above-indicated purpose at no charge.

2. Maintenance and arrangement

(a) Installations necessary for the aviation school consist of one hangar, one workshop, one small house for administration, one petrol depot, and one ammunition depot. Location, dimensions, and arrangement of the installations must be submitted to the R.L. representatives' approval, details are in supplement I.

(b) The premises in the plant building necessary for depots and lodging are built and repaired according to information presented in supplement II[42] so that placing airplanes and accessories within the depots

and personnel in lodging can be carried out in full order and with observing proper safety rules.

The R.L. takes upon itself work on building premises for the aviation
school, rebuilding and restoring depots and lodging rooms (according
to supplements I and II).

The S.G.M. assumes expenses for this work of building, rebuilding,
and restoring. The above-indicated work must be completed no later
than in three months, that is, no later than on 13 June of the current
year.

3. Personnel

(a) The S.G.M.'s personnel.

The S.G.M. provides the following personnel for the aviation school:
one head of the aviation school, one instructor-pilot, one his assistant
(conditionally), two foremen, one master on armament, one assistant
master. For managing plant depots and stored materials: one depot
manager.

For the school course on aviation: 6–7 pilots at every course.

(b) The R.L.'s personnel.

One assistant head of the aviation school for supporting the school
administration in all questions arising in connection with school operation. Twenty foremen for aerodrome maintenance, among them: fourteen
technician-mechanics, two joiners, one saddler, one house painter, one
blacksmith, one welder. Several of them must be able to talk German.
The S.G.M. shoulders the expenses on maintaining twenty indicated
foremen according to standard rates accepted by the R.L. and corresponding trade unions.

The accommodation and nourishment of the indicated personnel
are accomplished by the R.L. as agreed with the head of the aviation
school.

The S.G.M. notifies the R.L. in proper time about its personnel
coming to Moscow.

The supposed arrival: the depot manager and one or two foremen—
in the second half of May. The head of the school with the rest of
personnel—in the middle of June. Student pilots—in the middle of July.

One may need the personnel given by the R.L. in the second half
of June. The S.G.M. commits itself to communicate more exact information about dates of the arrival of its personnel in proper time.
The necessary guard for the aerodrome and plant depots is given by

the R.L.; the S.G.M. assumes expenses on maintaining the guard at current rates.

4. Transportation and arrival of materiel

Airplanes, aviation accessories, as well as other materiel necessary for arranging aerodrome and depots, come to the R.L.'s address through the Leningrad port. The arrival of the first transports is expected in the beginning of June. Further transportation from Leningrad to the aerodrome (to the depot) is assumed by the R.L. The S.G.M. assumes the related expenses. The S.G.M. notifies the R.L. in proper time about the arrival of the transport to Leningrad and communicates information concerning the volume of arriving load. The R.L. takes measures on obtaining permission for duty-free importation of the load.

5. Training

Separate school courses may last four weeks supposedly. Thus, the first course, if started on July 15, will be completed in the middle of August. The interval between separate courses will be one week long, which under favorable conditions will allow four courses to be completed over 1925. Questions associated with rooms and use of the aerodrome, together with the R.L.'s detachment being there, are settled by immediate dealings of the detachment commander with the school administration taking account of mutual practical needs.

The physician attached to the aerodrome also attends the aviation school as accidents occur.

The S.G.M. pays for these services, the scope of which will be defined later on. The aviation school brings conventional sanitation equipment (litters, dressing, etc.). The R.L. provides the school with the necessary combustible materials (petrol, oil) in accordance with their prime cost. The R.L. transfers a special area to the school for ground target shooting practice with live cartridges. Armament and ammunition are brought by the school with it.

6. In case the school is liable to liquidation, the R.L. consents to accept all constructions at the aerodrome built anew and being needed for the aviation school according to prices fixed by a mixed commission comprising representatives of the R.L. and S.G.M.

7. Note: supplements indicated in articles 1–6 cover the most important and fundamental questions concerning construction, arrangement, and operation of the aviation school in Lipetsk and the depot for aviation materiel. Mutual rights and obligations of the R.L. and S.G.M. are

fixed in these articles. All subsequent wishes and needs that arise in putting the above-presented agreement into practice should be satisfied on a friendly basis by the R.L. and S.G.M.

On the R.L.'s side   Baranov
On the S.G.M.'s side   Lit[43]

Supplement No. 2 to the Protocol on Lipetsk.
Location, dimensions, and arrangement of constructions
being built at Lipetsk aerodrome for the S.G.M.'s aviation school

(1) The location of buildings is seen from the accompaning krokis.[44]

(2) Hangars: three premises, each with an area of 18 × 18 m, are united in a single hangar as indicated on the presented construction plan. The hangar wall looking toward the aerodrome can be entirely opened owing to the sliding door. In accordance with sketches presented during negotiations, each short-side wall of the hangar will have windows and one door. The back wall will have windows and two doors. Instead of internal walls, being needless with united premises, three or four poles will be placed as supports (constructions) for the roof.

The floor will be made of concrete. The rest of the hangar will be built according to accompanying sketches of 18 × 18.

(3) Premises for the workshop: the construction will be built of stone. Dimensions, layout, doors, windows, and heating system are seen from the accompanying plan. The floor is of concrete.

(4) The small house for administration: the building will be erected of wood according to the accompanying sketch. The floor is of wood.

(5) Depots for petrol and ammunition will be built after erecting constructions of articles 2 and 4 under the agreement with the head of the aviation school and his deputy.

(6) Prices for above-indicated buildings and equipment are as follows:

Hangar (three united premises)	40,000 rubles
Premises for the workshop	12,000 rubles
House for administration	9,000 rubles
Depots for petrol, etc.	2,000 rubles
Total	63,000 rubles

The cost should be as small as possible. The estimate must not be exceeded.

TsGASA. F. 33987. Op. 3. D. 295. L. 4–11. Copy.

*   *   *

RECORD OF SOVIET-GERMAN TALKS ABOUT AVIATION

March 24, 1926

The Question of Lipetsk

OBERSTLEUTNANT VILBERG. Last year in Lipetsk, at the favorable support of the Red Air Forces, the premises were given and the buildings were constructed for the fighters' school. In summer the courses started to work for the first time. At the kind assistance of the Red Air Forces (RAF), the competitive flights had been organized that have given the very valuable experience. I hope that this experience was valuable for you too. That circumstance that our airplanes turned out to be stronger is accounted for by the fact, that our engines of 480 horsepowers were used while the Russian engines have only 300 hp. These flights have given valuable tactical experience as well. Good initial successes of the last year in the field of the fighters' school induced us to continue and develop the preparation of the personnel and to widen Lipetsk together with the RAF this year. By the end of May, the new hangar will be finished. This year we wish to organize the courses for fighters but with double the number of the participants. At the same time, we wish to begin preparation of the observers, by organizing the courses this year and by collecting the old, experienced observers possessing the experience of the war. They will renew their experience and then will be able to train the new staff by themselves. For this purpose, some quantity of airplanes of the more contemporary types, namely, the wooden airplanes of firm Heinkel HD-17 with Nepir engines of 450 hp will be transported. We hope, this summer, to set in motion the airplane of the same firm, but provided with the engine BMW of 600 hp, type HD-33. This will be a splendid airplane for the long-range reconnaissance and the more for day bombing. Particularly, we underline that the airplane HD-17 (Heinkel provided with the

Nepir engine of 450 hp) shall not be considered as absolutely up-to-date, for which purpose, the engine possessing a minimum 600 hp is required. Further, we want to put right testing of such materials and subjects that we shall consider to be appropriate for introduction in the forces in Lipetsk alongside with the school of fighters and observers. To inform you of what may be tested first—it is a motor gun. For this we are only waiting for the coming of appropriate weather. Then, on the arrival of the airplanes in summer, we suggest testing a series of appliances: the wireless telephone intended for communication between the airplane and the ground, and the new construction for the filming performed from the airplane. When the new airplanes being built by the German firms abroad will be ready, they also will arrive for performance of the practical tests. The following types will arrive: the HD-17; HD-33; the two-seat fighter *Albatross* with the BMW/6 engine of 600 hp intended within the limited sizes for reconnaissance; toward the end of the summer, evidently, one more airplane Junkers (K-Mittelstück)—the middle bomber—will arrive. Fifteen bombers have been ordered by you.

Of particular interest to us are the tests connected with bombing. We have no data about the probability of hit. We would like to perform the tests in this field, but this will be possible only the next year as we have neither materials nor drawings: all this had been destroyed after the war and everything shall be done anew. I don't know if you possess experience in this field. We also have no devices for aiming and bombing. We know only that there are contemporary apparatuses abroad securing much more accuracy of hit than it was at the end of the war. In conclusion two more remarks: (1) we want to try this summer to organize in Lipetsk a photographic enterprise and a small dockyard equipping it with the machines necessary for performance of the experiences; (2) we aspire to develop with the future experiences a new type of the military aircraft in the Junkers firm. It is still not clear for us what type of fighter, bomber, or reconnaissance aircraft it will be. But in any case, in the following year together with the Junkers firm, a new type of the contempory military aircraft will be created by us.

COMRADE MUKLEVICH. For our part you can calculate on the most full assistance and support. Mr. Litt has already let us know about everything. All the required shall be done in Lipetsk. The airfield is to be widened evidently. Our squadron, which very likely, hampers you, shall not be withdrawn, but the airfield can be widened. This, probably, will require some expenses, but this question shall be specified later with Mr. Litt. On our part, we shall take all measures to ensure the uninterrupted and the right work of the school.

VILBERG. Are there any wishes concerning the schools and experiences on the part of the RAF?

COMRADE MUKLEVICH. We should like to connect by this or that way, your preparation with our one, but this talk will be in the future. If this coincides with the wishes on the German side, then everything possible shall be done on our part to take participation in the work. If on the German side, the corresponding wish will be expressed, we could, for example, organize the tactical exercise with the other arm of the service in which the German pilots can take part.

VILBERG. We are very thankful to you for the proposal to connect our and your preparation of the personnel. This question shall be considered in details in the place. We are also very thankful for the proposal with respect to the tactical exercises. Do you mean to perform it in the form of the maneuvers?

COMRADE MUKLEVICH. Yearly, our definite units accomplish their preparation by performing the maneuvers on a large or small scale. If this coincides with the wishes of the German side, those maneuvers that will take place in this region can be used without organizing any special maneuvers for our aims.

VILBERG. Already yesterday, the question about such maneuvers was present in other talks. We welcome the participation of our pilots in the maneuvers in this or that form. This question shall be worked out in detail later. It might be possible, for example, to distribute our observers in your flight detachments or to forward our officers in your aviation headquarters for the opinions exchange. At last, there is a possibility that this or that airplane of the school can take part in the body of your detachment. But it is difficult to say now, if the school will be ready for this. In any case, we welcome this idea and thank you for it.

GENERAL VETSELL. We extremely welcome the established cooperation in this matter.

COMRADE MUKLEVICH. There are especially little conflicts because there are no commercial moments. Everything is based on the idea of cooperation.

CSASA. F. 33988. Op. 3. D. 78. Sh. 93–96.

*   *   *

KEPT IN SECRECY: INFORMATION ABOUT LIPETSK

January, 1929

1. Expenses connected with major construction:

1925	rubles	120,000
1926	rubles	230,000
1927–1928	rubles	750,000
TOTAL:	rubles	1,750,000

2. PROPERTY:

(1) Aircraft 62	(7) Rifles 6
(2) Motor cars 19	(8) Carbines 6
(3) Horses 24	(9) Mausers 17
(4) Radio stations 2	(10) Flare pistols 19
(5) Bicycles 16	(11) Bomb ammunition 45
(6) Machine guns 213	

TOTAL: rubles 4,500,000

3. Current expenses for the whole time, i.e., salary for the workers, fuel and lubricants, taxes, and so on: rubles 3,000,000

In sum utilized: rubles 8,600,000

The aircraft carried out by leasers mostly adhere to the contemporary but already becoming out-of-date (Zakrep D-B) types.

The school is equipped very well.

For 1927/28, 20 pilots and 24 test pilots have been trained.

> Chief of Fourth Headquarters Control of the WPRA
> BERZIN
> CSASA. F. 33987. Op. 3. D. 295. Sh. 81.
> Original.

*   *   *

TELEGRAM OF LOGANOVSKY TO VOROSHILOV

August 1, 1932
Kept in secrecy

In reply to your letter No. 4204 of July 28, this year, I inform you on the part of Torgsin that the defects in the supply of its shops in Kazan and Lipetsk[46] that service the "friends" had actually taken place.

I have proposed to the Torgsin management to delete these stations from the local krai offices of the Torgsin conductance and subordinate them directly to the management, putting the questions of these stations' supply under a special observation.

On July 29, this year, the assistant of the management chairman has gone to these stations, he is entrusted in the place to eliminate all defects and to ensure uninterrupted work in the future.

Assistant of the People's Commissar of Foreign Trade
Loganovsky
CSASA. F. 33987. Op. 3. D. 148. Sh. 143.
Original.

*   *   *

REPORT OF BERZIN TO VOROSHILOV

July 3, 1933
Kept in secrecy

I report: the military attaché of the German, Colonel Hartman asks for the reception with the assistant of the chairman of the RMF Comr. Tukhachevsky to which he wants to put a series of questions from the Reichswehr Command about the work of the Lipetsk station. I ask your instructions about the possibility of the reception of Hartman by Tukhachevsky.

Berzin[47]
CSASA. F. 33987. Op. 3. D. 504. Sh. 2.
Original.

* * *

REPORT OF VRID ASSISTANT TO CHAIRMAN OF THE
FOURTH CONTROL OF THE WPRA HEADQUARTERS
DAVUDOV TO VOROSHILOV:[48] THE CORPSE OF THE KILLED PILOT
IS BEING SENT BY "FRIENDS" TO THE GERMANS

July 4, 1933
Kept in secrecy

I report: this July 2, during the time of the training flights of the Lipetsk station, two German Fokker D-13 airplanes had a mid-air collision. At this, one pilot successfully jumped with a parachute from an altitude of 700 m; the second pilot, Herr Pol, jumped from the airplane at an altitude of 50 m and died from the impact. Two Fokker D-13 airplanes are put out of commission. The corpse of the killed pilot is being sent by "friends" to the Germans.

Davudov
CSASA. F. 33987. Op. 3. D. 504. Sh. 3.
Original.

* * *

TOMSEN AND DANDORF TO FEDOROV[49]

July 16, 1933
Kept in secrecy

1. . . . On July 10, at a distance of 20 km from the Lipetsk town, due to engine operation shutdown, the crash of the FD-13 aircraft piloted by the student pilot Lange took place. . . . Reason for the engine shutdown is the leakage of water from the radiator due to damage of the cylinder jacket.

2. On July 13, during the training flights on the airfield, the student pilot Lange caused a rough landing of the FD-13 aircraft, due to which the aircraft landing gear was dented and the aircraft was nosed over. . . .

3. On July 14, during the training flights on the airfield, the student

pilot Shlichten, the leading pilot in the team, directed the team to the landing along the diagonal through the landing, neutral, and takeoff zones. . . .

All of the above described incidents once more underline a weak discipline in the air of the students and insufficiently accurate organization of flights proper; nonetheless, the faults are left almost unpunished.

> Commanding Officer of Unit A5
> Tomsen
> Headquarters Chief: Dandorf
> CSASA. F. 33987. Op. 3. D. 504. Sh. 47–48.
> Original.

*   *   *

KESTRING TO EGOROV ABOUT LIQUIDATION
OF SCHOOL IN LIPETSK

> July 22, 1933
> Moscow

On January 11, this year, Colonel Kestring informed the chairman of the WPRA headquarters Egorov that the Reichswehr Commander was supposed to cease the training of the pilot-fighters in Lipetsk in autumn of 1933.[50] The grounds that have initiated the Reichswehr Commander to take these measures are known to the Red Army. However, once more it is affirmed that, unfortunately, the necessity of the hard economy makes us take this step. With the present financial position of the State, the further expenses of the large amounts intended for the work of this station do not pay itself. This is aggravated by the fact that the equipment to be used till now has been worn; the further work with the station in Lipetsk in 1933 would call forth the new large capital costs, which the Reichswehr could not produce without detriment to the rest of its interests.

Proceeding from these reasons, the commander of the Reichswehr has come to the final conclusion to cease the training in Lipetsk. The sincere wish of the Reichswehr, in spite of ceasing the training activity, is the continuation of the mutual activity of both armies, in particular in the field of aviation for a number of years. Therefore, the commander of the Reichswehr especially would welcome: (1) the mutual exchange of the officers and specialists for visiting the technical structures, factories, and flying schools; (2) the mutual exchange of information and the experiences in the field of tactics and technique. The commander of the Reichswehr is persuaded by the expediency and necessity of the joint activity in the field of aviation, and he welcomed any suggestion of the Red Army and the Red Air Forces, having the further deepening in the joint activity within the limits of our possibilities. As for the buildings and structures in Lipetsk, the following is being proposed. To transfer the structures and all equipment remaining in Lipetsk, as its return to Germany is not occurring, to the full disposal and control of the Red Air Forces. The Red Air Forces are granted the full and boundless right to use this establishment. The transmission of the property will be produced by the leader of the Lipetsk station to the Russian representative.

The commander of the Reichswehr on behalf of the Reichswehr thanks the Red Army and the Red Air Forces for the long-term hospitality in Lipetsk.

> CSASA. F. 33987. Op. 3. D. 504. Sh. 52–53.
> Original.[51]

* * *

REPORT OF BERZIN TO VOROSHILOV:
FORWARDING THE REVERSE TRANSPORT TO GERMANY
IS PLANNED FOR AUGUST 15

> July 29, 1933
> Kept in secrecy

I report: Presented by the "friends" concerning the Kazan and Lipetsk stations are the below inventories:

1. the property subject to reverse transport to Germany;
2. the property subject to transfer to the AFA and MMA;
3. the property of the Kazan station that can be sold to the WPRA.

Forwarding the first large reverse transport to Germany is planned for August 15. The flight of the three aircraft of the "friends" from

Lipetsk to Germany through Moscow and further along the line of Deruluft will take place on reception of your permission. The authorized persons of the AFA, MMA, and OGPU PD should consider to conduct the custom examination of cargo, avoiding the infringement of the forwarding secrecy, on stations of Kazan, Lipetsk, and Tomka. To avoid the prolongation of the term for the liquidation of the enterprises, your instructions are necessary for the chairman of the MMA and AFA about the quickest decision of the question concerning the purchase of the required property of those of the stations to be eliminated.

Appendix: the inventories of 15 sheets.[52]

Berzin

. . . INVENTORY No. 2 of the property subject to transfer to the Air Force Administration (AFA).

Aircraft and engines . . . ; (2) Aviation materials, engine shop, arms shop, electrical station, photolaboratory, writing materials, autotransport and horse park, telephone station, the main storehouse of the casino and linen storeroom, ambulance (all structures with the equipment, the x-ray apparatus, the mountain sun, medicaments, dressing and instruments . . .); real property: (a) the camp, (b) the airfield, (c) the polygon, (d) other real estate; . . . the house in the Bukhanovsky garden, the boat landing-stage, the house with the flat of TOMSEN, the house with the flat of Dandorf. All private property of the station personnel is not taken into account for the transmission.

The Property of Lipetsk Station

INVENTORY No. 1 of objects subject to the reverse transport.
1. Aircraft and engines:
   Junkers B-33
   Junkers K-47
   Junkers A-48
   4 engines Siemens-Jupiter from Dornje DO.P.
   Special parts DO.P. (spring legs, wheels, and so on).
2. Aviation materials: parachutes, respiratory apparatuses, instruments, compasses.
3. From the engine shop: all the measuring instruments, gauges

and templates, spare parts and special tools for the BMW-6, Siemens-Jupiter, Junkers L-5.

4. Arms shop (all arms available on the station, all ammunition, bombs and fuses, photo machine guns, optical sights, reflex sights with the accumulators belonging to them, etc.); the training models (the model of the machine gun, the model for the fixed installation); the machines for equipment of the cartridge belts; the machine-gun turrets (of the Vikkers types); the devices for bombing; measuring instruments; arms bags with tools. . . .

5. The shops: different measuring and test instruments.

6. Electrical station: receiving and transmission radio stations.

7. Photolaboratory: (training photo material, all card material).

8. Writing materials: (servicing library, literature library, important archives materials, technical drawings, typewriters).

9. Autotransport and horse park: none.

10. Telephone installation: none.

11. Main storehouse (winter clothes of the German personnel, clock, theodolite, binoculars).

12. Casino and linen storeroom (part of linen, silver plate).

13. Ambulance (separate instruments, microscopes). . . .

CSASA. F. 33987. Op. 3. D. 504. Sh. 78–83. Original.

*   *   *

BERZIN'S REPORT TO VOROSHILOV:[53]
FLIGHT FROM LIPETSK TO GERMANY IS PLANNED BY "FRIENDS"

August 20, 1933
Kept in secrecy

The flight of three "Junkers" aircraft from Lipetsk to Germany through Moscow and further along the line of Deruluft is planned by the "friends" between 25 t[his] m[onth] and 5 September. The "friends" ask for permission to order their aircraft to the airfields of Smolensk and Vitebsk in case of an emergency landing. Pilots: Blumenzaat, Heinz, Makrazki, Foss, Teetsman, Blume, Ressing are flying the aircraft. The chief of the Air Forces Comr. Alksnis has no objections against the flight of three aircraft of the "friends." On my part, I would suppose that it is possible to allow the flight of the three aircraft on the line of Deruluft, indicating only civil airfields for the emergency landings.

I ask your instructions.

> Berzin
> CSASA. F. 33987. Op. 3. D. 504. Sh. 152.
> Original.

*   *   *

"KAMA"

It is impossible for us to realize the mass production of tanks due to the Versailles treaty.

> K. von Hammerstein-Ekword, the chief
> of the Reichswehr Land Forces Control

Extract from information of the Fourth Reconnaissance Control of the WPRA Headquarters:

"KAMA" is the tank school in Kazan. It had started to form since 1926. The German people have built schoolrooms, a shop, and a training field, having spent about two mln marks. The tank test sample is already sent. They promise to deliver training tanks in March of 1929.

*   *   *

THE MAIN TREATY BETWEEN VIKO-MOSKVA[54]
AND KA-MOSKVA[55] ABOUT TANK SCHOOL ORGANIZATION

Further in the text Viko-Moskva and Ka-Moskva will be called "Viko" and "Ka."[56]

> October 2, 1926
> Moscow
> Kept in secrecy

The following agreement between "KA" and "VIKO" is being concluded about organization of VIKO in the former kargopolsky barracks of the tank school in Kazan:

(1) The KA delivers VIKO three stables and the living rooms for use . . . from the barracks structure for the location of the materials and for the school personnel dwelling. Three stables are delivered now, and the rest, as they cannot be delivered earlier, not later than May 15, 1927.

(2) The VIKO gets the right, together with the KA units, to use the adjoining country as the training field and the shooting ground quite near the barracks . . . as well as the polygon being at a distance of 7 km to the south-east of the barracks and the means of communication between both fields. The order, turns, and the terms for using the polygon are established by the chief of the garrison.

(3) The VIKO bears the expenses in sum of 125,000 rubles for displacement of units and military-educational schools located in the part of the premises, the former kargopolsky barracks, to be cleared out for the school. . . .

(4) The VIKO bears the expenses for the buildings and premises repair indicated in Item 1.

(5) The connection to the Kazan electrical power station will be performed to illuminate the living and working premises as well as to supply electrical power to the school shop. . . .

(6) The KA performs the repair and rebuilding of the living and store[57] premises for the materials and ammunition as well as the construction of the connection to the power mains in Kazan at the VIKO cost. . . .

(7) Till the living premises are released, the KA has given VIKO the required flats for the personnel and the leader of the school, namely, the barrack flats for only 15 to 17 men. . . .

(9) The leadership of the school is subordinated to the VIKO. The leader develops the program of studies with the desires of the KA taken into account. The KA appoints the assistant for the leader of the school, who is simultaneously a representative of the KA.

(10) The KA places at VIKO disposal the appropriate technical personnel for the shop, the staff for protection, as well as the workers. . . . The VIKO bears the expenses for keeping the whole above-indicated staff on trade union rates as well as the expenses required for keeping

the school leader assistant in compliance with the rates approved by the KA. The rating of the employees is performed on the ground of the additional agreement.

(11) The VIKO bears all the expenses for the arrangement and keeping of the tank school; the expenses for keeping the VIKO personnel, both the permanent and the temporary ones, including all the expenses for the communication services and electric energy; the expenses for the purchase of metal, educational supplies, the fuel, and raw material. The KA renders assistance in acquisition of the latter on more favorable conditions.

(12) The VIKO must observe the labor legislation of the USSR as well as all sanitary, fire protection, and other rules according to those effective in the USSR laws. The VIKO is responsible for the proper execution of the above rules in the course of its activity.

(13) The term for opening the tank school is planned for July 1927, provided that at this term all the building works will be finished and the property required for practical studies will be delivered.

(14) In the first year of existence of the school, the VIKO renders the more possible quantity of places for the variable staff of the KA, but beginning from the second year, the exact relation of the places offered for the variable staff of the both parts is established. The KA bears the expenses for keeping and quartering the variable staff of the KA, the expenses for the fuel and ammunition, as well as for the significant damage resulting from KA's fault. If the KA personnel is on the VIKO allowance, the expenses shall be paid by the KA on the rates approved by the KA.

(15) The present agreement is made for 3 years from the date of its signing. In the case that not one of the parties orders the cancellation of the agreement before 6 months of its expiration, the agreement is effective for one year more. On expiration of the agreement, the tanks, the property reserves, the armament, the equipment of the shops, and the stock of the school is returned to the VIKO. The buildings are transferred to the KA. In the case that the KA would express a desire to acquire the subjects of the technical equipment purchase at VIKO expense, they are estimated by the parity commission and its value is compensated to the VIKO.

Representative of "KA": Berzin
Representative of "VIKO": Litt[58]

Appendix No. 2[59]
Temporary Preliminary Staff of "KAMA" School

(A) I. Personnel of VIKO: 1 headmaster, 1 assistant, 1 engineer, 1 head of production, 1 doctor, 1 foreman, 1 storehouse manager, 3 teachers (artillery, machine gun, radio), 5 teachers (instructors) for the ride training, 16 students (vari[able]. to this number). Total: 42 men.

  II. Personnel of KA
   (a) With the leadership: 1 assistant.
   (b) Technical personnel: 1 joiner (master), 2 joiners (apprentices), 1 metalworker (master), 4 metalworkers (apprentices), 1 painter (master), 6 drivers, 1 mechanic, 1 tinman, 2 painters (apprentices), 1 tinsmith, 1 electrician, 1 saddler. Total: 23 men.
   (c) Executive personnel: (1 messenger, 1 housekeeper, 1 cook, 3 employees, 1 watchman (yardkeeper).
   (d) Protection personnel: 7 men. As required.
   Total: 30 men plus the protection personnel.
(B) Property (preliminary calculation)
   (1) Machines: 3 tanks, 1 caterpillar tractor (with trailer), 2 trucks (with trailer), 2 passenger cars, 2 motorcycles.
   (2) Shops: mechanical shop, lathe shop, mounting shop, smithy shop, joiner shop, saddler shop, painting shop.
   (3) Storerooms: spare parts storeroom, storehouse for fuels, storehouse for property and reserves.

Appendix No. 3
Study Program of "KAMA" School

I. Curriculum.
It is supposed for the present time, after finishing the construction works and on the delivery of the materials:
(1) To begin the preparation (training) of the personnel to be trained. It weill take about 12 weeks. It is calculated that 5 Russians will take part in this.
(2) The following course, from approximately August till September, shall proceed with training of the first part of variable staff within

the troop as the least tactic unit. It is calculated that 10 Russians of the variable staff will take part.

(3) The further cycles (courses) of the 1928 year, mainly in the summer months, shall be aimed at gradual growth in work and number of trained students, as well as at the firsthand acquaintance with the work of the company commander and its control organs, as soon as the number of machines will allow personnel to deal with the work within the company and higher formations.

The number of Russian participants is established on the base of the experience of the 1927 year.

II. Training Procedure

The practical training on the machine (individually and in formation) in all possible positions takes place in parallel with the theoretical learning of the materials and its application.

1. Theoretical part
   (a) Knowledge (study) of tanks.
      (aa) General information about different types.
      (bb) The types at the "KAMA" school, its main parts, construction, and use.
   (b) Knowledge (study) of weapons and ammunition: guns (cannons), machine guns, automatic machines, pistols, grenades.
   (c) Knowledge (study) of means of communications.
   (d) Study of motors.
   (e) March, arrangement in place, guarding.
   (f) The common principles of a fight, mutual action with other kinds of weapon, independent tasks of the tanks.
   (g) Special principles of fight: of separate tanks, of the company, of the troop.
   (h) Transfer of reports (information).
   (i) Evaluation of the land and reading the map.
   (j) Main information about the gas fight.
   (k) Transport and supplement to the battlefield (ammunition, fuels, and equipment).
   (l) Equipment maintenance.
   (m) Safety precautions, fire protection, how to behave oneself when the machine is on fire, and the arrangement in the place.

2. Applied part
   (a) Operational training. Gradual transition from simple exercises

Fig. 1. *(left)* General von Seeckt, Reichswehr Chief— "Germany lies between the West and the East. It should not merge with either of them."

Fig. 2. *(bottom)* General von Lüttwitz during inspection of troops in Zossen, March 1920.

Fig. 3. *(top)* Parade of "Steel Helmet" militarist organization, 1924.

Fig. 4. *(left)* Vorovsky, Litvinov, and Chicherin, Genoa, 1922. Alliance with Russia was Germany's only way to requite the Versailles humiliation.

Fig. 5. *(top)* Doctor Walter Rathenau, signatory of Rapallo Treaty with Russia, 1922.

Fig. 6. *(bottom)* Reichskanzler Cuno, advocate of cooperation with the USSR.

Fig. 7. *(top)* Major-General
Adam, the Reichswehr's
General Staff Chief.

Fig. 8. *(right)* Stresemann,
who initiated the "exposures"
of secret contacts between
the Reichswehr and the USSR.

Fig. 9. *(top)* At the Reichswehr's autumn maneuvers, 1932. From left to right: Commander-in-Chief of the First Military District General von Hasse, Reichswehr Minister (Minister of Defense) General von Schleicher, General von Fritsch.

Fig. 10. *(bottom)* President Hindenburg and behind him General K. von Hammerstein-Ekword.

Fig. 11. *(top)* Graff Brockdorff-Rantzau, the German Ambassador to the USSR in the Kremlin.

Fig. 12. *(bottom)* Before the flight to "Lipetsk," Major Felmi *(left)* and Colonel von Mittelberger.

Fig. 13. *(top)* German experimental detachment in "Tomka." Von Sicherer *(second from left, above)*, head of the station for joint chemical experiments and application of poison gases.

Fig. 14. *(bottom)* In experiments with chemical bomb-dropping the Soviet side provided the place, the people, and the aircraft. The Germans provided the bombs and some of the means.

Fig. 15. *(top)* Gas-shells fired by a light howitzer, "Tomka" station.

Fig. 16. *(left)* Iagodá, deputy chairman of the OGPU and Berman, the chief of the OGPU's general board of corrective labor camps, Belomorstroy.

Fig. 17. *(top)* Stalin, Ezhov *(on the right)*, and accompanying persons at the Moscow-Volga canal, 1937.

Fig. 18. *(bottom)* Voroshilov, Budenny, Levandovsky, Frinovsky, Tukhachevsky, Egorov, Yakir, Dybenko, Kamenev, Gorbachev, Orlov, and other persons before going out to Red Square for review of the troops of the Red Army in honor of the Seventeenth Party Congress, 1934.

Fig. 19. *(top)* Tukhachevsky, Kork, Budenny, Blyukher, Egorov, and others in a delegate group of the Seventeenth VKP (b) Congress, 1934.

Fig. 20. *(bottom)* We shall remember these people and the creators whom Stalin called "masses" and "small screws."

Fig. 21. *(right)* Hitler and military minister von Blomberg.

Fig. 22. *(bottom)* The fascists burn the books, Berlin, 1933.

Fig. 23. "God with us." By the beginning of the war Germany had one and a half million well-trained soldiers.

Fig. 24. *(top)* Check of prisoners in concentration camp Oranienburg.

Fig. 25. *(right)* On August 23, 1939, Ribbentrop arrived in Moscow. The nonaggression pact between the USSR and Germany was signed on the same day.

Fig. 26. On September 27-28, 1939, the "friendship" between the "socialist" state and the fascist regime was fixed during talks between Molotov and Ribbentrop. On September 1, 1939, Wehrmacht troops had invaded Poland. Before the war had even begun, the USSR and Germany had already established the frontiers.

Fig. 27. *(top)* General Guderian receives the Soviet representative Borovinsky to discuss the line of demarcation with him, Brest-Litovsk, September 20, 1939.

Fig. 28. *(bottom)* This parade of Soviet and German troops took place in honor of transferring the fortress Brest-Litovsk to the Soviet Command, September 22, 1939.

Fig. 29. June 22, 1941–after a battle. Perceiving Stalin's plan to move the Red Army into Europe, the leadership of fascist Germany was able to forestall him. Then the fascist Wehrmacht struck a blow directly against the Red Army.

on common terrain to difficult ones (riding) on any terrain. Overcoming the obstacles.

(b) Night exercises in driving, first with lights, then without, and with the enemy being illuminated by the projectors.

(c) Riding with the smoke screen.

(d) Exercises taking place in formation with giving of commands and orders.

(e) Exercises in march, mainly at night.

(f) Analysis of the country and exercises in the country estimation out on the training field. Reading the map.

(g) Firing.

(aa) Identification and determination of the target.

(bb) Determination and measurement of the distance.

(cc) Exercises in command.

(dd) Exercises in aiming (swinging board).

The exercises under (aa) to (dd) are carried out in the running machine (in motion).

(ee) Single firing performed from the machine guns and automatic pistols outside of the machine.

(ff) Single firing from the guns, machine guns, and automatic pistols at known (familiar) fixed and moving targets from the stationary machine and then from the moving machine.

(gg) Single firing on unknown targets under the same conditions.

(hh) Combat firing performed by a troop. Mutual actions of the troop, distribution of targets, mutual support.

3. Special reports on the transmission of reports (information)[60] and orders. . . .

(j) Tactical studies on camouflage.

(k) Exercises to be conducted in mountains, connected with loading on the railway, and taking into account the type of the tank, on the trucks. The instructions on the undermining work (obstacle) and damage to tanks that can get in the enemy's hands.

(l) Combat studies organized together with the other weapons.

(m) Technical studies.

(aa) Assembly and repair in the shop and in the country under fighting conditions.

(bb) Maintenance of machines.

CSASA. F. 33987. Op. 3. D. 295. Sh. 58–64. Copy.

*   *   *

UNDER THE OSOVIAKhIM[61] ROOF

1928[62]

Kept in secrecy

1. About ceasing the work of KAMA Building Commission

   (a) The building commission KAMA has been broken up as the preparation works have come to an end.

   (b) From August 1, 1928, "Technical courses of OSOVIAKhIM" are being formed on this territory.

   (c) The courses exist on the basis of the special Position[63] signed in December 2, 1926.

   The Courses are under the authority of "OGERS."[64] . . .

II. About observation of the rules of security

   (a) The life and the work of the course are accommodated to the common type of military organizations with a view to concealing the real host of the courses. Due to this, the personnel shall appear as the technical and teacher staff of the OSOVIAKhIM courses.

   (b) During study hours out of the barracks as well as at the official receptions, the constant and variable personnel of OGERS wears the WPRA uniform but without tabs. Outside of studies all the personnel can wear civilian clothes.

   (c) The correspondence in German is transported by a special delivery.

   The telegrams are only in Russian.

III. About relations between the Chief of the Courses[65] and the representative of the WPRA

   (1) The leadership of the administrative-economy and training-drill

life of the courses is realized by the Chief of the Courses to be appointed by OGERS following its instructions and directly subordinated to it.

(2) The control under the life and work of the courses in the part concerning PA[66] as well as introducing the different proposals for the study character is realized through the representative of the PA (assistant) directly subordinated to the PA.

Note: The name of "assistant" is mainly used for the conspiracy. The assistant's range of duties:

(a) To render all possible aid to the courses of the foreign organization in all its undertakings, removing the difficulties on its way and solving the questions for the most benefit of the courses.

(b) To take the necessary measures in acquiring the textbooks and means, different kind of materials, and subjects required for the uninterrupted work of the students at the PA prices.

(c) To carry out communication with the Soviet, industrial, and trade union establishments; to regulate the disputable questions with the local authorities; to be under the authority of correspondence, delivery of documents, and different references on behalf of the Courses Chief Assistant.

(d) To give assistance in quickly obtaining transport on the possible favorable terms for the courses as for the freight, taxes, and other advantages.

(e) To give assistance in obtaining certificates, identity cards, references, and other necessary documents.

(f) To engage and discharge the personnel in the German service (such personnel as household servants, drivers, dvornik, coachmen, guards, the workers in the shops, etc.). All actions listed above are performed by the PA representatives. The above personnel is considered to be the OGERS personnel and is subordinated to the Courses Chief as their service concerns it.

Note: The assistant (representative of the PA) has no right to impose the disciplinary penalty on the OGERS personnel.

(g) Engaging, discharging, and displacing personnel of the PA can be performed only by the assistant (the PA representative) on the order of the Courses Chief. In case the candidate to be nominated by the PA representative does not meet the definite requirements, the motivated rejection can be done by the Chief of the Courses.

If the PA representative discharges somebody of the personnel, he immediately lets the Chief of the Courses know, having presented the reasons for the discharge.

(h) To complete the Courses by the variable staff of the PA can be carried out by the assistant (representative of the PA). The variable staff is subordinated to the assistant of the Courses Chief, but with respect to school—to the Chief of the Courses.

The course-guarding personnel, including the staff of the offices (storerooms, etc.), is appointed by the assistant (the representative of the PA) and is subordinated to the latter in all respects.

Note: The Chief of the Courses has no right to inflict a punishment on the PA personnel.

(i) The assistant (representative) does not interfere in the order of the administrative-economy life of the courses except for the cases obviously contradicting the interests of the PA or the existing laws and positions of the USSR.

(j) The assistant shall control the proper following of the USSR laws by the administration of the courses.

(k) Seals and stamps are with the assistant (the PA representative) or the person responsible for it.

(l) In connection with the transfer to new functions due to which the work is complicated and the daily presence of the PA representative is necessary in the courses, a person for the commissions (a secretary) is appointed from the PA personnel for the assistant at the expense of OGERS.

CSASA. F. 33987. Op. 3. D. 295. Sh. 66–68.

*   *   *

IN SECRECY: INFORMATION ABOUT KAMA

January 1929

In 1926, the organization of the tank school in Kazan began. The leaseholders have built the schoolroom, the shops, and have equipped the training field.

At present, the following is available in the courses:
1. 1 test tank disassembled.
2. 6 cars.
3. 3 trucks.
4. 3 tractors of different types.
5. 2 motorcyles.

Since the beginning of the spring, the following subjects are expected:
1. 5 light tanks, 3 of them are armored.
2. 2 middle tanks.
3. 2 cars (Porsche and Citroen).
4. 2 trucks.
5. 3 tractors.

From March 15, the four-month training course is supposed to be conducted for PERMANENT PERSONNEL (5 or 7 of our comrades will be admitted).

From June 15 till November 15, the first course for VARIABLE STAFF is planned (10 leaseholders and 10 of our comrades). We have no data at our disposal about the expenditures incurred by the lease-holders; by rough estimate they have spent a significant sum of one and one-half million marks.

> Chairman of the Fourth Board of the WPRA Headquarters
> Berzin
> CSASA. F. 33987. Op. 3. D. 295. Sh. 80.
> Original.

*   *   *

VOROSHILOV TO STALIN:
"THE GERMANS ASK FOR OUR ASSISTANCE . . ."[67]

March 1929

. . . 2) With the opening of navigation, the Germans will transport 10 tanks to the Kazan tank school. The tanks have been made in Germany. The Germans ask for our assistance in the transportation of the tanks, which will consist in the following:

We conclude a fictitious agreement with the "Rheinmetall" firm about the purchase of these tanks for the WPRA. On arrival of the above tanks in the USSR, this agreement is eliminated.

In accordance with the Versalles treaty, Germany has no right to construct the tanks; therefore the act of formal purchase of the tanks by us protects the Germans in the case that the outer world will learn of it. Due to the above-mentioned, the German government will not be formally involved in that, and the industry will be responsible for the production and sale of the tanks.

I suppose we can meet this wish, as "the purchase of tanks" in any place will not cause political damage to us. The fictitious agreement could be concluded either by the war industry or by the Berlin trade representative. There shall be indicated in the agreement that the money due for the tanks has already been paid.

The quick arrival of the tanks in the USSR for the WPRA is very desirable.

CSASA. F. 33987. Op. 3. D. 295. Sh. 50.
Copy.

*   *   *

GRYAZNOV[68] TO VOROSHILOV ABOUT "TEKO"[69] WORK

March 14, 1932

The 3-year TEKO summer work experience provided the opportunity to train the chief personnel in the courses, in total, 65 men of the WPRA tank and mechanized units. The greater percent of the number of those sent on an official trip is combat officers and the teachers of the tactical and technical cycle of the armored higher schools and the smaller percent is engineering personnel (engineer-tankmen, engineer-artillerymen, engineer-radio operators).

. . . Briefing our engineers on the materiel of the German fighting machines as well as studying all the German materials: the drawings and the conclusions on the tests have allowed them practically to use the TEKO experience. . . .[70]

So, on the whole, the TEKO work is of great interest to the WPRA, till now from both the technical and the tactical point of view. . . .

The courses are the research laboratory for the technical, tactical, and methodical improvement of our officers. . . .[71] With a view to preserving the conspiracy and solving all the economic-domestic questions in the quickest time, form the TEKO as the official staff, the WPRA Scientific-Research Station.

> CSASA. F. 33987. Op. 3. D. 295. Sh. 113–14.
> Original.

* * *

PROVIDED FOR SENDING . . .
THE PROPERTY OF KAZAN STATION[72]

> July 29, 1933
> Kept in secrecy

Sheet A

Provided for sending:

1. Machines (wheel machines, truck trailers, 2 large tractors Daimler-Benz, 2 large and 2 light tractors Krupp, 2 large and 2 light tractors Rheinmetall).
2. Weapons and optical instruments: 2 cannons 7.5 cm Rheinmetall with the brake, air with run-up; one cannon 7.5 cm Krupp with the brake and air run-up; four cannons 3.7 cm (45–2) with the brake and air run-up; three 3.7 cm auto[matic] cannons with the accessories, 4 optical sights[73] are also attached to them; 1 machine gun 08/15

with the equipment; 3 machine guns, 13 with the equipment; 4 machine guns Seda with the equipment; 10 machine guns . . .[74] 15 with the equipment; 3 rifles 98; 5 automat[ic] pistols; 12 pistols, type 08; optics, stereoscopic telescopes, etc.; . . .
Ammunition: 800 of 7.5 cm training grenades
                    2000 of 3.7 cm training grenades, cartridges, grenades . . .
Tools: machine tools . . .
3. Electro-radio-techn[ical]. instruments and materials.
   Measuring instruments, voltmeters, capacitors, buzzer, oscillograph, receivers Telefunken, Lorents, transmitter, wire, scissors. . . .
4. Instruments and machines, measuring instruments, etc. . . .
5. Buildings.

Sheet C[75]

Transferred without compensation for the Red Army:
1. All constructions performed during the current years, including the normally installed machine equipment in the shops that, according to the inventory making, are estimated above 650,000 rubles . . .
2. The equipment for the shops (press, machine tools, saws, valves, the machine tool for pressing out the iron rolls) . . .
3. Equipping with furniture for the living and service rooms, casino, laundry at the cost of 180,000 rubles.
4. Radio instruments.
5. Equipment for target practice [shooting ranges] . . .

Sheet B

Supposed for sale to the Red Army:
1. Motor Vehicles
   1 BMW motorcycle with sidecar attached
   2 BMW cabriolets
   5 BMW two-seat
   1 BMW four-seat
   1 Mercedes-Benz limousine
   1 Adler limousine
   —Omnibus
   —Opel-blits truck

—Bussing-NAG cross-country vehicle
—Daimler-Benz, etc.
The total sum: 159,000 rubles.
2. Storeroom
   Production materials, tools, spare parts, etc. . . .

   Total: 90,500
3. Radiotechnical Equipment
   8 Telefunken receivers, transmitters, Lorents receivers. . . .

   Total: 10,970
4. Depot
   Oil tank for 50,000 liters, cisterns, etc. . . .
   Total: 18,000 rubles.
5. Weapon, optical accessories, and ammunition
   Tool machines and tools. . . .
   Total: 5,000 rubles.
   The total cost of the subjects to be offered for sale:
1. Autocars . . . . 159,000 rubles
2. Storerooms (content) . . . . 90,000 rubles
3. Radiotechnical equipment . . . . 10,970 rubles
4. Buildings . . . . 18,800 rubles
5. Weap[on]. and optical accessories and ammunition . . . 5,000 rubles

Total: 284,270 rubles

CSASA. F. 33987. Op. 3. D. 504. Sh. 80–94.

* * *

BERZIN TO VOROSHILOV ABOUT REMOVAL OF THE
REICHSWEHR MILITARY EQUIPMENT FROM USSR TERRITORY[76]

August 14, 1933
Kept in secrecy

I report:
   Following your directives about the liquidation of the "friends' "
enterprises in the USSR as soon as possible, from Kazan to Leningrad
on 11 of t[his] m[onth] the first transport with the "friends' " property
has been sent. It comprises the following:

(a) 4 large tractors,

(b) 2 small tractors,

(c) 1 eight-wheel machine, and

(d) 2 covered flatcars with fighting-machine armament, spare parts, and accessories.

The question about this transport departure was agreed upon with the YMM. Comr. Khalepsky has no objections against the departure of the above-mentioned "friends' " equipment to Germany.

I ask your permission for

1. Delivery of the license to pass the cargo to Germany through the Leningrad port;

2. Delivery of a USSR-Leningrad pass for a German team of civil mechanics, including 5 men, intended to ensure loading of the equipment on the ships.

Appendix: List of the equipment to be forwarded with the first transport[77] . . .

> Chairman of the Fourth Office of the WPRA Headquarters
> Berzin
> CSASA. F. 33987. Op. 3. D. 504. Sh. 105.
> Original.

*   *   *

"TOMKO"

As for the work on the chemical polygon at Prichernavskaya st., VOKHIMY considers it to be very valuable and useful for the WPRA.
> Ya. Berzin, Chairman of the Fourth Office
> of the WPRA Headquarters

From the report of the Fourth Reconnaissance Office of the WPRA Headquarters:

"TOMKO" is the enterprise for conducting mutual chemical experiments (testing new instruments and methods of application of poisonous substances in the artillery, aviation using the device-gas projectors, etc., as well as the new means and methods of degasification). Tomko has been established in 1926. The Germans have invested about 1 million marks in Tomko."

*   *   *

THE SOVIET-GERMAN TREATY ABOUT MUTUAL WORK IN TOMKO

1929

The draft of terms between the Russian Joint Company on pest control and application of the artificial fertilizers (named further as M) and the German joint company on usage of the raw material (named further as B) concerning the continuation of the mutual tests started in 1928.

. . . Both parties conclude the present treaty for the all-round and deep development of the question to be of interest; but every year not later than December 31, this treaty shall be renewed and approved by both parties. . . . In the case of cancellation of the treaty, B has the right to bring back the materials and instruments belonging to it, or to deliver them to other local enterprises, or to sell M at the assessed cost. The settlement of this question shall follow not later than after nine months in this case. The articles not shipped back to this term, not delivered to the other enterprises, or not sold, become the property of M. . . .

A. Preparation work

The preparation work of the economy and technical character in 1929 (Appendix 2 a and b) is performed by the training personnel to be forwarded by both parties. The training personnel shall arrive at Tomko till May 5, 1929. The training groups are headed by the leaders, whose rights and duties correspond to those of the M. and B. leaders. The necessary orders shall be made in due time by both parties so that the training personnel have at their disposal all the required materials. The training personnel of both parties performs together the additional buildings provided in the statement (Appendix 2). The latter shall be ended by June 10, 1929, excluding the highway and the railway siding. To perform these jobs, M. gets the required technical personnel. To perform mechanical tests, each party gives the necessary machines and accessories at his expense on a special agreement. The M. loans out, free of charge, the new tent measuring not less than 20 × 15 × 5 meters for use on the test field in addition to that in Tomko.

B. assumes half of the expenses on the hangar construction intended for 2 large and small agricultural machines. The required special vehicles with the special equipment shall be given by both parties in the quantity and of the type admitted necessary for realizing the program.

B. Performance of tests

The program for tests worked out in 1928 has been checked for two years by both parties and can be added, if necessary. The present program shall be approved by both parties not later than two months have expired after the moment of the given document approval.

B. gives the personnel for performing the tests in 1929 in the same quantity as in 1928, but provides one photographer and, if it is possible, in addition, 1 automechanic, 1 locksmith for the ground instruments, 1 cleaner of the vivarium, 1 clerk.

M. gives the same staff as in 1928, and in addition 2 drivers, 1 locksmith (motorcar), and 1 worker for the vivarium (knowing how to skin, if possible). Besides, M. gives 1 experienced joiner at B.'s expense. Both parties shall avoid changes in the personal staff, if possible, during the test time period, which is going on from June 10 till the beginning of December 1929, without interruptions.

Conditions for Performing the Tests with Missile Devices

1. The German tests with the missile devices are being performed during the summer of 1929. The duration of the tests is about four weeks.
2. The tests are performed with L. missile balls[78] solely.
   AIM OF TESTS:
   (a) To determine the action character of one L. missile ball.
   (b) To perform the test of flinging in large sizes on a definite area.
   (c) To solve the missile-technical questions.
3. For the time of performance of the tests, B. sends on a mission 1 specialist on flinging and 1 specialist-technician as the experienced personnel.

   Other necessary persons shall be taken from the Tomko experienced personnel. The D.[79] personnel departure will follow after the balls will be filled and ready for flinging. On the order M. gives the ranks required for the maintenance of three devices.
4. By June 1, 1929, for performance of the tests in Tomko the following will be delivered:

(a) 4 missile devices (one is as the standby).

B. has the right to forward the devices back to D. at any time after the tests are finished.

(b) 1,000 missile balls ready for use (exclusive of filling).

5. The filling of the balls is performed in the following quantity: 0.75 by the M. part and 0.25 by the B. part in a small installation.

M. takes care of the supply of the required material for filling in a quantity of 1,900 kilograms at least 90 percent of L. B., in its turn, delivers three tons of odol[80] necessary for obtaining 1,900 kilograms L.

6. M. ensures the transportation of missile devices and balls there and back at the lowest rate.

7. B. incurs the expenses on payment of the D. special personnel. M. pays the normal salary to the ranks to be given by M.; B. incurs their transportation expenses (according to the appropriate tariff) and the additional maintenance expenses, etc., in Tomko.

The supply of the necessary material for L. and its filing is calculated: M. at par, the approximate calculation shall be delivered to the B. party not later than at the end of February 1929 by the M. party. B. bears the transportation expenses of missile devices and balls.

Appendix No. 1
Administrative Instructions

1. The administrative leadership is in the hands of the M. leader. The B. leader, however, shall be preliminarily informed about the directions to be executed as the "administrative instruction," at this, all directions relating to the B. personnel and the M. personnel employed by B., and the directions touching technical questions go through M.

2. It is prohibited for all B. participants to make the acquaintance of the population, garrison, and foreign subjects. Accidental talks caused by necessity do not fall under this prohibition.

3. All the participants shall live within the range of the test area.

4. B. and M. leaders are responsible for ensuring that the B. and M. personnel should leave the borders of the test area only in cases of necessity. If the B. leader shall send somebody of the workers, in case of service need, to Volsk or Saratov, he informs the M.

leader about it. The latter has the right, if he considers it necessary in the interests of the deed, to protest against this sending. The B. and M. leaders immediately report to Moscow in such cases. The B. participants have the right to go for short trips along the Volga, preliminarily coordinated with the M. leader. Each time these trips are carried out along the routes established by the M. and B. leaders within the limits of Samara to Stalingrad. All the B. participants are supplied with identity cards by M. for the time required for the tests' performance. The B. participants are obliged to return these identity cards to the M. leader prior to each departure for Germany.

5. The out-of-service photographing can be performed by the M. and B. personnel, and each time with the consent of the M. leader. The out-of-service photographing of the tests, test buildings, and equipment as well as M.'s uniformed participants and Red Army men is prohibited. The leader has the right to look through all negatives, and in the case of detecting those contradicting the present prohibition, to eliminate them together with the positives available.

6. The work hours in the barracks, tents, and laboratories shall be reported to the M. leader beforehand.

7. It is prohibited to take out the instruments and materials from the places of the constant work to the other places (in particular, to the living rooms) without the M. or B. leader's permission.

8. The service instructions for the guard are given through the guarding chief. Out-of-service talks with the guard personnel are prohibited.

9. The program of each "test" day is compiled a day before by mutual discussion of it by the M. and B. leaders. The following changes are also inserted on agreement of the M. and B. leaders.

10. All the tests are performed in the presence of the M. leader or his assistant. As for the test work, the M. leader determines who of his personnel shall take part in the tests.

11. B.—leader.   M.—leader.

12. The present instructions are given to both leaders in Russian and in German. Both of them are responsible for familiarizing the personnel with it.

CSASA. F. 33987. Op. 3. D. 295. Sh. 25–27.
Copy.

*   *   *

INFORMATION ON TOMKO. KEPT IN SECRECY

January 1929

I. The following has been built by the leaseholders on Tomko enterprise by January 1 this year:
1. Barracks for habitation 5
2. Laboratories 4
3. Garage 1
4. Vivarium 2
5. Degasification chamber...............................1
6. Well with water pipes system 1
7. Equipment connected with the electrification of a settlement. Total invested already by the leaseholders for the construction is 180,000 marks, and together with the equipment their expenses are 320,000 marks.

    It is offered to invest 120,000 marks more the next year in this enterprise.[81]

II. As for the test research work, the following has been done:
1. Tested is the cistern for contamination of the ground.
2. The portable instrument for contamination "Minimako" and "NAG."
3. The device for pouring war gas (WG) from the air.
4. The samples of the distant chemical bombs.
5. Installation for filling the mustard gas.
6. Chemical fougasses bursting in the air.
7. Devices for degassing.
8. Protective suits—gas masks.
9. Devices intended for electrolytic determination of mustard gas.
10. Treatment and prophylactic means against the mustard gas affliction.

    Chairman of the Fourth Office of the WPRA Headquarters
    Berzin
    CSASA. F. 33987. Op. 3. D. 295. Sh. 79.
    Original.

*   *   *

INFIRMARY REGULATIONS OF TOMKO

1929[82]

1. The head B-physician distributes duties and observation in the infirmary. All M. and B. doctors in T[omko] are subordinated to him; an appointment of his assistants is especially regulated. M. sees to it that the head B-physician would obtain all the required according to his prescriptions, i.e., his recipes will be realized in one of the drugstores.
2. The B-physician deals with the reception and discharge of patients. He regulates their treatment and nursing. Treatment of the M. patients shall be entrusted to M-doctors. Insubordination to B. physician is not allowed.
3. The M. party delivers 5 (five) sets of the hospital beds with mattresses, 10 woollen blankets and bedding, and takes care of the underwear and bedclothes of the M-patient at his entry. All patients are provided with fresh bedclothes and underwear upon their entrance into the infirmary. The M-party takes care of the M-patients' allowance and, as it is possible, takes the physician's instructions and the expenditures required for a treatment into account at this.
4. The time for visiting the patients is established by the B-physician.
5. The B-physician keeps records of drugs and dressings at cost monthly. All medical property of the infirmary can be used following the B-physician's instructions. Nursing in the infirmary is performed by the B-physician's assistants.
6. The B-physician keeps all case histories in the infirmary. The copies concerning M-patients are delivered to the M-doctor after the patients are discharged from the infirmary.
7. The B-physician establishes the daily hours for out-patients; the treatments and distribution of the drugs, etc., is performed in compliance with Paras 2 and 5.
8. The cost of cleaning the infirmary, excluding the B-physician's flat, is especially counted and paid half by M. and B. The heating and lighting equally relate to the common expenses.

CSASA. F. 33987. Op. 3. D. 295. Sh. 28–29.
Original.

*   *   *

CALCULATION OF COSTS REQUIRED FOR RESEARCH WORK[83]
OF 1929 TO BE ACCEPTED IN HALVES BY B. AND M. PARTS

(a) Equipment of the camp and field
   (1) Autogarage and construction 7,500
   (2) 1 large reinforced concrete barrack
      (the B. storehouse for a laboratory) 1,500
   (3) 3 small reinforced concrete barracks (a storehouse for the
      car gasoline, gas chamber, meterological accessories) ... 1,500
   (4) Building and cementing the floors 4 times 1,000
   (5) Building the vivarium 2,000
   (6) Crane with load capacity of 2 t.................... 2,500
   (7) Motor for lighting 6,000
   (8) Gas-proof shelter............................... 4,000
   (9) Construction of the halt and the road to it 54,000
  (10) Roads, a camp, a test field 129,000
  (11) Wooden barracks for 100 P.[84] workers (P. cost) 30,000

                                                      239,000
  (12) Construction of a hangar intended for 6 aircraft 75,000

                                                      314,000
(b) Common expenses for the research work
   (1) 2 "Opel" 4P passenger cars 6,400
   (2) 1 caterpillar tractor with 2 trailers 20,000
   (3) 2 motorcycles with baskets 4,000
   (4) Chevrolet device for biological purposes 1,500
   (5) Spare parts for autocars 2,500
   (6) Motor trolley (for cargoes of 3 tons) 20,000
   (7) 6 horses 6,000
   (8) 2 platforms and carts 4,000
   (9) 2 carriages 5,600
  (10) 1 harness 800
  (11) A stable and equipment 1,500
  (12) Devices for degassing (platforms with the degasification
      tanks, vats, the roof for protection of the accessories,
      degasification pump, fan) 4,000

(13) The new building of a room for drying and annex   3,000
(14) Measuring tables with pegs.   3,000
(15) Device for filling, including the construction   9,000
(c) Various[85]
    (1) Improvement of the airfield   1,800
    (2) Photomaterial   1,500
    (3) Biological equipment, addition   1,500
    (4) Medic[inal] substances for treatment test
        performed with animals   800
    (5) Experimental animals   3,000
    (6) Allowances for them   3,500
    (7) Additional meterological equipment   1,500
    (8) —, —, —, additional equipment of
        chemical laboratories.   3,000
    (9) Allowances for horses   3,600

                                              93,500

(d) Materials and chemicals
    (1) Gasoline, oil for cars   20,000
    (2) Chemicals   30,000
(e) Unforeseen expenses, round   57,500

                                            515,000

For each part. . . . . .257,500 m[86]

CSASA. F. 88987. Op. 3. D. 295. Sh. 30.
Original.

*   *   *

ABOUT LIQUIDATION OF "FRIENDS' " STATION TOMKA[87]

August 8, 1933
Kept in secrecy

I report: In connection with the "friends' " station liquidation in Tomka, the list of the property to be exported from the USSR to Germany before 15 this month has been presented by them. The VOKHIM considers it necessary to buy only the experimental chemical motor provided with the Krupp chassis[88] from the listed property. As for the rest of the property indicated in the list to be exported from the USSR, the VOKHIM has no objections as this property is not of any value to the VOKHIM. . . .

> Berzin
> Chairman of the WPRA Military-Chemical Office
> Rakhimson
> CSASA. F. 33987. Op. 3. D. 504. Sh. 99.
> Original.

*   *   *

LIST OF TOMKA CHEMICAL PROPERTY TO BE EXPORTED

I. Personal property of participants (towels, beds, table-cloths, gramophone, chairs, rifles, goggles, blankets, etc.).
II. Service property: Equipment, pictures, typewriters, experimental machine (Krupp model)—1. Artillery guns, stereoscopic telescope, binoculars, protractor, optical sight, iron box, meteorograph, theodolite, barograph, anemograph, stopwatches, autograph of the sun's radiance, anemometer, compasses, aerial bombs, belts for parachutes, technical chamber, objectives and lenses, tachograph, altimeter, exhauster, areometer, balance, injectors, cable, microscope.

> Assist. of the Central Military-Chemical Polygon
> Gubanov
> CSASA. F. 33987. Op. 3. D. 504. Sh. 100.
> Attested copy.

*   *   *

REPORT OF BERZIN TO VOROSHILOV:
ABOUT RESULTS OF THE WORK IN KAZAN, LIPETSK, TOMKA

1931

The results of the work in Kazan and Lipetsk do not satisfy the Administration of the YMM and YBBC entirely as the "friends" deliver the newest technical objects subject to tests in insufficient quantity, sometimes limiting themselves to the aged types [such aircraft as Fokker Do-XIII], and do not always share all the materials and information obtained from the research and training-experimental work with us. . . . As for the work on the chemical polygon located near st. Prichernavskaya, VOKHIMY considers it very valuable and useful for the WPRA.

. . . It is desirable to introduce the following improvements:

1. On chemical works in Tomka [st. Prichernavskaya]:
    (a) To bring to an end the works with the viscous mustard gas in field conditions (using it by artillery, aviation, combat chemical machines, and degasification).
    (b) To complete the work with "pfificus" and new PS (poisonous substances].
    (c) To use the liquid degassing device . . . [application of the Krupp cistern].

In connection with the development of our own works in 1932, it is desirable to transfer the "friends" from the Central Military-Chemical Polygon (CMCP) territory to the other place.

2. On aviation in Lipetsk:
    (a) To intensify the import of the newest technical objects, especially the engines of large power, including the engines operating on heavy fuels.
    (b) To widen the experiences on communication. . . .
    (c) To deliver all technical objects that, we think, will be valuable for the WPRA, even if for the pay.
    (d) To perform the joint studies on bombarding from high altitudes and firing from heavy machine guns over arms and on creating the smoke screen as well.
    (e) To perform testing of aircraft provided with the pressurized cabin under winter conditions and to solve other technical questions. . . .

3. As for the tank courses in Kazan, it is required:
    (a) To intensify an import of the newest samples of the materiel.
    (b) To bring forward the questions concerning the leadership and compiling the study program, having handed over a common leadership of the work of the courses to our part.

General Adam, the chief of the Reichswehr truppenamt, coming on November 9, 1931, will possibly touch upon the following questions:

(1) Exchange of opinions on the questions of the operative character in case Poland will take the field.

(2) Unification of gauges for the artillery and automatic weapons of the WPRA and the Reichswehr.

(3) About military reports.

(4) About our cooperation in the future in our joint enterprises: the tank courses in Kazan, the experimental work on the chemical polygon, st. Prichernavskaya and the aviation work in Lipetsk. . . .

Berzin
CSASA. F. 33987. Op. 3. D. 375. Sh. 110–11.
Original.

* * *

BERZIN TO VOROSHILOV: "LIQUIDATION OF THE "FRIENDS' "
ENTERPRISE IS TAKING PLACE AS QUICKLY AS POSSIBLE . . ."

August 31, 1933
Kept in secrecy

I report about the completion of the following actions:

I. Germany

The liquidation of the "friends' " enterprise is taking place as quickly as possible and will be finished by September 20–30.

1. On August 15, the liquidation of st. Tomka will be completed. The technical personnel of the "friends" has left Tomka and the station has passed into the hands of the VOCHIMU on 15.08.

2. The Kazan st[ation] is planned to be liquidated in the period 7–10 September. The last "friends' " transport will leave on September 5. The remaining technical personnel, with the station leader at the head, will leave for Germany on 8 September. The station property presenting some interest for the YMM is bought from the "friends." The payment in rubles is 220,000.

3. During the period from 20 to 30 September, the "friends' " station in Lipetsk will finally be liquidated. At the present, one transport with the equipment has been sent, and 3 aircraft of the "friends"

[Junkers A-48 (2 aircraft) and B-33 (1 aircraft)] have left Lipetsk for Germany by the Deruluft route at 29.08. . . . The acceptance at the station passes without incidents.

The "friends," however underline their desire to continue the co-operation with the WPRA. This was also officially declared by General Lutz (the chairman of the Reichswehr motorization forces) when in Moscow. . . .

CSASA. F. 33987. Op. 3. D. 458. Sh. 101–4.
Original.

*   *   *

BERZIN'S REPORT TO VOROSHILOV:
ABOUT CEASING THE PRODUCTION ACTIVITY OF ALL
ENTERPRISES ORGANIZED BY THE REICHSWEHR IN THE USSR[89]

October 14, 1933
Kept in secrecy

I report: in compliance with your order to take all measures for the quick and harmful curtailment of all "friends' " enterprises located in all stations (Tomka, Lipetsk, Kazan), the activity of the "friends" is completely stopped, their property is exported to Germany, and the personnel of their enterprises has left the USSR.

At 12 t[his] m[onth], the enterprise office will stop existing. At the beginning of the negotiations, the "friends" tried to drag out the enterprises' liquidation, evidently supposing that in the course of the negotiations some changes would take place and their staying in the USSR would be prolonged for an uncertain time. Once certain, however, of the futility of this attempt, the "friends," with a view toward "saving face," curtailed the enterprises by themselves in a relatively short time, declaring that it completely coincided with their wishes, and that the up-to-date situation required new forms of cooperation, which would be reserved for the future after liquidation of the enterprises. This was also declared by the Chairman of the Reichswehr Motorized Forces, General Luts, when in Moscow before.

Taking into account the Reichswehr's interest in preserving the friendly relations with the WPRA, and mainly, the cost of the return freight back to Germany, the "friends" had no objections to our claims to have this or that object from the equipment and armament. Namely:

(a) They have left a large quantity of the property on all stations, mainly, the buildings and equipment, free of charge.

(b) They have sold that property that the WPRA was mostly interested in.

(c) They have made significant concessions in price for the equipment sold to the WPRA.

The plan approved by you provided for the liquidation of the enterprises in Tomka by August 15, the enterprises in Kazan by October 1–15, and the enterprises in Lipetsk by October 1, t[his] y[ear].

Actually the liquidation has passed as follows:

I. Tomka. The liquidation of the station was started on 26 July, 1933. In compliance with our requirements, the "friends" have brought into order and repaired all the equpiment to be left starting in July. The liquidation was finished on August 15, and by the 16 of August, nobody from the "friends" was present in Tomka, and this station was handed over to VOCHIMU.

Free of charge, the VOCHIMU was in the possession of all buildings created by the "friends" such as the hangar, the mechanical shop provided with all equipment, machines, and a full set of tools and instruments; all equipment of the filling station of the pump type, electrostation and water-tower with the new motor installation, fully providing the works in the given region; the garage including 6 cars and 3 trucks and a trailer; the equipment of the marsh outfitting shop, chemical laboratory; a degassing shop, casino, technical materials, reactives, household articles, etc. On the approximate count made by the MEB,[90] the total cost of the equipment left in Tomka is 40,000–50,000 gold rubles.

We have bought the test fighting-chemical machine of the Krupp type, paying 5,000 rubles in Soviet banknotes to the "friends" (as they stated, they had paid 15,000 marks for it).

The "friends" have exported: artillery guns with the spare parts, one car, sports goods, various tools, a cine-camera, a microscope, and different technical and economic property. All listed above has no importance for us according to the VOCHIMU chief's opinion.

Two cars and 2 platforms have passed the border through Sebezh on 29.8.33 (August 29, 1933) and 2 platforms through Leninport at

11.9.33. The remaining and acquired property in Tomka is being used for development of the polygon in Tomka and a part of it for the Institute of Chemical Defense.

II. Kazan. The liquidation of the station was started on 20 July. The property of the "friends" has left Kazan by the three transports on 11.8, 19.8, and 4.9. By 6 September none of the "friends" was in the place.

The property given to the YMM free of charge is estimated to be worth about a million rubles by the most modest calculations. It consists of the reequipped and built-anew buildings of a storehouse of fire . . . ,[91] habitable buildings, radiolaboratory, guard room, cooperative, refrigerator, gasoline storehouse for 20 tons of fuel, electrostation, reconstructed water-tower, garage with the compressor installation, shops (assembly, tool machine) in good condition, . . . systems for central heating, garage and storeroom, drainage, shooting range, well-organized roadway, building materials, etc. Acquired by the YMM is the property for a total sum of 220,000 rubles: autocars and tractors with spare parts, drainage pipes and instruments, refrigerator and dining-room equipment.

Exported to Germany are 6 large and 4 small tanks, one 8-wheel machine with spare parts, equipping, armament.

All the evacuated cargo of the Kazan enterprise has passed the border through Leninport on 4, 11, and 18 September this year.

III. Lipetsk. The liquidation began on 19 July, t[his] y[ear]. The aerodrome was handed over on 18 August, polygon on 20 August. The liquidation was finished on 11.9, and the "friends" left Lipetsk on 14.9.

The property handed over free of charge to the AFA is of significant value. Besides the buildings (4 large hangars, aerodrome office, shooting range, habitable houses, a dining-room, 11 new habitable barracks for personnel) built by the "friends," they left a number of shops such as the motor, machine gun, and armory, the aircraft repair shop, a laboratory, the garage with full equipment, the electrostation, a photolaboratory, and so on. In addition, 15 aircraft with engines and spare parts, 8 fuselages, all transport (7 cars, 10 trucks, 1 autocistern, 2 aerosledges), an automatic telephone station, the main material storehouse with the equipment, the equipped infirmary, a camp, an aerodrome, polygon, etc.

Sold to the AFA for 13,500 rubles is the property, mainly spare parts for the BMW engines, camera guns, cameras.

Exported to Germany are 3 aircraft (in summer), all machine guns,

4 Siemens-Jupiter engines with special parts, all parachutes, breathing apparatuses, some tools, spare parts for engines Junkers-15, weapons, ammunition, camera guns, optical sights, radio station, cameras, archives, winter clothes, silver, etc.

The AFA was not interested in acquiring anything from the property exported by the "friends." The transport from Lipetsk (7 cars) has passed the border on 11.9 and 30.9 through Leninport and on 19.9 and 20.9 through the Sebezh.

In spite of a special regime introduced in the process of liquidation, the work was well organized at all stations; the relation to the "friends" was quite correct on our part. This was noted at the final banquets and talks arranged by the "friends" in places. The "friends" underlined the great significance of the continuation of the friendship relations between the Reichswehr and the WPRA in some new form at the final banquet given by the German military attaché, Colonel Hartman, and at the response banquet on our part with the participation of the representatives of the Foreign Relations Department, of the WPRA Mechanization and Motorization Board, of the Military-Chemical and Air Forces Administrations.

Berzin
CSASA. F. 33987. Op. 3. D. 504. Sh. 160–65.
Original.

*　　*　　*

"BERSOL"

. . . To be considered it is necessary to advance the idea of breaking-off with them [the Germans] for the Bersol deed.
From decision of the CPSU(B) CC Political Bureau
Commission on special orders

June 30, 1926

On May 14, 1923, there was signed an agreement about the construction of the poisonous substances production plant. The technological aid in creation of this establishment was rendered by the German concern of Stolzenberg. This plant has become the "child" of the mixed Soviet-German stock company "Bersol." This enterprise, however, for various reasons, has not existed for a long time, and the stock-owners were obliged to close it.

* * *

KEPT IN SECRECY: PROTOCOL NO. 38 OF MEETING OF
CPSU(B) CC POLITICAL BUREAU ON SPECIAL ORDERS

May 12, 1926

There were present: Unshlickt, Chicherin, Iagodá, Avanesov, Shklovsky, Mrochkovsky, Galperin, and Gailis.

Listened to:	Resolved:
1. Bersol	1. Since the German part did not fulfill its duties on the founding agreement[92] in spite of the delay till May 1, in compliance with the treaties performed between U. and S.,[93] it has been resolved to carry out the decision of the Commission[94] made on 9 January 1926, in life.
	2. Offer the German part to invest 500,000 rubles within a month, on account of 1,000,000 intended for additional equipment and re-equipment of installations T and H[95] to be performed by the Russian side, and the required money sums for a fulfillment of other duties relating to the German part on the plant to be conditioned by the treaty and not performed by 1 May. The cost of the works listed above is 2,400,000 rubles by the preliminary calculations of the Russian part. At this, the plan of financing of these works by the German part shall be established not later than June 1.
	3. The Russian part in Bersol Office shall enlist the services of specialists to make more accurate preliminary calculations and to work out estimates.
	4. As the season for building works has come

(should it not be used, the works on the plant will be postponed for one year more), issue 1,000,000 rub. to "Metachem" into the account for the German part as appropriations for the immediate start of work on the plant by the Russian part.

5. Prepare the Commission's decision about the necessity to start building the other plant independent of the Germans, and not waiting for when Bersol will put its plant into service.

2. About AUER's[96] project concerning the production of combat protective masks.	2. The project shall be rejected without paying 75,000 marks for drawing up the project, as it does not correspond to the conditions of the preliminary agreement.

Chairman Unshlikht
CSASA. F. 33987. Op. 3. D. 151. Sh. 72.
Copy.

* * *

KEPT IN SECRECY: PROTOCOL NO. 38 OF MEETING OF CPSU(b) CC POLITICAL BUREAU ON SPECIAL ORDERS

June 30, 1926

Present were Comr. U., Ch., E., Av., Mrochk., Galp., and G.[97]

Listened to:	Resolved:
The German part proposal on "BERSOL"	After three years' work together with the Germans on equipping the chemical plant producing the OS in Ivaschenkovo, the German part systematically didn't fulfill its obligations,[98] constantly dragged out all business questions, and as resulted from the test starts, productions T. and H., installed by the Germans, showed their complete failure and unserviceability.

Therefore, it is necessary to advance the idea of breaking off with them as with the Bersol deed.

1. Accept the proposal of the German part to deliver to the Russian part all works on the "Bersol" plant at the German's expense till they are finished.

2. Five hundred thousand rubles shall be completely and immediately invested, and the rest of the sums provided for the reequipment shall be invested within the 4-month term. At this, the coordinated plan for financing these works shall be approved by the German part not later than at 15 July. It is the final term and not subject to further prolongation.

3. In case the financing plan is neither approved nor fulfilled, it shall be considered as a renunciation of the fulfillment of the founding agreement obligations and a repudiation of the agreement. This done, perform the necessary work on the plant at your own expense, having compensated them for the value for the property that shall be used by us in reequipment with the losses incurred by us to be considered.

4. Offer the "Metachem" to start the reequipment and additional equipment of the plant immediately, beginning with the most necessary jobs.

Chairman Unshlikht
CSASA. F. 33987. Op. 3. D. 151. Sh. 35.
Original.

*   *   *

UNSHLIKHT'S LETTER TO THE POLITBURO OF THE CK VKP(b)
[CENTRAL COMMITTEE OF THE ALL-RUSSIAN
COMMUNIST PARTY OF BOLSHEVIKS]

Copies to: Rykov and Voroshilov

November 22, 1926
Strictly Confidential

In my letter of November 12 (No. 1641) I adduced a number of arguments on the problem of Bersoli (plant) concerning the necessity of the urgent solution of this question and taking appropriate measures that would instigate the Germans to break off relations with us. During the last several months I have sent several letters to Comrade Krestinsky on the same line to be further forwarded to Mr. S.[99] But for the reason of Comrade Krestinsky's being on holiday and S.'s resignation, those letters were handed to the proper quarter. As for Mr. S.'s deputy General Gaye[100]—he entered into the post only on October 25. Any realistic discussion during his first meeting with Comrade Krestinsky was naturally impossible, since the meeting was of general outline; that is why more detailed discussions concerning the Bersoli plant were postponed until November.

On his part Comrade Krestinsky has changed his former opinion and now advises against our being in a hurry to break off [relations with the Germans]. This runs counter to the adopted Politburo resolutions and to the policy we pursue of breaking off relations with the Germans.

Owing to this fact, this question is to be solved within the shortest period of time so that Comrade Krestinsky can have certain instructions from us well before the negotiations with General Gaye start. I regard our policy of breaking off relations with the Germans as the only correct one. Later it is necessary to put stronger pressure on the Germans to obtain a final answer from them so that our relations (whatever their direction may be) would become completely clear by the time the secret equipment is delivered and installed at the plant (May–June 1927). During negotiations special attention should be paid to the financial point of the problem in general as per our memorandum[101] to the Germans of July 6 of the current year.

At the same time I regard it impossible to receive an advance without our financial plan being preliminarily adopted root and branch.

With all said, I pray the "Bersoli" question be solved at the next Politburo meeting.

> Enclosure: Draft resolution[102]
> With communist regards.
> Unshlikht
> CSASA. F. 33987. Op. 3. F. 151. Sh. 1.
> Original.

*   *   *

FROM UNSHLIKHT TO STALIN:[103] "THE GERMANS ARE READY TO RECOGNIZE THE 'PROJECTILE EPISODE' AS WELL"

> January 12, 1927
> Strictly confidential

The latest secret-service information proves more definitely the correctness of our opinion of Stresemann's involvement in the exposures recently made.[104] Moreover, there is an indication of the fact that, with their Foreign Ministry being informed, the Germans are ready to recognize the 'projectile episode' as well.

The carelessness with which they treated the past exposures campaign makes their version plausible. It is clear to me that if this proves to be politically advantageous for them, further exposures are likely to take place. With this in view, I consider it necessary not to confine ourselves only to the discussion of the Bersoli questions, but to consider our relations with PBM at tomorrow's session of the Politburo, taking into account the reasons I stated in my letters of December 31, 26.

> With communist regards.
> Unshlikht
> ZGASA. F. 33987. Op. 3. F. 151. Sh. 27.
> Copy certified.

*   *   *

STRICTLY CONFIDENTIAL: MINUTES NO. 40 OF THE
SESSION OF CK VKP(b) RE: SPECIAL ORDERS

January 12, 1927

Present: Commission Member: Un., Li., Yag.
Invited Mr., Eg., Ga., Be.[105]

Heard:	Decided:
About Bersoli:	(a) As per letter from the Germans of January 11, 1927, the Bersoli agreement is to be considered cancelled. Compensation detriment to our defenses due to failure of fulfilling it should not be limited only by the Bersoli plant, but should be attributed to all our military affairs with them. Comrade Mrochkovsky is to be charged with drawing up a memorandum for its further delivery to the Germans after it has been checked [agreed upon] with NKVD.
	(b) Reconsideration of our relations with the Reichswehr is necessarily to be put before the directive instance.
	(c) On account of the Bersoli plant having become our exclusive property, it is to be transferred to the VSNKH SSSR.
	(d) In view of the importance of the plant for our defenses, urgency, and a high amount of reequipment work to be carried out, it is necessary to reorganize it into an independent unit with other OV industries attached to it so that such a form of organization and administration be coordinated by VSNKH with RVS.

Chairman Unshlikht
ZGASA. F. 33987. Op. 3. F. 151. Sh. 28.
Copy certified.

*　　*　　*

THE "BERSOLI" PLANT SHOULD BE
TRANSFERRED TO VSNKh SSSR[106]

> January 21, 1927
> Strictly confidential
> Personal

In accordance with the resolution of the directive instance, the plant "Bersoli" is to be transferred to VSNKh SSSR. The amount of reconstruction work to be carried out is high; whatever delay in resolving the questions raised may cause a delay in its completion and make the fulfillment of the deadline (autumn of the current year) impossible. Meanwhile, international situation urgently demands a timely fulfillment of supplying the outlined OV (Toxic Agents). So far we have not had plants that produced OV. A small exolchim installation and the Olginsky plant of the VOKHIM trust under construction are experimental—they may be called experimental—but not a large plant production that could be able to meet the needs of the Red Army in case of war.

The Bersoli plant is still the only one plant that produces OV on a large scale and will be the only one to be relied upon in the near future. That is why a timely launching of the plant is of highest importance for us now. In order to complete the construction of the plant in time, it is necessary to solve the question of transferring the plant under VSNKh jurisdiction at our earliest convenience. This is above all necessary for the urgent solution of the questions of production and organization and financing. The plan for reequipment is to be ready by February 1 when, after it has been approved, orders on equipment should be made. The confirmation of the plan cannot be made by the present management board, since it is not authoritative enough to do this.

With regard to the work to be performed at the plant, a question will be raised as to its financing. According to the decision of the directive instance, the reequipment of the plant should be based on 2,500,000 rubles of the estimate. The 1,000,000 rubles allocated earlier have been fully spent. The work needs further financing for its further development.

In light of the above said it is necessary to urgently solve the question of affiliation of the plant to VSNKh and to organize the management of the plant charged with launching it.

As for the organization of the management of the plant, taking into account the paramount importance OV will play in the future war, I consider it correct to combine the organizational trial lines of OV VOKHIM of the trust and gas-protection business in one production unit, thus creating an independent trust within the plants: Bersol, Olginsky, Bogorodsky, gas-protection, and experimental laboratories. The new association of the plants should be given the name "Military Chemical Trust." This is the only way to solve the task of supplying the Army with OV.

Another very important problem can be solved after the establishment of an independent OV trust. It will gather those few specialists on OV that we have now in one group. The necessary number of workers, chemists, and engineers that know the OV production technology will be trained at the plant; a school will be established of the trained, disciplined personnel, capable, in case of war and necessity of rapid development of such industries at our other plants, to be moved there for installation, launching, and instructions.

To ensure appropriate contacts with Military-Chemical Administration, I regard it necessary to include one representative of VOCHIM in the management board of this new trust.

> Please, inform me about the results.
> Unshlikht
> ZGASA. F. 33987. Op. 3. F. 87. Sh. 73.
> Original.

*   *   *

TO THE CHIEF OF THE MILITARY POLITICAL ADMINISTRATION, COMRADE TOLOKONTSEV[107]

> February 1, 1927
> Strictly confidential

In accordance with the resolution of the directive instance and proceeding from the assumption of the necessity to transfer the "Bersoli" plant under the jurisdiction of VSNKh SSSR, the RVS addressed you on January 21 with the request to solve the question of the acceptance of the plant. Despite the fact that more than ten days have passed, the question has not yet been solved. No proposals on your part have yet been made to RVS. The construction matters are urgent by the way. The plan of reequipment of the plant and the question of financing the work must be considered urgently, because the money allotted has been fully spent. A delayed solution of the above questions will undoubtedly cause a delay in launching the plant, and the latter will produce harmful effects on our defense potential. The RVS once again reminds you of the necessity of immediate solution of the question concerning the acceptance of the plant. Its further delay with all the consequences ensuing therefrom will be through the fault of the VRU VSNK.

> *Narkomvoenmor* and RVS SSSR Deputy Chairman
> Unshlikht
> ZGASA. F. 33987. Op. 3. F. 87. Sh. 72.
> Original.

*   *   *

TO COMRADE STALIN

> February 4, 1927
> Strictly confidential

The "Bersoli" constituent agreement was sanctioned to be cancelled by the Politburo resolution of February 13, 1927. The terms of the agreement remain to be cleared up.

Since in the statement of the German side of January 11, 1927, the question remains open; we made an enquiry on January 20 as to the terms of cancellation of our relations in this matter. In their reply of January 31 of the current year, the Germans propose the following terms of cancellation of the Bersoli agreement:

(1) They leave with us all the things of material value and financial contributions they have made since the conclusion of the agreement without any reciprocal account and

(2) renounce all their rights given to them by the constituent agreement as partners of the business.

Thus, withdrawing from the business, the Germans leave with us all the things of material value, plant equipment, and premises without any counterclaims.

As for the loan of 750,000 rubles for "Bersoli" mentioned in their last request, it is of no value for the reason of its (as well as other German financial contributions) having been spent on other articles of material value that they leave here with us. Taking into account the fact that, first, in its resolution of January 13 of the current year the Politburo stressed the necessity of maintaining good-neighbor relations when liquidating joint ventures with RWM and, second, that a detriment to the defenses as a result of a delayed construction of the plant under existing circumstances cannot be presented to them in the form of monetary claims, I suggest that the conditions of the German side be accepted without any additional counterclaims on our part.

Please bring the question to a solution at the next Politburo session.

> With communist regards.
> Unshlikht
> ZGASA. F. 33987. Op. 3. F. 151. Sh. 80–81.
> Original.

NOTES

1. The document is addressed to Frunze.
2. What is meant is the pilot-training school in Lipetsk and its head Lit-Tomsen.
3. German radiotelegraph company.
4. We suppose it may be Yakov Fishman, the chief of the military chemical command.
5. The famous German optical company in Jena, of particular interest to the Soviet side, which acquired various optical equipment for military purpose (sights, range finders, etc.).
6. Apparently, L. G. Ginsburg is the representatives of the people's commissariat of defense. He worked over a long time as an assistant military attaché in Germany.
7. Schwarz was the member of a control council on questions of Junkers and cooperation of the Soviet side.
8. N. von Dreise is a German designer, the owner of a small-arms factory. A machine gun is named for him. The test of the Dreise machine gun is the case at point in the document.
9. F. Fisher is the German minister of defense.

10. The question is of Unshlikht's negative opinion of some points of interrelations with the Reichswehr.

11. The full listing of addressees reads: "To Stalin, Secretary of the TsK VKP(b) (*Tsentral'nyi Komitet Vsesoiuznoi Kommunisticheskoi Partii (bol'shevikov)*—Central Committee of the All-Union Communist Party (of bolsheviks), CC ACP[b]), to Comrade Uglanov, secretary of the MK (*Moskovskii Komitet*—Moscow Committee, MC) VKP(b), to Comrade Kuibyshev, people's commissar of the RKI (*Raboche-Krest'ianskaia Inspektsiia*—Workers' and Peasants' Inspection, WPI), to Comrade Voroshilov, people's commissar of military and naval affairs."

12. These materials are not available.

13. In 1925 the military aviation of the USSR had purchased 119 Fokker D-11 fighters abroad.

14. It was formed on September 21, 1920, for testing aviation materiel.

15. Duks is an aircraft-production plant in Fili (in 1917 there were 370 airplanes there), which subsequently received the name GAZ No. 1.

16. Three years later, on April 11, 1929, Baranov, chief of the RKKA (Raboche-Krest'ianskaia Krasnaia Armiia—Workers' and Peasants' Red Army, WPRA), in the letter to Voroshilov, on the contrary, pointed to the high technical qualities of the BMW-IV motors being purchased at the BMW company for installation on Heinkel-type fighters and for other needs of the RKKA (TsGASA. F. 33988. Op. 3. D. 131. L. 21, 22.).

17. So is in the document.

18. AVIAChIM is a society of friends of air and chemical defense and industry of the USSR.

19. VSNCh is the acronym for Vysshii Soviet Narodnogo Khoziaistva—Supreme Soviet of National Economy, SSNE.

20. Olsky is a deputy chief of the OGPU [Obiediniennoie Gosudarstvennoie Politichieskoie Upravleniie—United State Political Administration, USPA].

21. NAMI [Nauchno-Avtomotornyi Institut]—Automotor Research Institute, ARI; TsAGI [Tsentral'nyi AieroGidrodinamicheskii Institut]—Central AeroHydrodynamic Institute, CAHI.

22. Vaurik is a confidential person of the German Ministry of Defense; Gilder is counsellor of the German Plenipotentiary Representation in Moscow.

23. It is likely Rantzau.

24. Professor G. Junkers (1859–1935) was the German aircraft designer and industrialist who founded the German airplane-production works Junkers.

25. Representative of the Junkers Company.

26. Representative of the Junkers Company.

27. Von Schlieben is a minister of the German government who gave this statement in the course of a talk with Baranov, chief of the VVS RKKA [Voenno-Vozdushnyie Sily Raboche-Krest'ianskoi Krasnoi Armii—Air Force of the Workers' and Peasants' Red Army, AF WPRA] and representatives of the German government and Junkers-Dessau company.

28. Krianga was a jurisconsult of the UVVS RKKA [*Upravleniie Voenno-Vozdush-*

nykh Sil Rabochekrest'ianskoi Krasnoi Armii—Air Force Command of the Workers' and Peasants' Red Army, AFC WPRA].

29. The first copy was sent to Dzerzhinsky.

30. Horsepower, the English unit of power.

31. There is a specification of the value in the margin of the document: 542658.

32. Meters.

33. Seemingly, it means: authenticity certified.

34. Likely, the administrator of the affairs of the RVS.

35. The text of the document is damaged.

36. The document is sent to the Politburo of TsK VKP(b).

37. The text of this letter is not available.

38. The resolution on the document: "No objections. Voroshilov."

39. R.L. is the Soviet side (the abbreviation-cipher is not interpreted in the document).

40. S.G.M. is the German side (the abbreviation-cipher is not interpreted in the document).

41. The former aerodrome of the RKKA.

42. There is a supplement 2 to the document in which the repair of all the school premises is described in detail; its cost is determined in the amount of from 25,000 to 30,000 rubles. Supplement No. 2 is not presented.

43. Lit-Tomsen.

44. Kroki is a sketch-map of the most important country elements prepared using the topographical methods of field sketching.

45. Figure is absent.

46. The supply of everything necessary for the tank school in Kazan and the airfield in Lipetsk is what is meant.

47. Voroshilov's instructions, appended on document, run as follows: "Don't accept. Let him inform the person dealing with the foreign military attaché. V[oroshilov]."

48. Resolution of Voroshilov on the document runs as follows: "The copy to comr. S[talin]. V[oroshilov]."

49. This document is directed by the chairman of the foreign sector of the Military Air Forces Control of the Workers' and Peasants' Red Army (WPRA) Fedorov, by order of Alksnis, to Voroshilov. In the document, the Lipetsk school is camouflaged as "the fourth aviation detachment of comr. Tomsen No. 39 cc.," unit A5.

50. On July 26, 1933, the Chief of the Fourth Intelligence Control of the WPRA headquarters Berzin secretly informed Voroshilov that the German military attaché, Colonel Gartman, delivered to the chief of the department of foreign affairs, the addressed Voroshilov, an explanation from the Reichswehr commander on the question of the liquidation of the enterprise of the "friends" in Lipetsk. Voroshilov put a resolution: "The copy to comr. Stalin. V." On August 4, 1933, the secretary of the People's Commissariat of the Navy and the chairman of the RMF Antonov in secrecy reported to the Political Bureau of the CPSU(b) Stalin: "By the order of comr. Voroshilov, I forward the copy of the material presented by the chief of the Fourth Office of the WPRA headquarters on the question of liquidation of the 'friends' ' enterprise in Lipetsk" (CSASA. F. 33987. Op. 3. D. 504. Sh. 49–51).

51. The identical text of the document in German is present.

52. Published partially. For the inventory of the Kazan station, refer to section "Kama."

53. The document is forwarded to Tukhachevsky as well.

54. VIKO is the German part.

55. KA is the Soviet part.

56. The more accurate definition is in the document text.

57. So in the document text.

58. Lit-Tomsen.

59. The text of Appendix No. 1 is not available.

60. So stated in the document text.

61. The document is very carefully ciphered. It may be only guessed that under the roof of OSOVIAKhIM (Society for the promotion of defense, the furthering of aviation and the chemical industry) the tank school was organized where the Soviet and German cadres of tankmen had been trained.

62. The document is dated by the content.

63. The text of the Position is not available.

64. The abbreviation is not revealed in the document.

65. The Chief of the Courses was the Reichswehr General Lutz. In 1933, he filled a post of the chief of the Reichswehr mechanized forces. In August 1933, Berzin told Voroshilov about Lutz's desire to come to Moscow and to pay a number of visits to the high-officer persons of the WPRA, including the YMM Chief Khalepsky, and to thank them for mutual cooperation in the K station. "August 20, this year, is the most acceptable time of Lutz's arrival in Moscow (according to Hartman): I ask your instructions. Who is to be paid a visit?" (F. 33987. Op. 3. D. 504. Sh. 105. Original.)

66. The abbreviation is not revealed in the document.

67. The document resolution reads as follows (judging by the signature, it belongs, supposedly, to Stalin): "About tanks. We can't strike a fictitious bargain. 26.3.29."

68. Gryaznov, I. K.—the assistant to the WPRA mechanization and motorization administration chairman.

69. The abbreviation is not explained in the text. Supposedly, it is the courses intended for preparation of the chief staff of the tank and mechanized units of the WPRA at the KAMA tank school.

70. Listed is what German achievements have been used in the Soviet tanks: T-28—suspensions of the Krupp tank; T-26, BT, and T-28—the welded casings of the German tanks; T-28 and T-35—the internal location of the team in the nose part; T-26, BT, T-28—observation instruments, sights, the idea of coupling the gun with the machine gun, electrical and radio equipment.

71. The term for training in the courses (six months) is determined in the report.

72. This document is a supplement to the report of Berzin to Voroshilov (July 29, 1933). The report is published in section "Lipetsk."

73. So stated in the document.

74. Omission in the document.

75. The order of letters in the document is being preserved.

76. On the document is the resolution of Voroshilov: "Agreed to. Voroshilov. August 15, 1933."

77. Given further is the detailed (on fifty sheets) description of the cases' content, the Reichswehr equipment prepared for shipment from the USSR. The list of the reverse transport is signed by the inspector of the Moscow customhouse and by the responsible person of the Reichswehr (the signature is made in German—illegible).

78. Missile devices with poisoning substances.

79. It is possibly from Germ. *Deutsch,* i.e., German personnel.

80. Poisonous chemical substances.

81. So stated in the document.

82. The date is established on the basis of the early text analysis of the documents relating to this period of time.

83. Tomko is meant.

84. Evidently Russians.

85. Expenses.

86. Marks.

87. The station is inconsistently called both "Tomko" and "Tomka." On the document Voroshilov's resolution: "No objections. V. August 4, 1933."

88. For the experimental tests.

89. The document is also forwarded to Tukhachevsky, Egorov, Gailis.

90. Evidently, the Military-Economy Board is meant.

91. Apparently, ammunition is supposed. The document is damaged.

92. Unfortunately, the text of the agreement is not available.

93. Unshlikht and, quite possibly, von Seeckt.

94. The text of this decision is not available.

95. T and H are the installations for the production of poisonous substances.

96. The German firm.

97. Unshlikht, Chicherin, Egorov, Avanesov, Mrochkovsky, Galperin, evidently, Gailis.

98. So is the idea expressed in the document.

99. General von Seeckt is meant.

100. General Heye.

101. Text is not available.

102. Not given.

103. The document is forwarded to the Politburo of the CK VKP(b).

104. For some time the German-Soviet cooperation was concealed from the public, until an article in the English newspaper *Manchester Guardian* of 1926 let it out. This was followed by a government crisis in Germany and the resignation of Prime Minister Marx's cabinet. The Social-Democrats in the Reichstag organized a demarche because of the projectiles being delivered to Germany from the USSR.

105. Present apparently were Yagodá, Mrochkovsky, Egorov, Gailis, possibly Berzin. The abbreviation "Li." cannot be interpreted.

106. The document is sent to Tolokontsev; copies to Voroshilov, Dybenko, and Fishman.

107. Copies sent to Voroshilov, Dybenko, Fishman.

4

The Program of Cooperation
Was Rather Wide

The Germans are the safety-valve for us, with whose help we can now study military achievements abroad, . . .

I. Uborevich, Chief of Arms RKKA

When it was impossible to perform experiments with new types of weapons in Germany and to train officers' personnel, Russia had great value as a convenient place for experiments and training.

Küllental, Reichswehr General

LETTERS OF FISHMAN FROM GERMANY

Letter A

March 10, 1925
Berlin
Strictly confidential

Dear Comrade,[1]

1. On the eighth of this month I visited Dessau on the invitation of Junkers' directors. I visited the aviation and engine departments and factories that produce radiators, baths, etc. It looks like all the departments work at full capacity. In the aviation department several large

209

G-23 (planes) are being built similar to the one that arrived in Moscow yesterday. As I was told, twelve pieces were being built.

One of the planes seems due to be delivered to Turkey. I suppose some of them are intended for Spain as well. For the time being they are equipped with weak engines (capacity of both is 400 HP[2]) as in the Versailles treaty, but I was told the planes were designed for much stronger engines.

Apparently, the Junkers firm actively participates in the struggle of the Germans with the Moroccans.[3] Mr. Saksenberg, the principal technical administrator of the aviation plant, whose brother is in Moscow now, leaves for Morocco in three weeks. The G-23 will be used as a bomb-carrier and gas-sprayer. Such experiments on the G-23 have already been made in Germany. Anyhow, Saksenberg let the cat out of the bag at dinner. Whether they have anything to do with ours is still difficult to say. But I think they have, as Stolzenberg, who is to take part in our experiments, is also involved in the actions of the Spaniards against Morocco.

The cores can easily be transformed if necessary, changing a plane into a bomb-carrier or a gas-carrier with a carrying capacity (without fuel) of 1.2 tons, 500 km of action range, and 170–80 km range. The diagram of such transformation was demonstrated to me. It was forwarded to Lose[4] by Saksenberg. The former is to demonstrate it to you in Moscow. If under test the G-23 indeed proves to have the ascribed combat characteristics, this will be regarded as one of the good up-to-date bomb-carriers. By the way, the Junkers pilots, with whom I had a private conversation, very much praise its flying properties.

It is for advertising purposes and out of the desire to show the flying properties of a G-23 in practice that a flight to Moscow by G-23 was undertaken; what is more, Moscow had not been notified by the firm of such a big plane flying to Moscow, as Lose told me. The notification cable was sent by myself only on the evening of the eighth.

Junkers is going to undertake a similar advertising flight from Moscow to Peking this summer.

The engine-building department works at full capacity. Besides standard low-capacity engines produced at the Junkers plant, 6-cylinder engines L-5 at 360 HP have been put to serial production.

The enterprise subsists mainly on the gains it gets from the production of commodities, sheet plates, radiators, etc. These divisions are at full swing already. To my question why a Junkers enterprise is not established on the same basis in our country, they answered that it was because the question had not been raised so far and that it was for economic principles that the metallic planes could be put on production in our country. Obviously, Saksenberg will discuss this point with you during his coming visit.

There is a scientific trial physical-and-chemical laboratory affiliated with the radiator factory (I KO) and it handles all the divisions of the enterprise. Here there is also a museum of different types of alloys and separate parts of the planes put to the flying tests in this or that way. The experience of the last war is taken into account. I cannot say that the testing laboratory is equipped very well. The building is small. Obviously, only control analyses on the production and acceptance of the stuff are made in the chemical lodging (two rooms). I have not noticed any traces of the research work to be performed. The rooms in which Prof. Junkers himself works might simply have not been shown to us.

The physical and chemical parts occupy a larger space, and there are several original-type testing machines. A new metallic duralumin[5] propeller is now put to the test and seems to be yielding good results. Its shortcoming is its weight being 30 percent heavier than those made of wood. A new alloy . . . mainly of magnesium (over 90 percent) and aluminum (about 6–7 percent) is now used for some parts of the plane; experiments on a new alloy that induces a small quantity of lithium are made too. Its admixture improves alloy strength. . . .

Unfortunately we were not allowed to be present there longer than we were—besides we were short of time—because we were in a hurry to catch the return flight to Berlin.

My general impression of the organization of the work at the enterprise is favorable. At the same time, there is an impression of a sort of amateurishness that I did not expect to see in the very heart of Germany now. Some processes are not mechanized well enough. This also concerns the engine-building division that, in this respect, is far behind even the Italian engine-building plants. The most striking impression is made by the large number of workers engaged in the process. Many processes are organized in an extremely primitive way in producing radiators; for example, zincing processes of large units are performed manually, moreover, no labor protection measures are taken. They have to work in a suffocating atmosphere, breathing in acid and zinc vapors. Low wages may possibly account for such a wide involvement of manual labor. An average skilled worker gets 70 pfennings per hour for 9 hours' working day. Defects that involve the equipment point as well to the lack of capital.

I have enjoyed a good reception by the firm and used a plane to come here and back.

2. Aerochemical experiments. I am still not allowed to approach the work at the plant despite my insistance. A specialist engaged in this production branch has informed me through Fischer that spade work is planned to be completed and be ready for tests in our country early in July. They ask us to prepare the people, the aerodrome, and three planes: 2 Fokkers and 1 Junkers I-13 by this time. I told Fischer once again about the abnormal way in which the work is performed; whereas the direction of the experiments will largely depend upon the sort, quality, and quantity of the materials, we are completely removed from their preparation. It would be very desirable if you could express your dissatisfaction with it.

3. Lit has got a permission to leave for a 1.5 months' holiday. The official pretext is treatment. Fischer is to come to Moscow to act for him. Recently the question was discussed at Seeckt's, who approved of Fischer's voyage. It is unclear why one has to send a special deputy from far away, while we have Niedermeier already.

Fischer is going with his wife. He is accompanied by Rad who will work at Glavvozdukhflot (Main Air Fleet) as an acceptor of planes.

I have the impression that Fischer has some concrete special mission and is bound for a longer time than he says he is. I wonder what Niedermaier's reaction to Fischer's arrival will be.

As I have written to you already, Fischer insistently recommends himself as a zealous supporter of the German-Soviet rapprochement. Now he believes that the propaganda among western German industrialists is especially important. He thinks that Stresemann's position will be weakened and believes this to be the only right way to succeed in the struggle against anglophile tendencies[6] in Germany.

4. . . . Reichswehr circles pin much hope on the candidature of Hindenburg.[7] As they are informed, the majority of the center will vote for Hindenburg, but not for Marx.[8] The struggle between the two names is now the main subject in the press campaign and in the political life

in Germany. A symptomatic importance is attached to the victory of one or the other for Germany's foreign policy in the East and for this reason is in potentiality a threat of the revanche in the West. Hindenburg is (at least, from the point of view of England) an obstacle for the earliest "relief of Europe" and continuation of the Soviet-German rapprochement.

Marx-Stresemann—that would mean Germany's compulsory joining the Nations League, a full adoption of the guarantee agreement for western and eastern borders, and cooling down of German-Soviet relations. Such are the mottos of both courses in foreign policy. What these names mean for the domestic life of Germany is, of course, clear.

The Entente states are naturally extremely interested in the outcome of the pre-election company. Lord D'Abernon, the English ambassador, is getting especially busy.

5. Professor Matchos, invited to deliver 2–3 lectures on Germany's industry, has left for Moscow (by plane) in company with Saksenberg. The GEFU intereceded for Moscow's visa. The invitation was apparently made on the initiative of GEFU-Moscow (Dr. Tylle) and Professor Levityn of Moscow. It has become clear during the talks with Fischer that Matchos plays a rather important part among western German industrialists. His report on the trip will much influence the Germany heavy industry's policy with the USSR. So an appropriate reception should be extended to Matchos.

6. There are no special radio stations at Reichswehr. The radio stations now used in the Army are available for sale at large radio firms. For your notice I send you a proposal of the Telefunken company, with which I have been in contact for a long time. Telefunken is ready to give us credits. Talks are conducted by Comrades Levichev and Khalepsky; the military department would do right if it participates in these talks as well. (The Telefunken materials are forwarded to the Intelligence Service for use.)

7. To fulfill Fischer's promise, I have received a secret report of the Reichswehr press bureau on the military equipment as of 1924 and January, February, 1925. (Forwarded to the Intelligence Service.)

8. Enclosed are the copies of the letter from the building firm Leinihe addressed to Stolzenberg and Guntzler's[9] threatening letter. Inquiries about Guntzler are being made. It would be safer if you could call Guntzler to Moscow and go into the case over there. I wonder how

well Guntzler may be informed of Stolzenberg's work here with us, how much information he can let out even if he confines himself only to complaints now taking place in the German party: otherwise, there may be troubles. . . .

10. Inquiries are being made as to the Austrian cartridge and pistol plant in Girtenberg. It used to be the biggest cartridge firm in Austria.

11. A new method of sound detection of the location. The communication is received by myself via GEFU. The invention is the prerogative of the Nurgetion firm. Its representative is Captain Meine who has a relation to the admiralty. All the equipment is made by the Siemens-Galske firm. . . . I regard this method to be of extreme value both for artillery reconnaissance and the Navy. The value of the method becomes the more greater due to a wide employment of smoke screens in the future war.

The firm's representative told me that Czechoslovakia had already made attempts to purchase such equipment at Siemens-Galske; it is decided, yet, against selling the equipment in question to any of the Entente countries.

12. Invention of a high-sensitivity igniter.

The igniter produces the explosion of the projectile upon contact of the striker with a water surface. The safety device gets released soon after the projectile has flown off, so the sensitivity of the igniter can be achieved without detriment to safety. Igniters of such a type are especially important for the employment of the chemical projectiles at sea, because they cause an instantaneous smoke- or poison-screen (conditional on tactics).

The inventor showed me a manufactured model, the picture of which please find enclosed. If you get interested in this invention, it could be possible to purchase it and to have negotiations with the inventors as to the production of such an igniter in our country. The materials and pictures have been forwarded to the Intelligence Service.

13. The Americans are conducting negotiations with Prof. Flamm, in addition to I.V.S. Such negotiations are now conducted by a special French mission through a Brazilian diplomat (confidential. Not subject to publicity not to compromise the source). Our Morved's (Sea Department) opinions about Flamm's submarines would be welcome. A year ago I began talks with him, but ceased it later, having failed to

receive due instructions from Moscow. This talk could be renewed, if necessary.

> With communist regards.
> Jacob
> ZGASA. F. 33987. Op. 3. F. 98. Sh. 649–56.
> Original.

*   *   *

Letter B

> March 20, 1925
> Berlin
> Strictly confidential[10]

1. Aerochemical experiments. In addition to #5 of my previous report,[11] I inform you that yesterday I was received by General Hasse, to whom I expressed my doubts, asking to be allowed to meet those who are directly engaged in designing aero-bombs and gas-sprayers. At first Hasse answered evasively, almost negatively; he pleaded the strict supervision of the Entente[12] countries and persistent observation on the part of the pacifist circles.

My answer was that while regarding the maximum caution in our relations as quite a necessary measure, yet I did not see any reasons for being so very anxious about allowing me a few rendezvous with some of their confidential people. This is the more important that these people . . . knew the purpose for which they designed the equipment. I also pointed to a number of particular inconveniences caused by a lack of information about the work and asked Hasse to help me get closer to their work. I added in conclusion that by making my work easier here, on this wise they make Lit's work easier in Moscow. Any obstacles imposed upon me here are sure to have an immediate effect upon his work there.

In the end Hasse agreed with my arguments and promised to inquire about the true state of things; he also gave instructions to Fischer that the latter put him in the know (to the extent permissible) within fourteen days, for it was necessary for our preliminary orientation and coordination of our tactical views in the field of aerochemistry. I shall have to meet with their specialists on one of these days for this reason. I do not think the results of my talk with Hasse are satisfactory. I am not sure if Hasse is likely to keep his word or if I shall be introduced to the appropriate people and shown appropriate things. The matter drags on extremely. It is not yet quite clear to me whether they are afraid of betraying their secrets or whether they merely do not want to disclose their technical unfitness.

It would be very desirable if you express your dissatisfaction to Lit concerning delays in the experiments and my not being allowed to approach their work.

2. Inspection of the factories. Hasse said definitely that I might begin the inspection of the military plants immediately after the report of the inspection commission[13] is published, that is, in 3–4 weeks.

3. Obtaining technical information. I asked to expedite the answers to various technical questions on artillery, machine gunnery, and chemical projectoring put to him long ago. I stressed that it was necessary for me to enter into direct negotiations with the appropriate specialists. It would expedite the answers so long delayed. For example, it is about 2.5 months since we have received any information from them about the German front line in the past war. Hasse gave me instructions that the information in question would be issued to me without delay; nor did he object to my personal talks with their spec[ialists].

4. In view of our having disturbing news from the eastern borders of Germany and in view of the answer of the German government concerning the guarantee treaty, I asked Hasse what would be their reaction, should Poland undertake any aggressive actions. Hasse's answer was that it could hardly be expected from the Poles to initiate such actions, since, if any, England would undoubtedly stand up against them.

Hasse answered negatively to my question whether there were any guarantees from Englishmen that they would do this. He also added that in case of the encroachment of the Poles upon eastern Prussia, they would not stop at opening military actions.

According to the information from the Reichswehr secret service, no movement of the Polish regiments in the direction of the German borders have been observed so far.

5. Fischer has informed me that now Romania is entered into negotiations with France on making a military alliance against the USSR.

The initiative comes from Romania. The negotiations are mainly devoted to the formation of a permanent base from Constantza for French warships. They are conducted by England's consent. According to Fischer, the source is quite reliable.

With communist regards.
Ya. Fishman
ZGASA. F. 33987. Op. 3. F. 98. Sh. 664–65.
Original.

*   *   *

Letter C

April 3, 1925
Berlin
Strictly confidential[14]

1. Auer's gas-protection mask.

Yesterday (IV.2) I visited Auer's gas protection-mask factory accompanied by Major Auer. Major Auer (who has nothing to do with the owner of the factory) accompanied me . . .[15] as a Reichswehr (representative) for assistance.

The board of directors of the factory was represented by Prof. Kvazebad and the technical manager Dr. Engelgardt. The results of our meeting are as follows:

A. Organizational matters.

(a) They agree to delegate to Moscow their representatives authorized for signing the treaty.

(b) Their representatives (obviously Dr. Engelgardt) will bring samples of their gas-protection mask for tests.

(c) Should the results of the test prove to be quite satisfactory, the samples will be put into large-scale production.

(d) Otherwise, some other mixed type, a synthesis of our and their experiments, may be chosen as a basis for production.

(e) As regards the trade and administration forms of the enterprise (a concession, a joint company, or any other independent venture supplied technically by them)—this point will be discussed in Moscow.

(f) The production of industrial and fire-gas masks for sale in a peacetime period must be the basis of the organized venture.

(g) The USSR government (and, maybe, the Reichswehr) guarantees a certain annual order for combat gas masks. . . .

The most important thing is that they have agreed to delegate their people to Moscow with a gas-protection mask sample.

Please let me know when they can come. I think May (in one month's time) will be the right time for their visit. Our gas-protection commission could work out a program for gas-protection mask testing by this time. Representation of our specialists in the commission is extremely important. They must be absolutely confidential people—I would consider it expedient to come to Moscow myself by the time, if there are no objections on your part.

The new gas-protection mask has been show to me. I shall send you my comments with the next mail. . . .

2. The Reichswehr has still been supplied with gas-protection masks of model [19]18, part of which is produced at Auer's factory. But it is decided to supply the Reichswehr with the new model of Auer's gas-protection mask (most likely by the end of this year). The question of its mass production depends on whether the controversy will be solved with the inspection commission that thinks that, according to the Versailles treaty, Germany may not carry on any kind of work on gases, including the production of gas-protection masks as well. The Germans are, of course, of the opposite opinion and want to be given the right to produce war-protection means and to train the Army how to handle them. Whether the Reichswehr will guarantee part of the order in our country will much depend upon the solution of the above question.

3. Lately the Reichswehr officers with whom I met (Hasse, Fischer, Djunke, De-Grale, and others) have developed a more amiable attitude toward me; even more insistently do they speak of the rightness of our "joint work." I answer in tune. Fischer speaks much about it (evidently, on Hasse's advice); he has written and sent to the Nations League a whole report on the project. As I have written to you already, Hasse puts pressure upon the Nitrogen Syndicate. They suggest that similar steps in our favor should be taken by any branch of the German industry that may be of interest to our military industry.

I shall inform our plenipotentiary representative in Berlin of these opportunities, and yet it would be better if you communicate with Glav-concesscommission and VSNKH.

I do not expect any great results from the Reichswehr's putting pressure on patriotic feelings of German industrialists, but there may yet be some privileges. Why not use this opportunity?

4. The idea taken originally as the basis of the aerochemical experiments (laboratory and theory in Germany—large-scale experiments in our country) is now applied for other types of weapons.

Constrained by the Entente control, the Reichswehr grows willy-nilly into a backward army in Europe. General Staff is busy with theorizing, but is absolutely incapable of checking the training results in practice.

Intensive "training games" have been in progress both in the Reichswehr ministry . . . and both group commands (Berlin, Kassel) through winter on. One of the outstanding leaders of these games is General Hasse. On Thursday (IV.2), for instance, Hasse made a three-hours' report that he read in a close circle of the General Staff officers. As has become known, the topic of the report was devoted to the changes of the military tactics due to the broad involvement of the Air Fleet, chemical weapons, and tanks in the operations.

During our talk about the work, Fischer regretted very much that it was impossible to check in practice their tactical deductions and suggested that it could be possible to do it at some maneuvers in our country. They would attend some of our maneuvers as headquarters' advisors.

Fischer justified his proposal not only by the necessity of inspecting their theoretical work, but also by the advantage such a rapprochement of the leading groups of both armies might bring, since it could be so that we would ostensibly have to struggle together. Hence comes the necessity of the unity of opinions, unification of the military methods and techniques. I answered that there could hardly be any objections to such a disposition and that I would inform Moscow of all that, but, as I said, the unification should not be one-sided, which implied the full participation of the General Staff in the work of the German General Staff and vice versa.

To begin with, I asked him to give me a copy of Hasse's report or, at least, its extracts, a detailed program of their training games for the winter period and the officers' training program for division schools now housed at the General Staff Academy in the Reichswehr, and secret editions of their technical divisions.

Fischer's answer was evasive, yet he promised to give me something. It would be good if you put pressure upon the League in this matter.

Besides, I pointed to the necessity of giving due instructions to the German military press, so persistent in spreading cock-and-bull stories about the Red Army, similar to those I had refuted in the past (military-chemical experiments on the arrested in the Ukraine in the presence of Frunze).

Without encroaching on the freedom of views, we want only one thing—that already now the German military press has fostered—respect for the Red Army—its system and way of life, its power—by the Reichswehr people. They promised to put pressure upon the military press in view of this. In particular, Fischer spoke of the possibility to open a tank school in some of our armored units, such as an aviation school for training their people tank business. Lit might have already discussed this point with you.

It looks as though the Reichswehr executive group has steered a somewhat steadier course in our direction. It is now but an impression that I shall try to verify in the near future.

If my impression seems erroneous to you, please let me know it in good time so that I could regulate my relations with them. May I ask you to send me the instructions (if possible, concrete) with regard to the questions I touched upon in my report at your earliest convenience.

5. Yesterday I expressed to Seeckt through Hasse my condolences on behalf of RVS and our plenipotentiary on the accident that had occurred during the maneuvers when fording the Wester River.

Hasse thanked me very much for the attention; by the way, he asked me to convey his gratitude for the warm welcome Zenflieben, Lit, and others had enjoyed in Moscow.

Incidentally, the Reichswehr Germans highly appreciate an outward display of one's attention, and in view of this, I think it good if, generally speaking, they would be nourished with things like these now and then.

6. The three-engine plane that was built at the Junkers' plant (with the Entente's permission and at England's urgent request) is still taking advertising flights Zurich-Berlin-Copenhagen-Malmo-Berlin. Our

Plenipotentiary Delegation has received an invitation to participate in the flight.

> With communist regards.
> Ya. Fishman
> ZGASA. F. 33987. Op. 3. F. 98. Sh. 658–69.
> Original.

*   *   *

Letter D

> April 17, 1925
> Berlin
> Strictly confidential

Dear Comrade,[16]

1. This is to confirm my cable of IV.17 concerning the necessity to postpone the visit of the testing commission and Prof. Ipatiev to Berlin until the first days of the next month. The reasons for doing this are the following: the machine-gun tests can be expected only early in May. Schwartz will also be away till May 6, and without him the commission will not be able to be provided with due technical explanations.

As far as I know, the commission will get a clear idea only of the minor machine gun, which is already a mass-production unit.

The average machine gun to be demonstrated is a semi-homemade sample already in long use without having been tested. Thus, the technical defects revealed in testing may be accounted for by the defects of the sample.

The models of average mass-production units will be prepared only in August. Professor Ipatiev's visit late in April is not expedient either, since his visit to Schtoltzenberg's factory can be possible only after May 6. Besides, the already envisaged visits to some other factories are possible only at the beginning of May. Nor will Ipatiev find me here, as I leave for Italy in a couple of days and will only be back early in May.

2. Gas-protection mask. There is a finally established opinion, that the 13-mm caliber does not answer the purpose. They do not recommend

the employment of such machine guns either against tanks or airplanes. Now they are performing tests in Switzerland on the new 20-mm gas-protection machine guns.

The tests are said to be yielding good results. They will not be able to provide us with anything interesting in this respect. According to their information, all other countries are in the trial period yet as well.

3. Early in May a new model of the portable flamethrower, I mentioned in one of my previous letters, will be shown to me. It would be desirable to leave some instructions from our flamethrower men.

4. The old model of the 17-cm flamethrower with the rifled muzzle employed at the end of the last war cannot be regarded as corresponding to modern war requirements. They have agreed to sell us one or several units. We do not have such models. Comrade Dzerzhkovich of GAU[17] asked to purchase such a model as well. Please, confirm the necessity of purchasing this and in what quantity.

By now they have manufactured a new 15-cm motor-gun system of high hitting and firing range.

Theoretically, this motor-gun can also be employed against tanks and be a substitute for infantry weapons. The idea of a universal motor-gun is very interesting, though the model they have worked out bears serious shortcomings. This model will be shown to me.

5. The Army will now be supplied with a new type of hand grenade with a knock-down igniter. The cord is absolutely unhydroscopic; the combustion period can be precisely calculated mathematically; the danger of any overshoots is removed. They promise to show these models as well ("perpitus" is replaced with trotyte[18]).

6. One hundred fifty Fokkers are ready for delivery. They are loaded onboard the ship bound for Holland and are addressed to Rio de Janeiro. Later they will be readdressed to Leningrad. Please, let me know (preferably, by cable) at your earliest convenience the address of some private expedition firm in Leningrad, since it would be unwise to address the cargo to some state institution.

7. Nitrogen. On Monday I am to receive from Frank and Karo[19] a plan and a proposal for building a cyanamide-calcium factory, and an oxidizing and condensation plant. The details will be forwarded to you later.

8. Aniline syndicate. I have taken a similar position with regard to the aniline syndicate. Professor Geller was reminded of the great

military value of paint production and of the incorrectness of the position taken by the aniline syndicate in our relation. It is necessary that the syndicate should assist our aniline trust in every respect. To raise our paint industry is first of all a strategic question. In case of war, most of the German paint industry will get into the hands of France. Besides, we do not have a common frontier with Germany, so we cannot be sure whether Germany will be able to supply us with all necessary O.V. (toxic agents) and V.V. The strategic interests here are above trade interests (for fear of losing the market). They agreed with my arguments and promised to grope their way in the aniline syndicate. As they put it, they have connections there. Speak with the aniline trust (Landau and oth.)—in what way and to what extent can this new opportunity be used—and then give me appropriate instructions. I believe that in this case we can see more and be given a technical assistance that so far has been constantly denied to us by the aniline syndicate.

9. Transfer of the commercial industry from Reine. To verify the previous information, I told Schwartz and Frank of the necessity of gradual transfer of the chemical industry from Reine into Central Germany or to any other strategically advantageous place. Schwartz replied to me (with a triumphant smile upon his face) that they had long been busy with doing it and that "for known reasons," they could not acquaint me with details. So this is true that "Grizgeim-Elektr" is moved from Grizgeim to Witterfeld for strategic reasons. Witterfeld seems to become the place for concentration of the German chemical industry especially indispensable for military purposes. That means that the information about the missions of special Reichswehr commissions to Witterfeld, which we sent to you a few months ago, is now confirmed. We focus our attention on Witterfeld and will try to inform you of it in detail.

10. Early in the next week (21–22) I leave for Italy for talks with Fauzer and Kazale[20] (concerning nitrogen and other matters). Late in April or early in May I shall be back in Berlin. Frank leaves for Moscow on the nineteenth (this month), so our contacts are naturally broken off for some time (he will be temporarily substituted for by some other person). Schwartz will be absent also. Therefore my departure will not negatively affect the progress of our affairs.

> With communist regards.
> Jacob

11. This is to forward you *Militär-Wochenheft* No. 37 with the biased information on us (see p. 1138). I voiced my protest, first of all, against the contents, and second, against the abusive tone they use toward the Red Army. I told them that they could obtain correct information on our military agreements only from us, and that in view of our joint work and future plans, the Germans should be aware of the inadequacy of their tone when speaking of us in military press. They agreed with my arguments and promised to exert the necessary pressure.

12. Now about the "Big program" you wrote to me about. After the talks, I have the impression that they indeed have allocations only for aviation and tank schools. They show a serious interest in the Tula enterprise and are likely to be disposed to bear the expenses. All the rest is but a project without any financial basis, but with a desire to find such a basis. As an equivalent of their financial impotency, they are ready to give any assistance to our industry by exercising influence upon German industrialists.

Jacob
ZGASA. F. 33987. Op. 3. F. 98. Sh. 645–47.
Original.

*   *   *

Letter E

April 21, 1925
Berlin[21]

1. I leave for Italy tonight. Kazale and Fauzer have already cabled their reply and fixed the meeting. I shall have returned to Berlin by May 3. Schwartz is to return on May 5. The commission may get down to work on the sixth or seventh of May.

2. Transference of the chemical industry from Reine to Germany center is continuing. Simultaneously, administrative reorganization of the aniline syndicate is taking place. The actual amalgamation of the main chemical enterprises in Germany in one single enterprise is a question of the near future.

This strong organization will undoubtedly be able to build up our paint industry and nitrous compound industry, at will. That is why the nitrogen and paint industries must be part of our "Big Program." Our friends must help us break down the resistance of aniline syndicate. They have already agreed to do it in principle. Now everything depends on the fulfillment. What is Landau's opinion of this?

3. Frank left Moscow on the nineteenth. Lately he has shown a very friendly disposition to us. Before his departure we had breakfast together, during which he expatiated upon our common enemy—capitalism, which cared only about its own profit and was alien to "ideological" interests, etc. Tears almost in his eyes, he spoke of Hindenburg and tried to assure me that with him beside us "our" business would proceed big steps ahead. He appears to be seriously imbued with the idea of our joint work and seems less knavish than are the Gefists.[22] Lately Frank has begun to gain some weight in his office. I think he must be given a good reception.

4. On April 19, Comrade Chicherin cabled an inquiry as to the purchase of weapons in Hamburg for China. We are informed of the sales of Thompson guns. They are received in Hamburg by various countries from the firm representative, von Zeebek.

For China it is purchased by Kharbinskaya firm of the Kapustin brothers. They have already purchased 80 units and made an order for 220 more units. Kapustin is now on[23] Bern, but will soon come to Berlin. The weapons are apparently delivered by sea. Besides Thompson guns are purchased:

—by Poland (two w[eeks] a[go]) 160 units and now 200 units are bound for delivery. The Swede Loht is an agent for the Polish military department.

—by Estonia, 200 units are ordered. The agent is Hanz Swinal, Revel.

—by Romania, 300 units are ordered.

—Bulgaria has made a direct inquiry through New York.

—Yugoslavia and Czechoslovakia have made a common purchase of the Thompson patents. The guns are planned to be put into production at the Shkoda plant.

According to Zeebek, all these Thompsons were sold at 172.50 dollars. Zeebek is ready to sell them to us at 150 dollars.

If you decide to buy Thompsons, I think it will be right to agree with our friends—let them make the purchases as if they do it for themselves. Zeebek will obviously sell them at an even cheaper price. But we must not let him know that the purchase is made for us. . . .

6. Enclosed are activiated carbon samples from Ausig. No. 2 (in the small tube) is the newest product manufactured by the new method. Soon I shall send it to you in a larger quantity.

Pika does not agree with Ipatiev's estimation. I think he is a prominent specialist, whom it would not be amiss to pay. If is he who is in charge of the production of the activated carbon in Ausig. I shall meet with him in May and finally find out all the possibilities and terms.

> With communist regards.
> Jacob
> ZGASA. F. 33987. Op. 3. F. 98. Sh. 642–43.
> Original.

*   *   *

Letter F

> May 4, 1925
> Berlin

Dear Comrade,[24]

(1) I returned to Berlin on May 3.

(2) The scheduled nitrogen program in Italy has been fulfilled. I have visited Kazale and Fauzer's factories, got projects from them, and collected information on both firms. These data along with Frank Karo's projects give us all necessary elements for making an appropriate decision on the nitrogen problem. I plan to bring all these materials with me to Moscow in the middle or end of May, for I hope the work of the commission will have been completed by this time.

(3) The planes[25] have already been loaded on board two ships. One ship bears 50 units, spare parts, equipment for repair shops, and armaments; on board the other one there are 50 other units and spare parts.

The first ship is scheduled for Leningrad early in June; the other one, in a two weeks' time. Shtar[26] says that he has arranged it with Comrade Baranov so that the load will be forwarded to the address of Glavvozdukhflot, as they usually do when sending goods purchased in[27] the USSR. This does not coincide with the address you gave in your cable No. 69. In this view I ask you to inform me of how the load should be addressed at your earliest convenience. The reply must be given before May 15. . . .

> With communist regards.
> Jacob
> ZGASA. F. 33987. Op. 3. F. 98. Sh. 640.
> Original.

*   *   *

Letter G

May 14, 1925[28]

1. This is to inform you that the commission has got down to work: special space is allotted for studies. A detailed report on the work of the commission is sent to Metachim by Comrade Ginsburg. To prevent reiteration, my information will be supplemental. I participate in all the works of the commission.

2. The general impression of the reception of our delegation by the Germans is favorable. They have already agreed upon joint work (GEFU—Metachim) in optics and gas-protection masks. Regarding the M-treaty, they agree in principle to increase the order, but they make it dependent on price reduction.

Schwartz, Djunke, and others give to understand by hinting that the arrival of the old man is very favorable to us, but one has to wait, because he has to be very cautious. Generally speaking, the situation is not quite certain. On the other hand, our secret service informs us of possible changes that may occur in the whole department, and of Z.'s[29] and others' possible resignation. Soon everything will become clear. . . .

3. Today we visited the Hertz plant. Technical report will be made by Milch—he will be able to visit the factories again. I must note that

the factory is equipped rationally and lavishly from the point of view of mobilization. In each room there are necessary appliances for providing a rapid increase in productivity. Even in the rooms that are now employed as warehouses there are apertures for fitting machine tools. As Director Ipan says, in case of war, they could organize the production of artillery- and aviation-sights within 3–4 months. I think the time is exaggerated; they say so to calm the Entente. It will seem more realistic if reduced by 50 percent. One to one-and-a-half months are all the same a long period, that is why our friends are interested in organizing the production of military optics in our country; this must be taken into consideration during negotiations. The military optical industry in Bratislava (Czechia) will be cut off from Germany in case of war. By the way, Bratislav[a] lies on the Austrian-Czech border, they plan its immediate occupation in case of war. The Czech government insists on moving the factory inland now, but the management has so far succeeded in evading the requirement.

The inspection of military optics samples will take place next week in Berlin; after that the commission can also visit Bratislava.

4. Professor Ipatiev and Galperin told me about the formation of a special nitrogen commission at VSNKH and the allocation of the required sum of money for this. So I shall inform them of the results of the work carried out both here and in Italy. The materials will be sent in a day or two. By virtue of our friends (and this is a fact) it was possible to have broken down the resistance of the nitrogen magnate Karo in Germany who has written a project of CYANAMIDE CALCIUM, OXIDATION, AND CONCENTRATION for us. The project has not yet been handed to me, since at the last moment he became as obstinate as a mule. He wanted to receive a confirmation from Z., since, according to his information, we are conducting negotiations with France on delivery of military equipment to our country, etc.; in this latter case Karo, like an honest German (by the way, he is a Jew), refuses point blank to help us organize the nitrogen industry. Of course, I assured him of the absolute absurdity of such information, but the matter has been delayed all the same. He promised to give me a call in a day or two after his talk with Z. I have already informed Schwartz of this talk and asked him to keep in mind Z's coming conversation with Karo.

I have brought exhaustive material from Italy and the proposals of both firms—Kazale and Fauzer's.

Comrade Ginzburg told me that you ordered me to accompany Prof. Ipatiev during his planned visit to France and Italy. I think I shall manage to leave for France late in May.

We plan a preliminary visit to the large nitrogen plants in Munaverke and Pastrice. The talks regarding our admission there are in progress now. I think the situation will be clear early in summer, and then we can make a choice and at last get down to practical work.

5. I confirm my cable about the ship with 50 Fokkers on board ready for sailing from Szczecin and inform you that the ship will evidently leave port not on the twenty-seventh (as indicated in cable) but on May 30. I shall keep you informed of the progress of the matter.

Why did Frank give the address of the Dobrolet management?[30] We confirmed the Metachim's address.

6. Auer. As we know, besides gas-protection masks, the plant produces gas-protection uniforms. If this information is confirmed in the course of Metachim's negotiations, it will be necessary to extend the production.

7. Tomorrow we leave for the testing area for Dreise testing in Kummersdorf. Besides there will be tests on flamethrowers and gas-throwers and hand grenades, as I have informed you already. There are no appropriate specialists in the commission nonetheless.

With communist regards.
Jacob
ZGASA. F. 33987. Op. 3. F. 98. Sh. 633–35.

*   *   *

Letter H

May 26, 1925
Strictly confidential[31]

1. I have already recovered and have been participating in the work of the commission since V.26.

2. Today I have had a talk with Professor Geller. They were also represented by Schwartz. We were represented by Turov, Ginzburg, and myself. What Geller says does not coincide with Gefists' and Schwartz's statements.

According to the Gefists, the money has already been allocated for our joint organization for the production of Dreiser units, optics, and gas-protection masks. Geller said on the contrary, that there was no money, and that it was not yet known whether they could obtain it, that he tried to get the money and that we oughtn't cherish vain hopes, etc. The same can be said about the extension of the treaty. In one word, a very strange hitch. I think we must ask the Germans point blank: do they feel responsible for their works or are they playing games?

3. Geller, as representative of the General Staff, leaves for western Prussia on June 4 with the aim, as he puts it, to check the conclusions made after the training games and to pick up the information that will be used in making the strategic plan; he says they proceed from the idea of our joint warfare against Poland and from the assumption that Latvia and Estonia remain wait-and-see neutral countries.[32]

According to the secret-service information, movement of troops of irregular[33] German units can be observed along the Silesian border.

4. According to the latest information, the ship *Hugo Stinnes—IV* with 50 Fokkers and military equipment on board has arrived at Szczecin. She is due to leave the port on 2.VI for Leningrad and is due to arrive there on 6.VI. I shall cable you of the exact departure date.

5. Nitrogen. Karo has us on a string again. Ipatiev visited him and had a four-hours' talk with him at breakfast. The reasons for Karo's influence are not clear. Only today has Geller told me about Karo's proposal to Ipatiev to begin talks with the Bambag firm, manufacturing devices for oxidation and concentration. . . . Professor Mooze's speedy departure for Berlin would be very welcome.

6. Tomorrow we shall attend gas-protection mask testing.

> With communist regards.
> Jacob
> ZGASA. F. 33987. Op. 3. F. 98. Sh. 631–32.
> Original.

*   *   *

Letter I

January 16, 1929
Strictly confidential[34]

I have received a letter from Niedermeier informing me that:

1. Our proposal for expenses for the needs of the Red Army soldiers has been approved by Blomberg. Thus, our hard line has proved to be correct here as well, contrary to Kork's expectations.

The sum we win certainly is not big (about 1000 r.), but such an outcome can and must be a precedent for other, possibly larger, joint undertakings.

2. I have received a reply to my inquiry about the program—what will be shown to our three comrades in Germany: (1) visit to the gas-protection laboratory and performance of the experiments in it; (2) visit to Prof. W's chemical institute (obviously, Prof. Wirt); (3) visit to the Chemical-Technological Institute and participation in the test; (4) visit to the testing area; (5) visit to the gas-protection school; (6) visit to the Auer's factory (gas protection); (7) visit to Dreger and Ganzeatische factories (gas protection and production of smoke devices and smoke pots); (8) visit to the pharmacological institute (obviously, Prof. Fluri).

They promised to acquaint our comrades in detail with any questions they may be interested in. The program is wide enough to give us, if properly fulfilled, much valuable information.

I instructed the comrades (they have left already) to be very persistent and demand to be shown everything. There must be no closed doors for us.

In case they refuse to show anything, our comrades must say that they will report this in Moscow. Thus we shall have (1) one extra argument against them; (2) appropriate information for the Fourth Department.

3. In reply to my demand to give us new OV, I have received the answer that I quote below: "Our friends' [that's us] suggestion that we have discovered a new substance in the postwar period is not true. Neither our industry that works for peaceful purposes only, nor (as we are informed) any other state in the world have ever succeeded in creating a substance fit for our purposes." All the information now appearing in the press (pacifist) belongs to the "Land of fairy-tales."

We cannot be satisfied with such an answer. First, it is not the "peaceful" industry that is in search of new OV, but chemical institutes and laboratories, control over which is quite impossible. Second, their allegation that other countries do nothing in this direction is wrong, for I have information from the Fourth Department that much work has been performed on new OV in France (Prof. Bushe's laboratory).

Several hundred new OV have been synthesized there. Now we check the data and cannot say yet whether among them there is at least one (OV) fit to be regarded superior to those already known; and yet the fact that gigantic work is being performed on this problem in France has definitely been confirmed. And it is in France—the country that ratified the Geneva Protocol.[35]

I have doubts about the Germans' being ignorant of the above work. In any case, I told the comrades to demand to see all the experiments they have performed in this direction. If they claim that they have not succeeded, let them speak about their failures, let them show the new OV (though of low use) that they have synthesized.

4. In conclusion, Niedermeier asks to expedite the reply concerning amortization "in order to do away with the agreement."

> Chief of the Military Chemical Department RKKA
> Ya. Fishman
> ZGASA. F. 33987. Op. 3. F. 295. Sh. 1–2.
> Original.

*   *   *

Letter J

> February 28, 1929
> Strictly confidential[36]

I inform you that Comrades Rokhinson, Kartsev, and Blynov returned on 22.II (the current year) from mission, on which they were for about one month. The program proposed by our bosses was approved by our comrades with some amendments that they made in order to extend it and supplement it with questions that present interest to us.

They visited the following places:

1. Gas-protection laboratory, warehouses, gas-protection equipment

storehouses and repair shops in Spandau. Acceptance testing of gas-protection equipment with which various firms supply the Reichswehr is performed in the laboratory. A detailed description of the laboratory is made. Gas-protection equipment storehouses consist of several departments in which to store various gas-protection equipment. Accurate description of the warehouses is made. The repair shops do repairs to old gas-protection masks for training purposes. There are about 900 workers. The description is made.

2. Testing Area in Kümmersdorf. We have visited two types of gas-protection dugouts, Prof. Wirt's testing laboratory, attended the experiments on degasification of uniforms contaminated with yperite and on degasification of the forest by the "Total" device. A detailed description is made.

3. Prof(essor) Wirt's Laboratory at High Technical School (Scharlottenburg). Instruments for detection of yperite in soil have been examined (a quartz lamp, electroconductivity) and degasification of fabrics. A detailed description is made.

4. Professor Obermiller's laboratory (technological). During their visit to Dr. Obermiller's technological laboratory, Comrades Rokhinson and Kartsev were the witnesses of the experiment made on obtaining yperite by using a new method. The method is different from those we use in our laboratories. Their method will be checked up as soon as possible and, if results are favorable, will increase the productivity of the plants without their reconstruction and will make our yperite fit for spraying purposes.

5. Gas-protection business of "Auer" or "Degea" firms. They showed us in with reluctance. The inspection of the research laboratory and gas-protection business was cursory. The description has been made. By spring they will produce a pilot mask. The "Auer" plant laboratories are undoubtedly one of the main places of scientific gas-protec[tion] work, and the plant itself is one of the largest suppliers of gas-protection masks to the Reichswehr.

6. Gas-protection school.

Task of the school: training of officers and underofficers in gas-protection service. One hundred twenty to one hundred fifty people can be trained simultaneously. The duration of the term is about two weeks. School regulations, manuals, educational program, the museum, and premises are thoroughly studied, description has been made.

7. Dreger factory (gas-protection mask production) in Lübeck and Hanzeatische factory in Kiel have been visited as part of the program envisaged by bosses. Both factories are large production units. Dreger produced isolating and filtrating gas-protecting masks, Hanzeatische produces isolating gas-protection masks and chemical-assault devices (devices for contamination of the locality, hand grenades). The Design Bureau in Hanzeatische is closely connected with the Reichswehr and works on the instructions of the Design Bureau of the chemical department of Test Administration (Prüfwesen).

8. Professor Fluri's institute in Würzburg. Fluri is regarded among Germans as the most prominent specialist in the study of OV effects upon living organisms and is now a consultant at the Reichswehr.

The comrades visited laboratories and the vivarium and asked several special questions. A detailed description of the laboratory, questions, and Fluri's answers to their questions has been made. The official part of the program ended with the visit to Fluri's laboratory. Being aware of the fact that the answers they received to their questions as well as the procedure of the visit were of general character, our comrades asked for additional information and started a discussion.

The discussions gave interesting results, making the bosses provide the comrades with some interesting and valuable information. The talks with the German firms on the construction of the plant for thiodikligol production (raw material for yperite) in our country by the Germans that were held to help Glavchim have not been effective. The tentative sums mentioned by the firms are Goldschmit firm, 1,800,000 marks; Rom and Gaas firm, 800,000 marks—too high for a one-ton plant.

They had to refuse the first firm at once, the more so that it had agreed to do it on condition that the construction of the plant will be carried out in Germany and we could remove the plant to the Soviet Union after it had been constructed. The talks with the other firm have not yet been brought to an end, but there can hardly be expected satisfactory results. That is why our chemist Comrade Kartsev began simultaneous talks with a group of German chemists engaged in yperite production. Their proposal (now oral) gives a tentative sum of 300,000 marks, and a six-months' term (instead of the twelve months suggested by the above firms).

As soon as I receive official detailed proposals, I shall pass them on to Glavchim for discussion and making a decision. As a result of my trip, I have obtained the following secret information:

1. Secret material on production of various types of OV during the World War at plants of the largest industrial union—I.G.

2. A secret report with detailed information on OV and their admixtures, with physical and chemical constants, physiological effects, effects produced on metals, etc., used in the World War. This material is of special value, for it will save our laboratory work.

3. Description of the OV equipping procedure of projectiles and balloons.

4. Sixteen c/m gasolyte drawings.

5. Drawings of the dugout, its filter, and special construction of the "field filter" (trench flute).

6. Mist-protection ointment formula for gas masks.

7. Yperite-protection ointment formula for fabrics.

8. Proxylene cartridge.

9. Gopkalytre cartridges.

10. Drawings of the smoke-screen formation device from plane.

11. Drawings of OV pouring-out valve-devices for big planes.

12. Description of the device for yperite analysis.

Besides, the bosses promised to send the following materials in addition to the above ones (the list is forwarded to Comr. Kork):

(1) data on 16 c/m gas-projector; (2) a list of substances (several hundred) they tested during the World War in order to find[37] OV fit for using in battle with the testing results (extremely interesting); (3) a film *Gas-projector Firing*; (4) description of the sighting device for bombing and pouring out OV from altitudes.

Besides, the comrades have cleared up some technical and organizational questions and drawn up a plan of joint preliminary work to be performed in Tomsk this year.

*   *   *

A QUESTION OF NEW OV AND A TALK WITH BLOMBERG

At first all the Germans unanimously claimed (and Blomberg was the first to begin) that they do not have any new OV available and that if our comrades hoped to see something special, they would have to be disappointed. The answers to our questions if they had had any positive results in the research of new OV were schematic and seemed to be following certain instructions. While speaking, chief of the Reichswehr chemical testing department reached the point of regarding the work on new OV as completely useless. Professor Fluri, unlike the others, was more open, saying that "nobody will let real secrets out, but will keep them to themselves." Besides, it should be stressed that the Germans said in the most categoric way that it was impossible for our comrades to get acquainted with the research work of the I.G. plant laboratories; they were denied attendance at the process of proxilene production, to see pilot mask samples at "Auer" factory, to have a look at the drawings of the remote detonating fuse for aviachimbombs. As for the two latter units, they said they would be delivered to Tomka in spring. In the concluding talk after ordinary thanks for the material shown, our comrades told Blomberg that the valuable materials and instructions that they had received would be reflected in a detailed report to Moscow together with the information that in Germany no preliminary research works are performed, the fact being confirmed by their specialists. In reply, Blomberg referred to their foreign and domestic political difficulties preventing them from performing such work. Next day, during the talks with Com. Kork, the Germans said that they were depressed by our distrust and our suspicion of their concealing something from us. Saying that, he referred to our comrades and expressed his concern about the report to be made in Moscow by our comrades. . . .

To: Chief of the Military-Chemical Department YS RKKA
Fishman
ZGASA. F. 33987. Op. 3. F. 295. Sh. 13–15.
Original.

*   *   *

UBOREVICH'S LETTERS FROM GERMANY

Report on Stay in Germany (A)

June 18, 1926
Berlin

Dear Kliment Efremovich!

I am in receipt of your letter, which affords me the opportunity for observing our large-scale army maneuvers. I am very grateful to you for affording me this opportunity. It really means very much to me. Only after summing up the results of our army's demonstrating the extent of its battle preparedness at the maneuvers shall I be able to continue my work in the winter with wide open eyes. That is why I am so urgently asking you to authorize this trip of mine. On the Germans' part, as far as I can assess their attitude of mind, there will not be any suspicions. It cannot in any way hinder my principal work.

I am availing myself of the opportunity to inform you shortly of the work accomplished by me since 1 May, as well as of the program up to the end of August. During the past period I have gone on the following four official trips:

1. *April 30–May 8*—the Sixth Artillery Regiment. Acquaintance with battle training and firing exercises of the Reichswehr artillery. In this trip I was partly accompanied by Comrade Triandofilov, who must have already reported to you the fact.

2. *May 9–May 24*—a field trip through the third divisional military district. The scale of the trip: several infantry and cavalry divisions on both sides.[38] Participants—General Staff officers as well as several well-attested company and battalion commanders.

3. *May 30–June 10.* A field trip connected with General Staff officers' and "Gruppen Romm II" Services Chiefs' rear service duties. The trip was of most interest to us, for we were admitted to such kinds of exercises for the first time. Now questions of preparation of rear services became more or less clear to us.

4. *June 10–June 16.* A field trip directed at selection of instructors of tactics. Rather a lively and engaging trip, consisting in choosing from among well-attested officers the best ones having an evident inclination

for teaching. Besides, many questions relating to tactics (battalion and regiment) got at it in proper amount of detail.

All field trips were effected in cars with a heavy daily load. The trips were of undoubted benefit to me. The forthcoming expected work is as follows:

June—eight days—an official trip to *field engineer (sapper) exercises* in Ingoldstadt. Questions of river-crossing means and other questions of sapper service will be considered.

July—*getting an acquaintance with infantry training*—with attachment to the Fourth Infantry Regiment. A field trip on the lines of the AAD (Fifth Division). I am paying special attention to this trip, for I have for a long time—since the very moment of my learning of such exercises being conducted—strived for getting admission to them.

August—*acquaintance with cavalry training.* The Fourteenth and Seventeenth Cavalry Regiments. Maneuvers of intercommunication radio units and of four (Fifth, Sixth, Seventh, and Ninth Cavalry) divisions. Besides, I have asked for my being admitted to anti-aircraft firing exercises. Organized by Germany's Marine Force Department, they are being kept a strict secret. I am earnestly requesting you for Comrade Berzin's starting negotiations with the Germans in Moscow in your name concerning desirability of my being admitted to these exercises. My general view in this respect is that the Germans, even though deprived of the right to have a navy, have scored big successes in this sphere.

September—so far not finally settled. The German army's large-scale maneuvers are expected to start on September 21. General disposition of people here toward me is quite good. However I myself am always feeling much better when visiting military units than when contacting Ministry of Defense officials. On this I am finishing my rather long letter.

I am wishing you good health and every success in work.

My best regards to An. Serg., Joseph Stan., S.S., and Sem. Mikh.

> Uborevich
> TsGASA. F. 33987. Op. 3. D. 151. L. 3.
> Handwritten original.

*   *   *

Report on Stay in Germany (B)[39]

> January 13, 1929
> Berlin
> Strictly confidential

In addition to all the materials sent by me from Germany as current work, I think it expedient to summarize briefly the entire work accomplished by me during my stay here, chiefly in relation to the following questions:

(1) Reichswehr's technical development level; (2) political and military role of Reichswehr; (3) Reichswehr's relations with us; (4) appraisal of the Polish army and its strategic-mobilization potentials.

The results of my thirteen months' stay in Germany can be reduced to work in the following periods:

1. Winter period—Military Academy (third year), military schools, multifaceted examination of specific questions with Reichswehr specialists' aid; military exercises.

2. Summer period—four field trips: the first—an operational-tactical trip, organized by the General Staff; the second—an aviation trip; the third—a trip relating to rear supply services; and the fourth one—devoted to choice of instructors of tactics.

3. The next period—my stay in units of various arms of the service, artillery, infantry, cavalry, sapper-pontoon units, intercommunication units, anti-aircraft artillery exercises; and the conclusive period—attending four Reichswehr maneuvers (Fifteenth Regiment's maneuvers, maneuvers of the reinforced second and third divisions, and all-out manuevers).

As a task to be achieved in all these seasonal periods, I put not only personal perfection in certain questions, but also general acquaintance with the Germans' strategic, tactical, organizational, and technical views on the present-day army, methods of training troops, and basic principles of the German General Staff's structure and operation.

My working load has been rather big, so that I have spent seven and a half months on trips, and, therefore, I have not been able to systematize a part of the material gathered during them.

The methods of tactical training of troops appear to have been sufficiently studied by us. In this relation the Reichswehr has invariably met us halfway. It is quite different with the question of techniques, in which the Germans have been trying to hush up or give only incomplete information on the major part of their achievements.

When considering the military-technical level of the Reichswehr, or, to put it more accurately, of Germany, one ought to clearly delimit two questions:

first, officially existing armaments of the Reichswehr, which is barred by the Versailles Treaty from having aviation, heavy artillery, chemical means of warfare, tanks, etc.;

second, the items of military equipment and armaments, which have of late been created in laboratories and plants and tested (as far as possible in secret) by the Germans.

I am quite certain that for the thirteen months of my stay in Germany I have succeeded in discovering only a part of what the Germans have got by now. The general orientation of this military-technical designing activity of the Germans is apparently as follows:

(a) developing perfected specimens; (b) preparing industry for quick manufacture of such; (c) secret testing of the models in the Reichswehr units while simultaneously giving training in handling them to a part of the officers and soldiers; (d) a wide-scale use of foreign experience by manufacture of a number of arms and specimens abroad, in plants and works (which are actually German enterprises) in Sweden, Holland, and Spain. . . . I have at my disposal a good number of facts—officers' statements—showing that German officers had long-time access in America to studying chemical means of warfare in the Edgive [Edgewood] Arsenal (1927), to studying the latest tank models in the autumn of 1928, and to studying all military institutions of America during General Heye's official trip to this country in the autumn of 1927.

Therefore, one can't but state that the achievements of American military techniques are greatly accessible to the Reichswehr.

Another source of foreign experience is England, where German officers have access to tank and air force maneuvers. Good relations in questions of military techniques are also maintained by the Germans with Czechoslovakia. Of the character of work targets set before Germany's own industry, receiving significant subsidies for conducting all kinds of military experiments, one can judge, for instance, by the following statement of General Ludwig, managing the armament questions in the Reichswehr: in 1914 manufacture of a field gun, including preparation of working drawings, used to take nine months, whereas now they are striving for accomplishing the gun's manufacture within six weeks, this term not at all being a fantasy.

. . . One more observation on the general nature of Germany's military-technical work. It is striving for creating new, highly effective means of warfare, greatly exceeding those existing at present, and especially for properly training the army and imparting to the armaments a defensive nature, capable of withstanding the most powerful technique of the potential enemy (aircrafts, tanks, poison gases, etc.).

1. *Anti-aircraft gun.* The Germans have given me all the ballistic characterstics of this gun, covering 16 specific features of the design. . . . The gun's caliber is about 3 inches (7.5 cm), the initial speed— 88 meters a second. I am especially calling your attention to the height limit—height of firing—reaching 9.5 km, which twice exceeds that of our present-day anti-aircraft guns; range—16 km, which also twice exceeds the range of our guns. . . .

The gun has been manufactured at the "Rhein-Metall-Fabrik" in Düsseldorf. The firm is willing to offer us cooperation in organizing production of such guns in our country.

2. . . . *Device for anti-aircraft firing* by Prof. Pschor, manufactured by the "Siemens and Zeiss" Firm. . . . The device can be regarded as the last word in the technical progress in this field.

The device automatically defines the distance to the aircraft, the angle at which it is flying, the direction of the flight, and the speed (aircraft speeds now vary from 150–300 km).

I was present at five exercise firings with the aid of this device at the target, carried in the sky by an aircraft, and the results were surprisingly good. The Germans' general objective in employing anti-aircraft guns against the flying enemy squadron is such as to ensure hitting on the very first shot.

By all signs, this device and the new anti-aircraft gun, described above, will be greatly conducive to solving this problem. Despite all my efforts to find out to what extent the Germans are ready to render us assistance in arranging production of such a device, I failed to obtain a positive answer. . . .

Of course, I know of our inventors' works in this field at the works of weak electric currents in Leningrad and those of IGNATYEV, but I simply ought to stress here that in the Germans' case we have almost finished specimens, whereas our comrades' works will hardly be finished earlier than in 1.5–2 years, with their efficiency meanwhile remaining absolutely uncertain.

3. *Small-caliber field gun* to be engaged simultaneously against aircrafts and tanks.

Ballistic characteristics of an anti-aircraft machine gun, engaged against tanks: pierces the armor of over 20 mm thickness, i.e., that of all light and average tanks; its height limit—4200 m and maximum range—61.5 km. One should always have these ballistic data of the 2-cm machine gun at easy reach for comparing them with those of our heavy machine guns, with the aid of which we are going to fight against the enemy aircrafts in infantry units up to the size of a division. Our machine gun's height-limit of effective operation just slightly exceeds 1 km, whereas that of the German machine gun is four times more—4 km 200 m. . . . Against tanks our machine guns are practically useless. In addition to aforesaid anti-tank measures, I should like to mention an anti-tank mine, at which the Germans have also been working for a number of years and the mechanism of which they showed to me and Triandofilov in spring, and to our other comrades in autumn. . . . The mine produces such a bursting effect on a tank that it is rendered immobile.

The role of anti-tank mines for defense of fortified sectors in strategically important directions will apparently be rather signficant (Leningrad).

4. *Average mortar.* Its range has been increased to 4 km, a steel shield has been added for protection of the crew; the change from the marching order to the firing one takes as little time as in the case of an ordinary field gun. . . . I must note the exclusive accuracy of mortar firing. . . . The Germans' intention to use average mortars in their army is quite understandable, since they cannot count on immediately having at their disposal heavy artillery in great quantity because of it having been forbidden to them. Our position in this respect, in view of our poverty and the general backwardness of our heavy artillery, rather resembles that of the Germans, and average mortars might, therefore, prove to us very useful, especially if one takes into consideration the fact that in case of war we are quite likely to have before us very strong fortifications with barbed wire, trenches, and dugouts on the side of Poles.

5. Some special features of the organization of the infantry—ours and German:

(a) In respect to rifles there is no great difference, and our rifle can be regarded as sufficiently modern. . . . However, each fifth or eighth German rifleman, according to commanders' reckoning, will have on his rifle a telescopic sight, significantly improving his firing accuracy. Equipping our rifles with telescopic sights requires improvement of the steel the rifle's barrel is manufactured of.

Light machine guns. . . . Our light machine gun is quite competitive with its German counterpart of Dreise's design, but Germans are adjusting telescopic sights, improving accuracy of firing, even in light machine guns. As regards heavy machine guns, constituting the major part of infantry's armament, our backwardness in this sphere is rather great. German heavy machine guns are equipped with devices for thirty-second switch-over to firing at air targets. In our army even divisions have not got devices for a thirty-second switch-over to firing at air targets.

Yes, in our army even divisions have not got such devices. German machine guns, equipped with telescopic sights, ensuring fairly accurate firing up to 2.5 km, . . . have also got goniometers and range finders for firing from shielded positions. . . . My résumé is as follows: we ought not to grudge expenses for equipping infantry's armaments with telescopic sights, for they will surely be repaid by better results in battle and greater economy of cartridges; and, second, we ought to improve our heavy machine guns to the standard such machine guns have reached in the German army.

6. *Field artillery.* As regards 3-in field guns and howitzers, there is no essential difference, excepting the circumstance that Germans have almost entirely abandoned using shrapnel in view of its high cost and uncertainty of effect and have switched over to high-explosive shells.

. . . Of fairly great interest is the view on further development of field artillery of General Ludwig, chief of all the Reichswehr's armaments. He considers field guns and howitzers of now-existing types to be far from perfect and their large-scale production without first modernizing them to be hardly expedient. According to him, especially inadequate is the gun-carriage system, hampering field guns' carrying on effective all-round fire at tanks. . . .

Germans are assiduously working at the manfacture of some improved specimens of heavy artillery. I have not succeeded in obtaining detailed information, but the "Rhein-Metall-Fabrik" Firm, in the person of its designer General Schirmer, assured us that in this field they were ready to share with us some of their achievements.

The Reichswehr's Political and Military Role

The Reichswehr was formed of volunteer corps and army divisions that remained after demobilization and were for a number of years engaged in suppression of revolutionary movement in Germany. The Reichswehr deserves our attention for many reasons: first, from the viewpoint of its adaptation for maintenance of internal order of Germany; second, to the extent Germans have succeeded in perfecting the Reichswehr in order to adjust it—under the highly unfavorable conditions of the Versailles Treaty—for solving the problems of Germany's foreign policy . . . ; and, third, how useful contacts with the Reichswehr and acquaintance with its activity can be for improving the training of the Red Army. The Reichswehr's strength is fixed and includes about 4,000 officers, 20,000 noncommissioned officers, 75,000 rank-and-file soldiers, who, together with officials, make a 100,000-man army, divided into 7 infantry and 3 cavalry divisions. The Reichswehr is a regular army with long terms of service (12 years for privates and noncommissioned officers and a minimum of 25 years for officers).

. . . Judging by the views of General Seeckt, who remains up to now a main ideologist of the Reichswehr (see his book *Gedanken eines Soldaten* [Thoughts of a soldier]), General Blomberg's speeches during a number of field trips, Defense Minister Grener's speech at large-scale maneuvers, and the talk with Organization-Mobilization Department Chief Mittelberger, the Germans' organizational-strategic outlooks in regard to their armed forces are roughly reducible to the following propositions:

1. For a number of years to come the Reichswehr will remain a small, professional peacetime army.

2. In Germany one sees an impressive upgrowth of industry and of technical achievements, opening great prospects for creation of the newest up-to-date means of warfare.

3. In Germany there are strong half-military political class organizations (Steel Helmet, Republicans, and Rote Front).

4. The presence at Germany's borders of much more numerous armies of potential enemies (France, Poland, Czechoslovakia) . . . having huge advantages in the period of war. . . .

The Reichswehr leaders' activity consists in work with industry officials at testing grounds, in lecture halls, and most of all, in issuing secret instructions. The whole of the Reichswehr's army training at military exercises and tactics lessons is being carried on not only within the limits of organizational measures imposed on Germany by the Versailles Treaty, but most frequently with an orientation toward organization of a modern army, regarding which they have got their own views and intentions. . . .

Soldiers' average level of literacy is as follows: 10 percent of them have secondary education . . . , 40–50 percent of them come from workers, 35–40 percent—from peasants. . . . The Reichswehr's major soldier mass politically stands more to the right than social-democracy, in a number of cases tending toward German nationalism.

Material conditions of soldiers are rather good. . . . As regards the prestige of a Reichswehr soldier, it is also high—thanks to a number of measures taken in the country to improve it.

. . . In their relations with soldiers officers are invariably polite, quiet, cool, and very persistent, and in general quietness, politeness, equanimity, and persistence are considered to be the best qualities of any commander. Some extent of impulsiveness is notable only in Bavarian units, where officers sometimes permit themselves to shout somewhat rudely during lessons. The German army's officer corps—about 4,000 officers—represents an exceptionally interesting group of military specialists. . . . Officers' political orientation—this is more right, significantly more right than social-democracy. The majority of officers is for firm bourgeois dictatorship, for fascism. . . . Very popular among them are Hindenburg, Seeckt, and—as a clever diplomat in foreign policy— Stresemann. The officers' attitude toward social-democracy is in the main hostile. It should be noted that the most reactionary-minded is the navy, which, however, I have not succeeded in visiting. . . .

The most influential group of the Ministry of Defense—and, namely: Grener, Heye, Blomberg, Schleicher, Stühlnagel, etc.—are on the whole continuing Seeckt's policy on Seeckt's and Gessler's resignation. They consider themselves to be the continuers of the best traditions of the German general staff of the World War years.

The Reichswehr, as it is at present, if it proves impossible to find ways to demoralize it, represents a serious force, capable of suppressing leftist movements and even Germany's parliamentary system. . . .

The Reichswehr from the viewpoint of foreign policy. . . .

1. The possibility of revenge, of grappling in the near future with France and cancelling the Versailles Treaty by force of arms—almost

nobody speaks of it in earnest as if it were tomorrow's task. On the other hand, high officials hold very little belief in the possibility of close, peaceful rapprochement with France.

2. The prevailing opinion is that the Versailles Treaty knots can be cut best of all by force of arms in a new war, and it is necessary to make proper preparations for it. . . .

France's policy, aimed at rendering Germany unarmed, apparently has not been a full success.

The Reichswehr's influence on industry seems to be extraordinarily great. As is generally known, the Reichswehr has been forbidden to carry on any mobilization work in regard to manpower as well as technology and industry; but my conversations with a number of officers show that such work is being intensively carried on and there are signs of a transition to a big army. . . .

Heinkel's fighter aircraft, Rohrbach's bombers, or Junkers' aircraft, adjusted for night bomb-dropping—all these show that as regards aviation, Germany now is not an unarmed country. . . .

Chemical means of warfare have been forbidden to the Germans, but nobody in the world now doubts that they are doing comprehensive work in this sphere, and, judging by their repeated statements, it is in it that the greatest surprises can be expected. Germans are building in their country both light and heavy tanks, making use of all the newest achievements in technology.

General conclusions on the Reichswehr from the viewpoint of Germany's imperialist policy can be reduced to the following:

1. The Reichswehr is beyond any doubt seeking ways of transition to a big army capable of waging an external war.

2. Germany's rich industry is being systematically made ready for this purpose.

3. The public mood is being cultivated in the sense that the possibility of revocation of the Versailles Treaty by force of arms is not excluded.

4. Belief in peaceful rapprochement with France is very meager.

5. At present they do not speak in Germany of taking revenge immediately, considering conditions to be still inopportune and premature for it.

. . . Talks with some prominent Reichswehr officials show at the same time that settlement of the eastern question cannot be reached before that of the western one, because settlement of the western question is to be looked for in Germany's relations with England and France. In other words, more clear to us, it means that settlement of the eastern border question is being shifted to a later time or until the moment of Poland's having serious complications in its relations with us. . . .

Concluding my report, I would like to sum up our relations with the Reichswehr as they appear to me from my detached viewpoint. First of all I wish to dwell on the spring of 1928—the time of Grener's and, as a result of it, the right Social-Democratic government's accession to power. This period was, in my opinion, the worst one in our relations, and, judging by statements of certain persons, made subsequently in conversation with me, most people thought that Grener would stop our joint work. General Blomberg's group, which came to our country for the purpose of attending maneuvers and inspecting joint enterprises, came as a matter of fact on a check-up visit, undertaken with a view to decide to what extent our cooperation could be further expanded. Blomberg's group returned to Germany with a *very favorable impression of our country, of the reception given to them,* and on the whole gave a positive appraisal of the Red Army's growth as an important international factor in the future war; but at the same time Blomberg's group *found the condition of a number of their enterprises unsatisfactory,* putting the blame for it on the lack of skill of the enterprises' chiefs, appointed by the Germans, and on some of our representatives' hampering of the work. Most complaints concerned Comrade Fishman. Of three enterprises inspected by them, they gave praise to the aviation group, but remained dissatisfied with chemical experiments as inadequately organized and with the tank-development depot as being only at the stage of starting work.

Subsequently the Germans came to a conclusion about the necessity of developing these enterprises and procuring additional financial means for this purpose, although—it ought to be noted—the state of the Reichswehr's budget is extremely strained. As I came to know, Blomberg had succeeded in obtaining money for expanding chemical experiments with great—up to a scandal—difficulty.

The Germans regard their affording the opportunity to many of our comrades for coming to Germany in order to attend maneuvers, to go on field trips, and to stay in Reichswehr units for a long time as a very good service rendered to us. I think that in the near future they are going to ask for a similar favor from our part, that is, for our inviting several of their representatives to come to our country for a long-term stay.

My opinion on this question is as follows: the general state of our foreign relations and cooperation is such that Germany affords to us the only opportunity for studying military achievements abroad, and that through cooperation with the army, which has attained highly interesting achievements in a good number of fields. . . . As a result of my stay in Germany, I have succeeded in getting acquainted with the methods of training of General Staff officers, methods of organization of field trips, of training troops through arrangement of maneuvers—in short, with all principal questions of formation and training of a peacetime army. In this relation it ought to be stated that we have already gained much useful learning and know-how, but there still remains plenty of work to be done in our country to go over to more adequate methods of the army's battle training. . . . Now we must focus our attention on making use of the Germans' technical achievements, and that, chiefly, in the sense of our learning to produce in our country, as well as to operate and apply, the latest means of warfare: tanks, improved models of aircrafts, anti-aircraft and anti-tank artillery, mortars, anti-tank mines, intercommunication means, etc. . . .

Reichswehr representatives Beschnit and Ludwig, in reply to my statement on the technical assistance question, suggested that it would be good to consider questions separately one by one, and, in particular, raised a question as to the possibility of organization for them in our country of testings of a number of interesting achievements, which they found it difficult to carry on in Germany. I answered that it apparently might be of benefit to both sides. . . . German specialists, *including military specialists, stand immeasurably higher than ours.* I believe, we must buy these specialists' services, cleverly win them over to our side, in order to catch up promptly on what we are lagging behind. I do not think that German specialists might prove politically worse and more dangerous than our Russian specialists, and, in any case, there is much to be learned from them, with the price being hardly higher on the whole.

> Uborevich
> TsGASA. F. 33987. Op. 3. D. 295. L. 141–83.
> Original.

*   *   *

UBOREVICH: "THE REICHSWEHR IS PRESENTLY STANDING AT THE CRITICAL TURNING POINT . . ."

. . . It is necessary to say in a direct way that to all appearances the interest for the Red Army was not very high until the autumn of 1927; at present the breakthrough is becoming apparent in this sense. . . . To the known extent the Reichswehr is presently standing at the critical turning point in its relationship with us. The direction in which these relations will develop partly depends on us. . . . The administrative staff of the Reichswehr (Grener, Heye, Blomberg) put forward the proposals to strengthen further our relations and to expand the cooperation between both countries. . . .

> Uborevich
> TsGASA. F. 33987. Op. 3. D. 329. Pp. 1–145.
> Original.

*   *   *

FROM EIDEMAN TO VOROSHILOV

> February 11, 1927
> Absolutely confidential

The Report

Here I present the copy of the report of Comrades Krasilnikov and Svechnikov, the lectures of the Academy, that were entrusted to me, about the impressions of the attitude of the administrative circles of the Reichswehr to the Soviet Union, these impressions were received during their official visit to Germany.

The appendix: the above mentioned.

> Eideman,[40] the head of the Academy.

*   *   *

TO COMRADE EIDEMAN, THE HEAD OF THE
MILITARY ACADEMY OF THE RKKA

The Copy

Absolutely confidential
To his own hands

(Impressions of the attitudes of the administrative circles of the Reichswehr toward Soviet Russia.)

From the impressions received by us and private talks with individual
representatives of the General Staff who are close to the political life
of Germany, it is possible to conclude that the Reichswehr, in general,
and the General Staff, in particular, take an extremely negative attitude
toward the existing social and parliamentary system led by the Social-
Democratic party. The governmental crises and inner-party struggle are
painfully echoed in the administrative circles of the Reichswehr. The
pacifism naturally meets the most negative attitude in these circles. The
whole number of facts that humiliate the dignity of Germany and come
from part of the allied commission kindle more chauvinistic attitudes
of mind, not only within the Reichswehr, but also among the wide
petty-bourgeois sections.

The inevitability of revenge is obvious. There is a draught in everything pointing out that revenge became a dream of the General Staff,
meeting support from the extreme right-wing fascist groups in Germany.
It is believed that the necessary precondition for successfully conducting
a war is the establishment of the dictatorship and bringing the parliamentary system to naught. However, it is necessary to make the reservation that the monarchic idea had gained a relatively limited number
of supporters. Therefore, it is possible that the reaction will not be oriented
toward monarchy, but it will be directed toward the fascist system.

The military circles perfectly realize the impossibility of a single
combat with France at this moment, having Poland and Czechoslovakia
at the home front. Therefore, these circles are anxious about searching
for respectful allies, the support of which could render definite assistance
or, as a last resort, neutralize the eastern states in case of war and
by this action give Germany the time required for industrial mobilization
and the deployment of a massive army, about the scale of which one

may judge, taking into account the results of operative games of the General Staff (in the last game, 165 infantry divisions and 2 air-force divisions took part). The bloc with France and the gradual overcoming of chauvinistic feeling toward France on the part of military men and right-wing political circles are hardly probable, especially while humiliating conditions of the Versailles treaty exist. The hate of military circles in France is extremely sharp. The (tactical) studies within the General Staff and in the Academy demonstrate that the army is making preparations for a war with France and Poland.

The bloc with England meets a lot of obstacles, first of all, because England supports and can't help supporting Poland in its anti-Russian policy, the hostility to which is extremely sharp in Germany, particularly in the military and right-wing circles. Second, the military support of England on the continent isn't highly assessed, especially during the first phase of war, very severe for Germany. Finally, the proximity of England and France in a political respect is a restraining factor in relations with England.

Italy, which is a military ally, does not satisfy the German General Staff at all for reasons of purely geographical character and partly because of the Austrian problem.[41]

Therefore, because of the circumstances, the German General Staff, according to our observations, sees the only effective force, capable to give growth to its military power, as friendly relations with the Soviet Republic. The presence of the common enemy, Poland—dangerous for Germany because of the geographical conditions—pushes the German General Staff farther on a way of close rapprochement with Soviet Russia. The middle circles of officers of the General Staff who are on the active list in the Reichswehr of the Ministry do not conceal their hostile attitude to France and Poland and their sincere sympathy with the Red Army. The latter was manifested from the side of the representatives of the Reichswehr during a period of our official journey.

First, the attitude toward us was restrained and polite. The subsequent joint work, with our active participation, gave us an opportunity to observe the gradual manifestation of sympathies and friendly attitudes on the part of literally all the officials surrounding us, not only in Berlin itself, in the Reichswehr of the Ministry, but also in local areas (in Dresden, in the infantry school, and in Munich in the staff of the infantry division and in the Pioneer school[42]). We watched their intentions to demonstrate to us as much as possible and to give us an opportunity not only to learn methods of training of officers' corps, but also to receive comprehensive materials of a factual character. At the farewell audience, the head of the General Staff General Wetzel, and the commander of the Reichswehr General Gal, as well as the leaders of tactical training of the third-year students and the officers of the General Staff, expressed especially benevolent attitudes toward us, the representatives of Soviet Russia. Short speeches made during these audiences and the farewell banquet were devoted to good wishes and hopes for further rapproachment, to mutual studies of both armies and, hence, to relations between Germany and Soviet Russia.

In conclusion, it is necessary to note that though sharp hesitations are possible in the foreign policy of the German government, inside the Reichswehr, particularly in the General Staff, friendly feelings, conditioned by a hope of military support coming from our side, may be saved for a long period of time, and the administrative circles of the General Staff may be used in the purpose of exerting pressure on the government in favor of Soviet Russia.

> Svechnikov
> Krasilnikov
> TsGASA. F. 33987. Op. 3. D. 148. Pp. 76–78.
> Attested copy.[43]

*   *   *

FROM BERZIN TO VOROSHILOV:
"I WOULD CONSIDER IT EXPEDIENT TO CONTINUE
THE PRACTICE OF EXCHANGE OF COMMANDERS . . ."

> 1928
> Absolutely confidential

[The commemorative paper devoted to the problem of exchange of the commanders of the RKKA and the Reichswehr.]

1. The Lit has announced that at the beginning of March the Reichswehr has the intention to send on an official journey Colonel Mittelberg[er] (the closest assistant to the head of the Reichswehr on Russian

problems Heye) to the USSR to make acquaintance with German institutions in the USSR (the pilot school in Lipetsk and the tank school in Kazan) and with the training institutions of the RKKA, including the military Academy and some military units. . . .

It is possible to demonstrate to Mittelberg[er] the following schools and units in Moscow: the Military Academy, the Moscow Artillery school, the TsIK[44] school, and probably "Vystrel"[45]—if he will insist—as well as the first regiment of the proletarian division.

2. The question of sending the commanders of the RKKA and the officers of the Reichswehr to maneuvers and tactical schools was raised by us (by me under the order of Comrade Tukhachevsky) and by the Germans.

Last year we participated in[46] the field journeys, tactical studies, and maneuvers of the Reichswehr. The group included the following comrades.

In the field journeys

1. Feldman—L.V.O.[47]
2. Zhuev—first department of the staff of the RKKA.
3. Bobrov—M.V.O.[48]

In maneuvers and tactical studies

1. Fedko—the head of the district's staff
2. Triandafil(l)ov—the head of the department of the staff of the RKKA.
3. Dubovoy—the commander of the corps.
4. Batorsky—the head of the staff of the cavalry corps.
5. Kuibishev[49]—the head of the department of the staff of the RKKA. . . .
6. Nechajev—the commander of the artillery regiment.
7. Gigur—the assistant to the chief of the department of the RKKA's staff.

Totally, 11 men.

In addition to the above-mentioned number we sent comrades Uborevich, Eideman, and Appog on an official journey. Consequently, in 1927 we sent 14 persons totally on an official journey to Germany.

Germans sent the following officers on a mission in 1927.

1. Lieutenant-Colonel Smolke
2. Major Krato
3. Colonel Galm
4. Major Fischer

5. Colonel Müller

6. Major Hot

I would consider it expedient to continue a practice of exchange of commanders this year to such an extent that took place in 1927. This problem must be solved yet again in order to select candidates and, accordingly, to prepare them in relation to the language and to the organization and tactics of the Reichswehr.

> The head of the fourth department of the RKKA's staff
> Berzin
> TsGASA. F. 33987. Op. 3. D. 87. P. 125.
> Original. Printed in three copies.

*   *   *

FROM VOROSHILOV TO STALIN

> December 28, 1928
> Absolutely confidential

I ask you to raise the following questions at the next Politburo session:

1. About the arrival in the USSR of Colonel Mittelberger, the closest assistant of General Heye, the head of the Reichswehr's department on Russian issues.

2. About the reciprocal official journey of the commanders of the RKKA and the Reichswehr to Germany and to the Soviet Union for participation in military trainings and maneuvers in 1928.

As to the essence of these questions, I make the following report.

The Reichswehr wishes to send Colonel Mittelberger on a mission to the USSR for making an acquaintance with the German institutions that we have in Lipetsk and Kazan and with some training institutions of the RKKA.

I believe that because the Germans gave the respective workers of the RKKA, Comrades Uborevich, Eideman, Appog, an opportunity to arrive in Germany for training, we have no formal cause not to satisfy the desire of the German commanders.

The question about the reciprocal exchange of the commanders in order to organize their participation in the field training and the maneuvers of the RKKA and the Reichswehr was simultaneously raised by us and the Germans. Last year's experience (on our maneuvers and tactical trainings seven officers of the Reichswehr took part, and for the same purpose we sent eleven commanders of the RKKA on a mission to Germany) gave the RKKA very valuable results.

I would consider it expedient to organize a reciprocal journey of commanders this year at the level of 1927.

> With communist regards.
> Voroshilov
> TsGASA. F. 33987. Op. 3. D. 87. P. 123.
> Original.

*   *   *

TO THE POLITBURO OF THE TsK OF THE VKP (b),
TO COMRADE STALIN

> March 1929
> Strictly confidential

I ask that the following questions be raised at the Politburo for discussions.

1. This year the Germans will invite eight of our commanders plus three comrades to the summer training and maneuvers of the Reichswehr. These men are to be from those who are now in Germany.

Simultaneously the Germans ask for permission to send to the maneuvers of the RKKA the same number (8 men) of their officers and, in addition, 4 officers including inspectors of the engineering corps of the RW, who will be present at the field trainings of the RKKA for a month.

The official journey of the workers of the RKKA to Germany made last year gave very positive results. Having this in mind I consider it necessary to accept the proposal of the Germans.

We nominate the following comrades to the official journey this year:

1. Comrade Yakir, the commander of the UVO.[50]
2. Comrade Zomberg, the commander of the VI corps.[51]
3. Comrade Stepanov, the head of the department of the RKKA's staff.

(They are now in Germany.)

4. Comrade Egorov A.I., the commander of BVO.[52]

5. Comrade Danenberg—the commander of division "24."[53]

6. Comrade Katkov—the commander of the 40th regiment.

7. Comrade Ventsov S.I.—the commander of the 15th regiment.

8. Comrade Kalmykov—the commander of the 1st corps.[54]

9. Comrade Mezheninov S.A.—the assistant of the head of the UVVS.[55]

10. Comrade Fedotov—the head of the First Leningrad Artillery school.

11. Comrade Rosynko—the head of the Artillery of the MVO.[56]

The above-mentioned comrades, excluding comrades of the VKP (b). . . .

> Voroshilov.
> TsGASA. F. 33987. Op. 3. D. 295. P. 50.
> Original.

* * *

REPORT NO. 11: FROM KORK TO VOROSHILOV

April 8, 1929
Strictly confidential

1. The summer working of our commanders in Germany.

I have failed to obtain comprehensive information about forthcoming work this summer. The information that I had an opportunity to obtain in the Ministry is probably known to you, because last week that information was conveyed from the Ministry to Moscow to Niedermeier, who certainly has transmitted it to the fourth department.

The Germans ask us to send a new group of commanders on a mission here by 10 June. Comrades Latsis and Longva's departure from here is arranged for 8 June.

In a general way the plan of work during the summer months looks like the following.

On 15 May the work will come to the end at the third year of the Academy. Up to 8 June our commanders will be given an opportunity to observe the combat training of the cavalry and infantry, and comrades Latsis and Longva will also watch artillery. These trainings are planned to take place on training fields: the fourteenth and seventeenth cavalry regiments on the Königsbrück training field at a distance of 30 km to the northeast from Dresden, and the fourteenth infantry regiment on the Altengrabow training field at a distance of 35 km to the northeast of Magdeburg. Comrades Latsis and Longva, in addition, visited the third division of the third artillery regiment (I do not know yet when the trainings of the division will take place). The group (5 men) will be divided into two parts (3 and 2 men) as the Germans consider the joint traveling of all the group to be undesirable, having fear that it will be noticeable for the strangers; for our commanders this partition is comfortable too, because it is easier for a small group to gain understanding of all the questions and to get all the explanations.

Since 10 June we'll begin joint work with 8–10 commanders (11 men totally) who are expected to come here. The Germans consider it is necessary to divide our commanders into groups consisting of 3–4 men. Comrade Yakir has a desire to continue working with his group (Yakir, Somberg, Stepanov). Consequently, comrades who are sent to the official journey will be divided into 2 groups consisting of 4 men each. It is necessary to do it in Moscow. I must report that the desires of our comrades to pass from one group to another in a process of work provoked Germans' objections. (Germans must report in advance to the local authorities about names of our commanders and the time of their staying in every place, and they do not want to make corrections later.) The above three groups will visit the training fields from 10 June to the end of July.

In June the training of the thirteenth infantry regiment is to take place in Münzingen.

In Württemberg, at a distance of 40 km to the west from Ulm, the trainings of the seventh and tenth Caucasian regiments, and in Königsbrück in Saxsony at a distance of 30 km to the northeast from Dresden; and the trainings of the second field-engineer battalion in Klausdorf at a distance of 40 km to the south from Berlin; in July the training of the fourth artillery regiment in Jüteborg at a distance of 70 km to the southwest from Berlin, the second artillery regiment in Königsbrück, and the trainings of the eleventh and twelfth cavalry regiments in Neuhammer in Silesia at a distance of 60 km to the northwest from Liegnitz will take place.

In August the following training is to be conducted in the presence of our commanders.

a. The tactical training of the twelfth infantry regiment in Königsbrück.

b. The fortification trainings of field-engineer units of the first group of troops of the Reichswehr.

c. From 10 to 25 August trainings of the radiotechnical units of the Reichswehr and the first combat group.

d. From 27 August to 4 September the training of field-engineer units in connection with construction of bridges on the Elba and Weser rivers.

Three or four of our commanders are invited to take part in each of these four training courses. In September the Germans intend to conduct:

a. The tactical training course of the seventeenth and nineteenth infantry regiments in motorized formations of the second group of troops. They invited four or five of our commanders to Germany.

b. The autumn tactical training course (small maneuvers) of the first infantry division in eastern Prussia with invitations sent to three or four of our commanders. The maneuvers are planned to last for four days, from 11 to 14 September inclusive.

c. The great maneuvers of troops of the second group of the Reichswehr, the time of the maneuvers is arranged from 16 to 21 September; the area of the maneuvers is selected near Württemberg; only two or three of our commanders, including the military attaché, are invited to these maneuvers. The Germans explain such a limitation by the fact that these maneuvers will be observed by military attachés from other countries.

Besides all that, three of four of our commanders (including Jakir) are invited to take part in journeys: journey devoted to PO defense,[57] journey for studying the rear service (supplies), field journey to the sixth division (with the means of communication), and visit to a district field journey. The time and place of these journeys are not reported to me yet.

More detailed information is not at my disposal yet. I am going to speed up the reception of the information, but I'll hardly manage to get anything new earlier than in two weeks.

2. In the Ministry I reminded them of the guns ordered from Boffors two times in the week past. Beshnit, as before, claimed in a talk on

3 April about political difficulties for the Reichswehr connected with participation in speeding up the solution of the problem, and because the Germans already had time to receive a dispatch from Gerstenberg about our refusal to conclude a fictitious agreement concerning an order for tanks, Beshnit, as might have been expected, stated: "It is more difficult for Germany to receive guns ordered by the Red Army from Sweden, than for the USSR to conclude a fictitious agreement with the German company providing an order of tanks." In the meanwhile on 6 April I was informed in the Ministry that Blomberg, as before, gave assurances that he was ready to do his best in order to help us in receiving guns and that, in connection with this, on 8 April, General Ludwig is going to conduct negotiations with me apropos the ordered guns. The essence of these negotiations will be described in a supplement to this report.

3. About a shipment of tanks. On 3 April I made an announcement to Beshnit that we encountered insurmountable difficulties connected with the conclusion of a fictitious agreement with a German company concerning an order of tanks. Our military department has not yet got the consent of the government to conclude the agreement. We ask Beshnit to report to Blomberg about the problem. It appeared that our refusal is already known from Gerstenberg's report. The further discussion of this problem did not take place. Having an intention to make it clear whenever Germans, nevertheless, plan to ship tanks, I received the former reply from Beshnit; they are going to begin a shipment of tanks when the navigation starts, i.e., when the Leningrad port opens.

4. Our chemists under the leadership of Comrade Robinson have carried on negotiations about production of yperite, trying to obtain equipment to produce yperite using Mayer's method. The negotiations came to nothing because of the high cost of the equipment. Now with the assistance of the Ministry and through this ministry Golzern-Grimme Company has sent a proposal about selling us a third stage of the system of yperite production. I ask you to issue an instruction about studying the proposal within the chemical department and to send me instructions about what I may answer to the company (through the company).[58]

5. Professor Smitz was in Berlin on 5 April and made a report about the work done to Alexandrov in my presence in the engineering department. In a talk with me Professor Smitz made an announcement that engineer Elze, the representative of the Rheinmetall concern, came to his place in Braunschweig and made an offer for obtaining ready-

made drawings for us from Rheinmetall, instead of preparing new ones. It is necessary to believe that the work has been done in accordance with a directive from the Ministry. The results of the work were reported by Smitz to the design[59] and testing bureau of the supplies department, but it is unknown what Smitz was told about. He also visited the intelligence department of the Ministry.

His work has not yet been finished at all, and what he did was really carried out for two or three weeks, but when he came to know about his summons to Moscow, Smitz introduced a number of design changes into the construction of both the howitzer and the gun. These changes improved the quality of the designed weapons. He received drawings of a new gunsight for a light mortar for us from the supplies department. Furthermore, he has presented a draft of a long-range (20 km) gun of a caliber of 42 lines (10.67 cm). Smitz left Berlin for Moscow on 7 April and all his drawings will be sent by Comrade Alexandrov on 8 April. I am going to arrive in his design bureau in Braunschweig not later than the beginning of May, when the prototypes of new weapons being developed will already be produced.

Appendix: the proposal of the Golzern-Grimme Company.[60]

> Kork, the military attaché
> TsGASA. F. 33987. Op. 3. D. 295. Pp. 33–34.
> Original.

* * *

FROM YAKIR TO VOROSHILOV

> 1929
> Germany

Dear Kliment Efremovich.

I have not written to you for a long time because I expected that my weekly letters are reported to you. As you know from those letters we finished the winter period of work in the third year of the Academy and we have just begun our summer works. The works started with journeys for us together with administrative personnel. We have tactical, rear, operative, and, presently, air-training courses that will take place in Bavaria on the aircrafts. I was sending both my reports and materials to them concerning all the journeys; therefore I am not going to repeat them. Two weeks have already passed since our summer comrades arrived. The third group, Zis-Jakovenko, Ventsov, and Katajev, have already returned from a rear division journey and it is leaving for troops. . . .[61] The second group is working in a camp for Caucasian regiments; one of these days the group is going to return and is going to continue its program (the weakest).

Our group, instead of the field-engineer battalion, has been sent on a mission to the aviation facilities. They will make an air journey later, then they will begin a visit to troops' camps. In that way everything normally corresponds to the "program." All the comrades are engaged with interest in work. . . . By this post I am sending a report letter about a field journey made by the first division. I ask you to take an interest in this letter, because it says something completely new in comparison with the past materials. It tells about difficulties of an internal nature that R.W. faces. . . . It tells about undoubtedly new positions and searches that the Reichswehr is obliged to do because of its isolation from the masses.

In two words the situation may be described as follows. It is necessary to make preparations for war in the right way; for this purpose we should prepare officer cadres (the significant number of them may come from lower strata, from noncommissioned officers). . . .

Judging by the experience gained from a journey of the first division, the work stumbles upon a clear lack of understanding from officers. . . . I had a lot of work to do recently in connection with making these journeys for the last time, with the necessity to make notes and remarks in a short period of time, with necessity to give some help to new comrades present for the first time.

I should like to ask you, Kliment Efremovich, to issue an order and to give advice on the following problem. In June and August we shall be engaged in visiting troops, and the second half of August and a part of September, in spite of a lack of maneuvers, will probably become a period of all the army trainings, of motorized units, forcing a crossing over the rivers, and so on. As I had already said, I had been promised that they would demonstrate to me the shooting of the anti-aircraft artillery with modified sighting devices and controls at the end of trainings. So I ask you to issue instructions in a timetable concerning my orientation. The period of my twelve-months' stay here finishes on 6 December. Up to that date, as it is clearly seen now, we must not wait, doing nothing, because it is doubtful that they will show anything interesting and new. The question is if I should try to obtain a demonstration of an anti-aircraft artillery, a stronghold, and something more (they wanted to show it to me personally) after September, or if I should take an orientation upon my return in September. . . . I wish you well. I am waiting for your early reply.

Yours.
Jakir
Excuse me for my dashed-off letter.
TsGASA. F. 33987. Op. 3. D. 295. Pp. 222–24.
Original.

*   *   *

FROM BELOV TO VOROSHILOV:
ABOUT THE PREPARATION OF REICHSWEHR OFFICERS

October 7, 1930
Germany

. . . Dresden[62] and many other schools of the Reichswehr undoubtedly became a focus of an educational experiment of the German army. It would be useful for us to try to attain permission from the Germans in order that some of our commanders could stay in these schools for a long time. . . .[63]

When I see how brutally German officers from second lieutenant to general work on themselves, how they work on the preparation of units, how they achieve results, I feel a pain inside me because I come to a realization of our army's weakness. I want to shout at the top of my voice about the necessity of intensive training, decisive alteration of all weak commanders for a shorter period of time if possible.

We have got excellent human material in the Red Army man. We have good perspectives to provide the army with equipment. We need commanders who are competent in military and technical respects; we must make them, it is one of the tasks of today. . . .[64]

In the German Reichswehr there is no place for failure to execute an order.

TsGASA. F. 33987. Op. 3. D. 348. P. 104.
Original.

*   *   *

FROM EGOROV TO VOROSHILOV:
"I AM STAYING HERE, IN GERMANY . . ."

February 15, 1931

Dear Kliment Efremovich.

With my whole heart I am sending you, my dear friend, my comrade-in-arms, and beloved head and leader, my warmest congratulations on the day of your glorious jubilee. Certainly, I would be extremely pleased to see you these days and to express personally the feelings exciting me, like a child, in connection with the days of your historical jubilee.

It is through your combat and revolutionary way that there was a great number of events and phenomena, exclusive in their significance, and they are now becoming more and more salient and loom like giants not only on the ground of the really stormy and heroic days of the past Civil War, but also in the perspective of the near future, in balance of which there is a column of so-called "inevitable collisions." I say that these days I, like a child, am caught by a special feeling of gladness and, at the same time, pride. Really, I am tied to you by the historical days of combat work. The whole epoch of a struggle in the South against the principal (in essence) forces of all the Russian counterrevolution (Denikin and Vrangel) and then the Polish campaign in 1920 took place with our (your, Semyon Mikhailovich Budenny's, and my) mutual and friendly participation.

With what an enthusiasm I recall this close mutual combat work that was performed under the direct, factual leadership of our heartily beloved Iosiph Vissarionovich Stalin. When you take into consideration that for solving problems history requires a great number of people who are capable of manifesting the greatest qualities of mind, will, hardness, decisiveness, and whole-hearted devotion to Lenin's mission and come to know that our Soviet Union has such people as Iosiph Vissarionovich and Kliment Efremovich, it becomes more joyful, and the cheerfulness, like a live spray, fills all the fibers of our organisms.

Is it not desirable in such days to be together with you and to convey these lovely feelings and emotional experiences to you? I have not such an opportunity because I am staying, as they say, under Fremde (i.e., a strange land). But, however, the work, for the sake of which I am staying here in Germany, convinced me, and it is necessary to think that it serves as a sufficient ground and justification of my personal absence. I wish you, dear Kliment Efremovich, many years of living and good health, so needed in order that year after year our valiant Red Army will grow further and perfect itself in all the fields of its combat training, and in a case of military conflict it will crush any mortal enemy encroaching upon the revolutionary rights and sovereignty of the Soviet Union.

> Yours.
> A. I. Egorov
> TsGASA. F. 33987. Op. 3. D. 56. P. 62.
> Original.

*   *   *

FROM BERZIN TO VOROSHILOV:
ABOUT OUR RELATIONSHIP WITH "FRIENDS"

> November 6, 1931
> Absolutely confidential

Our relationship with "friends," in general, has the following structure.

1. Mutual educational-official journeys, demonstrations of military units. 2. Joint educational enterprises: tank courses in Kazan, experimental works at the chemical proving ground near the station Prichernavskaja and in an aviation institution in Lipetsk. 3. Rendering us some assistance from the side of German industry (an agreement with Rheinmetall and establishing business relations with Zeiss). The results, in

general, of the reciprocal cooperation are the following for the year passed.

In 1931, for the purpose of studying military and technical, operative, tactical, and other problems, the following groups were sent on a mission to Germany.

I. The General Army Group

1. The commander of the Byelorussian military district Comrade Egorov. 2. The commander of troops of the north Caucasian military district Comrade Belov (the second and the third year from 12 December 1930 to 6 June 1931). 3. The commander of troops of the Middle-Asian military district Comrade Dybenko (the second and the third year from 12 December 1930 to 6 June 1931). 4. The assistant to the head of the GUPO Comrade Kruchinkin. 5. The student of the eastern faculty of the Military Academy Comrade Raizenstein (interpreter). 6. The student of the main faculty of the Military Academy Comrade Delova (interpreter).

II. Military and Technical and Armaments Group

1. Deputy to the head of Armament, Comrade Efimov.
2. The head of the military and technical department Comrade Sinjavsky.
3. AU-department Comrade Zheleznjakov.

Studying the systems, armaments, organization of the Waffenamt; problems of organization, and arming of technical troops; acquaintance with plants.

From 10 February.

III. The Group of the VOSO

1. The head of the third department of the staff of the RKKA Comrade Appog.

Studying the problems of mobilization of railway and mobilization transport.

From 28 January 1931 to 3 April 1931.

2. The assistant to the head of the third department of the staff of the RKKA Comrade Jenokjan.

3. The head of the third department of the staff of the RKKA Comrade Pavlov.

4. The military representative at the Moscow juncture Comrade Nikitin.

5. The head of the Central Mobilization department of NKPS (transport ministry) Comrade Ljamberg.

IV. The Staff Group

1. The former military attaché Comrade Putna.

2. The head of the staff of the Belorussian military district Comrade Ventsov.

3. The head of the staff of the north Caucasian military district Comrade Belitsky.

4. The head of the staff of the Ukrainian military district Comrade Kruchinsky.

5. The head of the staff of the Moscow military district Comrade Meretskov.

6. The head of the staff of the Leningrad military district Comrade Dobrovolsky.

7. The assistant to the head of the first department of the staff of the RKKA Comrade Obysov.

8. The head of the staff of combat training Comrade Tkachev.

9. Comrade Stern, in disposal of the NKVD.

Studying the organization and the system of the staff service.

From 28 March to 20 June 1931.

V. The UMM Group

1. Comrade Ratnerm in disposal for the UMM. 2. Comrade Hlopov, in disposal of the UMM.	For improving qualifications at the German tank-training course.	From 20 February to 20 April 1931.

VI. The Topographical Group

1. The head of the seventh department of the staff of the RKKA Comrade Maximov. 2. The cartographical department of the staff of the RKKA, Comrade Jukov. 3. The topographical department of the staff of the Siberian military district, Comrade Demanovsky. 4. The geodesical department of the seventh department, Comrade Fedorov. 5. The Leningrad topographical school, Comrade Mortjaghin.	The study of the organization of topographical works and the material part.	From 29 May to 1 August 1931.

VII. The Group of Specialists

1. The commander of corps Comrade Timonenko. 2. The commander of the corps of UVUZ Comrade Gorbachev. 3. The teacher of "Vystrel" Comrade Ushinsky. 4. The assistant to the head of the RVS department Comrade Orlov.	Acquaintance with method of training the troops in a field, acquaintance with organization of training of the cavalry, problems of usage and methods of training of the artillery. Visiting artillery proving fields.	From 4 June to 1 August 1931.

5. The adjunct of the military and technical academy Comrade Struselba.

Presence at the combat shooting of the anti-aircraft artillery.

6. The adjunct of the military and technical academy Comrade Sakrner.

Visiting plants.

7. The assistant to the head of the communications institute of the RKKA Comrade Kokade-jev.

VIII. The Military and Technical and Armament Group

1. The head of the AU Comrade Siminov.
2. The head of the second sector of the AU Comrade Drosdov.
3. The head of the sector of the VOHIM Comrade Hailo.

Studying the weapon system, the organization of the Waffenamt; acquaintance with proving fields and plants.

From 20 August to 5 November 1931.

IX. The Group of the Department of Military Stud-Farms (VKZ)

1. The head of the department of the military stud-farms Comrade Alexandrov.
2. The assistant to the head of the department of military stud-farms Comrade Davidovich.

Purchase of pedigree horses.

All the above groups presented reports and materials on a mission, admitted in the respective departments as very valuable for the RKKA.

From the side of the Reichswehr the following persons were sent on a mission to the RKKA during 1931.

1. Kestring in the fifty-fifth division in Kursk (eight days).
   Kestring in the eleventh division in Orenburg (eight days).
   Kestring in the fifty-seventh division in Sverdlovsk (ten days).
   Kestring in the third Caucasian division in Berdichev (five days).
2. The group of artillerists composed of Lieutenant-Colonel Mer-

chinsky in the fifty-first artillery regiment in Odessa (fourteen days) and Captain Kruse in the seventh artillery corps of artillery regiment in Pavlograd (ten days).

3. Captain Ashenbrenner who is a pilot in the twentieth aviation brigade in Kharkov (during first, fifth month).

4. The Caucasian group composed of Major Model in the ninth division in Rostov, Captain Horn in the tenth Caucasian division in Prochladnaja (fourteen days each).

5. The group of leading officers of the Reichswehr composed of four persons: Colonel Faighe at the district maneuvers of the MVO (the Moscow military district) from 15 to 20 September, totally six days; Colonel Brauchitsch at the district maneuvers of the Byelorussian military district; Lieutenant-Colonel Keitel and Captain Krechmer from 21 to 24 September, totally four days.

6. The head of the veterinary department of the first group, professor Lurs (from 17 to 28 October, eleven days) in Leningrad, Moscow, and Rostov.

On return the above groups, at least outwardly, expressed complete satisfaction with their stay in the RKKA.

> Berzin
> TsGASA. F. 33988. Op. 3. D. 202. Pp. 122–24.
> Original.

* * *

LEVANDOVSKY'S LETTERS FROM GERMANY[65]

Letter A

> 28.02.1933
> Berlin

. . . The local internal political position presents itself today in the following view: the Nazis in their election zeal during the last eight–ten days, besides brutal repressions as regards the Communist Party, are occupied in the most barefaced way and systematically with the hounding of the Soviet Union and, of course, not only with the knowledge but also with the obvious connivance and direct patronage on the side of government. Suffice it to show, for example, the following headlines with arching letters on the enormous (2 m and more) posters on the posts: "*Lieber in Luebthaus in Deutschland als freie Arbeiter in Soviet Union*"[66] or "*Jagt die Moskauer zum Teufel,*"[67] etc.

And, at last, the insolence of the local authorities reached the point that this morning from thirty minutes past seven near the entrance to the Soviet boarding house at Geistbergstr.,[68] there were put three commissioners of criminal police and four policemen who required everyone who came out from the boarding house to present passports; three comrades who accidentally didn't have passports were delayed and sent off to the police division (at the present moment, two of them have been discharged); our counsellor in the Ministry for Foreign Affairs made a protest that received the insolent reply that "since we know that the German communists are constantly associated with this house, naturally that is our policy now and in the future." I consider that our political representation made a mistake when it didn't react to the mentioned posters in good time, but today it wants to protest, and against that; at least, of course, it is something at last, but I think that our silence encouraged this pack, and they came to direct attacks against us. One more interesting detail: a rather great fire took place in the "Reichstag,"[69] and this morning all the press declares that the communists set the Reichstag on fire and that during the fire in the building there was arrested a *Dutch communist* who has *confessed* that he performed arson. As you see, it is a provocation that is not very thin, but in any case it is unmistakable.[70] Owing to this today the communist faction of the Reichstag is being arrested in batches; it was pronounced as judgment to arrest the whole faction.

2. A few days ago, the paragraph about the anniversary of the Workers' and Peasants' Red Army was in *Völkischer Beobachter*[71] (Hitler's newspaper) under the heading "Roter Moerder Tag,"[72] as well as the phrase "Die Vertierte Rote Armee"[73] in *Preussische Zeitung* (fascist semi-official organ in East Prussia). In connection with it I immediately made a categorical protest to Iodl,[73] saying that "we didn't pay attention to the bark of this press till Nazis [sat] at the head of the government, but now, since the government performs a responsibility for this press, I require [you] to give instructions about terminations of such disgraceful attacks against the Red Army."

Iodl was very embarrassed, said that we know that the Reichswehr, after all, didn't join with such tricks, and in conclusion he said that he will inform the Reichspressechef[75] through General Adam to take the necessary measures. I declared *that for the present* I had been satisfied with his answer, which I will report to my authorities. I think that it is not harmful if you[76] will make such a declaration to Hartman. In any case, I consider that we (the Red Army) shall not pass over such facts.

CSASA. F. 33987. Op. 3. D. 497. Sh. 79–80.
Original.

* * *

Letter B

17.03.1933
Berlin

[Letter] *No. 5. 5.03.33. Quite secretly. Copy.*
. . . the facts informed earlier by me, letters of Schmidt and von Fischer—show a desire to emphasize the Reichswehr line to keep and strengthen a friendship with us. . . .
[Letter] *No. 7. 5.03.33. Quite secretly. Copy.*
. . . In the present letter, I want to inform you that our further studies are planned from 1.03 to 12.04.
. . . In this letter, I will specify the extracts from the Ministry's decision regarding 1.03 to 12.04.
(1) to 20.03—we participate in the studies of the third year in Berlin (in class).
(2) 20.03–25.03—participation in educational group studies of first year.
(3) 27.03—Visit of Reichsarchives in Potsdam.[77]
(4) 28.03—Acquainting with A.—Bates Lb i Döberitz.[78]
(5) 29.03—Visit to troop library in Berlin.
(6) 30.03—Participation in survey of Un Affs Deht—Rdos. I rim Döberitz.[79]
(7) 31.03–1.04. Acquainting with artillery school and commun-

ication school and also with Abteilung in Lüterbow.[80] Should an opportunity arise—participation in studies of Abt. B.

(8) 2.04–8.04—Visit to der Waffenschulen[81] in Dresden, Munich, and Hanover.

(9) Visit to the sports school in Kümmersdorf.[82]

(10) Acquainting with shooting range in Kümmersdorf.

(11) 12.04—Participation in studies of Wach-Batterie in Döberitz.[83]

Spalke[84] additionally reported that after Easter we will attend a theoretical course during one week, approximately, then—a ten-day field journey, and after it the summer period of education will begin. . . . I think that from 12.04 to 1.06 we will succeed in becoming acquainted with engineering units, intelligence detachments, motorized units, sanitary and veterinary institutions, and also the education of General Staff after the academy, a visit to industrial districts—Rheinmetall, Essen, Ruhr, etc., and defenses. It is our desire to receive the decision on orienting information connected with our further stay, since in early May it is necessary to submit an educational application for the summer period. . . . If you will accept the decision to keep us for the whole summer studies including maneuvers, we desire to receive your instructions on what additional questions shall be included for our studies and work.

Signature: Levandovsky
CSASA. F. 33987. Op. 3. D. 497. Sh. 70.
Certified copy.

*   *   *

Letter C

19.07.1933
Berlin

. . . The comparison (with the German army) is mainly necessary to show once more the colossal achievements the Red Army has made in combat training under your[85] leadership and how it began to surpass some capitalist armies, for example, the German army, in the present-day stage of the field of practical theory and scientific orientation extended to problems of the highest tactical and operational art. The colossal, diametrically opposed difference between the historical tasks of the Red Army as an army of victoriously advancing socialism, as an army that is the vanguard of world social revolution, and the German army as an army of decaying capitalism, as an army suppressed and hands tied by Versailles ideas, becomes a chasm dividing the basic advanced conditions of combat progress of the Red Army from the German army trudging along after it. . . . Proceeding from the concrete international situation, political-historical tasks, and industrial technical possibilities of countries, there is developed the military doctrine that is the basic general line in the construction of armed forces and in combat training.

"The well-performed five-year period strengthened the defense of the Soviet Union. Now the socialist industry can produce all the modern defense guns on a mass scale and provide the Red Army with the necessary quantity, if the class enemies dare to attack our frontiers. The five-year period gave modern fighting equipment to the Red Army" [from the Order of the People's Commissar and Chairman of USSR's Revolutionary Military Council Voroshilov, 23.02.1933].

The responsible circles of the Reichswehr's officers feel our primary position to be especially this; they speak about the Red Army: "Yes, your country is a free and independent country that has not been connected with Versailles, and you can receive for national defense absolutely all of what is dictated in the interests of any country. And suffice only one order of government for it. We have the wrong way. . . ."

Yes, our country is the country of victorious socialism, a free country that has been subordinated to no capitalist state. At last, the great thing— it is the country led in its socialist struggle and construction by Lenin's Bolshevik party with its leader Comrade Stalin. Under Party leadership our country created and trained, namely, such an army, which having all the facilities for modern struggle in the present-day stage of its training not only overtakes but also begins to surpass the German army in the field of strategic thinking.

The German army has been deprived of modern engineering, for at present it cannot guarantee that the country will be safe from various accidents. . . . The German army, lacking the latest means for combat, is the army that became obsolete in the present stage and is backward in military-technical relations compared with other advanced armies and, of course, the Red Army.

They don't play and study the whole operation and the total battle, and one can make a conclusion on the basis of a large number of private talks that they don't know these principles. . . . The level of general education and the cultural level of the commander before enlisting in the army is the decisive factor determining the methods of his training. In this relation the low level of the general-education training of our commanders is obvious. Owing to it, our army shall expend very much time, forces, and means to make our commander a competent man, capable of doing well in the complex requirements of the modern control of troops in battle. . . .

The recruitment features of commander training in the German army are as follows: highly skilled cadres of teachers, small educational groups (15–20 men), students with good training in general education, simple forms of tactical and operational situations, and a single, methodical plan developed definitely throughout the whole army. . . .

The airborne troops aren't mentioned and are spoken of nowhere. In frequent talks a rather large part of the officers calls the airborne troops branch a "Utopia."

We have.[86] Regarding the condition of our situation and training, the motorized units are the means of wide, great, and decisive maneuvers. The motorized formations in connection with infantry forces offer the possibility to concentrate a massive, powerful attack by infantry forces in the necessary place and in necessary time.

They have.[87] The difference in use of motorized units between our and German installations is absent. The presence of a great quantity of motor vehicles in the country permits them to use this transport for wide maneuvers, the more so, since the condition of the roads (highways) is favorable to it. The wide-track railway system permits them to apply widely the combined maneuver of railways and motorized transport.

Conclusions. The obvious pictures from comparison of studies of our army with Germany's permits one to make the following conclusion:

1. Regarding the conditions of a technically equipped army, many-sided operational and tactical studies, and depth of problems, our Red Army ranks higher than the German army.

2. In the present-day stage the German army is not a model for our commander.

Levandovsky[88]
CSASA. F. 33987. Op. 3. D. 505. Sh. 46–78.
Original.

*   *   *

"GERMANY IS AT AN EXTREMELY HIGH LEVEL OF MOTORIZATION, MECHANICAL ENGINEERING, AND ELECTRICAL ENGINEERING . . ."

1–10.04.1933

. . . It seems to us that in the field of motorization, artillery weapons, and communication facilities the Germans stand much higher than they reveal to us. We are convinced that Germany is at an extremely high level of motorization, mechanical engineering, and electrical engineering. . . . Our higher schools are of mass production, but they have the forge for production by the piece, i.e., strictly on order; and our schools have less exposure to wartime conditions than German ones. The political education in the general syllabus doesn't take as much time as it shall take in the Army of the Proletarian State. . . . We have a tendency in schools to convert self-training into the collective and brigade one. It is quite necessary for a commander to acquire skills for independent work. Great stress is laid on it in German schools, and as a result quite independent commanders are really produced.

V. Levichev[89]
K. Levandovsky
I. Dubovoy
V. Primakov
S. Uritzky
CSASA. F. 33987. Op. 3. D. 505. Sh. 1–25.
Certified copy.

*   *   *

LEVICHEV'S LETTERS FROM GERMANY[90]

Letter A

25.04.1933

[Transcript of talk between V. N. Levichev with Colonel Schmidt.[91]]

COLONEL. . . . If the contradictions between the Soviet Union and Germany were absent up to now, today especially, that is out of the question. A strong-powered Germany is in the Soviet Union's interests and, on the contrary, a strong Soviet Union is in Germany's interests. . . .

VASILY NIKOLAEVICH. . . . Ultimately, it is necessary to understand that the Red Army is an inseparable part of the USSR and that its relations with the Reichswehr are determined by the general state relations.

COLONEL. The Reichswehr is a part of Germany also. In the last years it[92] stood aside from political events, but owing to changes in the state system it will now approach the people more and more. The essence of the new system accepts the contradictions between the Soviet Union and Germany. Both in the Soviet Union and in Germany the point is about the *building of socialism,* only owing to the failure of the realization of socialism in international ways, Germany constructs this socialism in national ways. . . . Though the Soviet Union had hoped that Germany's child would be born with red hair,[93] he was born with brown hair. . . .

Levichev
CSASA. F. 33987. Op. 3. D. 505. Sh. 26–28.
Original.

*   *   *

Letter B

13.06.1933
Quite secretly

(1) I informed only the chief of the Russian department, Iodl, without any reasons and explanations, about business trips of "friends" to us and about work in Tomka and Kazan. . . .The information about the

reduced program and especially the refusal of experiments in Tomka evoked a flush on his face and small sweat droplets. After registering and repeating the obtained information, he said that the case with Tomka is especially sorrowful and unexpected for them. . . .

(2) This week I saw only one aircraft G-38-Junkers. The machine is imposing and by its appearance it is close to the flying wing, since all that has been hidden in the wings and the fuselage is barely discernible above the wings and under them. . . .

By its design data the cockpit resembles the front cabin of R-6. . . .[94]

Levichev
CSASA. F. 33987. Op. 3. D. 497. Sh. 160–62.
Original.

*   *   *

Letter C

19.07.1933
Berlin
Quite secret
Personal

Dear Klimenty Efremovich!

During the trip for studies of the fourth communication battalion I accidentally got into the concentration camp at the township Hochstein (it means "high stone"). We knew that here now is the "Communist" concentration camp, and that admission is not allowed there. We were let in the camp but with certain delay. The following picture was revealed in the inner fortress: the narrow yard has been flooded with armed SA[95] occupied in cleaning weapons and apparently preparing to relieve the guard. Among this yellow-shirted sea there turned up individual ragged and barefooted figures with beer mugs in hands—these were the prisoners returning with soup from kitchen. Casting a glance at the yard I saw five ragged, barefooted figures standing erect facing a wall. The impression was that they had been leaned against the wall for shooting; three armed SA persons stood behind them. . . . I tried to peer into the faces of the persons leaned "against the wall" and clearly made out that they were young boys exhausted to a great extent. . . . At departure from Hochstein one officer said: "Obviously, Hitler deals seriously with his political opponents." Then as if for some excuse he added: "You also dealt awfully with enemies of the revolution." I explained to him very distinctly that there can be no comparison with us—"we struggle with counterrevolutionaries, with a class of oppressors, but tortures are not allowed as regards them; Hitler is called 'leader of the national-socialist working party' and yet he keeps workers, as we saw, in concentration camps." On the whole the passing glimpse of the camp shows that pieces of information that have appeared in the newspapers not only have been overrated but they also, apparently, are mild. Indeed, what greater physical, and especially moral, mockery for political prisoners can be invented than this barefoot "drill" over stones and, at last, a position at attention against the wall. . . . The official representatives of state power in the camp are absent. The SA and confined "Marxists" have been set against each other as political enemies, but the daily calls of "leaders" are set on the ruthless-cruel extermination of Marxism. Even in Frik's order on completing the "revolution" where all the "revolutionary acts" are forbidden as regards "masters," even the Jews receive freedom in the struggle with "Marxists." And these representatives of a "cultural nation" dare to inflame a "help campaign for starving Volga's Germans," ostensibly out of "human sensibility," when they starve and exhaust a full hundred thousand workers in the concentration camp. . . .

The opposition to the Reichswehr is inflated without foundation. I spent July as a whole in trips to units; the program has been drawn up so that I get to see the units of all the service arms. . . . Generally, I see anything new and unknown here, but I had to see many small articles, especially in control, which gives strength and steady order to the whole work. The same is true in the equipment. The small improvements and devices sometimes are made easily and accelerate the work better than other machines. As before, the reception is attentive enough. . . .

Your

V. Levichev
CSASA. F. 33987. Op. 3. D. 504. Sh. 38–45.
Original.

*   *   *

FROM DISPATCH OF OGPU SPECIAL DEPARTMENT CHIEF GAY
TO VOROSHILOV[96]

8.06.1933
Quite secret,
for personal delivery only

There was sent for perusal the withdrawn material of the German military attaché in Moscow Hartmann at the pretext of his talks with representatives of Workers' and Peasants' Red Army Staff Suchorukov and Schrott relative to the sending of students to Germany at the Academy school.

German embassy in Moscow.   Quite secret
Military attaché   Translation from German

Moscow, 3.06.1933

Transcript of Talks with Representatives of the Red Army

2.06.

(1) There are present from the German party Colonel Hartmann, Captain Harps, and General Genov substituting for the DM[97] head. There are present from Russian party: Suchorukov and Schrott.

(2) *Course of talks.*

(a) The telegram No. 124 from 30.05 came on June 1 at noon and contained the following text: "The Russian military attaché said that in spite of TU[K]H[achevsky's] assurances the experiments in TO[mka] cannot take place. Owing to the same reason no Russian students will be sent to KA[ma]. We ask for an acknowledgment of a telegram from Staff of R.[98] In the future do not undertake measures until the sending of more accurate directives.

Stülpnagel.[99]

On June 2 Suchorukov declared to us that the Red Army isn't capable of sending students to KA in 1933 since it has no budgetary funds. Suchorukov evaded a question whether this declaration is a final refusal concerning combined work in KA.

Since Suchorukov didn't open the conversation, I made known to him the circumstance that according to the information received by me from Berlin—in spite of Tukhachevsky's assurance, in spite of combined talks, and in spite of assurances of coordination emphasized more than once during the recent stay of Wa A,[100]—the production of experiments in TO has been abolished for the last time.[101] Here is the impressively unreliable evidence of not only Fishman, who after all is known to a sufficient extent in this connection, but also Deputy People's Commissar on Military Affairs Tukhachevsky. . . .

One can only suppose that these political reasons, evidently, stipulated the decision of the Russians. As I see it, one can bring up the following opinions on this pretext:

(a) In respect of a supposition that here it is a question of a decision dictated by some motive connected with a given moment, no grounds have taken place. The given decision is important for it, too. It has been accepted—as it is discovered after the event and as it has been proved—already rather long ago.

(b) The supposition that as the Russians feel they are getting on in the corresponding field they can refuse the help and coordination on the side of Germans can be related to Li[petsk] and To[mka][102] but on no account to KA[ma], in relation to which until now the Russian side excited interest. If we even thought that given supposition is correct, it would be quite unnatural if the coordination would be performed until the beginning of educational courses, but at the last moment— by tricks and unlikely provisos—we would be turned out.

(c) To suppose that some other state is willing to undertake the instructor's work that has been performed by us up to now—with extensive personnel and investment of material means—(in this case, in the first place, one can mention France)—at present is groundless. Contrary to this, it is impossible to deny this circumstance that coordination of such a kind can be foreseen in the future.

(d) The supposition that during its talks about a nonaggression pact with Russia France stipulated the break-off of the military coordination of Russia with Germany is, of course, the most probable thing. . . . It is quite possible that until the moment of final entrance into a non-aggression pact Russia felt free in its actions; therefore up to now it didn't refuse coordination in form of the combined experimental stations. The final ratification of a nonaggression pact could force Russia to make corresponding conclusions from former promises as regards France. . . .

Russia tries to attain emancipation from any military-political "burden" to have a possibility to accept its own decisions, freeing itself from any "obligations" and having "clean hands" in the presence of total freedom of decision, at the moment of the coming changes in the field of political and military power regrouping. . . .

> Hartmann
> CSASA. F. 33987. Op. 3. D. 497. Sh. 146–56.
> Original.

NOTES

1. The letter is addressed to Frunze.
2. Horsepower.
3. There was a conflict of interests among French, Spanish, and German monopolistic circles in Morocco.
4. Lose is, evidently, a Junkers' representative.
5. Duralumin—the same as modern duraluminum.
6. Pro-English.
7. Hindenburg, P. von—president of Germany from 1925 through 1933, surrendered the power to fascists, charging Hitler to form the government.
8. Marx—head of the German government's cabinet who resigned in 1926.
9. The letter is not available, and Guntzler fails to be identified.
10. The letter is addressed to Frunze with a copy going to Berzin.
11. The text of the report is not available.
12. Such works were prohibited by the Versailles treaty.
13. Soviet-German Commission on the control over the joint work.
14. The letter is addressed to Frunze, with a copy going to Berzin.
15. Omission in the document. Obviously, a Reichswehr authorized person.
16. The letter is addressed to Frunze.
17. The Principle Artillery Commission.
18. Trotyte (or troostyte)—a structural component of steel.
19. Frank James is a German physicist, a foreign corresponding member of the USSR Academy of Sciences (1927); Karo Nikodem—a German chemist, a foreign corresponding member of the USSR Academy of Sciences (1925).

20. Italian firms.

21. The document is addressed to Frunze.

22. GEFU member.

23. So runs the document.

24. The letter is addressed to Frunze.

25. "Fokkers." See Fishman's previous letters.

26. The person is impossible to identify.

27. So runs the document. It is implied—"for the USSR."

28. The letter is addressed to Frunze.

29. Von Seeckt.

30. "Dobrolet"—The Russian Association of the Voluntary Air Fleet. Founded on 17 March 1923 in Moscow with the aim of developing civil aviation to deal with various branches of the economy on a commercial basis.

31. The letter is addressed to Frunze and Krestinsky.

32. So is the idea formulated in the document.

33. Irregular troops are troops that do not have a unified permanent organization or else that differ from regular troops in the system of service in the Army, etc.

34. The letter is addressed to Voroshilov, its copy to Berzin.

35. The Geneva Protocol (1925)—international agreement on ban of using asphyxiating, poisonous, and other gases and bacteriological weapons in war. It was ratified by the USSR In 1928.

36. On February 8, Fishman reported to Voroshilov: "I inform you that Gerstenberg, responsible for guest reception, asked me if we would agree to abandon our claims for amortization. I answered him that I would ask your instructions. According to your telephone instructions of today, I informed the Fourth Department, to be forwarded to Kork, that in case they refused to pay the amortization claimed, we decline all rent responsibility. Gerstenberg will be informed about this next week. Chief of the Military Chemical Department US RKKA Ya. Fishman." (ZGASA. F. 33987. Op. 3. F. 295. Sh. 19. Original.)

37. So runs the document.

38. So it is in the document.

39. The document was sent to Voroshilov, who acquainted himself with it on January 15, 1929.

40. Autograph by Eideman.

41. The Austrian problem related to the territorial claims of Germany to the regions that split from Germany after its defeat during the First World War after the disintegration of the Austro-Hungarian Empire.

42. The Pioneers were members of the personnel of the engineering corps in the German army. In the Pioneer school the students were trained in engineering corps studies.

43. In the copy of the document "attested" received more precise definition: "The document is printed in one copy from the manuscript, exactly with the original. For assignment with the head of the Academy. Trotsky."

44. Situated on the territory of the Kremlin.

45. "Vystrel" was the high officers' school. It was founded in 1918. The school was in Solnechnogorsk of Moscow.

46. According to the text of the document.

47. Leningrad military district.

48. Moscow military district.

49. N. V. Kuibishev was the head of the command department of the RKKA since 1927.

50. The Ukrainian military district.

51. The commander of the 6th corps.

52. The Belorussian military district.

53. The commander of the 24th division.

54. The commander of the first infantry corps.

55. The assistant of the head of the department of the Air Force.

56. The head of the artillery of the Moscow military district.

57. Anti-aircraft defense.

58. At this point the text is underlined and Comrade Voroshilov writes: "What does Comrade Fishman know about defense? Voroshilov."

59. In accordance with the document.

60. The appendix is not in our possession.

61. The ellipsis marks in the text of the letter are given because the document is handwritten and is impossible to read in a lot of places.

62. Belov marks significant benefits in training German soldiers in comparison with Soviet ones by an example of the Dresden school.

63. The text from Belov's personal note to Voroshilov follows further on.

64. Belov underlines the illiteracy of some commanders of the RKKA. In his opinion "those who do not study and hold posts are criminals to the Revolution."

65. M. K. Levandovsky was a general officer in command of the Siberian military district. All the letters have been addressed to Voroshilov.

66. "Better to be in prison in Germany than to be a free worker in the Soviet Union."

67. "Chase the Muscovites to hell."

68. Soviet political representation at Geistberg Street.

69. The Reichstag was the German parliament, which lost importance after the Nazis' coming to power.

70. The burning of the Reichstag was a provocation instigated by the Nazis soon after Hitler's appointment as Reichschancellor.

71. *Völkischer Beobachter* was the name of a newspaper, which was the central organ of the Nazi party.

72. "Congress of red murderers."

73. "Brutal Red Army."

74. Alfred Iodl, colonel-general of the German-fascist army, was one of the main Nazi war criminals. In August 1939, he was appointed as staff chief of operational leadership of the supreme high command and became one of Hilter's main advisors on operational-strategic problems. He among other major war criminals was brought

before the International Military Tribunal in Nuremberg and on October 1, 1946, was sentenced to death and was hanged.

75. Leader of the German State Press.

76. K. E. Voroshilov.

77. Potsdam.

78. Artillery units in military center Döberitz.

79. Artillery units in Döberitz.

80. Artillery battery in Lüterbow.

81. Military flight schools.

82. Wyunsdorf.

83. Participation in military studies at Döberitz.

84. Major Spalke was the Russian sector chief of the Russian department in the German General Staff.

85. Voroshilov.

86. In Workers' and Peasants' Red Army.

87. In Reichswehr.

88. The content of the given letter is highly contradictory. The features of the author's style have been kept.

89. From 1 to 10 April this group of Soviet commanders visited the infantry school in Dresden, the artillery school in Juterborg, the engineering school in Munich, and the cavalry school in Hanover.

The report about the survey of the Reichswehr's educational institutes was prepared by V. N. Levichev (in 1933–34 he was the military attaché in Germany).

90. The letters were sent to Voroshilov.

91. Schmidt was the chief of the German military academy.

92. Germany Army—Reichswehr.

93. A hint at the Soviet idea of world revolution.

94. The letter goes on to speak about Soviet specialists in Munich (Vozlyublenny, Uralsky, Bakunin-Amelin, et al.).

95. SA—abbreviated from German Sturmabteilungen: assault detachments, in 1921–45 half-military formations of the National-Socialist Party.

96. Voroshilov's signature on the document is dated June 14, 1933.

97. Defense Ministry.

98. Reichswehr.

99. We don't provide information about him.

100. Wa A—Boards of Arms in Reichswehr.

101. Suchorukov cited the absence of budgetary funds and justified the hard position by the examples of German specialists who arrived with families to work in the USSR.

102. Suchorukov also explained the refusal of combined work in Tomka by budgetary difficulties.

5

The Year 1933: Never Had Relations Been Maintained in a Tenser General Political Atmosphere

Our public opinion, as well as the public opinion of the whole world, cannot but perceive the contradictions between the official statements of the chancellor . . . about the unchanged character of Soviet-German relations and these daily acts of hostility.

N. Krestinsky, Deputy People's Commissar of Foreign Affairs

I give myself 6 to 8 years of time to wipe Marxism off the earth. Then the army will be able to carry out an active foreign policy, and the goal of the German people's expansion will be reached by an armed hand. This goal will, evidently, lie in the East.

A. Hitler, March 2–3, 1933

"THE GERMANS . . . CANNOT ANY LONGER RECKON WITH THE VERSAILLES RESTRICTIONS"

From Berzin's dispatch to Voroshilov

January 21, 1933

The Germans make this appointment[1] officially, stressing that they cannot any longer reckon with the Versailles restrictions that forbid them to have military attachés in foreign states.[2]

285

Simultaneously, the Germans appoint military attachés to England, Poland, France, America, Italy, and to other countries, trying to partially break through the Versailles front.

The appointment of Hartmann[3] to our country will hardly introduce anything new into their intelligence work here, because they already have their representative in the USSR; therefore I think it would be expedient to agree to Hartmann's appointment as military attaché to our country, unless there are any objections of a political character on the part of the People's Commissariat of Foreign Affairs (PCFA).[4]

Request instructions
Berzin

Biographical Data on Lieutenant-Colonel Hartmann

Forty-five years old, Bavarian by nationality. A regular officer in the old imperial army. Graduated from the General Staff Academy before the World War. The main arm of the service—artillery. Till 1932 served as a staff officer with the headquarters of the seventh Bavarian artillery regiment. Since 1932 has been attached to Reichswehr Ministry and has worked in the Intelligence Department studying the Red Army and the USSR. During the Reichswehr maneuvers in 1932, escorted a group of our commanders headed by Comrade Garkavy. Understands the Russian language, but speaks poorly. Hartmann is an energetic officer, an expert in artillery.

Chief of the Fourth Department of the Red Army Headquarters
Berzin
CSASA. F. 33987. Op. 3. F. 497. Sh. 11–13.
Original.

*   *   *

GERMAN INTELLIGENCE ABOUT THE RED ARMY[5]

February 19, 1933
Top Secret

General estimate of the Army. The potential of the Army has generally reached the degree where it is capable of waging a defensive war against any enemy. In the event of an attack launched against the Red Army by modern European armies of the great powers, their victory today will be doubtful. Having numerical superiority, the Red Army is capable of waging victorious offensive war against its direct neighbors in the West (Poland, Romania).

The transition of industry to military production in the Soviet Union will be easy, because the whole of it is controlled by the state apparatus. . . . The Red Army has achieved obvious successes in personnel training as compared with previous years. The German prototype is clearly seen here. Despite all measures, the experience of the Civil War has not been properly studied. The construction of the armed forces has on the whole been completed. The time has come to mold initiative and strong-willed commanders of all ranks. However, . . . there is a danger that this goal will not be achieved in due time, and that the middle-rank commanders will stick to the scheme and the letter of the manual. The weak point of the Army is that all commanders, from platoon to regiment commander, are not yet efficient enough. Most of them are capable of dealing with problems at the level of only a noncommissioned officer. Despite all efforts, the problem of the Red Army commanders has not yet been solved. But the general value of the Army has risen, and it is now capable of successfully waging defensive war against any enemy. Its numerical superiority makes it quite possible to wage offensive war against direct neighbors of the Soviet Union—Poland and Romania.[6]

Adjutant Special under Chief of the Fourth Department
of the Red Army Headquarters
Sviridenko

Our conclusion

A general review of the material shows:

1. The location of infantry and cavalry units—which till 1932 was not confidential—fully reflects in this respect our legal and official data sometimes communicated to foreign military representatives staying in the USSR.

2. The data on units whose location is confidential are incomplete and inaccurate as compared with the real situation at the time.

> Chief of the Fourth Department of the Red Army Headquarters
> Berzin
> Adjutant special
> Sviridenko
> CSASA. F. 33987. Op. 3. F. 457. Sh. 41–43, 46.
> Original.

* * *

"THE SECRET SOVIET-GERMAN PACT REMAINS VALID . . ."[7]

From the Report of the American Ambassador to Germany
Mr. Dodd to the United States Foreign Minister[8]

March 8, 1933
Top secret

It is difficult for a foreigner to understand the attitude to socialists here. Nobody believes the official version of setting fire to the Reichstag, according to which Dutch arsonist Van Der-Lubbe named Stampfer, chief editor of the *Vorwärts,* the initiator of the crime. Even if it is true, German public opinion won't believe it. Stampfer is one of the most cautious and conservative representatives of German Social-Democracy. . . . The election day ended in sporadic[9] attacks against socialists, communists, and Jews. . . .

On Saturday before the election day, Chancellor Hitler broadcast to the German nation on the practical application of Bolshevism and

Communism, as reflected in the situation in the Soviet Union. I had seldom heard a more bitter, aggressive accusation. . . . The content of this broadcast, evidently, indicated that the relations between Germany and the Soviet Union would be subject to changes. But nothing of the kind has happened. On the contrary, both sides emphasize the stability of the existing relations. . . . In the interview given to the *Angreifer,* the Berlin organ of his party, Hitler once again reaffirmed that nothing would damage the friendly relations between the countries, unless the USSR thrusts its communist ideas on German citizens or conducts communist propaganda in Germany. Any such attempt would at once make any further cooperation between these two countries impossible. Similar assurances of good intentions were given by the USSR. The *Izvestia* responded in the same tones, saying that the Soviet government, which had proved to be able to maintain in peace and harmony vast trade relations with fascist Italy, would stick to a similar policy in its relations with fascist Germany. It demands only that the Hitler government refrain from hostile actions in relation to Russians and Russian establishments in Germany.

Indeed (in this connection I respectfully draw your attention to my report of December 19, 1932),[10] there should be not the slightest misgiving with regard to the Russian-German relations. Mutual economic interests of these countries are a stronger tie than various differences of opinion on the home policy. Germany has to preserve its relations with Russia as long as its own interests are endangered by friendship between France and Poland. Russia, on its part, agrees to wait till the downfall of Hitler, seeing in the German communist movement a successor to his power. Meanwhile, the secret Soviet-German pact, under which a certain number of aircraft and armament factories have been built in the USSR under German control, remains in force, and neither the Hitler government nor the Soviets are willing to annul it. . . .

I can give you information on two prolonged meetings between Papen[11] and the French Ambassador to Berlin, during which they discussed in detail a possible defensive and offensive alliance against the "Soviet threat" as a home policy necessity for both countries. . . . The Italian government has recently published some paragraphs of certain treaties between the countries of the Little Entente[12] that have a distinct anti-Soviet orientation . . . (a paragraph has just been published concerning the agreement reached between Yugoslavia and Romania in Belgrade in 1929). In the event of an attack by Soviet Russia against Romania, Yugoslavia agrees that Romania would send its troops to the border threatened by the USSR, provided that Yugoslavia would dispatch three divisions to Hungary as occupational forces to protect itself from Soviet aggression. . . .

We may conclude that Danzig[13] will cease to exist as a free state. The leaders of the League of Nations will have to find another, more satisfactory solution of the corridor problem before Europe is involved in another war, with its terrible devastations and losses of human lives and resources for an insignificant reason. Now that the USA has finally decided to take an active part in the solution of major European problems to ensure universal peace, Danzig and Memel should not be lost sight of.

CSASA. F. 33987. Op. 3. F. 504. Sh. 63–77.

*   *   *

"THE VALUE OF THE ARMY [THE RED ARMY]
MUST BE RECOGNIZED AS RELATIVELY HIGH . . ."

From the Report sent to Berlin by Hartmann,
the German Military Attaché to the USSR

March 27, 1933

A characteristic feature of commanders is a fear of responsibility. . . . They are even recommended not to express their opinion before their superiors clearly formulate their own judgment. . . . Nonetheless, the value of the Army must be recognized as relatively high, especially as it is in the process of further consolidation. . . . The industry of the country is still unable to satisfy the most vital mass-scale needs. . . . A possibility of full or partial provision of the mobilized Army with all necessities should be entirely ruled out. . . . The essence of the preparation for a future war is the idea of defense against the intervention prepared by Western countries, imparted to the Army and the people. . . . I don't share the opinion that the Red Army is capable of waging a defensive war against any enemy, because the general condition of the country does not let the Army deploy all the necessary forces (e.g., in the Far East). The might of the Soviet Union, as seen by the outside world, rests upon its little-known military power, almost invulnerable ample spaces, impossibility to study its inner state, and, finally, on those numerous obstacles that the potential enemies of the USSR have to overcome in their own countries. All these circumstances serve to enhance the prestige of the Soviet Union, providing endless opportunities for playing foreign policy games. . . . The aforesaid does not negate the correctness of and the need for military cooperation and, on the contrary, this cooperation should be even enhanced.

CSASA. F. 33987. Op. 3. F. 505. Sh. 217–20.

*   *   *

FROM BERZIN'S REPORT TO VOROSHILOV:
BOKKLEBERG IS EXPECTED TO VISIT MOSCOW

March 29, 1933
Top secret

Herewith I submit for your approval the plan of demonstration of our defense industry to the Reichswehr Chief of Armaments General Bokkleberg, invited to the USSR by the Deputy People's Commissar Comrade Tukhachevsky in response to the demonstration of the German defense industry enterprises [14] arranged for him in Germany. Bokkleberg is expected to come to Moscow in late April.[15] . . .

Confidential

The Plan of Demonstration of the Defense Industry Enterprises
to the Reichswehr Chief of Armaments General Bokkleberg

(Examination of the Central Aerohydrodynamic Institute, reception by Tukhachevsky; examination of the First Aircraft Factory, radio plant; examination of the artillery maintenance plant in Golutvino; examination of the chemical plant in Bobriki; reception by the Chief of Staff of the Leningrad Military District Comrade Yakovenko; examination of the Krasno-Poutilovsk Plant [without the tank-production facility]; visit to the Military Technical Academy; examination of the proving ground in Louga; examination of the armament plant in Toula; examination of the Kharkov tractor plant, examination of the Dneproges, examination of the twenty-ninth moto-building plant in Zaporozhye; trip to Massandra; examination of the Kalinin gun factory in Moscow; reception by the Chief of Staff Comrade Yegorov; farewell dinner on behalf of Tukhachevsky; on May 24 departure to Berlin.)

CSASA. F. 33987. Op. 3. F. 497. Sh. 103, 104–6.

*   *   *

FROM KRESTINSKY'S JOURNAL:
RECEPTION OF VON DIRKSEN AND HARTMANN

April 3, 1933
Confidential

By preliminary agreement, Dirksen came to see me with the German Military Attaché Colonel Hartmann, to introduce him to me officially. Up to now, there was no official military attaché in Moscow, and only since April 1, military attachés have begun to function officially in all German embassies in major countries. The Military Attaché in our embassy in Germany has been functioning since 1925.

In view of the decision to present a demarche to the German government both in Berlin and in Moscow in connection with outrages against our citizens and economic organizations, I decided to take advantage of Dirksen and Hartmann's visit and have a serious talk on this topic. . . . After Dirksen had introduced Hartmann to me, I told the latter that I welcomed in his person the first official German Military Attaché to Moscow, and after that, having apologized for ignoring conventionalities and touched upon the relations between our countries, I told Hartmann that he began his work at a very difficult stage of the relations between the USSR and Germany. Close cooperation between the Reichswehr and the Red Army has continued for over eleven years. I stood at the cradle of this cooperation, continue to promote it, know very well its ups and downs, and I had to tell Hartmann that never before had our relations been maintained in such a difficult general political atmosphere as now. He is undoubtedly aware of numerous acts of violence against our citizens committed in Germany by National-Socialist storm-troopers, and very often by the police. He cannot but know about the search conducted at the Hamburg and the Leipzig subdivisions of our trade mission, about the indiscriminate search of our ships in Hamburg, and finally, I didn't have to remind him of a real campaign against the Deropa Company engaged in marketing Soviet petroleum products. The management board of the company in Berlin, its branches in Cologne, Dresden, Stuttgart, Munich, and in a number of other cities were subjected to numerous attacks and searches accompanied by unlawful arrests of the employees, including Soviet citizens, who were subjected to coercion and humiliation, but were finally set free due to the complete groundlessness of their arrests. Acts of robbery and plunder were also committed against some gas stations of the Deropa Company that sell gasoline by retail; sometimes, gasoline is taken by storm-troopers who come in their cars and do not pay for gas; in other cases gasoline is simply poured out. . . . All these lawless actions, arbitrary rule, outrage, and violence create a very tense atmosphere around our citizens and organizations in Germany. Our public opinion, as well as the public opinion of the whole world, cannot but perceive the contradictions between the official statements of the chancellor and other members of the government about the unchanged character of Soviet-German relations and these daily acts of hostility. Public opinion, naturally, attaches greater significance to deeds than to words and takes into account the facts of a sharp change for the worse in the Soviet-German relations. . . .

If the German government really wants to retain relations with the USSR as the Reichschancellor asserted and which have for a long time existed between the military departments of both countries, it is necessary that the government should immediately, with an iron hand, put an end to all these excesses. . . .

Hartmann said that the military department of Germany unanimously stands for maintaining friendly relations with the USSR and that War Minister Blomberg speaks in the same spirit at the government sessions. . . . Dirksen said that he was very grateful to me for my frank conversation, which was the more so well timed as the colonel would two days later go to Berlin and, still keeping in memory my warnings, would be able to pass them on to his superiors.

> N. Krestinsky
> CSASA. F. 33987. Op. 3. F. 497. Sh. 81–84.
> Attested copy.

*   *   *

FROM VON DIRKSEN'S LETTER TO HITLER: "BOLSHEVISM IN RUSSIA IS NOT ETERNAL"

April 1933

. . . We cannot afford to weaken our positions in the East of Europe, thus aggravating our relations with Russia. It is particularly important for the German national policy. . . . We must struggle against our political isolation, and in this struggle, our agreements and treaties with Russia must continue to serve as the jumping-off ground that has already brought us so many political benefits.

Bolshevism in Russia is not eternal. The development of the national spirit, which evolves now in the whole world, will finally envelop Russia as well. Bolshevism, itself, with its poverty and mistakes prepares the ground for this. We must keep it in the focus of our attention.

Historically, we should keep good relations with Russia, with which sooner or later we will undoubtedly again have direct borders.

Under the circumstances, we must be particularly cautious about those home-policy and police actions that may directly undermine our relations with Moscow.

CSASA. F. 33987. Op. 3. F. 497. S. 87.

*   *   *

GENERAL BOKKLEBERG: "JOINT WORK WITH THE RED ARMY IS EXTREMELY DESIRABLE"

From the Report on the Trip around the USSR
between May 8 and 28, 1931

May 1933[16]

. . . The goal of the trip: (a) acquaintance with the Soviet defense industry; (b) return visit to the trip of Deputy People's Commissar Tukhachevsky to Germany.

General impressions: . . . The People's Commissar Comrade Voroshilov and Chief of Staff Yegorov stressed that joint work was possible when the big politics of both governments pursued the same goals. The well-known statement by Rosenberg is judged by Soviet authorities as hampering joint work.[17]

Comrade Tukhachevsky, at a lunch in a narrow circle, repeatedly stressed that Germany, to extricate itself from the difficult political situation, should as soon as possible have an air fleet of 2,000 bombers.[18]

. . . The enterprises seen by the delegation produced a favorable impression on its members and demonstrated the great successes achieved as a result of implementation of the first five-year plan.

An excellent impression was produced on them by the pilot school in Kacha and its chief Orlovsky.

The opposite impression was produced by the sight of the Red Army soldiers in the street: they mostly wear threadbare, dirty clothes and don't have a military bearing.

Industrial objects: CAHI produced a very good impression. The radio factory in Moscow, 350 engineers, 1,600 workers. Transition to martial law has not been prepared.

GAZ No 1 (former Dux): 4,500 workers. An excellently equipped plant. . . .

Golutvin mechanical shops: 3,000 workers. Successful upgrading of artillery hardware.

The Bobriki chemical industry complex: super-modern enterprise.

The Tula small-arm factory: 20,000 workers. Monthly output is 1,500 rifles, Maxim and aircraft machine guns, 10,000 sporting guns, and 6,000 small-caliber rifles. Sixty to seventy percent of production capacities are used for military production.

The tractor plant—Kharkov: 13,000 workers. The output—140 tractors a day.

The aircraft factory—Alexandrovsk—5,000 workers. Monthly output: 50 Jupiter 450 hp engines and 200 M-11 100 hp engines. A new M-58 700 hp engine has been constructed. A modern plant, efficient management, loaded to capacity.

The small-arms factory, Kalinin: 3,000 workers. Produces 4.5-cm. tank guns and 7.62-cm anti-aircraft guns.

Special observations: With regard to armaments, Comrade Tukhachevsky expressed the following ideas: the best weapon against tanks

is a tank. There are three types of tanks: a light, fast-moving reconnaissance tank, a medium, and a heavy combat tank. The principal
armament is the 4.5-cm tank gun, while the 3.7-cm gun is of little use.
As regards the aircraft armaments, Comrade Tukhachevsky thinks that
large combat planes and bombers must have 3.7-cm guns, rather than
2-cm guns that are little effective for firing at aircraft with metal structures.
A fighter with two engines and four coupled machine guns was seen
at the Dux plant. CHAGY is testing an all-metal aircraft weighing 17.5
tons with a 5-ton loading capacity, 5 engines, and 236 km/hour speed.

General conclusion: (1) There is no indication that in view of an obvious famine, the Soviet power could be overthrown in Russia. (2) The newly built industrial enterprises everywhere produce an excellent expression.
Within the next ten years, the Soviet Union will achieve its goal, i.e., complete
liberation from foreign dependency. (3) Taking into account the immensity
of Soviet plans, joint work with the Red Army is highly desirable not
only for military-political, but also for military-technological, reasons.[19]

CSASA. F. 33987. Op. 3. F. 505. Sh. 135–37.

*   *   *

KRESTINSKY TO VOROSHILOV:
ON NEGOTIATIONS BETWEEN AEROFLOT AND LUFTHANSA

May 16, 1933
Personally
Top secret[20]

The German government applied to us through Dirksen here[21] and
through our embassy in Berlin with the following two proposals-requests.

1. The German Lufthansa air company has long been in negotiations
with our Aeroflot on the organization of a joint air route between Shang-
hai and Berlin. There is even a preliminary agreement on this matter
between the aforesaid organizations, but a final reply on our part has
been delayed, because both the military department and the People's
Commissariat of Foreign Affairs have had doubts on this score. . . .

2. The second request of the Germans is that irrespective of whether
the agreement on organization of a joint air route is concluded or not,

we should give permission for a single flight over our territory of three German airplanes designed to serve the route Urumchi-Shanghai. We denied this request, because in the atmosphere of tense relations with the new German government we did not want to do a favor for the German government. But officially, we justified our refusal by the fact that western China was plunged into an uprising and therefore such a flight was poorly timed. . . . Our repeated refusal to this request may be regarded by the Germans as unwillingness to do them a favor. . . .[22]

We agreed with OGPU on complying with certain requests made by the Germans concerning German citizens. But those are insignificant problems in which the present German government is comparatively little interested. But by a compromise on the airplanes' flight we will raise Dirksen's stock in the eyes of such an influential person as Goering.

In Berlin, the problem of the flight has been and is raised before our embassy by Milch, State Secretary of the new Ministry of Aeronautics and Goering's closest assistant in this Ministry. This very Milch is a long-standing head of Lufthansa. . . .

It is important for us to show Milch our gratitude for this service of his, so that we can in the future take advantage of his influence on Goering. For these two reasons concerning our relations with Dirksen and Milch, the People's Commissariat of Foreign Affairs, which initially came out against permission for the flight of airplanes, is now in favor of such permission.[23] . . .

> With comradely regards.
> N. Krestinsky
> CSASA. F. 33987. Op. 3. F. 497. Sh. 141–42.

*   *   *

ON GENERAL BOKKLEBERG'S TRIP TO TULA, KHARKOV, DNIEPROGES, AND SEVASTOPOL FROM MAY 17 TO 24, 1933[24]

> May 25, 1933
> Top Secret

On May 16, General Bokkleberg's group consisting of General Bokkleberg, Colonel Hartmann, Lieutenant-Colonel Tomas, Captain Krebs, and Engineer Pollert, escorted by the Deputy Chief of Foreign Relations Department Comrade Shrot, left Moscow and arrived in Tula at 8:00 A.M. on May 17. In Tula, they saw the "Small Arms Factory," paying the greatest attention to the technological process of production. . . . While we were viewing the machine-gun department, Bokkleberg asked me to tell my superiors that he wanted to receive our "Degtyarev" light machine gun in exchange for their "Dreise" light machine gun. The plant produced a very good impression, and they noted that in all shops most workers were young people who showed great skill in their work.

[Bokkleberg asked Vannikov][25] how many shots the barrel of our machine gun could endure during continuous fire. The director of the plant said that it could withstand 100 thousand shots. Bokkleberg shook his head and, turning to me with a puzzled look, said that it was impossible, because to his knowledge in all armies machine-gun barrels didn't withstand more than 20 thousand shots. Later, this misunderstanding was cleared up, and Bokkleberg was told that our machine-gun barrel endured 15 thousand shots. Besides, Bokkleberg was informed that the annual output of the plant did not exceed 6 mln rifles. During the lunch given on the occasion of the guests' arrival, Bokkleberg noted that we could be proud of having arranged a highly efficient production of weapons, and at the present time, despite a high level of technology in Germany, there is something to learn from the USSR and from the Red Army. . . .[26]

Hartmann complained to me about Bokkleberg's behavior as unworthy of a Prussian officer: he got drunk at the reception, and after we had left, he behaved indecently, finally falling under the table. . . . At the same time, Hartmann mentioned the excellent behavior of our commanders in Germany whom he escorted, adding that during his stay in the USSR he did not see a single drunk commander. . . . In Kharkov, the Germans were shown the tractor plant. The up-to-date American equipment and machinery attracted their attention, and engineer Pollert accurately put down in his notebook the technological process that aroused his interest. Bokkleberg asked me whether the plant produced tanks, to which I answered that the tractor plant did not produce tanks. The great scope of production and the vast territory of the shops and the plant in general stunned the guests. Bokkleberg said: "I would like to have a magnet that could at one stroke throw the plant over to Germany. You have something to be proud of." . . .

Despite the obsolete equipment and the not-quite-rational organization of production, the motor-building plant[27] produced a quite satisfactory impression on them. They saw the work of the new M-58 engine at the testing station. After they had seen the plant, they went to the Dnieproges. . . .

Bokkleberg and others more than once said: "To decide to build such a huge structure, one must have an iron will and iron nerves. The creators and initiators of this construction will go down in world history. . . ." On May 20, we arrived in Sevastopol. . . . The group was received by the Navy Commander-in-Chief Kozhanov and Chief of Staff Doushenov. The conversation had an official character. Having learned that Comrade Kozhanov had served as our naval attaché in Japan, Bokkleberg asked his opinion about the strategic plans of a probable war between America and Japan in the Pacific Ocean and about the combat training of both navies. After the reception, we proceeded to the air school in Kacha, where the guests were present at training flights and examined classrooms, shops, and barracks. . . .[28]

Conclusions: (1) Enterprises in Tula, Kharkov, Dnieproges, and Sevastopol produced an obviously favorable impression on the group,[29] demonstrating the great achievements of industry, which created ample opportunities to organize mass-scale production of armaments and to equip the Red Army with military hardware. Bokkleberg and the others did not conceal their envy toward the USSR, which has constructed such giants as the Kharkov Tractor Plant and the Dnieproges.

(2) The group repeatedly said that the Reichswehr and the military industry of Germany had a great deal to learn from the USSR. Bokkleberg emphasized the great common will to reconstruct the country and to enhance the defense capacity of the USSR.

(3) The group was under the impression that it was shown very many things, though they had expected to see more confidential types of armaments (tanks, up-to-date engines, etc.), but during the whole trip they did not demand to see anything else. Most favorable conditions were created on their route, and everywhere they were accorded a warm and courteous reception.

(4) Bokkleberg's group was most of all interested in technological processes, in the chemical structure of steel and materials, and in production capacity in peacetime and during the mobilization period. No information was given to them on the latter questions, and our people just kept tactfully silent.

(5) Rather conspicuous were clashes between Hartmann and Bok-kleberg over the excessive drinking of Bokkleberg, Tomas, Krebs, and Pollert, over their behavior "unworthy" of a German officer.[30]

(6) Estimating the situation in Germany, the group concluded that Hitler's statement in the Reichstag would bring about an armed conflict with France and Poland, but later it turned out that the "nervousness" of the group was unfounded, because Hitler's speech assumed a moderate tone, thus arousing the group's resentment, disappointment, and depression over the hopeless situation in Germany.

> Deputy Chief of the Foreign Relations Department
> Shrot
> CSASA. F. 33987. Op. 3. F. 497. Sh. 143–48.
> Original.

*   *   *

FROM THE DIARY OF VINOGRADOV, COUNSELOR OF THE
USSR POLITICAL REPRESENTATIVES IN GERMANY

> July 8, 1933
> Berlin
> Secret

At the military reception for the Political Representatives, I had to talk a lot with the Chief of Ministerialamt von Reichenau.[31] Reichenau turned out to be talkative company, and he even seemed to have looked for an occasion to talk about Soviet-German relationships with somebody of the officials of the Political Representatives. Most solemnly and categorically Reichenau several times declared that the Reichswehr is, as it used to be, for the development and extending of Soviet-German friendship. . . . Reichenau confirms that General Blomberg is extremely influential on Hitler about the questions of foreign policy and that Blomberg often influenced and will influence Hitler in respect to changing former foreign policy directives of National-Socialists to the USSR. According to Reichenau, Hitler "has rid himself" of his fantastic projects for the Ukraine,[32] etc. . . . Reichenau emphasized that if parallel organizations attached to other ministries are little by little eliminated, the

Reichswehr had and has no rivals at all. Hitler acknowledged that the Reichswehr was and would be the base for the armed forces of Germany and he keeps acknowledging it. The Reichswehr is not subject to unification and all rumors about the would-be purge in the Reichswehr, about the replacement of the leaders, etc., are nonsense. We control the situation in full, said Reichenau, hinting that the Reichswehr leadership does not depend on Hitler, but quite to the contrary. . . . In answer to my leading remark that some years later Germany would be better armed and, thus, it would increase its proportions, Reichenau said, "I don't know whether we are completely armed, but it is quite clear that in some years we shall be much stronger than today." Encouraged by my questions about French-German relationships Reichenau went on: "If the French have at least a grain of political sense, they will have to conclude a political union with us. Nothing interferes with this union, as we are not making claims against Alsace and Lorraine, which used to be and always will be a dissatisfied region bringing troubles for the state owning it."

This union will not aim at the USSR, but it may aim at England; trade and industrial competition with the latter had already led us to the war of 1914. The French-German union cannot be dangerous for Italy, which is now under the mouths of cannons of the English Mediterranean Fleet. If the position of the English Mediterranean Fleet is weakened, Italy will be able to show much greater colonial activity, as it used to, due to the French-German military agreement. Poland, due to the French-German military union, will have to agree to the revision of its western frontiers and will be satisfied with a compensation, say, at the expense of Lithuania. I consider Reichenau's clear declaration that the Reichswehr is ready to enter the military agreement with France to be extremely important. It shows that the Reichswehr leaders are seeking the agreement with the French, as under Papen and under Schleicher. This agreement will inevitably be of an anti-Soviet character. One should take into account that the Reichswehr is really influential on Hitler and, unlike the latter, takes a quite sober view of possibilities both for German-English and German-Italian relationships, and using failures of foreign policy of (German) fascism in Rome and London will attempt to influence Hitler for preparation and realization of the French-German agreement. The recent interview of Goering for the French press is significant in this respect. . . . Reichenau was obviously discontent with our agreement with England and accused us of compliance.

... Reichenau asked me, how to explain the *Kündigung*[33] of some German military works in the USSR. ... Our military relationships are not self-sufficient values; they are but a function of political relationships between the two countries. If the political relationships are aggravated, if representatives of the German government and of the National-Socialist party are overtly calling for war against the USSR, one cannot be surprised that the function of these determining political relationships is also undergoing some changes. ... Reichenau declared that Germany would never let itself be drawn into an anti-Soviet adventure, because the events of 1914 had taught the Reichswehr a very good lesson. ...

Blomberg ... tried to emphasize specially that, despite all the events of recent months, the Reichswehr, as usual, like the German government, is for political and military collaboration with the USSR. We know from the German military that before having accepted our invitation and making a speech, Blomberg visited Hitler, who approved both his visiting us and the contents of his speech. At the beginning of his speech Blomberg pointed out that Soviet-German relationships. being quite friendly over the course of many years, were recently *betrübt and verwirrt*.[34] But this period is already over, and the relationships between the Great Soviet Union and his country are put on a solid base. In the political sphere they are determined with the prolongation of the Berlin agreement. Economic relationships are being developed *und sind ausgezeichnet*.[35] In the military sphere the long-termed collaboration is going on, and he is glad to greet the representatives of the Red Army present. The interests of "the socialist Soviet Republic" coincide with those of Germany, as both countries strive to support peace and do their best to prevent war.

Vinogradov
CSASA. F. 33987. Op. 3. D. 504. L. 20–26.
Witnessed duplicate.

*   *   *

FROM THE DIARY OF KHINCHUK,
PLENIPOTENTIARY OF THE USSR IN GERMANY[36]

July 8, 1933
Berlin
Secret

1. VII. Hammerstein had breakfast made on the occasion of the departure to the USSR of our red commanders after more than six months'
staying here. The following persons were present at the breakfast: Hammerstein, von Kunzen (Oberst-Leutnant), Stülpnagel (Oberst), Sodenstern (Oberst-Leutnant), Tippelskirch (Oberst-Leutnant), Spalke (Hauptmann), Scholl (Hauptmann), Krebs (Hauptmann).[37]

Hammerstein made a speech on the topic of the traditional friendship
of the two armies, the Soviet Army and the German one. He was answered
by our Siberian red commander Comrade Levandovsky, who pointed
to the great importance of our commanders' staying here and expressed
his regret that the conditions of the German army made it impossible
to study all the novel military and technical refinements in full.

3. VII. I had supper made on the same occasion. The following
persons were present: Reichswehrminister von Blomberg, Oberst-Leutnant von Sodenstern, Oberst von Reichenau, Chief Heeresleitung Gen.
von Hammerstein, Oberst-Leutnant Schmidt, Hauptmänner—Spalke,
Funk, v. d. Decken, Scholl, and Oberst-Leutnant Kunzen. For our part:
Levichev, Shnitman, Levandovsky, Primakov, Dubovoy, Uritsky,
Khinchuk, Girshfeld, Vinogradov, and Borisov. I made a short speech,
expressing gratitude to the officers of the German Reichswehr for their
sympathetic attitude to our military commanders who had been working
in Germany. I pointed out that it was impossible to tear away the military
part of Germany from the country as a whole and that was why the
established friendship between the two armies (the Soviet Army and
the German one) was of special importance. I pointed out that in the
future the friendship between the two armies and the two states (the
USSR and Germany) should strengthen. The answering speech was made
by Blomberg. He thanked me for the flattering words addressing the
officers who had been receiving and accompanying the Red Army officers
during their stay in the Reichswehr. The relations of the Reichswehr
and RKKA (Workers' and Peasants' Red Army), he goes on, emerged

long ago and is based on the common interest. . . . There is every pre-condition between the RKKA and the Reichswehr to strengthen their friendly relationships on the principles of trust. The two kinds of people, i.e., diplomats and military, know what war means and how terrible it is. Common efforts of the diplomats and military of such a large country as the Soviet Union and of new Germany will manage to maintain equilibrium in Europe. . . .

I told Blomberg about the difficulties that I had to experience due to the sudden attacks of policemen and storm-troopers against our offices and our Soviet citizens. I pointed out the demonstration called in connection, supposedly, with the starving Germans in the USSR. . . .

Kinchuk
CSASA. F. 33987. Op. 3. D. 504. L. 27–29.
Witnessed duplicate.

* * *

THE SECRET-SERVICE INFORMATION:
THE SOURCE IS IN CONNECTION WITH REICHSWEHR CIRCLES[38]

September 4, 1933
Top secret

According to the German military attaché, Dirksen informs that Russia is removing its troops from its western frontier (Poland). Only a small part of these troops was sent to the Far East, but all the other forces were sent inward, the country fearing troubles on the ground of food shortage.

The rapprochement with Poland is perceptible in the very fact that the USSR has already given Poland bigger orders for iron delivery. But despite all this and future information as well, the Reichswehr ministry, under the influence of the Reichswehr's commander and chiefs T.A. and T.S.,[39] is still for collaboration with Russia, as they are of the opinion that the General Staff of the Red Army keeps its promise. The Russian military attaché has just approved it again. The collaboration in the sphere of military investigation (teamwork on the Russian territory at what is forbidden by the Treaty of Versailles) will be, however, by

15.9.33. temporarily suspended. The refusal of the future exchange of officers and military information was not intended.

Unfortunately, the USSR refused to send its officers to Germany for the present training period; this fact greatly clouded the relationships with Germany. Germany answered to that with the refusal to send German officers for Russian autumn maneuvers. The military attaché colonel H., who has recently arrived in Berlin, will report on the condition of military relationships between the USSR and Germany and in accordance some new directives will be developed. (Hitler wanted to dismiss both Adam and Hammerstein.) The chief of the main administration of the Reichswehr Adam assumes command of the fourth division from 1.10.33. in Munich. . . .

As to the relationships with the USSR, the position of the Soviet Union at the conference on disarmament will be crucial. The publication in many newspapers (starting with articles in Russian newspapers) of the information on the collaboration with Russia in the past years made a thrilling impression and the former opinion of the Reichswehr Ministry of Foreign Affairs was shaken. Now one can say that at the conference on disarmament Germany will utterly deny military collaboration with the USSR, if there is talk about this collaboration.

CSASA. F. 33987. Op. 3. D. 504. L. 153.

* * *

FROM THE LETTERS OF DR. VON TWARDOWSKY,
COUNSELOR OF THE GERMAN EMBASSY IN MOSCOW

Letter A

September 18, 1933

Dear Tippelskirch![40]

. . . An American, well acquainted with the situation here, told me about the condition of agriculture: "From the point of view of humanity, what has happened this year[41] is awful." There is no doubt about it. On the other hand, this year starvation means unconditional strengthening of the Soviet regime in the countryside: members of collective farms especially have up to now been utterly convinced that the Soviet government would not let them die of starvation. As a result, the incentive for work has up to now to them been the question, to what extent could they convert the grain they possessed into money in order to satisfy their vital needs. Last autumn the peasantry came to the conclusion: there is no sense to work, as either we shall not be able to buy anything for the money we get for the sold grain, or the very grain will be taken away from us. Thus, why should we work? As a result a considerable part of the crop was lost as the harvest was not gathered in. Now the Soviet government clearly showed the peasants that if they say, we don't work, they [the government] will simply let them die of starvation. As a result, the incentive to strive to get money was changed to another one, being the panicky fear of death of starvation, and this condition urges the peasants to work, gathering in the harvest with all their might. The government showed its merciless weapon, and the peasantry has to yield to it. I don't share this appreciation in full, but much of it is, for sure, true. . . .

(3) On the question of Soviet-German relationships I had a rather sharp conversation with Litvinov, whose opinion is the following: what have I to do with these fine words, if the actions of the German government are developing in a different direction?

The fact that he (Litvinov) was hurt by the attacks against his person in the German press gave me the occasion I wished: to send a written protest against shameless oaths addressed to German ministers Goering and Goebbels, published in the newspaper *Trud* [Labor]. . . .

If the period of detente does not come now, the Russians will be able to make further rapprochement with the Poles and French, to make more than they really wished, just in order to step on our foot. . . .

On Sunday I visited the Leningrad harbor; all the German ships— and they were about forty—had flags with the swastika on them, but no incident was reported.[42] . . .

CSASA. F. 33987. Op. 3. D. 505. L. 148–56.
Witnessed duplicate.

Letter B

September 19, 1933

Dear Tippelskirch![43]

. . . There exists a very strong trend in Russia, to leave us and become good friends of France. This strong trend is represented in the People's Commissariat for Foreign Affairs by Litvinov. Most Russians are ill-disposed. . . . I think, quite to the contrary, it is necessary to give the opportunity to oppose Litvinov's Francophile[44] policy, treating the friendship with Russia very carefully—without being ingratiating to our friends in the USSR, who, I think, still exist in the ranks of the ruling party and in *military circles.* . . .

Tukhachevsky, technical deputy of the People's Commissar for military affairs, organized a grandiose reception where the Russian military were present—our friend Uborevich among them, as it was also emphasized in the press. . . . We are greatly interested not to let the Russians leave us; we should not carry on the wrong policy of prestige. . . .

CSASA. F. 33987. Op. 3. D. 505. L. 157–62.
Witnessed duplicate

Letter C—To Von Dirksen[45]

September 25, 1933

. . . Maksim[46] is victorious, as all the time it is again and again grist to his mill, and the small David[47] with the pointed beard became desperate—but, of course, he has no such post as Nickolas,[48] to be able to become a partner of Maksim. . . .—even consider it doubtful, if Maksim let Nickolas go to Berlin now: perhaps, he will advise him to take another route. Pierre Cot was celebrated everywhere here. He saw the plant in Fili in the course of five hours and he visited a large motor plant in the course of three hours together with his whole staff, i.e., with the crew of three large airplanes or with his experts. Voroshilov did not arrive: he and Yegorov are at maneuvers. Tukhachevsky organized a grandiose reception in the evening.

CSASA. F. 33987. Op. 3. D. 505. L. 165–66.
Witnessed duplicate.

*   *   *

VON BLOMBERG TO VOROSHILOV

September 29, 1933
Berlin

Dear Sir People's Commissar!

The liquidation of the three experimental stations was over on September 15, 1933. With it the long-term period of close and friendly joint work has come to an end, which, perhaps, will be of constant benefit for the armies of the two states. On this occasion, I have a sincere wish to thank you, dear Sir People's Commissar, for important assistance, which you and the Red Army Staff had granted us, while we were occupied with the liquidation work. This very assistance let us finish the liquidation satisfactorily for the both parts.

I beg you, dear Sir People's Commissar, to express my gratitude to all those persons who took part in the liquidation, and I remain with the expression of high esteem.

Sincerely Yours,
Von Blomberg
CSASA. F. 33987. Op. 3. D. 505. L. 171.
Original is in German.

*   *   *

FROM COLONEL HARTMANN'S REPORTS
TO THE REICHSWEHR MINISTRY[49]

October 8, 1933
Top secret
The material is received by secret-service channels

[According to Hartmann's words] As early as April 1 of this year Russia has had an extremely reserved attitude toward us. At the reception organized for the occasion of Kestring's retirement and at the same time for the occasion of Hartmann's assuming the post, this could be perceived quite well from Yegorov's speech, who spoke on the deviation of the new national government from the right way. Hartmann sensed this especially acutely in Krestinsky at the reception on 3.4., who told Hartmann the following: "You are starting your activity in an extremely hard time, as our relationships are strained enough." Also, Krestinsky told Hartmann that the disparity between the words and deeds of the new German government made a very bad impression in the USSR, first of all, by the fact that the former economic agreement between the USSR and Germany seems to exist no more for National Socialists.

On 18.7.33. Hartmann informs that the military attaché visited the camp of Kubinka. . . . The preference for the French attaché was striking.

On 1.VIII.33. Hartmann informs about his trip to Leningrad-Luga, to the artillery school "The Red October." Hartmann appreciates everything he had seen in the following way: shooting skill is very high. The teachers and pupils are crack material. . . . Hartmann informs that he visited Smagin on 26.VII. . . . Hartmann proposes in this report to make the same conditions for Levichev, as the USSR command is making for Hartmann and Krebs.[50] On 31.VII. Yegorov made a very friendly reception and no disputable questions were touched upon there. The intrusion into Hartmann's flat was but a robbery and has nothing to do with any other attempts.

CSASA. F. 33987. Op. 3. D. 505. L. 139–46.

*   *   *

DRAFT OF THE LETTER OF THE FOURTH DIRECTORY
OF THE RKKA STAFF TO THE GERMAN WAR MINISTER
ABOUT THE RKKA AND REICHSWEHR RELATIONSHIPS

October 1933

Dear Sir Minister!

With a sense of deep satisfaction I should point to the fact that the measures known to you[51] have had no aggravations for friendly relationships between the RKKA and the Reichswehr.

I believe that the collaboration, which lasted many years between the two armies, will, without doubt, leave its deep impression on the future RKKA and Reichswehr relationships and will serve as a benefit for both armies.

I dare to assure you, Sir Minister, that the representatives of the RKKA command and the Reichswehr representatives in the USSR have done their best to preserve the basis for future close collaboration of the two armies.

Highly esteeming the importance of friendly connections between the RKKA and the German army for securing peace in Europe, and expressing to you my warmest gratitude for your letter, I remain highly esteeming you.

Sincerely Yours[52]
CSASA. F. 33987. Op. 3. D. 504. L. 159.
Original.

*   *   *

FROM THE REPORT OF THE
USSR POLITICAL REPRESENTATIVES IN GERMANY[53]

December 31, 1933[54]
Confidential

. . . 1933 was the turning point in the development of Soviet-German relationships. Fascists' coming to power in Germany put the realization of longstanding anti-Soviet projects of Hitler and Rosenberg onto the agenda of German foreign policy. The final goal of these projects was the creation of the anti-Soviet block of West European countries under the leadership of Germany for the campaign against the USSR and for its division. The proximate task was the subjugation of the Baltic lands to fascist influence and the support of Ukrainian separatists. The first attempt to carry out this project, undertaken by German fascists through Rosenberg, Goering, and Hugenberg in March–July 1933, was a complete failure. The USSR answered the fascist provocation with a series of pacts on the definition of the aggressor and on nonaggression concluded with neighboring countries, and also with strengthening its relationships with France, Poland, and Italy. . . .

Thus, instead of weakening the USSR, the fascists found themselves confronting the greatly increased international importance of the USSR, which was the natural result of the successes of the first five-year plan accomplished in the course of four years by the Party, working class, and kolkhoz peasantry of the USSR under the genial leadership of Comrade Stalin. . . . Fascists' coming to power was accompanied by a raging terror not only with regard to workers' and communist organizations in Germany, but also with regard to the Soviet offices and citizens who stayed on the territory of Germany in 1933. In the course of 1933 fascists made forty-seven arrests of Soviet citizens, nine officials of Soviet organizations in Germany among them. . . .

Since July 1933 the campaign surrounding the so-called "starvation" in the USSR has been spread. This campaign is unprecedented in the history of anti-Soviet campaigns in its range. In August the violent personal persecution of Comrade Litvinov developed in connection with his stay in Royat.[55]

The year 1933 was undoubtedly the turning point in the development of the Soviet-German relationships.

The increase in German armament and the difficulties of the expansion toward the west and southwest of Europe will urge Hitler to further aggravation of the relationships with the USSR.

Soviet-German commodity circulation in the first nine months of 1933 was 45.7% less in comparison with the same period of 1932; German imports from the USSR are 37% less and German exports in the USSR are 49.9% less. Considerable reduction of total commodity circulation and especially the reduction of German exports into the USSR indicates a rather strong, absolute active-balance reduction (61.1%) of the Soviet-German trade balance for Germany.[56]

CSASA. F. 33987. Op. 3. D. 476. L. 2–127.
The original.

*   *   *

FROM THE BOOK BY HANS VON SEECKT:
GERMANY BETWEEN WEST AND EAST[57]

1933

. . . As every human activity, every culture, every power and policy are based on mind, thus, territory is the first principle of the development of the nation. . . . Germany is bound by a certain territory, and the main question is whether it wants to be preserved as Germany, or, speaking the political language, to be converted into a French satrapy, or to become one of the Soviet republics. The accomplishment of the second possibility has its precondition in the refusal by Germany of its fighting position between East and West; it would mean the end of the German mind. . . . On its way to its future Germany cannot count on the support of England. . . . France, the repository of the future of Germany! If it is so, there are only three ways ahead for the future: subjection, agreement, and fighting. . . . Originally Germany was always to fight on two fronts, and on one of them it always fought against France. . . . The bipartite task of Germany (maintenance of its influence in the West and expansion of its national possessions in the East) is the tragedy of its history, due to the geographical position of the country. . . . The mention of Poland is leading our thoughts to the East. . . .

Poland itself appears before us as a link between our discussion on the position of Germany in the West and East. . . . The Peace Treaty of Versailles created a new Poland, which is based on the wrong geographical and historical preconditions and which has no unity, based on the identical population. The whole structure of Poland was created under the omen of the idea of creating a power in the East, surely, a hostile one to Germany. The establishment of the western frontiers of Poland was subjected to this goal. These frontiers not only meant the immediate advantage for Poland and as great a damage for Germany as possible, but also they were to aggravate extremely the hostility between the two states and to separate citizens of the neighboring countries and to make the unity between the neighbors impossible. That is why the Polish Corridor was created behind the screen of the vital necessity of the territorial connection of Poland with the sea; thus, eastern Prussia was partitioned off from the Reich. . . . The goal was reached. The created condition is so unbearable that the comedy of Locarno, where Germany was guaranteed French frontiers, cannot be repeated again with regard to eastern frontiers.

. . . There will never exist friendship between Germany and Poland, but a truce, advantageous for the both parts, could be concluded on the ground of the establishment of frontiers tolerable for Germany. . . .

Finally, Lithuania has not yet recovered from the surprise that it has become a state. It still uses as far as possible the weakness and long-suffering of Germany. Sooner or later it will have to decide, if it wishes definitely either to make Germany its enemy or to fall into Polish hands. So far, it serves as a barrier (a fastening) between Germany and Russia.

. . . This country [Russia] is so varied in its form, climate, and soil, so varied in its population, but it constitutes a solid powerful mass, which presses both Manchuria, China, India, and Persia, and the North and West of Europe. This country can concede lands of the Far East to Japan, it can lose Poland in the West, Finland in the North, and it still remains great Russia; only points of pressure on the environing world move. In conditions of the greatest collisions it can change its state form crucially, but it remains that Russia that will not let itself be excluded from world politics. . . .

Mongol cruelty, Caucasian audacity, Mohammedan piety, German sense of order, French mind—all these qualities were adopted by the great Russian soul that recast and Russified everything. . . . At present Bolshevism is that stronghoop, which unites the union of the United Soviet Republics. . . .

We are of the opinion that one should fight Bolshevik influence more severely than it is being done now. . . . Russia fears that some day Germany will give its friendly relationships with the East in exchange for the gift in the West. . . .

Bound with native soil, bound with its fate, Germany lies between the West and the East. It should not merge with either of them. It should remain free, it should remain the master of its fate. The preconditions of the freedom and supremacy are health, unity, and power. Thus, the ground of every foreign policy is our striving to become healthy, united, and powerful again.

CSASA. F. 33987. Op. 3. D. 505. L. 79–128.
Translated from German.

NOTES

1. Meaning the appointment of Hartmann as military attaché to the USSR.

2. See Article 179 of the Versailles Treaty, p. 29.

3. In this document, the spelling is Hartmann, while other documents use the spelling generally accepted in the literature: Hartman.

4. In connection with Hartmann's appointment as military attaché, Colonel Kestring, representative of the Reichswehr, gave a farewell dinner in his apartment on January 23, 1933, on the occasion of his departure from the USSR. After Berzin had got approval from Voroshilov (January 19, 1933), the dinner was attended by Deputy People's Commissar for Military and Naval Affairs and Chairman of the Revolutionary Military Council Tukhachevsky, M. N., with wife; Chief of the Red Army Headquarters Egorov, A. I., with wife; Chief of the Foreign Relations Department Soukhorukov, Deputy Chief of the Foreign Relations Department Smolin and Shrot.

(CSASA. F. 33987. Op. 3. F. 497. Sh. 9. Original.)

5. This material was taken from a so-called "information book," which contains important intelligence data. By the German estimate, "regular personnel of the Red Army by the spring of 1932 totaled about 600,000 officers and men, and according to official data it was 562,000 strong. Altogether there were 21 army corps, 71 infantry divisions which included 43 territorial and 1 infantry brigade (Uzbekistan), 4 cavalry corps, 13 cavalry divisions, 3 cavalry brigades. . . . Altogether there were 2,000 aircraft. The Navy had "a total of 21 pennants."

6. A conclusion drawn by the Intelligence Department on the basis of the material of the German intelligence is appended to the document.

7. The document was received through agents on June 29, 1933.

8. This is how it is worded in the document; the right wording is the "US Secretary of State."

9. Separate.

10. We don't have it.

11. Franz von Papen was Vice Chancellor of Germany from January 1, 1933.

12. The Little Enténte is the political alliance of Czechoslovakia, Romania, and Yugoslavia in 1920–38.

13. Article 102 of the Versailles Treaty runs: "The main Allied and United Powers pledge to turn Danzig . . . into a Free City. It will be placed under protection of the League of Nations."

14. In the autumn of 1932.

15. The document contains a note made by Voroshilov on April 1, 1933: "To Comrade Stalin. By way of reciprocation we have to show the Germans our plants and certain military units. If you have no objections, I will give instructions to those who are escorting the Germans as to how they should behave during the 'guests' ' travel around our country. Voroshilov." On May 10, 1933, Berzin sent top secret information to Voroshilov about the dinner that Dirksen would give at 8:30 P.M. on May 13 on the occasion of General Bokkleberg's arrival in Moscow. Invitations were extended to Voroshilov, Tukhachevsky, Yegorov, Budenny, Orlov, Kork, Yefimov, Mezheninov, Soukhorukov. Voroshilov gave his decision: "All those may go. V. May 12, 1933" (ibid., Sh. 135).

16. Berzin submitted the document to Voroshilov on September 26, 1933.

17. Alfred Rosenberg was a theoretician of fascism, editor of the main organ of the Nationalist-Socialist party, and one of the main German fascist war criminals. He was executed in Nuremberg by the sentence of the International Military Tribunal. We are not in possession of his statement.

18. Three times, Voroshilov using a blue pencil heavily underlined these words written by Bokkleberg about Tukhachevsky.

19. The latest achievements of Soviet military technology were, as a rule, demonstrated in parades and invariably attracted the attention of the Reichswehr representatives. On May 1, 1933, Hartmann stood at the base of the Mausoleum together with the "group (3 people) of 'friends' from the enterprises management." Their invitation had been sanctioned by Voroshilov. (CSASA. F. 33987. Op. 3. F. 458. Sh. 35.)

20. The copy of the document was sent to Deputy Chairman of OGPU Iagodá.

21. In Moscow.

22. The document has a postscript: "We must do our best to keep Dirksen, who is friendly to us, in Moscow."

23. Voroshilov put his resolution on the document: "This is a matter for the Politburo. To which it must be addressed. I, personally, have no objections" (V. May 13, 1933).

24. The document was submitted to Voroshilov by Berzin.

25. The director of the plant.

26. Then the document contains information about the dinner, about Bokkleberg who didn't remember that he had had a trip to the Yasnaya Polyana, about Captain Krebs who had lost his notebook, and "the neighbors" (i.e., the NKVD people) who took advantage of that.

27. Meaning the twenty-ninth motor-building plant in Zaporozhye. The Germans were met by the plant director.

28. In the next part of the document it is noted that in Sevastopol they saw homeless children.

29. Such was the wording of the document.

30. As Hartmann put it, "They got as stinking drunk as swine."

31. Walter Reichenau was, in 1930–33, chief of staff and later commander of a military district.

32. The idea of annexation of the western regions of the Ukraine existed since World War I.

33. *Kündigung*—a calling off or giving notice.

34. "Troubled and confused."

35. Excellent.

36. The contents of the document reminds us of the recent period, when the collaboration of the two armies was at its zenith. Of course, in 1933 this was over. But at the official reception both Hammerstein and the Soviet political representative followed diplomatic etiquette.

37. The military titles of the Reichswehr figures are written this way in the document.

38. The document is prepared by the chief of the Fourth Directorate Berzin and the temporarily acting chief of the Third Department of the Directorate Bogov for Voroshilov. It is sent also to the chief of the Staff of the RKKA, OGPU (Security Police) Comrade Artuzov.

39. The abbreviation does not allow deciphering.

40. Tippelskirch was Counselor of the German Ministry of Foreign Affairs. The letter was received through the secret service. On October 19, 1933, Deputy Chairman of OGPU Prokofyev sent its text to Voroshilov. The duplicates of the letter were sent to Stalin, Raganovich, and Molotov. The document was witnessed by the secretary of the OGPU Special Department Gurov.

41. In 1933 terrible starvation afflicted the grain-producing regions. The government doomed many hundreds of thousands of people to death by starvation, while spending millions of rubles for armaments.

42. The reference is to the anti-fascist demonstrations.

43. This von Twardowsky letter was received through the secret service.

44. Pro-French.

45. Von Twardowsky's letter was received through the secret service. It is witnessed by the secretary of the OGPU Special Department Gurov. The contents of the letter testify that the split in the Soviet leadership was taking shape between the supporters of the pro-German trend (Krestinsky) and those of the pro-French one (Litvinov).

46. Maksim Maksimovich Litvinov.

47. Apparently, Lev Mikhailovich Karakhan.

48. Nickolai Nickolaevich Krestinsky.

49. The material is sent by the chief of the Third Department of the RKKA Staff Nikonov to Voroshilov and also to Tukhachevsky and Yegorov.

50. I.e., to restrict both sides' acquaintance with military objectives.

51. The evacuation of enterprises.

52. Apparently, Voroshilov's signature was to follow.

53. The report was prepared in order to involve the body of officials of the political representatives in the USSR common work at the preparation of the XVIIth party

congress. Some chapters are written by Bessonov, Vinogradov, Yoffe, Troyanker, Izanson, Levitin, Gasyuk, Girshfeld. The report is signed by the political representative of the USSR in Germany Khinchuk (January 4, 1934, Berlin).

54. The date when the report was made.

55. In France.

56. The following tables were attached to the report:

Soviet-German Trade in 1929–1933
(in relative figures, 1929—100, calculated on the basis of prices)

	1930	1931	1932	1933
German exports into the USSR	121.7	215.4	176.8	94.0
German imports from the USSR*	106.5	74.8	64.6	44.9

Reduction in Soviet exports of the most important goods
into Germany for the first nine months of 1933 in comparison to
the same period (calculated on the basis of physical value)

Goods subject to various protectionist measures	% of reduction in comparison to 1932
wheat	–38.8%
rye	–76.4%
barley	–87.4%
maize	–86.1%
leguminous crops	–28.9%
fowls	–64.5%
butter	–66.1%
eggs	–86.0%
fish and fish produce	–66.0%
plant oils	–91.4%
oil-cake and oil-yielding	–23.8%

57. "A very interesting and almost trustworthy document. Intelligent Germans, even fascists, cannot think differently. K.V." This resolution was written by Voroshilov on the following document, reported to him and Yezhov:

The Fourth GUGB (Security Police) Department of the NKVD (People's Commissariat of Internal Affairs) received from the agent connected with the German government circles the following secret-service information: the political and military testament of General von Seeckt was handed over to Hitler by

---

*being calculated without platinum imports, involving German customs statistics in pure commodity circulation and constituting (per 1000 marks) in 1929—25.5; 1930—10.1; 1931—4.3; 1932—13.3; 1933 (1/X)—6.0.

Blomberg, on the day of Seeckt's funeral. According to the terms Hitler gave one copy of the testament over to Fritsch.

Seeckt's testament is said to coincide approximately with the framework of his brochure (1933) *Germany between East and West*. In his testament Seeckt implores Hitler not to be prejudiced against Russian problems and Russian political and military figures; then, Seeckt affirms, it will be easy to come to an agreement with the Soviet Union. By the way, Seeckt places his confidence in the following statements:

(1) Germany has no common frontier with the USSR;

(2) The USSR had nothing to do with the Peace Treaty of Versailles;

(3) The USSR did not object to the arming of Germany, because in the course of several years the USSR actively supported German armaments;

(4) The USSR demands no reparations from Germany;

(5) The USSR is not the rival of Germany [gap in the document];

(6) At present from the inner-political point of view Germany fears Bolshevism less than ever;

(7) Both Germany and the USSR are autarkic, that is why they have more in common with each other than with democracy;

(8) Relationships of Turkey and the USSR prove the possibility of the most intimate and best relations between Germany and the USSR;

(9) Over a course of many years the USSR has been on friendly terms with Italy.

Seeckt requires that the Germans should improve their relationships with the USSR as soon as possible, to secure Germany not only from the danger of war on two fronts, but also from the danger of a multi-front war. At present this danger is much more actual for Germany than under Bismarck and Schliffen. Seeckt warns insistently against the union with Japan, counting its unreliability, and also because it can damage the agreement with England and America and will not let it start friendly terms with China.

In the circles of the War Ministry the contents of this testament are said to be met with almost unlimited approval.

> Deputy of the Chief of the Fourth GUGB Department
> of the NKVD of the USSR, GB Major Shpigelglaz

(CSASA. F. 33987. Op. 3. D. 1036. L. 126–28.)

Epilog

Dearly Bought Collaboration

Every historian, like every person, has his own opinion of this or that event. He can interpret it in his own way, especially if he is susceptible to the ideological syndrome. That is why I am not thrusting my conclusions on the readers, but am calling upon documents to speak.

In the thirties "the Stalinist hurricane" in fact swept away everybody who had had something to do with the Reichswehr. Not making claims to an all-sided description of the inner political situation in our country of that period, I want to tell fragmentarily, using just several documents, about the tragic end of two Soviet marshals: Tukhachevsky, who was called "Red Napoleon" by the Germans, and Voroshilov's close friend Yegorov.

Thus, readers can make their conclusions themselves . . .

*　　*　　*

TUKHACHEVSKY: "HITLER'S MILITARY PLANS"[1]

March 29, 1935

. . . The frenzied, ecstatic policy of German National Socialism is pushing the world toward a new war. But in its frenzied militarist policy National Socialism runs across the firm peace policy of the Soviet Union. This peace policy is supported by tens of millions of proletarians and working people of all the countries. But despite the fact that capitalists and their

319

underlings inflame the war and risk anti-Soviet intervention, our Red Army and our socialist industrial country on the whole will convert any aggressive army into an army of ruin, and woe unto those who break their own frontiers themselves. There is no such force that could win our socialist kolkhoz country, the country with its enormous human and industrial resources, with its great Communist Party, and the great leader Comrade Stalin.

Tukhachevsky
CSASA. F. 33987. Op. 3. D. 400. L. 238.

* * *

"TUKHACHEVSKY'S FALL IS OF CRUCIAL MEANING"[2]

April–May, 1937

The real causes of Marshal Tukhachevsky's fall are not clear so far; one should suppose that his great ambition resulted in contradictions between him and calm, sober-minded, and well-thinking Voroshilov, who is wholeheartedly faithful to Stalin. Tukhachevsky's fall is of crucial meaning. It shows cleary that Stalin has the Red Army under his thumb.

CSASA. F. 33987. Op. 3. D. 1009. L. 41.

* * *

ADDRESSING THE COURT-MARTIAL, STALIN ACCUSED TUKHACHEVSKY, YAKIR, UBOREVICH, KORK, EIDEMAN, FELDMAN, PRIMAKOV, AND PUTNA . . .[3]

June 2, 1937

This is a military and political plot. This is the original work of the German Reichswehr. I think that these people are puppets of the Reichswehr. The Reichswehr want us to have a plot and these gentlemen set to organize it. The Reichswehr wants these gentlemen to deliver them military secrets systematically, and these gentlemen informed them of military secrets. The Reichswehr wants the actual government to be slaughtered, and they set themselves to execute this, but they failed. If the war broke out, the Reichswehr wanted everything to be ready for the army to begin sabotage in order that the army was not ready for defense. This was what the Reichswehr wanted and they had been preparing this. . . .

Cited: *Izvestia* of the CPSU. CC. 1989.
No. 4. S. 54, 64.

*   *   *

TUKHACHEVSKY'S GOOD FORTUNE AND DEATH

June 24, 1937

His good fortune in the Civil War having become proverbial (by the way he routed Denikin), his quick-as-lightning attack on Poland, and successful severe neutralization of a great peasant rebellion in Central Russia in 1921—thanks to these he was called "Red Napoleon" in the Kremlin. "The good fortune stood at the cradle of this lucky man," said Colonel Sergei Kamenev several years ago. Though Colonel Kamenev, being Trotsky's right hand, created the basis for the Red Army, Mikhail Nicholaevich Tukhachevsky, nevertheless, should be acknowledged as the only creator of the Red Army in its actual form. Its existence in actual form Stalin owes to Tukhachevsky alone. . . .

But when Stalin still had full confidence in Tukhachevsky and made his projects for the future of the army he had created, Kaganovich a year ago started to whisper about him that, perhaps, he [Stalin] would have to be deeply disappointed in Tukhachevsky, who was given dictatorship in military affairs.

. . . Early in May "the evidence" was collected of the supposed preparation of a coup with the Red Army forces. The accusations against Tukhachevsky were collected in full and declared for all those present by the People's Commissar: Tukhachevsky was preparing the coup to declare a national military dictatorship with himself at the head. . . .

Undoubtedly, Tukhachevsky was the most outstanding of all the red commanders and he cannot be replaced. Someday history will tell us what his part in the organization of this army really was. . . . None will ever know, what was going on at the trial. . . . The fact suggests some reflections that three so well-known representatives of the younger generation, as Uborevich, Yakir and Eideman, joined Tukhachevsky. . . . Taking into the account the suicide of Gamarnik, who was responsible for the political condition of the army and also belonged to the younger generation, the case became still more serious. Tukhachevsky wanted to be the "Russian Napoleon," but he showed his hand too early, or, as usual, he was betrayed at the last moment. Kaganovich-Stalin are again masters of the country and the International is victorious. But is it for long?

Deutsche Wehr.
CSASA. F. 33987. Op. 3. D. 1049. L. 257–58.

* * *

BENES: "WHAT COULD HAVE HAPPENED IF TUKHACHEVSKY, NOT STALIN, HAD WON IN MOSCOW"

From the Record of the Conversation of Alexandrovsky,
Soviet Political Representative in Czechoslovakia with President Benes

July 4, 1937
Prague

Benes kept talking to me in the course of 2½ hours, and he was speaking all the time almost solely on the topic of inner processes going on in the USSR. He started the conversation with the question, what I thought of the meaning of the trial of Tukhachevsky and Co., but after some rather general phrases on my part, he interrupted me declaring that he wanted to tell me his interpretation in detail in order that it would be clear to me what reasons he was guided in his policy toward the USSR.

As the first premise to the whole conversation Benes put the statement that so-called events in the USSR did not surprise him at all and did not frighten him, as he had been waiting for them for a long time. Also he was nearly sure that the winner would be "Stalin's regime."

. . . He welcomes this victory and considers it to be the strengthening of the might of the USSR, being the victory of the adherents of peaceful defense and of collaboration of the Soviet Union with Europe. . . .

Benes declared that he considers Soviet foreign policy in recent years to be the USSR gambling on the West European democracy of the French, English, and Czechoslovakian type as on its ally in the fight for peace and against fascism.

Benes declared that he thought his support had been the USSR under the Stalinist regime, but neither Russia nor democratic Russia, as those in Moscow suspected him to have been. . . . Since 1932 he has spent all the time in a decisive fight between Stalinist policy and that of "radical revolutionaries." That is why the latest Moscow trials, Tukhachevsky's trial among them, were not unexpected for him. . . .

Benes especially emphasized that, according to his confidence in the Moscow trials, especially in Tukhachevsky's trial, the matter was not spies or diversions, but direct and clear conspiratorial activity with the purpose to overthrow the actual regime. . . . Tukhachevsky, Yakir, Putna (almost all the time Benes named but these three), of course, were not spies, but they were conspirators. Tukhachevsky is a nobleman, an officer, and he had friends in the official circles not only in Germany, but also in France (since their imprisonment in Germany and Tukhachevsky's attempts to escape). Tukhachevsky was not and could not be the Russian Napoleon. But Benes can well imagine that the mentioned qualities of Tukhachevsky plus his German traditions, supported during the Soviet period with his contacts with the Reichswehr, could have made him very open to the German influence during the Hitler period, too. Tukhachevsky could not have at all realized that he was committing a crime while having contacts with the Reichswehr. Especially, if one imagines that Tukhachevsky considered the only salvation of his Motherland being a war side by side with Germany against the rest of Europe, the war, which was the only means left to provoke the world revolution. One can even imagine that Tukhachevsky thought himself not to be a traitor, but even a rescuer of the country. . . .

In connection with the above said, it is worthwhile to note that Benes told me the following in strict confidence: during Tukhachevsky's stay in France last year, Tukhachevsky had quite private talks with his personal French friends. These talks are known quite well to the French government and, through it, to Benes. In these talks Tukhachevsky

developed quite seriously the theme of possible Soviet-German collaboration, also under Hitler, so to say, the theme of "a new Rapallo."
Benes says that these talks troubled France a little. Developing the thesis
of "the subjective factor" Benes, by the way, said that a number of
persons could be guided with such motives as dissatisfaction with their
status, craving for glory, unprincipled adventurism, etc. In this connection
he mentioned Yakir and Putna once again. About the latter Benes knows
that he was near Warsaw with his twenty-seventh division and, obviously,
he "could not accept the fact that the glory of the subjugator of Warsaw
had escaped him."

In the same connection Benes mentioned Iagodá. He suggested that
Iagodá knew everything about the plot and played a waiting game,
to see what it would come to. A drunkard, debauchée, and unprincipled
person, Iagodá could have attempted to play the role of Fouquet of
the epoch of the Great French Revolution. . . . Benes declared frankly
that the political police in all states is a mob of bandits and twins[?]

Benes was sure of the victory of the "Stalinist regime," namely,
because this regime did not lose morale, while shouters of the permanent
revolution did apparently not rise to the morale. In Moscow the traitors
are being shot, and the so-called European beau monde is horrified.
This is hypocrisy. Benes not only understands quite well, but in fact
approves of the Moscow line of action. Moscow continues its life in
the epoch of revolution. . . . Stojadinovics[4] asked to tell Benes the following: "Well, Benes, you have got into trouble with your Russians.
Perhaps, it would be more correct to keep aloof, like Yugoslavia does.
What will Czechoslovakia do, when the Soviets fall to pieces?"

Benes reminded that in a conversation with me (it seems to have
happened on 22.IV. this year) he said that the USSR could agree with
Germany, why not? I answered that I remembered it and admitted that
I was then very much surprised with this part of the conversion, being
quite out of Benes's usual frame of mind. Laughing slyly, Benes answered
that at that time he could not explain to me the hidden meaning of
the past conversation.[5] Benes asked me to consider his explanations
to be top-secret ones and then he said the following: since this January
Benes has received indirect signals about great intimacy between the
Reichswehr[6] and the Red Army. Since January he has been waiting
for what this will come to. The Czechoslovakian envoy to Berlin Mastny
is quite an established informer. . . . In Berlin Mastny had two con-

versations with the outstanding representatives of the Reichswehr. Mastny took the photos of them, but it seems, he did not understand their meaning himself. Benes even doubts if the representatives of the Reichswehr realized that they betrayed their secret. But for Benes it became clear from these conversations that there was a close contact between the Reichswehr and the Red Army. Benes could not know that it was contact with the traitors. The problem arose for him, what to do, if the Soviet government would really come back to a policy of "a new Rapallo." In this connection Benes asked a rhetorical question, what the means to defend Czechoslovakia was, and I answered plainly to this question that in this case Czechoslovakia should have also made an agreement with Germany. It would have been the beginning of Czechoslovakian dependence, but it was the only way out. Hitler is not striving at all to destroy Czechoslovakia immediately, but he wants "a union" with it. Speaking of Czechoslovakia, it could have meant dependence, vassal status, but Benes spent so many years to get free from the Austrian yoke that he would not adopt the German one. Benes said that Moscow had to consider his declarations most seriously and to understand once and for all that Czechoslovakia wanted to be free in the full meaning of the word. It would never accept any dictate, but it would fight for its freedom and for European peace. As this is also the task of the USSR, Czechoslovakia, of course, is the ally of Moscow, and Benes's policy takes the invariability of Soviet-Czechoslovakian friendly relationships as an axiom. No shots, no inner changes can shake this friendship. In this connection Benes also asked this question: "What could have happened if Tukhachevsky, not Stalin, had won in Moscow?" In this case Czechoslovakia would have had to maintain the friendship with Tukhachevsky's Russia. But in that case Czechoslovakia would have had to reach an agreement with Germany, and this would again be the beginning of dependence either on Russia or on Germany, as the Russia of Tukhachevsky would not be ashamed to pay Germany with Czechoslovakia. Benes repeated again that he considered the Moscow trials to be a sign of the strengthening of the USSR, and that his concept of the friendship with the USSR had been and was the main ground for Czechoslovakia to realize its foreign policy.

CSASA. F. 33987. Op. 3. D. 1028 [1]. L. 107–14. Original.

*   *   *

EVIL IRONY: IMPARTIAL ACCUSATIONS AGAINST STALIN
WERE HEARD ON THE PART OF FASCIST LEADERS

From Rosenberg's Speech at the Nürnberg Congress of the
NSDAP (National Socialist German Workers' Party)[7]

September 3, 1937

The White Sea canal and the Volga-Moskva canal . . . , these great constructions were built by both political prisoners and criminals. For these and like constructions were gathered from the whole Soviet Union the best representatives of the Russian nation who did not wish to obey the Bolshevik system, as well as members of other nations of the Soviet state languishing under the yoke of red imperialism, and they were sent in the two directions: into the European part to build these canals and military plants; into the East, first of all to build the railway track, which could be beyond the reach of Japanese cannons with the purpose to alleviate the offensive against Japan in the Far East. About 800,000 criminals and political prisoners from the Ukraine, the Caucasus, and Cossack regions are working at this Baikal branch. They often work when it is 50–60° below freezing. In the forced labor camps along the White Sea canal there were placed in inhuman conditions about 300,000 prisoners who died while working, and they were replaced with other prisoners sentenced to death and with exiles, often from German colonies. . . . The establishment of the White Sea canal recently cost many hundreds of thousands of human victims. As if mocking this terrible extirpation of people, the central organ of the Communist International *Moscow Pravda* (from September 8, 1936), informed that the canal was built with "handsome spades," and the central organ of the Red Army, *The Red Star* (April 29, 1937), called these human torments unheard yet in world history the greatest victory of "socialist humanity"! This extirpation of people in the name of socialism and liberation of labor was executed mostly by the former Jewish chief of the ChK (Extraordinary Commission) Iagodá. Iagodá joined to it a cunning system of extortion, promising many prisoners, who still had some treasures, to alleviate their fates at the cost of giving him, perhaps, the last hidden treasures. These treasures, got by extortions, Iagodá and his partners sent over to other states, which made other rascals, who did not seize upon such earnings, envy him, and later he had to yield to them. His immediate subordinate . . . was Moses Berman,[8] who controlled the forced labor camps of the whole Soviet Union. With sadistic cruelty this Berman drove the prisoners from all the Soviet Union into the icy deserts of Asia and towards the White Sea or he drove them to destruction in tens of thousands in Siberian concentration camps. His deputy was Solomon Firin.[9] . . . In this way violence, having no precedent in their cruelty in world history, is going on over the best still-living Russian people and people of other nations of the Soviet Union.[10] . . .

CSASA. F. 33987. Op. 3. D. 1009. L. 390–91.

* * *

YEGOROV: "I WOULD BITE THROUGH THE THROAT OF ANY, WHO DARED . . . TO APPEAL TO REPLACE THE LEADERSHIP"

February 28, 1938

To the People's Commissar for Defense of the USSR, Marshal of the Soviet Union Comrade Voroshilov, K.Ye.

I have presented you with my conclusions on the main questions, which were posed in confrontation against me by the enemies of the people. With all possible responsibility for myself, for my actions and behavior, I am reporting again and again that my political basis, which has been the ground of my life during the last twenty years, now and to the end of my life is our great party of LENIN and STALIN, its principles, grounds, and its general course.

During all those twenty years, while I implemented all the tasks of the Party and was fighting for their realization, there was not the smallest cloud, which could provoke even the slightest doubt about me, nor was there hesitation with regard to the rightness of the Party tasks, nor criticism of the leadership. I never had these and none will dare to tell the contrary. On the same grounds my relationship to your person was based. I am emphasizing this decisively and I am declaring it, whatever and whenever traitors and spies spoke about me in this respect.

I am not sinless. I admit what I told and what I was told on certain moments of practice. But I say decisively that I would bite through the throat of any who dared speak and appeal to replace the leadership. My political base was and is unshakeable. Not a single drop of dirt has spotted my political image and it is clean, as it used to be in the course of all the twenty years of my being in the ranks of the Party and the Red Army. Realizing this, it is still more difficult to experience all of this situation around me. I felt still worse, as I had known about the extreme baseness and high treason of my former wife, for which I am greatly responsible morally.[11]

Dear Kliment Yefremovich! I feel extremely deep moral depression. I know and realize that the evidence of the enemies of the people, despite their crying foulness and calumny, should be checked up thoroughly. But I should say one thing, i.e., of course, the Party should get exhaustive evidence for the final decision of my fate. The decision will be the consequence of the analysis of the enemies of the people's evidence against myself and the analysis of my personality in the totality of all my personal qualities.

If I had in my conscience and soul even an iota of guilt with regard to my political connection with the gang of enemies and traitors of the Party, Motherland, and people, I would declare it directly and frankly, not now, but in the first minutes, when the Party speaking through Comrade STALIN declared that those who would plead guilty would not be punished, and simply so, first of all to Comrade Stalin himself and to you. But there is no factual cause for pleading guilty, no questions of my political guilt to the Party and Motherland as their enemy and traitor.

I may and I should be punished for my defects, faults, blunders, and negligence in my practice; for my political blindness and scatter-brainedness; for the absence of due class and revolutionary vigilance. I may and I should be punished for philistinism, unworthy for a good Bolshevik, around which the gang of criminals and spies acted. This is indisputable and I am pleading guilty for this all. But I cannot plead guilty for any political connection with enemies, traitors, and spies, as it has never existed in reality and I was not guilty of it in any form and value. There was no, there is no, and there will never be such matter. I am swearing to this with all my life-being.

Dear Kliment Yefremovich!

I gave a note to STALIN petitioning to receive me at least for several minutes in this very hard period of my life. There is no answer. I want to tell him in a private talk that all that radiant past, our common work on the front, remain for me and will remain in the future the dearest moments of my life, and that I have never let anybody blacken that past; moreover, I have never let and I cannot let this past be defamed, let it be in my thoughts, and become not only in my thoughts, but in fact the enemy of the Party and people. I beg you, Kliment Yefremovich, to help me to be received by Comrade STALIN. All my hard experience would immediately disappear like a load off my mind.

I want, I need extremely to be morally calm, as one always becomes after having talked with Comrade STALIN.

I declare to you once again, to my direct chief, comrade in arms of the fighting days of the Civil War, and to my old friend (you said so in your congratulation on the occasion of my fiftieth birthday) that my political honesty is unshakable both toward the Party and toward my Motherland and people.

Sincerely yours,
Marshal of the Soviet Union:
A. I. Yegorov
CSASA. F. 33987. Op. 3. D. 56. L. 120–22.
Original.

*   *   *

"I AM . . . ABSOLUTELY SINLESS AND CLEAN
TO THE PARTY AND MOTHERLAND"

From the Letter of Yegorov to Voroshilov

March 3, 1938
Top secret

Dear Kliment Yefremovich!

I have just received the decision of my expulsion from the number of candidates to the members of the RCP(b) CC. I confess this most severe for me party political decision to be absolutely and solely right, as the stability of the RCP(b) CC authority demands it, being the leading organ of our great party. This is a principal and indisputable ground. I am quite conscious of it in my mind and understand the political essence of the decision.

I beg your pardon, Kliment Yefremovich, for my bothering you with my letters. But, I hope, you understand that this is a very hard experience for me, which is constituted of two essentially quite different moments.

First, the unimaginable and indescribable situation of the political sullying of me by the enemies of the people, and secondly, the killing fact of the crying crime of the high treason of my former wife. The second one, i.e., my former wife's treason, is the indisputable fact, while the first one, that is the political sullying of me by the enemies of the people and traitors, is quite unexplainable, and I have every right to call it the tragic event of my life.

How can this terrible situation around me be explained, if there is no political basis for it, and there was no occasion when I was called, or someone in my presence called me, to turn against the Party leadership, against the Soviet power and the Red Army, i.e., I was recruited as a conspirator, enemy, and traitor?

In the course of all twenty years of my work, I have never heard the like calls and suggestions anywhere or from anyone. I declare that I would immediately give anyone who could dare to suggest to me the act of such a treason over into the hands of our organs of the NKVD, and I would first of all report to you about it. This attitude was known to everyone of the enemies' gang and nobody dared ever to suggest this to me in the course of all my twenty years-long period of work.

Dear Kliment Yefremovich! I have been all those twenty years in the ranks of our dear Red Army, starting from the first days of its origin, while on the front in 1917. I spent in its ranks years of especially heroic struggle, where I spared neither my strengths nor my life, firmly walking along the path of the Soviet power after I had broken irrevocably with my past (the officers' milieu, narodnik ideology, and absolutely every relation with anybody of non-Soviet elements or organization). I have broken off with them and have burnt all big and small bridges, and there is no such force that could have returned me to these for me old and dead people and to their positions. In this I am also absolutely sinless and clean to the Party and Motherland. You, Kliment Yefremovich, are a witness of my work on the fronts and of my devotedness to the Soviet power, and I am appealing to the leader of our Party, the teacher of my political youth in the ranks of our Party, Comrade Stalin, and I dare to believe that he will not refuse to approve my devotedness to the cause of the Soviet power. The blood I shed in the ranks of the RKKA fighting against the enemies of the battlefields welded me together with the October Revolution and our great Party. Is it possible that now, in the days of victory and triumph of socialism, I have slipped onto the precipice of high treason to my Motherland and my people, the treason to the cause to which I have devoted myself since the moment of my acknowledgment of the Soviet power—my strength, mind, conscience, and life? No, this has never been and this will never be.

I am ashamed, dear Kliment Yefremovich, to appeal to you again and to call upon you to believe my declaration. But being not guilty to the Party, Motherland, and people, being no enemy and traitor to them at all, I can swear to the Party, to Comrade Stalin, and to you at the cost of my life that around me (except my former wife's treason; and I have a special moral guilt for this) there is an unexplainable tragic situation, and I am dying in it, being not guilty at all of treason as an enemy and traitor of the Party, Motherland, and people.

> Yegorov
> CSASA. F. 33987. Op. 3. D. 56. L. 187–90.
> Original.

* * *

FROM THE REPORT OF THE MAIN DIRECTORATE
OF EMPIRE SECURITY OF GERMANY

1938

It is all the same, whether the government is called Nazi, fascist, or Soviet, the principle is the same. The dictator's will is the law. It is strictly subjected to this will. The property is confiscated completely.

. . . Patriotism becomes blind obedience to the ruling class. . . . The Dictator swings his censer over the nation cynically and insensibly. All this is the return to barbarism and slavery. Compromise between despotism and democracy is impossible. . . .

> Bundesarchiv. Reichssicherheitshauptamt.
> R58/1094.
> Jahreslagebericht
> 1938 des Sicherheitshauptamts.
> Band I.

*   *   *

GERMAN HISTORIAN S. HAFFNER: "IT IS NO USE CRYING OVER THE UNBORN CHILD OF HISTORY"

. . . One can say with confidence: in Berlin, like in Moscow, in the course of nine months, since June of 1937 till February of 1938, nearly all traditional bearers of the German-Russian military friendship of the Rapallo[12] period had disappeared from the ranks of command, and in Moscow simultaneously—from the ranks of living beings. If a military coup against Hitler and Stalin were possible, in the course of these nine months it finished its existence. It is no use crying over the unborn child of history. And still—what a lot could both countries have been saved with such a coup d'état! Instead bad fate appeared. But immediately on the eve of this seemingly inevitable clash there appeared another sharp turn in the course of both countries and the most incredible episode of this incredible history: the pact of Hitler and Stalin from August 23, 1939. . . . The second Rapallo became the prelude to the fight to the death. . . .

> S. Haffner, *The Pact with the Devil. Fifty Years of German-Russian Relations*, p. 90.

*   *   *

THERE WERE FOUR DAYS LEFT BEFORE
WORLD WAR II BROKE OUT . . .

August 27, 1939
Top secret[13]

On August 27 the German military attaché, General KESTRING, visited the Foreign Relations Department and made his congratulations on concluding the nonaggression pact between Germany and the USSR. And Kestring declared that he, supposedly, expressed the same thought as early as five years ago. After Comrade Stalin's report at the eighteenth party congress Kestring, in his words, reminded him again of the possibility of establishing friendly relations with the Soviet Union, but then it was met with mistrust in Germany. Ribbentrop, in Kestring's words, before his flight to Moscow kept doubting the possible success. His [Ribbentrop's] doubts, says KESTRING, disappeared only when he had visited the great man Comrade Stalin in person and heard his clear and provoking no-doubts formulation of questions.

After that he returned to the embassy, had a telephone talk with Hitler, reported to him his considerations, and received his agreement.[14]

> The Chief of the Foreign Relationships Department of the NKO
> (People's Commissariat for Defense)
> Colonel Osetrov
> CSASA. Op. 3. D. 1237. L. 413.
> Original.

NOTES

1. Tukhachevsky's article was published in *Pravda* on March 31, 1935. It was issued with considerable correction by Stalin's hand, who changed the title itself: "The Military Plans of Nazi Germany." The fragment of the article is published here without the correction, just as Tukhachevsky had written it.

2. From the secret review of foreign policy events for the period of April 23 to May 12, 1937, issued by the Directorate of the Military Forces (Wehrmachtamt) attached to the German War Ministry.

3. On June 11, 1937, the secret court-martial took place. The trial was short,

unjust, with no advocates and no right of appeal. On June 12, at night, all the accused were shot.

These also would pay with their lives for the "friendship" with the Reichswehr: Ya. I. Alksnis, E. F. Appog, I. P. Belov, Ya. K. Berzin, M. I. Baranov, M. V. Viktorov, I. K. Gar'kavy, I. N. Dubovoy, P. E. Dybenko, A. I. Yegorov, V. I. Zof, N. D. Kashirin, I. K. Kozhanov, L. M. Karakhan, N. N. Krestinsky, N. K. Levandovsky, V. N. Levichev, S. A. Mezheninov, K. B. Radek, A. P. Rozengoltz, L. D. Trotsky, I. S. Unshlikht, I. A. Khalepsky, and many, many others. Ya. B. Gamarnik would commit suicide; V. K. Blyukher would perish in Lefortovo prison; Ya. M. Fishman, K. A. Meretskov, G. G. Yastrebov, and others would be repressed.

But the main dramatis personae of these events would remain exempt. During those years the Soviet and international community was under the false impression that Stalin, Voroshilov, and the political and military leaders on the whole were, supposedly, not privy to secret connections with Germany. But could the dictator of the totalitarian state be ignorant of all this? The published documents say "no." Stalin knew everything. Quite another matter, the lie was always his main weapon in the fight for keeping power. Besides, he managed to play one person against another. Thus, Tukhachevsky, Yakir, Uborevich, Kork, Eideman, Feldman, Primakov, and Putna were sentenced to death by their "comrades-in-arms": marshals Budenny and Blyukher, army commanders of the first rank Shaposhnikov and Belov, army commanders of the second rank Alksnis, Dybenko, Kashirin, and division commander Gorbachev. Many of them would soon themselves become hostages of Stalin's mortal circle.

4. M. Stojadinović was Prime Minister and Minister of Foreign Affairs of Yugoslavia.

5. The German historical literature believes that in Tukhachevsky's case Stalin and Hitler played together for the first time. On Hitler's charge the chief of the political police Heydrich fabricated compromising material against Tukhachevsky, which was given surreptitiously to Stalin with Beneš's assistance, and it was handed over to the court-martial of the marshals.

6. In the conversation the word Reichswehr is used traditionally, although since 1935, the Wehrmacht had already been established in Germany.

7. Addressing the same congress, Hitler told about millions of people who fell victims to starvation in the USSR, and Goebbels, speaking about millions executed by shooting in the USSR, described the internal policy of the R.C.P.(E.) as "the bloody practice of hysterical and criminal political madness" (CSASA. F. 33987. Op. 3. D. 750. L. 47, 48).

8. M. D. Berman was chief of the Main Directorate of Corrective Labor Camps of OGPU. He had been awarded the Lenin Order but was shot in 1938.

9. S. G. Firin was chief of the White Sea–Baltic corrective labor camp. He was also awarded the Lenin Order.

10. Repressions were executed not only against the Soviet citizens, but also against foreigners in the USSR, the Germans among them. The secret letter of the deputy of the People's Commissar for Foreign Affairs Potyomkin to Stalin, dated July 9, 1937, testifies to this:

German chargé d'affaires informed the People's Commissariat for Foreign Affairs that in Kharkov the German citizens were sentenced to shooting: Friedrich Besgertz, Reinhold Rindler, and Friedrich Bolles. The embassy is petitioning to substitute shooting for some other measure of punishment. The cases of the citizens named were investigated by the court-martial of the Kharkov military district. The condemned were accused of espionage and diversion actions. As the shooting of the three German citizens can lead to undesirable consequences (up to now there has been no case of shooting of German citizens), the NKVD considers it to be expedient to substitute for the high measure of punishment of the condemned ten years of imprisonment. (The duplicates of the document were sent to Molotov, Voroshilov, and Kaganovich.) (CSASA. F. 33987. Op. 3. D. 1009. L. 230.)

11. Yegorov's wife, T. A. Tseshkovskaya, was accused by the organs of the People's Commissariat for Internal Affairs of high treason.

12. In Germany as early as June 30, 1934, according to Hitler's order on the night of "long knives," nineteen top commanders of the storm-troops of the SA (Storm-Troopers), with Roehm at the head, and about fifty-nine commanders of the lower echelon were killed. General Schleicher, who knew many negative things about Hitler and his assistants, was killed together with his wife in his own house that same night. As Mikoyan testifies, in 1934 Stalin expressed his admiration with the way Hitler destroyed his political rivals.

Confidential information of the Investigation Directorate of the RKKA on 1937 generals named the representatives of the Reichswehr who wanted "to agree with the Red Army peacefully": von Hammerstein-Ekword, von Fritsch, Reichenau, Beck, von Blomberg (CSASA. F. 33987. Op. 3. D. 1036. L. 235–36). With the war approaching, Hitler decided to shake up the leading war staff considerably and to get rid of the generals, who were not convenient for him. In 1935 SS (Blackshirts) set up a file on von Fritsch, accusing him of homosexuality. Goering charged von Blomberg with the fact that his wife was a prostitute. After that von Blomberg sent in his resignation and Hitler became commander-in-chief.

13. The document was sent to the deputy of the NKO of the USSR, the chief of the Fifth Directorate of RKKA, commander of the division Proskurov.

14. On September 28, 1939, only two years after the severe order N 96 of the People's Commissar for Defense Voroshilov dated June 12, 1937, where he declared the discovery of the plot of traitors and counterrevolutionaries who acted in favor of German fascism, Voroshilov and the army commander of the first rank Shaposhnikov, on the one hand, and the representatives of the Chief Command of the Wehrmacht, on the other, would submit military minutes, coordinating the actions of Soviet and German troops in Poland in September 1939.

Index of Names

Adam, Gen. V., 271, 305; description of, 188–89; and discussion questions for Russians, 124–25—n. 138; meets with Tukhachevsky, 102–103; in negotiations with RKKA, 113–18; quote from, 49; on tank development, 104; and Voroshilov, 101, 105–108. Letter to Voroshilov, 110–11

Albatross, 15, 155

Aleksinsky, Count I. P., 42

Alexandrovitch, V., 33, 45—n. 14

Alexandrovsky, S., 112, 322–25

Alksnis, Ya. I., 96, 113–18, 123—n. 111, 149, 164; in conspiracy, 333–34—n. 3

Amelin, 284—n. 94

Andreev, 45—n. 13

Angreifer, 289

Antonov, A. S., 40–41, 47—n. 36, 205—n. 50

Antonov-Evseenko, V., 47—n. 36, n. 37

Appog, E. F., 253, 265, 333–34—n. 3

Artushof, 64

Ashenbrenner, Capt., 111, 269

Auer, Maj., 195, 217

Ausem, 45–46—n. 18

Avanesov, 194

Averin, 139

Bainhorn, E., 100

Bakunin, M., 284—n. 94

Bamberger, 77

Baranov, P. (M.) I., 23, 120–21, 127, 137–39, 204—n. 16, 227; accused as traitor, 333–34—n. 3; describes Lipetsk, 150–54; issues statement to Junkers Company, 143–44. Letter to Voroshilov, 142–45

Batorsky, 253

Bauer, O., 32, 44—n. 4

Beck, 335—n. 12

Bekarevitch, 46—n. 21

Belitsky, 266

Belov (Below),* 23, 265, 283—n. 62,

*In the documents names are sometimes inconsistently spelled. Variant spellings appear in parentheses.

283—n. 64, 333–34—n. 3. Letter to Voroshilov, 262–63

Benes, E., 322–25, 334—n. 5

Berdiaev, N., 31

Berg, E. S., 36

Beria, L., 47—n. 38

Berman, M., 327, 334—n. 8

Bersol (Bersoli), 22, 61, 69, 193–94; agreement on cancelled, 202–203; protocols on, 194–95, 195–96; operations at cancelled, 199; terms of liquidation of, 201–202; transfer of operations from, 200–201

Berzin, Ya. K., 14, 166, 238, 314—n. 4, 315—n. 15; accused as traitor, 333–34; assesses German intelligence on Red Army, 288; on Bliumkin's behavior, 45—n. 13; quote from, 178; reports on cooperation, 68–75. Secret information: on Lipetsk (January 1929), 157; on Kama (January 1929), 173; on liquidation of Tomka (8 August, 1933), 186–87; on Tomko (January 1929), 183. Reports to Voroshilov: (29 January 1927), 65–66; (1928), 252–54; (1931), 187–89; (6 November 1931), 264–69; (21 January 1933), 285–88; (29 March 1933), 291–92; (3 July 1933), 158; (29 July 1933), 161–63; (14 August 1933), 177–78; (20 August 1933), 163–64; (31 August 1933), 189–90; (14 October 1933), 190–93

Beschnit (Beshnit), 249, 258–29

Besgertz, F., 334–35—n. 10

Bessonov, S., 316–17—n. 53

Bliumkin, 45—n. 13

Blomberg, Gen. W. von, 14, 73, 83, 91, 237–38, 244; as administrator, 231, 259; and relations with USSR, 249, 293, 300, 304–305, 335—n. 12; and Hitler, 302, 317–18—n. 57. Letter to Voroshilov, 308

Blum, 15

Blume, 163

Blumenzaat, 163

Blynov, 232–35

Blyukher, V. K., 88, 333–34—n. 3

Bobrov, 253

Bokkleberg (Bokkelberger), Gen., 26, 291–92, 294–96, 297–300, 315—n. 15

Bolles, F., 334–35—n. 10

Borisov, 303

Brauchitsch, Col. W. von, 25, 269

Briand-Kellog Pact, 122—n. 90. See also Kellogg Pact

Brockdorff-Rantzau (Rantzau), U., Count, 14, 17, 50, 51, 56, 57, 119—n. 4

Brodovsky, 66, 120—n. 46

Bruchmüller, 68, 120—n. 53

Brusilov, 46—n. 21

Budniak, 133–35, 139–40

Budnievich, 77

Budenny, S. M., 263, 315—n. 15, 333–34—n. 3

Bukharin, N. I., 33, 39, 45—n. 11, 57

Burtsev, V. L., 42

Bushe, Prof., 232

Butyrin, 77

Byulov, von (von Bülow), 101–102, 123—n. 120

Chesterton, G. K., 9

Chicherin, G. V., 14, 32, 44—n. 3, 64, 194; authority of questioned, 88;

and "conference in pyjamas," 16–17; on German armaments, 56–57; and purchase of Hamburg weaponry for China, 225; and Vygand, 40. Letter from Trotsky, 33
Communist International, 50, 53, 326
Cot, P., 307
Cuno, W., 17, 18

D'Abernon, Lord, 213
Danenberg, 23, 256
Danilov, Yu. N., 42
Danzig corridor, 109, 124—n. 137, 290
David, 307, 316—n. 47. *See also* Karakhan
Davidovich, 268
Davudov, 159
Dawes Plan, 62. *See also* Dowers Plan
Decken, von der, 303
De-Grale, 218
Delova, 265
Demanovsky, 267
De-Monzy, 51, 119—n. 13
Derevtzov, 113–18
Derop, 89, 122—n. 97
Deropa Company, 293
Deruluft line, 100, 149, 162, 163, 190
Dirksen, G. von, 104, 109, 120—n. 48, 315—n. 15; introduces Hartmann to Krestinsky, 292, 293; on joint air route, 296–97; Litvinov describes reception of, 87–89; quote from, 127; and Stomyanov, 79–81. Letters: from Twardovsky, 307; to von Byulov, 101–102; to Hitler, 294
Djunke, 218, 227
Dobrolet, 229, 284—n. 30
Dobrovolsky, 266
Dodd, W. E., 288–90
Dolgorulov, Count N. D., 42

Dosdov, 268
Doushenov, 299
Dowers Plan, 49, 50, 51, 52, 119—n. 3
Dreise, N. von, 203—n. 8
Dubovy (Dubovoi), I. N., 23, 253, 275, 303, 333–34—n. 3
Dybenko, 23, 265, 334—n. 3
Dzerzhinsky, F. E., 8, 14, 39, 133–35
Dzerzhkovich, 222

Edgewood (Edgive) Arsenal, 27, 240
Efimov, 265. *See also* Yefimov
Egorov, A. I., 14, 256, 265, 314—n. 4; dinner guest at Voroshilov's, 101. Letters: from Kestring, 160–61; to Voroshilov, 263–64. *See also* Yegorov, A. I.
Eideman, 250, 253, 254, 320, 322, 333–34—n. 3. Report to Voroshilov, 249–52
Ekkener, Dr., 97–98, 123—n. 113
Elze, 259–60
Engelgardt, Dr., 217
Enukidze, A. S., 101, 123—n. 124
Erbet, J., 51, 119—n. 12
Ertsberg, M., 32, 44—n. 4
Esterlen, 67
Ezau, Prof., 129

Faige (Faighe), Col., 25, 269
Fauzer, 223, 224, 226, 228
Fedko, 23, 47—n. 36, 253
Fedorov, Count P. M., 42–43, 205—n. 49, 267
Fedotov, 256
Feldman, 253, 320, 333–34—n. 3
Firin, S. G., 327, 334—n. 9
Fischer, Maj., 66, 212, 213, 218, 253; in correspondence with Levan-

dovsky, 271; on French-Romani-
an negotiations, 216–17; proposes
attendance at RKKA maneuvers,
219–20; researches status of aerochemical experimentation, 215–
216
Fisher, F., 120—n. 49, 203—n. 9.
Letter to Lit-Tomsen, 129–30
Fishman (Fischman), Ya. M., 14, 67,
82, 84, 85, 280; accused as traitor,
333–34—n. 3; complained about,
247; in military-chemical department, 22, 120, 203—n. 4; on talk
with Blomberg, 235–36. Letters
from Germany: (10 March 1925),
209–15; (20 March 1925), 215–17;
(3 April 1925), 217–18; (17 April
1925), 221–24; (21 April 1925),
224–26; (4 May 1925), 226–27; (14
May 1925), 227–291; (26 May
1925), 229–30; (16 January 1929),
231–32; (28 February 1929), 232–
35. Reports to Voroshilov: 22,
284—n. 36
Flamm, Prof., 214–15
Fluri, Prof., 231, 234, 236
Foss, 15, 163
Fradkin, A., 144–46
Frank, J., 120—n. 45, 129, 223, 226,
229, 281—n. 19; on building
cyanamide-calcium factory, 222;
Moscow stay of, 225
Fritsch, 317–18—n. 57, 335—n. 12
Frunze, F. E., 8, 14, 49–53, 220
Funk, 303

Gailis, 194, 207—n. 89
Gal, Gen., 252
Galm, Col., 253
Galperin, 194, 228

Gamarnik, Ya. B., 322, 333–34—n. 3
Garvaky, I. K., 333–34—n. 3
Garkavy, 286
Gasyuk, 316–17—n. 53
Gay, 279–81
Gefists, 225, 229–30
Gelger, 101, 123—n. 123
Geller, Prof., 129, 222–23, 229–30
Geneva Protocol, 232, 284—n. 35
Genov, Gen., 279
George, David Lloyd, 17, 37
Gerens, Prof., 77
Germanovitch, 23
Germes, A., 17
Gerstenberg, 96–97, 259, 284—n. 36
Gessler, 66, 67, 120—n. 44, 245
Gigur, 253
Gilder, 136–37, 204—n. 22
Ginsburg (Ginzburg), L. G., 129, 146,
203—n. 6, 227, 229
Girshfeld, 303, 316–17—n. 53
Goebbels, J., 306, 334—n. 7
Goering, H., 298, 306
Goltzman, 100, 123—n. 117
Gorbachev, M., 267, 333–34—n. 3
Gots, A. R., 36
Grener, V., 14, 244, 245, 247, 249
Griesmann, 77
Grigorovich, 77
Gryaznov, I. K., 174–75, 206—n. 68
Gubanov, 187
Guchkov, A. I., 42
Guderian, H., 21
Gukovsky, I. E., 32, 45—n. 9
Guntzler (Gunzler), 213–14, 281—n. 9

Haal, 149
Haffner, S., 23, 332
Hailo, 268
Halm, Gen., 84

Hammerstein-Ekword, H. von, 91
Hammerstein-Ekword (Hammerstein), Maj. Gen. K. von, 14, 91,
92, 105, 121—n. 72, 303; in
conversation with Hungarian
envoy, 118; and Hitler, 305; quote
from, 164; talks with Voroshilov
and Kullental, 82–85; seeks peace
with Russians, 335—n. 12
Harps, Capt., 279
Hartmann (Hartman), 25, 158, 193,
271, 279, 286, 297, 314—n. 3;
appointed military attaché, 314—
n. 1, n. 4; assesses the Red Army,
290–91; on collapse of collabora-
tions, 280–81; complains of Bokkleberg's behavior, 298, 300; meets
with Krestinsky and Dirksen, 292–
93; reports to Reichswehr ministry, 309
Hasse, Maj. Gen. P. von, 14, 16, 218,
219, 220; assists in aerochemical
inspection, 215–16
Heinz, 163
Heisemann, 137, 138, 143
Helz, Max, 88, 122—n. 92
Henderson, A., 91–92, 122—n. 104
Hering, H., 112, 125—n. 143
Hertz, 53
Heydrich, 334—n. 5
Heye, Gen., 23, 27, 67, 83; attempts
to improve German-USSR rela-
tions, 249; governmental position
of, 120—n. 36, 245, 253; seeks
German involvement in Bersoli, 61
Hilger, Gustav, 44—n. 2
Hinchuk. *See* Khinchuk
Hindenburg, P. von, 212–13, 225, 245,
281—n. 7
Hitler, A., 43–44, 305, 325, 333, 334—

n. 7; and the "night of long knives,"
335—n. 12; conspired with Stalin,
334—n. 5; quote from, 285;
receives von Seeckt's testament,
317–18—n. 57; on relationship
with USSR, 288–89; and status of
Reichswehr, 300–301. Report
from Dirksen, 294
Hlopvo, 267
Hofmeister, Capt., 92, 102, 103, 113–
18
Holtz, Count, 55
Honischen, 149
Horn, 25, 269
Hot, Maj., 254
Hotenhof, 64
Hugo Stinnes IV, 230
Humbold, H., 91–92, 122—n. 103

Iagodá, G. G., 35, 36, 38, 46—n. 19
Iodl, A., 270–71, 276, 283–84—n. 74
Ipan, 53, 228. *See also* Shpan
Ipatiev, Prof., 221, 226, 228, 229, 230
Ivanov, 77
Izanson, 316–17—n. 53
Izvestia, 57, 289

Jenokjan, 265
Jukov, 267
Junkers Company, 18, 50, 61, 72, 104;
and aircraft development, 69, 74,
102; bribery involving, 133–35;
contracts for military plant, 127–
28; cost overruns and, 130–33; and
Fili, 129–30; liquidation of agreement with, 146–47; new proposals
of, 139–40; operations at, 209–12;
receives compensation for factory,
148–49; resolution of bribery
charges, 137–39; situation with,

142–45; USSR disappointment with, 143–44

Junkers, Prof. G., 51, 136, 137, 211, 204—n. 24

Kaganovich, 321, 322
Kalmikov (Kalmykov), 23, 256
Kama, 19, 21–22, 280; organization of, 164–70; and OSOVIAKhIM, 170–72; secret information on, 173; tank school at, 71–72. *See also* Kazan
Kamenev, Col. S., 110, 321
Kaminsky, 18
Kangelari, 45—n. 13
Kaniya, 118
Kapustin, 225
Karakhan, L. M., 333–34—n. 3
Karo, N., 222, 226, 228, 230, 281—n. 19
Kartashev, A. V., 42–43, 47—n. 39, 232–35
Kartsev, 233
Kashirin, N. D., 333–34—n. 3
Katajev, 42, 261
Katkov, 23, 256
Kazale, 223, 224, 226, 228
Kazan, 73, 82, 106, 265; liquidation of, 161–62, 177–78, 189, 191; property inventory of, 175–77; results of work at, 187; Russian expectations for, 115–16
Keitel, Lieut.-Col., 25, 269
Kellogg Pact, 87–88. *See also* Briand-Kellogg Pact
Kerensky, 36
Kestring, Gen., 101, 123—n. 122, 124—n. 135, 314—n. 4; on friendly relations with Russians, 333; on German military support to USSR, 24–25; itinerary of in

RKKA mission, 268; quote from, 150. Letter to Egorov, 160–61
Khalepsky, I. A., 178, 206—n. 65, 213, 333–34—n. 3
Khinchuk (Hinchuk), 125—n. 140, 303–4, 316–17—n. 53
Klim, 67
Koba, 103. *See also* Stalin
Kokadejev., 268
Kopp, V. I., 15, 32, 33–34, 44—n. 2
Kork, A. I. 14, 23, 231, 235, 236; accused as traitor, 320, 333–34—n. 3; as dinner guest, 101, 315—n. 15; military rank of, 120—n. 37. Letter to Voroshilov, 256–260
Korka, 73
Kornuel, Col., 92
Korzun, 77
Kotov, 23
Kovalevsky, Count E. P., 42
Kovtyuh, E. I., 124–25—n. 138
Kozhanov, I. K., 299, 333–34—n. 3
Krasilnikov, 70
Krasin, L. B., 14, 43
Krasnilkov, 249, 250–52
Krato, Maj., 253
Krebs, Capt., 297, 300, 303, 309
Krechmer, Capt., 269
Krestinsky, N. N., 14, 33, 45—n. 10, 61, 309; accused as traitor, 333–34; journal entry of, 292–93; quotes from, 25–26, 285; as Russian negotiator, 17–18, 197. Letter to Voroshilov, 296–97
Kretchmer, 25
Krianga, 139, 204–5—n. 28
Kruchinkin, 265
Kruchinsky, 266
Krupp Company, 25, 50, 83, 117; agreement on technical assistance,

77–79; representatives' discussion, 75–76; and tank building, 107; and types of technical assistance, 15, 24, 93

Kruse, Capt., 25, 269

Ksandrov, 77

Kuibishev, V. V., 14, 204—n. 11, 253, 283—n. 49; delivers message to Politburo, 93–95

Kulik, G. I., 82, 121—n. 74

Küllental, Col., 82–85, 92, 209

Kunzen, von, 303

Kurakin, Count I. A., 42

Kurtzius, 88, 89–91, 122—n. 91

Kvazebad, Prof., 217

Landsberg, 128

Latsis, 23, 256–57

Lavrov, 41–42

Lebedev, P. P., 16, 36

Lejava, A. M., 32, 44—n. 5, 44–45—n. 7

Lenin, V. I., 8, 14, 32, 38, 39. Letter from Trotsky, 33

Leplevsky, 124—n. 136

Levadovsky, K., 275

Levandovsky (Levadosky), 23, 283—n. 65, 303, 333–34—n. 3. Letters from Germany: 269–71, 271–72, 272–75

Levichev (Levitchev), V. N., 23, 213, 275, 284—n. 89, 303, 309; accused as traitor, 333–34—n. 3. Letters from Germany: 276, 276–77, 277–78

Levitin (Levityn), Prof., 213, 316–17—n. 53

Lino, 133–34, 135

Lipetsk, 59, 67, 73, 85, 280; agreement on signed, 120–21—n. 58; camou-flaged as, 205; description of, 150–54; discussion on, 154–56; flying school at, 70, 71; inventory at, 162–63; joint educational enter-prises at, 265; liquidation of, 161–62, 189–90, 192–92; operation of, 19–20; Russian expectations for, 113–15; secret information on, 157; work at, 187

Lit-Tomsen (Lit, Litt), Col. von der, 19, 70, 120–21—n. 58, 128, 129–30, 150–54, 155–56, 166, 203—n. 2, 212, 215, 216, 220, 252

Litvinov, Gen., 67, 108, 306; diary entry of, 87–89. Letter from Unshlikht, 62–65

Ljamberg, 266

Loganovsky, 158

Loht, 225

Lomov, G. I. (Appokov), 39, 46—n. 34

Longva, 23, 256–57

Lose, 210, 281—n. 4

Ludwig, Gen., 84, 243, 249, 259, 121—n. 79; statement of, 240–41

Lunev, P. F. (N.), 19, 53, 61, 119—n. 16; report of, 128–29

Lunyov, 66–68

Luther, 50, 119—n. 5

Lutz, Gen., 21, 190, 206—n. 65

Makrazki, 163

Maksim, 307, 316—n. 46. *See also* Litvinov

Maliuguin, 46—n. 21

Maltzan, Baron, 16, 50, 51, 119—n. 4

Mannstein, von, 25, 104

Mark, 144–46

Marx, 212, 213, 281—n. 8

Mastny, 324–25

Matchos, Prof., 213
Maximov, 267
Mehonoshin, K., 100
Mein Kampf, 43–44
Meine, Capt., 214
Memel, 105, 109, 124—n. 132, 290
Mentzel, Lieut. Col. V., 17
Merchinsky, Lieut.-Col., 268–69
Meretskov, K. A., 266, 333–34—n. 3
Messing, 122—n. 105
Mezheninov (Mejeninov), S. A., 23, 256, 96–97, 315—n. 15, 333–34—n. 3
Mezhlauk, 133–35
Mikoyan, A. I., 79, 80, 121—n. 68
Milch, 297
Militär Wochenblatt, 84, 122—n. 84, 122—n. 85
Minkh, 36
Mirbakh (Mirbak), Count, 33, 45—n. 13
Mirk, Gen. von,, 84
Mittelberger, Col., 72, 73, 113, 244, 254; travels to USSR, 72, 252–53
Moabit, 13
Model, Maj., 25, 269
Molodtsov, 77
Molotov, V. M., 56–57, 120—n. 23
Moltke, 96
Mooze, Prof., 230
Morozov, S. V., 36
Mortjaghin, 267
Moscow Pravda, 326
Mrochkovksy, 194, 199
Muklevich, 154–56
Mulich-Hoffman, 139
Müller, Col. 254
Müller, R. D., 18, 29—n. 7

Nasha Pravda, 41

Nechajev, 253
Neuman, 121—n. 81, 127. *See also* Niedermeier
Neumeier, 77
Nickolas, 307, 316—n. 48. *See also* Krestinsky
Niedermeier, Col. O. von, 15, 112, 121—n. 81, 212, 231, 256; biography of, 127; and cooperation between armies, 73; as intelligence agent, 72; personality of, 102; proposed as intermediary, 84. Letter to Tukhachevsky, 109–110
Nikitin, 266
Nikultsev, 46—n. 21
Noske, G., 32, 44—n. 4
November Revolution, 45—n. 16

Obermiller, Prof., 233
Obolensky, I. L., 32, 45—n. 8
Oborin, 77
Obysov, 266
October Revolution, 37
Olsky, 133–34, 204—n. 20
Onufriev, 130–33, 135
Oradovsky, V., 144–46
Orlov, 267, 315—n. 15
Orlovsky, 295
OSOVIAKhIM, 170–72

Papen, F. von, 289, 301, 314—n. 11
Pasmanik, D. S., 42
Pastukhov, 77
Pavlov, 266
Petrenko, 124—n. 135
Pika, 226
Pollert, 298, 300
Potyomkin, 334–35—n. 10
Primakov, V., 23, 275, 303, 320, 333–34—n. 3

Preussische Zeitung, 270
Pschor, Prof., 24, 241
Putna, 96, 124–25—n. 138, 266, 320; accused as traitor, 323, 324, 333–34—n. 3

Rad, 212
Radek, K. B., 13–14, 44—n. 2, 333–34—n. 3
Raizenstein, 265
Rakhimson, 186–87
Rakov, D. M. (Osetsky), 36
Rantzau, Count. *See* Brockdorff-Rantzau
Rathenau, W., 14
Ratner, E. M. (Elkind), 36
Ratnerm, 267
Red Napoleon, 319, 321. *See also* Tukhachevsky
Reichenau, von, 300–301, 303, 316—n. 31, 335—n. 12
Ressing, 163
Rheinmetall (-Fabrik), 102, 117, 174, 241, 243; and tank building, 107; contracts with RKKA, 93–95
Ribbentrop, 332
Rindler, R., 334–35—n. 10
Robinson, 259
Roehm, 335—n. 12
Roisch, P., 17
Rokhinson, 232–35
Rokov, V., 39, 46—n. 32
Rosenbaum, 144–46
Rosenberg, Baron von, 17
Rosenberg, A., 295, 315—n. 17, 326–27
Rosynko, V., 256
Rote Fahne, 89, 122—n. 99
Rozengoltz (Rozenholz), A. P., 17, 69, 100, 333–34—n. 3

Russian Napoleon, 322, 323. *See also* Tukhachevsky
Rykov (Rykhov), A. I., 39–40, 43, 46—n. 33, 47—n. 37

Sacks, 137
Sakrner, 268
Saksenberg, 210, 211, 213
Samsonov, 36, 37–38
Savich, Ya. I., 42
Scheidemann, F., 33, 45—n. 16
Schirmer, Gen., 243
Schleicher, Maj. K. von, 16, 112, 245, 301, 335—n. 12
Schlez, 136
Schlieben, von, 137–39, 140, 143, 204—n. 27
Schmidt, Col., 271, 276, 284—n. 91, 303
Schöl, 137, 143
Scholl, Capt., 303
Schpitalsky, Prof., 61
Schubert, von, 66, 88, 120—n. 47
Schwartz (Schwarz), 129, 203—n. 7, 221, 224, 227, 228; and transfer of chemical industry, 223
Seeckt, H. von,, 14, 18, 45—n. 17, 63, 220; ideologies of, 244, 245; quotes from, 31, 312–14; and relations with USSR, 15, 25; on tank warfare, 20–21; testament of, 317–18
Semisotov, 21
Senitsky, 46—n. 21
Shaposhnikov, 333–34—n. 3, 335—n. 14
Shatilov, P. N., 42
Shklovsky, 194
Shnitman, 303
Shpan, 119—n. 17
Shpigelglaz, 317–18—n. 57

Shrot, 297–300, 314—n. 4
Shtar, 227
Shtern, 124–25—n. 138
Sicherer, Ludwig von, 21
Siemens, 24
Siemens and Zeiss, 241
Simonov, 268
Simons, 136
Sinjavsky, 265
Skylansky, E. M., 14
Smirnov, S. A., 42, 77
Smitz, Prof., 259–60
Smolin, 314—n. 4
Smolke, Lieut.-Col., 253
Sokolnikov, 43
Somberg, 257
Sondenstern, von, 303
Soukhorukov, 314—n. 4, 315—n. 15
Spalke, Major, 272, 284—n. 84, 303
Spiradonova (Spiridonova), 33, 45—
    n. 15
Stalin, I. V., 8–9, 14, 101, 333; and
    antigovernment conspiracy, 320–
    21, 333—n. 1, 333–34—n. 3, 334—
    n. 5; as dictator, 331–32; and
    knowledge of Reichswehr con-
    tacts, 123–24—n. 128; as leader,
    90–91, 263–64, 273, 335—n. 12.
    Letters: from Onufriev, 130–33;
    from Unshlikht, 57–62, 198, 202–
    3; from Voroshilov, 103, 146–47,
    174, 254–55, 315—n. 15
Stampfer, 288
Stepanov, 23, 255, 257
Stern, 266
Stojadinovic, M., 324; 334—n. 4
Stolzenberg, 68, 69, 72, 120—n. 54,
    210, 213–14
Stomonyakov, B., 79–81, 121—n. 67
Stresemann, G., 50, 69, 119—n. 6, n.

20, 212; involvement of in corrup-
    tion, 198; policy of toward Russia,
    54, 55, 213; popularity of, 245; and
    relations with Reichswehr, 62–64
Struselba, 268
Stülpnagel (Stühlnagel), 91, 245, 279,
    303
Sukhorov, 102–3, 124–25—n. 138, 279,
    280, 284—n. 101, 284—n. 102
Svechnikov, 70, 249, 250–52
Sviridenko, 287, 288
Sychev, K. I., 42

Tchernov, V., 36
Teetsman (Teezman), 163
Teko, 174–75
Telman, E., 122—n. 93
Tiele, Dr., 64
Timofeev, E. M., 36. See also Litvinov
Timonenko, 267
Tippelskirch, 303, 305–6, 307, 316—
    n. 40
Tissen, F., 50, 119—n. 9
Tkachev, 266
Tolokontsev, 77, 201–2
Tomas, Lieut.-Col., 297, 300
Tomka (Tomko), 19, 21–22, 122—n.
    86; costs of research at, 185–86; de-
    scription of, 178–82; disappoint-
    ment with, 107; experiments at, 70,
    71; infirmary regulations at, 184;
    inventory for export, 187; liquida-
    tion of, 161–62, 189; preliminary
    research for, 235, 236; results of
    work at, 188; Russian expectations
    for, 116–17; secret information on,
    183; separation of, 84–85
Trepper, General, 85
Triandifilov (Triandafilov, Triando-
    filov), 23, 24, 237, 242, 253

Trotsky, L. D., 8, 14, 38, 39, 44—n. 3; accused as traitor, 333–34—n. 3; on payment to Junkers, 148–49; political turmoil and, 42–43; and relations with Germany, 44–45—n. 7, 45—n. 12, 51. Letters: to Kopp, 33–34; to Lejava, 32; to Lenin et al., 33

Troyanker, 316–17—n. 53

Trubetskoy, N., 42

Trud, 306

Tseshkovskaya, T. A., 327, 331, 335—n. 11

Tukhachevsky, 14, 23, 42–43, 321–22; accused as traitor, 320, 323–24, 325, 333–34—n. 3; on armaments, 295–96; and Bokkleberg's visit, 291–92, 294, 295–96; farewell to from Neidermeier, 109–110; issues orders against civil disruption, 41, 47—n. 35, 47—n. 36; negotiates with Reichswehr, 113–18; and official receptions, 101, 102, 307–308, 314—n. 4, 315—n. 15; orders joint training, 253; and Reichswehr officials, 102-3, 104, 158; relates Hitler's military plans, 319–20; on Tomka and Kama, 280; on USSR combat capabilities, 25, 125—n. 141; visits Germany, 26

Turov, 229

Twardovsky (Tvardosky), von, 101, 123—n. 123. Letters: from Dirksen, 194; to Dirksen, 307–308; to Tippelskirch, 305–306

Tylle, Dr., 213

Tzergibel, 123—n. 106

Uborevich (Uborevitch), I., 14, 23, 24, 47—n. 36, 95; accused as traitor, 320, 322, 333–34—n. 3; favors pro-German position, 102; quotes from, 127, 209; on state of relations with Reichswehr, 249; training in Germany, 253, 254. Letters from Germany: 237–39, 239–48

Uglanov, 204—n. 11

Unshlikht, 14, 18, 23, 44–45—n. 7; accused as traitor, 333–34—n. 3; on Bersoli, 199, 200–201; focuses on supply issues, 129; protocols on Bersol, 194–95, 195–96. Letters: to Litvinov, 65–65; to Politburo, 197–198; to Stalin, 57–62, 198, 202–3; to Tolokontsev, 201–202

Uralsky, 284—n. 94

Uritsky, S., 23, 275, 303

Uryvayev, 77, 95

Van Der Lubbe, 288

Vannikov, 298

Vasiliev, 41

Vaurik, 18, 136–37, 204—n. 22

Vedeniapin, M. D., 36

Ventsov, S. I., 23, 256, 261, 266

Vesnik, Ia. I., 46—n. 22

Vetsell, Gen., 156

Viktorov, M. V., 333–34—n. 3

Vilberg, 154–56

Vinogradov, 300–2, 303, 316–17—n. 53

Virt, I., 14

Vitkovsky, 144–46

Volia Rossii, 36

Völkischer Beobachter, 270, 283—n. 71

Volkmann, 129

Voroshilov, K. E., 14, 283—n. 58, 295, 315—n. 18, 326; and Adam, 105–108, 110–11; attends maneuvers, 307-8; declares plot of traitors,

335—n. 14; and dinner guests, 314—n. 4; and German internal affairs, 123—n. 106; on flight of "friends," 164–65; order by, 273; personality of, 320; in public ceremonies, 26, 88, 92; quote from, 49; and Reichswehr, 82–85, 111, 113–18; and Soviet-Polish relations, 101, 109. Letters: from Alksnis, 149; from Baranov, 142–45; from Belov, 262–63; from Blomberg, 308; from Davudov, 159; from Egorov, 263–64; from Gay, 279–81; from Goltzman, 100; from Gryaznov, 174–75; from Kork, 256–60; from Krestinsky, 296–97; from Loganovsky, 158; from Yakir, 260–62; to Berzin, 161–63; to Molotov, 56–57; to Stalin, 103, 146–47, 174, 254–55, 315—n. 15; to Stalin and Politburo, 255–56. Reports from Berzin: (29 January 1927), 65–66; (1928), 252–54; (1931), 187–89; (6 November 1931), 264–69; (21 January 1933), 285–88; (29 March 1933), 291–92; (10 May 1933), 315—n. 15; (July 1933), 158; (29 July 1933), 161–63; (14 August 1933), 177–78; (20 August 1933), 163–64; (31 August 1933), 189–90; (14 October 1933), 190–93

Vorwärts, 89, 122—n. 99, 288
Vozlyublenny, 284—n. 94
Voznesensky, 46—n. 21

Vygand, 40, 46—n. 35

Wetzel, Gen., 67, 120—n. 50, 252
Widenfeld, 50, 119—n. 7
Wilde, 129
Wirt, Prof., 231, 233

Yakir, I. E., 14, 23, 255, 257; accused as traitor, 320, 322, 323, 324, 333–34—n. 3. Letter to Voroshilov, 260–62
Yakovenko, 291
Yashka, 128
Yastrebov, G. G., 333–34—n. 3
Yefimov, 315—n. 15. *See also* Efimov
Yegorov, A. I., 23, 292, 295, 308; accused as traitor, 319, 333–34—n. 3. Letters to Voroshilov: 327–29, 329–31. *See also* Egorov, A. I.
Yeshov, 317–18—n. 57
Yoffe, S., 149, 316–17—n. 53
Yurovsky, S. S., 66–68, 120—n. 42

Zarzar, V., 100
Zeebak, von, 225–26
Zeiss, 24, 119—n. 17, 129, 265
Zenflieben, 220
Zensonov, 36
Zeppelin, Count S., 123—n. 12
Zheleznjakov, 265
Zhuev, 253
Zis-Jakovenko, 261
Zof, V. I., 333–34—n. 3
Zomberg, 23, 255
Zyonarev, 119—n. 1